EMPIRIE UND THEORIE
DER SPRACHWISSENSCHAFT

Band 7

Edited by
Jadranka Gvozdanović

Lexicon of
Baltic Mythology

MARTA EVA BĚŤÁKOVÁ
VÁCLAV BLAŽEK

Translation
HANA BĚŤÁKOVÁ
MARTA EVA BĚŤÁKOVÁ
VÁCLAV BLAŽEK

Universitätsverlag
WINTER
Heidelberg

Bibliografische Information der Deutschen Nationalbibliothek
Die Deutsche Nationalbibliothek verzeichnet diese Publikation
in der Deutschen Nationalbibliografie;
detaillierte bibliografische Daten sind im Internet
über *http://dnb.d-nb.de* abrufbar.

Englische Lizenzausgabe des Titels
Encyklopedie baltské mytologie (LIBRI, Prag, 2012)

Funded by the Faculty of Arts of Masaryk University,
Brno, Czech Republic.

The original work in Czech language was supported by
Grantová agentura České republiky (Czech Science Foundation).

UMSCHLAGBILD
© Daniela Běťáková

ISBN 978-3-8253-4866-3

© 2021 Universitätsverlag Winter GmbH Heidelberg
Imprimé en Allemagne · Printed in Germany
Umschlaggestaltung: Klaus Brecht GmbH, Heidelberg
Druck: Memminger MedienCentrum, 87700 Memmingen

Gedruckt auf umweltfreundlichem, chlorfrei gebleichtem
und alterungsbeständigem Papier

Den Verlag erreichen Sie im Internet unter:
www.winter-verlag.de

Contents

Preface

The book you are holding represents an updated translation of the book that was first published under the title *Encyklopedie baltské mytologie* by the Czech publishing house LIBRI[1] (Praha 2012), as part of an edition of encyclopaedias dedicated to individual mythological traditions and religious systems. Our book was the first of its kind in this series, thanks to its systematic etymological analyses and the number of primary sources that had to be consulted. The topic of Baltic mythology is a half-forgotten field of study that, in Czech works at least, enjoyed a far greater attention 150 years ago. Nowadays it is mostly studied by Lithuanian and Latvian scholars, but it remains at the fringes of interest elsewhere in Europe. Only several articles on Baltic mythology have been written by Czech authors and it has been touched upon in translations of Baltic fiction. And yet, the tradition of Czech Baltic studies had already been founded by the writer and translator František Ladislav Čelakovský (1799–1852). This book hopes to remedy this blatant omission and to open up to its readers the so far nearly concealed area of Lithuanian and Latvian folklore, which in many ways has wondrously preserved ancient Indo-European archetypes.

Because it is the first monographic treatment of Baltic mythology in not only a descriptive, but also a historical, linguistic and comparative perspective, we thought it expedient to accompany the text with illustrative examples from our primary sources. We therefore frequently quote both selected passages from chronicles and official documents on the one

---

[1]   In his letter addressed to Václav Blažek, dated the 20th Feb 2013, the director of the publishing house, Dr. Karel Žaloudek, wrote: Nakladatelství Libri nemá námitek proti vydání překladu *Encyklopedie baltské mytologie* v angličtině. Předpokládám, že případné anglické vydání nebude kopírovat vydání české (grafická úprava a obálka), protože na to jsou také autorské smlouvy. ('The publishing house Libri has no objections to publication of the English translation of the *Encyclopedia of Baltic Mythology*. I suppose that the English translation will not copy the Czech edition concerning its graphic layout and jacket').

hand, and parts of folk songs – *dainas* – on the other hand. The translations in the text itself are usually ours (unless stated otherwise) and we
place the original text (Latin, German, Old English, Old Russian, Polish,
Lithuanian, Latvian, Finnish etc.) in footnotes or, in the case of *dainas*,
in the text itself. By this practice, we want to make possible further study
of authentic, but usually hard to come by sources, to scholars of Baltic,
Indo-European, Fenno-Ugric, mythological, ethnological or historical
studies, as well as any curious person from the general public. Our etymological conclusions represent the latest level of knowledge; in many
entries we even present brand new solutions. We were ourselves surprised
how often there exists a unique parallel between mythological names in
the Baltic region and in ancient Italy. We believe these are independently
preserved archaisms that open new possibilities for the reconstruction of
the Indo-European pantheon.

The book we offer you aims to be an encyclopaedia of the mythology of
Baltic nations; we must, therefore, clearly define which nations are concerned. The contemporary political term "Baltic nations" encompasses
Lithuanians, Latvians and Estonians, i.e. the main ethnicities of the three
small states at the Eastern shore of the Baltic Sea. However, the concept used in this book is based on the viewpoint of linguistics, compara-
tive-historical linguistics in particular, where the Lithuanian and Latvian
languages represent the Baltic branch of Indo-European languages; while
Estonian belongs to the Balto-Finnic branch of the Finno-Ugric group of
Uralic languages.

Originally, there were more than two languages in the Baltic branch
of Indo-European languages. At the time of English Revolution, there still
existed the language of old Prussians, originally spoken approx. from the
mouth of the Vistula River to the river Neman (Lith. Nemunas), i.e. in the
area of today's Warmian-Masurian Voivodeship in Poland and the Russian Kaliningrad Oblast.

Chronicles recording events from the 12th and 13th centuries inform
us about other Baltic tribes. Curonians, who lived in the west of Latvia,
participated in the ethnogenesis of Western Lithuanians, who are called
Žemaitians, but partly also of Latvians themselves. To the south of the
Gulf of Riga and the river Daugava there lived Semigallians; further to
the east there were Selonians. To the north of Daugava there was the territory of Latgalians. (In the Latvian language, there exists to this day a Latgalian dialect, actually deserving of the status of an autonomous language

with its specific phonetics.) These three tribes and a part of Curonians formed the modern Latvian nation.

The Lithuanian ethnic group has since the Middle Ages been divided into the Western, Žemaitian (Samogitian) group, i.e. "Lowlanders", and the Eastern, Aukštaitian group, i.e. "Highlanders". The same distinction survives to this day in Lithuanian dialects. At the mouth of the Neman River resided the Skalvian tribe, presumably part of the larger Prussian ethnic group. To the south of the middle reaches of the Neman and to the north of the Narew River, there was the territory of Sudovians, while to the east of Prussians and to the west of Lithuanians lived Yotvingians. Some peculiarities of the southernmost Dzūkian dialect of the Aukštaitian Lithuanian are usually ascribed to the influence of the tribal dialect of Yotvingians. They probably also played a similar role in the formation of the Belarussian language. Galindians, who lived to the South of Prussians, were in part assimilated by the ancestors of Poles and in part completely dissolved in the Migration Period of the 5th century.

Many regional names in the Baltic area preserve the names of the tribes listed above: Aukštaitija (Eastern Lithuania), Žemaitija or Samogitia (western Lithuania), the Curonian Spit (a sand-dune spit in the Baltic Sea, divided between the territories of Kaliningrad Oblast and Lithuania), Kurzeme or the historical Courland (western Latvia), the historical Livonia (northern Latvia and southern Estonia; Livonians were a Finno-Ugric tribe), Zemgale (southern Latvia), Latgale (eastern Latvia). Even Latvia itself got its name from the Latgalian tribe: *Latvija*. The meaning of this word is not clear, unlike the meaning of the name for Lithuania (*Lietuva*), which is formed from the name of a rivulet, *Lietava*, which in turn is derived from the Lithuanian word *líeti* "to pour". Similar names appear in Central Europe as well, most notably in the name of the river *Leitha* (Hungarian *Lajta*, Czech *Litava*) on the Austrian-Hungarian border, which historically divided the Austrian-Hungarian Empire into Cisleithania and Transleithania.

Around the year 1200, the Baltic tribes inhabited an area about three times as large as they do in the present. During the centuries, the largest territory was lost in the east, south and south-west; in the north and partly also north-west, on the other hand, the borders at that time lay further to the south and south-west than they are now. Older borders of the Baltic dialectic continuum can only be determined on the basis of toponymy. Vanagas (1980, 119) defined a conservative version: north – the northern border of Latvia and the towns of Pskov, Toropec, Zubcov, Kalinin; east – the towns

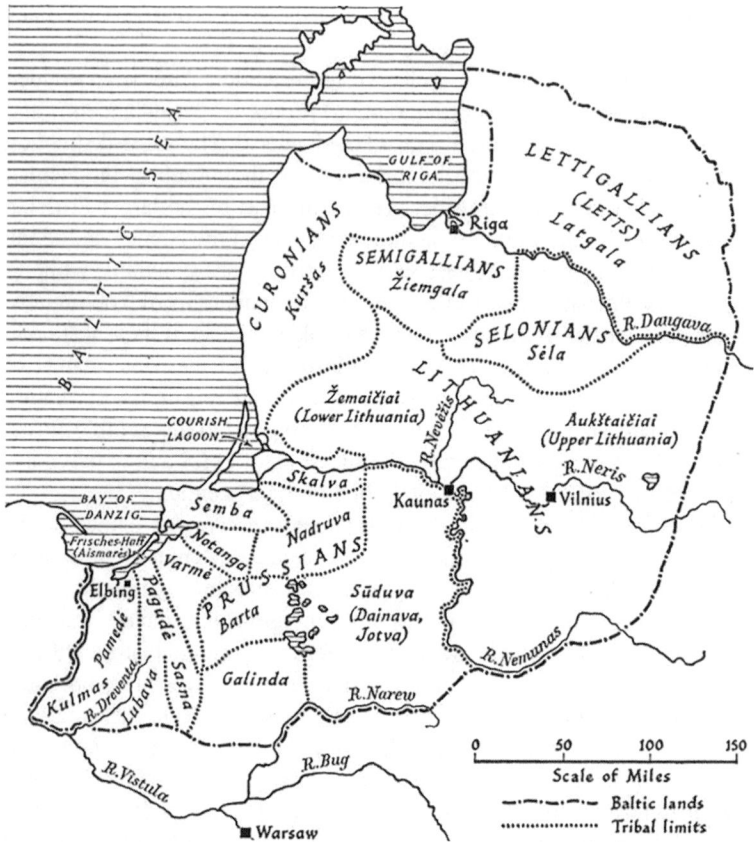

Baltic tribes and provinces around 1200 according to M. Gimbutas 1963, 23
See <https://en.wikipedia.org/wiki/Baltic_languages#/media/File:Baltic_Tribes_
c_1200.svg> – visited on June 2, 2021

Moscow, Kaluga, Orel, Kursk; south – the rivers Seym, Pripyat, Western
Bug; west – the Vistula River. Other Baltic scholars argue that the area in
which Baltic-type toponyms occur is much larger. The western border is
moved much farther, into the basin of the upper reaches of the Havel River
in south-eastern Mecklenburg (see Schall 1964, 1966; Toporov 1966a,
b). The eastern border, mapped in great detail in a series of studies by the
Russian scholar Toporov (1972, 1982, 1988, 1989, 1997a, b), reached to
the eastern banks of the upper reaches of the Volga River. The northern

border is defined by the shores of the Baltic Sea and the southern border of the Finno-Permic languages. If we accept the occurrence of Balt. place names, especially names of rivers, to the west of the Vistula River, only the southern border is left to define. There is an unspoken agreement as to its being identical with the mountain ranges on the southern border of Poland, although no explicit definition has ever appeared, not even in the latest studies (Orel 1997; Popławski 2001). However, Baltic place names, especially names of rivers (most notably Úpa, concordant with Lith. *upė* "river", Latvian *upe* id.; further *Brlenka* vs. Lithuanian *burlýnas* "thick mud", Latvian place-name *Burliņi*; *Cidlina* vs. Latvian *Ciduļ-upe*, Lithuanian *Kìdul-upis*; *Metuje* vs. Lithuanian *Medujà*; *Trutina*, today *Trotina* vs. Lithuanian *trúotas* "granite; whetstone, grindstone", Latvian *truõts* "whetstone, grindstone"), cross the Polish-Czech border and stand witness to the presence of a Baltic population in Eastern Bohemia before the arrival of the Slavs (Blažek 2003a, 2004b, 2006).

It is very difficult to date ethnic processes that took place in a time for which there are no written sources. Archaeological dating can be called upon to some extent – it is, nowadays, quite trustworthy thanks to dendrochronology – but no artefact can tell us anything about its maker's ethnicity or language unless they had left behind their signature as well. But not even a signature or a name present an unambiguous proof of the ethnicity. Gauls liked to use prestigious Roman names from the 1st century AD onward; the name of Maroboduus, the Marcomannic king, was apparently Celtic; and the name Attila, ascribed to the leader of the Huns, is possibly Germanic (there are other theories). The names used nowadays come from a variety of sources as well – in the English-speaking world, there are not only Germanic names used, but also names Celtic or Norman in origin, as well as Biblical, Greek, Roman and others. Archaeology, therefore, can date its finds of material culture but cannot discern who had used or made them.

This is an area where historical comparative linguistics can help. If it is presented with a representative sample of vocabulary, it can not only categorise a given language genetically into a higher taxonomy, but also determine a whole chronology of certain phenomena, namely e.g. to date the separation of hypothetical proto-languages. As archaeology uses the radiocarbon method to date fragments of originally organic material and genetics can pinpoint when two species began to differentiate, so linguistics can discern when two or more related languages began to arise from what had originally been one proto-language. This method was already invented in mid-20th century by Morris Swadesh who named it glottochronology. Since then, his method has met with harsh critique rather than warm reception. However, several linguists have tried to revise it into a reliable method. Out of these attempts, the most successful results are yielded by the recalibrated glottochronology of Russian scholar Sergei Starostin. Its application and results are based on a detailed etymological analysis of test samples from the basic vocabulary of the languages that are studied.

Application of Starostin's modified glottochronology confirms the old but often disputed hypothesis that the closest relation to the Baltic languages are Slavic languages. The method dates their separation into the first half of the 14th century BC. Around 800 BC, a group of tribal dialects split from the Baltic continuum, eventually to become the Prussian language. Slavic languages, in contrast, divided as late as the 6th century AD. Around the year 600, the central Baltic dialects separated as well; eventually, they constituted predecessors of Lithuanian and Latvian languages. A cause and effect can be discerned in these events. An expansion of Slavic-speaking tribes to the northeast caused not only the assimilation of older Baltic population in the East as far as the upper reaches of the Volga River, but also most probably a different development in the north of the Baltic area that led to the formation of Latvian language.

The same method suggests that the northern neighbours of the Baltic languages, Balto-Finnic and Saami languages, separated around the year 1300 BC, i.e. about 2–3 generations later than Baltic and Slavic languages. It is, therefore, both attractive and logical to assume that this later separation resulted from an expansion of Baltic tribes to the north and northeast after the Balto-Slavic unity had fallen apart. The long-time proximity of Balts and Balto-Finns led to more than 200 Baltic loanwords in the vocabulary of Balto-Finnic languages, including the names of some gods and demons, mentioned in this encyclopaedia (Thomsen 1890; Blažek 2004a). Baltic loanwords in Saami and Mordvinic languages, originally spoken to the east of the Balts, count in tens (cf. Hofírková & Blažek 2011; Vaba 1983). Word borrowing in the opposite direction is much rarer. Most of it is limited to relatively recent Estonian or Livonian influence on Latvian, but some older archaic loans can be found as well: Lith. *laĩvas* "ship", Latv. *laĩva* "boat", cf. Finn. *laiva*, Est. *laev* "ship, large boat", Liv. *lääja* "boat".[2]

---

[2]   Fraenkel I, 335.

Let us now leave aside the scholarly insights that historical linguistics and archaeology can give us about the ancient inhabitants of the eastern Baltic area, their neighbours and their mutual influences. Except for their immediate neighbours, the area remained until the High Middle Ages almost perfectly hidden from the rest of Europe. It is only briefly mentioned by historians and chroniclers, in the reports of merchants and Christian missionaries, but always only second-hand, on the say-so of other nations. For example, Roman historian Tacitus writes in his *Germania* at the end of the 1st century AD[3]:

"Upon the right of the Suevian Sea the Aestian nations reside, who use the same customs and attire with the Suevians; their language more resembles that of Britain. They worship the Mother of the Gods. As the characteristic of their national superstition, they wear the images of wild boars. This alone serves them for arms, this is the safeguard of all, and by this every worshipper of the goddess is secured even amidst his foes. Rare amongst them is the use of weapons of iron, but frequent that of clubs. In producing of grain and the other fruits of the earth, they labour with more assiduity and patience than is suitable to the usual laziness of Germans. Nay, they even search the deep, and of all the rest are the only people who gather *amber*. They call it *glasing*, and find it amongst the shallows and upon the very shore."[4] The name of the Aestyan people was in the Middle Ages used to designate the area of today's Estonia, but Tacitus was most probably describing the territory further to the South where Balts lived.

Another report about the eastern Baltic area comes from the 9th century. Its author was the Anglo-Saxon sailor Wulfstan. His information can be safely localised to the territory of Baltic Prussians[5]: "The Weissel

---

[3] §45. *Ergo iam dextro Suebici maris litore **Aestiorum** gentes adluuntur, quibus ritus habitusque, lingua Britannicae propior. Matrem deum venerantur. insigne superstitionis formas aprorum gestant: id pro armis hominumque tutela securumdeae cultorem etiam inter hostes praestat. rarus ferri, frequens fustium usus. frumenta ceterosque fructus patientius quam pro solita Germanorum inertia laborant. sed etmare scrutantur, ac soli omnium sucinum, quod ipsi glesum vocant, inter vada atque in ipso litore legunt.*

[4] Transl. Thomas Gordon (1910) <http://www.gutenberg.org/files/2995/2995–h/2995–h.htm>.

[5] *þæt Witland belimpeð to **Estum**; seo Wisle lið út of Weonodlande, lið in Estmere; se Estmere is huru fiftene mila brád. Þonne cymeð Ilfing eastan in Estmere of ðæm mere ðe Truso standeð in staðe, cumað út samod in Estmere,*

is a very large river, and near it lie Witland and Weonodland. Witland belongs to the people of Eastland; and out of Weonodland flows the river Weissel, which empties itself afterwards into Estmere [i.e. today's Pol. *Zalew Wiślany*, Germ. *Frische Haff*, Lith. *Aismarės*]. This lake, called Estmere, is about fifteen miles broad. Then runs the Ilfing east (of the Weissel) into Estmere, from that lake on the banks of which stands Truso. These two rivers come out together into Estmere, the Ilfing east from Eastland, and the Weissel south from Weonodland. Then the Weissel deprives the Ilfing of its name, and, flowing from the west part of the lake, at length empties itself northward into the sea, whence this point is called the Weissel-mouth. This country called Eastland is very extensive, and there are in it many towns, and in every town is a king. There is a great quantity of honey and fish; and even the king and the richest men drink mare's milk, whilst the poor and the slaves drink mead. There is a vast deal of war and contention amongst the different tribes of this nation. There is no ale brewed amongst the Estonians, but they have mead in profusion."

Because the Baltic tribes were not christianised, they had attracted the attention and captured the imagination of the Christian part of Europe since the 9th century AD. Gradually, Christian missionaries started to head there. One of the first to do so was a Czech man, St. Adalbert (Vojtěch in Czech), the former bishop of Prague († 997), known for his martyrdom

---

*Ilfing eastan of Estlande, Wisle suðan of Winodlande. Þonne benimð Wisle Ilfing hire naman, ligeð of þæm mere west norð on sǽ; for ðy hit man hǽt Wislemuða. Þæt **Estland** is swyðe mycel, þær bið swyðe manig burh, on ælcere byrig bið cyningc. þær bið swyðe mycel hunig fiscnað; se cyning þa ricostan men drincað myran meolc, þa únspedigan þa þéowan drincað medo. Þær bið swyðe mycel gewinn betweonan him. Ne bið ðær nænig ealo gebrowen mid **Estum**, ac þær bið médo genóh.* The description of Wulfstan's sea journey from Heddeby in Jutland to the Pruss. Truso was added to the Anglo-Saxon translation of ***Boc þe man Orosius nemned*** 'A Book Called Orosius', the work *Historia adversum paganos* by the Hispanic author Paulus Orosius, written around the year 417 AD. The translation was made in the years 888–893/897 by the famous Anglo-Saxon king Alfred the Great. The English translation here used comes from the book *The New Navigation and Discovery of the Kingdom of Muscovy* etc., by Richard Hakluyt, available online through Project Gutenberg: <http://www.gutenberg.org/cache/epub/4076/pg4076.txt> Visited on June 2, 2021. (See also Blažek, Hofírková, Kovář 2011, 197–198).

as, according to legend, he violated Prussian tribal laws. The missionaries were, however, only successful with individuals; and so, since the end of the 12th century, crusades were waged against the territory, benedicted by the pope, to baptise the locals by force. At that time, there already existed well-organised tribal princedoms in the area; Lithuania managed to resist the crusaders for 200 years. Later on, the Grand Duchy of Lithuania emerged, which was still expanding southeast at the time of the Hundred Years' War. It was not only the largest state in Europe at the time, but also the last European pagan country. Its christianisation only happened "from within" in the second half of the 14th century, forwarded by the Grand Duke Jogaila (the founder of the Jagiellonian dynasty, which also ruled in Poland and for a time in the Czech lands and Hungary as well). This era, when the journey of Hieronymus of Prague to Lithuania also took place, could have provided excellent resources on Lithuanian pagan religion and its mythology, but unfortunately only scarce written sources have been preserved. The later fate of Lithuania was as follows: It existed as an independent Grand Duchy, known by its tolerant policy towards its conquered provinces in today's Poland, Belarus and Ukraine. The Grand Duchy lasted till the 16th century when it entered a closer union with the Kingdom of Poland in the Union of Lublin. This large state, known by the saying "every other Pole is a *bojar* [6]", suffered from its own freedoms in the 18th century: there were too many noblemen with too many liberties (*liber vetum)* in state management, including the election of the ruler. In May 1791, the Polish-Lithuanian Commonwealth even adopted the first democratic constitution in Europe, but its existence was ephemeral – several months later the internally weak state fell prey to the Second Partition of Poland. At the end of the 18th century, the remaining territory was divided between Prussia and Russia in the Third Partition; Lithuania fell to the tsar.

Let us now return to the Prussians and the ancestors of today's Latvians. Unlike Lithuania, their territory was conquered by the crusaders and christianised by force during the 13th century. The Czech king Přemysl Otakar II. took part in two crusades in the years 1254–1255 and 1267–1268; he co-founded the town of Regiomontanum (Cz. Královec, Germ. Königsberg, since 1945 it is the Russian Kaliningrad). The territory was then held by religious orders, namely Livonian Brothers of the Sword and Teu-

---

[6]   Polish nobleman.

tonic Knights. Their language was Latin, although the mother tongues of most crusaders were various German dialects. This reflected on many areas. For example, chroniclers wrote all Old Prussian and Latvian words (including names of deities) using the German orthography of the time. Many German words worked their way into Old Prussian and Latvian. Notably, the only preserved Prussian dictionary is Prussian-German. Active contacts with the Holy Roman Empire of the German Nation and the fact that many Prussian and Latvian towns belonged to the confederation of trade towns known as *Hansa* (Hanseatic League) probably helped in transforming these two originally church states into Lutheran princedoms. The city of Riga was the first territory outside today's Germany to adopt Lutheranism. But from this time on, the fates of Prussia (this name, however, involved many territories), ruled by the increasingly powerful dynasty of Hohenzollern, originally Margraves of Brandenburg, and the territory of what is today Latvia began to differ. In short: Prussia was a Protestant princedom until World War I.; in 1701 it became a kingdom with German as its official language. The descendants of Prussian tribes lived there as serfs and their language gradually died out. In the 18th century, those who had the chance to study turned German and the rest adopted the language of Lithuanian immigrants. That is why the north-eastern part of Prussia came to be known as Lithuania Minor. That is also why the first work of Lithuanian fiction was created on Prussian territory – it was the poem *The Seasons* by Prussian-born pastor Kristijonas Donelaitis whose mother tongue was Lithuanian. The rulers of Prussia endorsed education and regarded the publishing of books in their subjects' mother tongue quite benevolently; Königsberg (Lith. Karaliaučius) therefore became an important centre of culture for the Baltic nations as well. For example, the book *Deliciae Prussicae oder Preussische Schaubühne* by Matthaeus Praetorius, the most comprehensive source of information on Baltic mythology, as well as many works of Lithuanian revivalists who could not publish in Lithuania, then part of the tsarist Russia, were published in the city. Thus, the occupation of *knygnešys* arose – "a books carrier", actually a smuggler who ran an even greater risk than usual by adding prohibited books to his cargo. This is also the reason why so many books in our list of sources were published in Königsberg.

In contrast, the territory of today's Latvia divided and re-united several times. At the end of the 16th century, it divided into Livonia (North), Latgale (East) and Courland (South and West) as a result of the Livonian War with the Tsardom of Muscovy. All three lands fell to the Polish-Lithuanian Commonwealth, but only Latgale was directly connected to it. (That is one of the reasons why Latgale is, unlike the rest of Latvia, even nowadays profoundly Catholic.) Livonia and Courland remained Protestant princedoms as fiefdoms of the Polish-Lithuanian state. Courland enjoyed an era of prosperity in the 17th century – manufactories were founded, the spiritual education of the subjects was attended to, villages were granted the status of towns and the princedom even bought overseas colonies – the St. Andrews Island on the West African coast and Tobago in the Caribbean. In the 18th century, Courland maintained an intense relation with Russia – the Duke Ernst Johann von Bühren (Biron) was very influential at the imperial court and had two grand palaces in the style of the Winter Palace in Petersburg built. His son, Peter von Biron, was an enlightened ruler who founded the first grammar school for his subjects of Latvian origin in the capital of Jelgava (Mitau). However, after the Third Partition of Poland (1795), Courland was seized by Russia which made it into one of its governorates.

Livonia, on the other hand, fell to Sweden right at the beginning of the 17th century, and it also experienced its "golden years" in some ways – the Swedish government was fervently Lutheran: it supported translations of the Bible, catechism and church hymns into Latvian, founded parish schools, while being on a watchout for manifestations of pagan behaviour. However, as stated in the entry → werewolf, hunts for → witches and werewolves were far less widespread and cruel in the Baltic countries than they were in Western and Central Europe. We owe many things to the Swedish rule; from the mythological point of view, it particularly concerns interesting reports of manifestations of paganism, where they were observed and what was their character. But in the year 1721, Sweden once and for all lost the Great Northern War (1700–1721) and Livonia fell to Russia. The same fate then followed for Courland and Latgale in the last Partition of Poland 70 years later.

Thus, in the 19th century, both Lithuanians and Latvians found themselves under Russian rule, gradually becoming aware of their national identity. The tsarist government did not pay much attention to Lithuania and in Latvia it gave free rein to the local German-speaking nobility. National revival in both countries is associated with a foreign city: for Lithuania, it was Königsberg, where the first Lithuanian-written magazines and Lithuanian folk songs etc. were printed and whence they were smuggled into Lithuania. The first work of Lithuanian fiction was also created near Königsberg. For Latvia, the foreign cities were the Estonian city of Tartu (Dorpat) and Petersburg in Russia, where the revivalists often studied, held their meetings and supported one another in their persuasion. Naturally, Lithuanian and Latvian mythology, especially folk songs and tales, became one of the cornerstones of national identity.

This had two kinds of effect. The first one is very useful for contemporary mythologists: The revivalists diligently collected oral literature and their collections still serve as some of the fundamental and most trustworthy sources of information on Baltic mythology. The other kind of effect is confusing. In their attempts to prove that the Baltic countries had had a great past, the revivalists created elaborate pantheons of "Pan-Baltic" deities, based on the Ancient Greek model. They mixed together indiscriminately conceptions of Prussian, Lithuanian and Latvian deities, and they distorted their names and created false etymology for them. Moreover, these works did not distinguish between reliable and unreliable resources; for example, the lists of objects of Latvian pagan faith were contaminated with Prussian figures, taken from the Prussian chronicler Simon Grunau. Many mythologists nowadays doubt the existence of these conceptions (e.g. the Pan-Baltic Prussian high priest *Kriwe*, *Krīvs* in a lettonised version). Surprisingly, even the Polish historian Teodor Narbutt created a similar pantheon, unquestioningly influenced by the Lithuanian collector A. L. Jucevičius whom most mythologists nowadays suspect of colouring up and adding to the oral literature he had collected. Narbutt himself completed the pantheon with deities of his own invention. Nonetheless, the works of both "researchers" gained such popularity that Lithuanians still consider some of the deities they created to be "old Lithuanian deities" and give their names to their children. The best known of these we therefore dedicate separate entries to, marking them as a creation of T. Narbutt. Nowadays, mythologists are convinced that a) deities common to all Baltic tribes were very few; b) their gods had no particularly organised hierarchy.

Beside Lithuanian and Latvian revivalists, Baltic mythology also attracted the interest of many scholars and writers from other countries in the 19th century. Foremost, these were German writers and scholars. German interest in the Baltic countries went back hundreds of years. Prussia, the hegemon of the German unification that culminated in 1871, was directly neighbouring with Lithuanian-speaking territories, and in the area of East Prussia, the Prussian language had been a living language only seven generations before the unification (till the end of the 17th century). Even Goethe or Herder took interest in Lithuanian songs, but here it is necessary to emphasise the work of Wilhelm Mannhardt (1831–1880), the librarian of the town library in Gdańsk (then the German Danzig), who collected and analysed the most important historical resources on Baltic mythology – relevant passages from chronicles, secular documents and church protocols – in his book *Letto-Preussische Götterlehre*. He worked on the book till the end of his – unfortunately short – life. The book was finally published in 1934 in Rīga and immediately became the corner-stone for the study of Baltic mythology; this book is no exception (mark the frequency of quoted source abbreviation LPG).

However, the study of Baltic mythology is made drastically difficult by the absence of sufficiently long texts of mythological content. Moreover, so far it has only been possible to work with limited secondary sources or with folklore material. An apt way to describe the situation is the Lat-vian mythologist Aldis Pūtelis's sigh: "If only we had a time machine…" The study of Baltic mythology would be best likened to archaeological investigations, or to a detective story without a detective to tell you who the culprit is at the end. The information is so grievously fragmented that describing most of the deities is similar to finding a single word and hav-ing to deduce the whole sentence. And not a single one of these pieces of information comes directly from a person who had grown up in this faith and still believed in it. Everything was written down either by people who did not believe in this mythology and wanted to exterminate it, and therefore described it as darker than it truly was; or by collectors who recorded oral tradition and received material by mail from other people. Very often, such texts were adapted so that it would be "fit for an educated gentleman," as the peasants often perceived the folklore collectors. It is no wonder, then, that a Baltic mythologist wishes to have a time machine to travel into 2nd century AD or whereabouts and to hear the myths people told and see the ways they sacrificed to their gods. So do not be surprised, dear readers, by the abundance of words such as "probably", "possibly", "apparently" in our encyclopaedia…

In spite of these problems, it is possible to put the individual pieces of information together into an interesting mosaic that shows at least a partial picture of Baltic mythology. It is a picture in which both Indo-European and Fenno-Ugric elements blend. No long sagas have been preserved, although it is possible that they existed earlier but nobody recorded them. Particularly in comparison to Nordic or Vedic mythology, elements of violence and fight play a much less significant part in Baltic mythology. With the Balts, we usually find little stories about individual characters. These stories are usually brief but the way they are told betrays a personal relation to all concerned characters. They are not great epics, and yet they will capture your imagination with unusual themes. Among the typical motifs are e.g. the activities of the supreme god → Dievas or the sky wedding (→ sky inhabitants, wedding) of the Sun and the Moon. Elsewhere, the god of thunder → Perkūnas (Latv. Pērkons) pursues → Velnias (→ velinas). We can find a cult of agricultural deities, the goddess of destiny and women in childbed → Laima, the goblin → *áit(i)varas* (Latv. pūķis or → vilce), the souls → vėlės (Latv. veļi) and → werewolves.

* * *

If the songs with mythological motifs in this book capture your interest, you can search online for musical groups that sing these songs. These include the Lithuanian groups VISI, Žalvarinis, Atalyja, Kūlgrinda, Sedula, Spanxti, Donis + Rasa Serra and the Latvian groups Iļģi, Rasa, Auļi, Skandinieki, Laimas muzykanti, Trejasmens, Auri, Grodi, Teiksma, Skyforger and Suitu sievas.

Acknowledgement

The first version of the present book (in Czech) originated thanks to synergy of The Foundation of the Czech Academy of Sciences (grant nr. IAA901640805), the supportive stance of the publishing house Libri, represented by its chief-editor František Honzák, and the text-editor Michal Schwarz. Extraordinarily useful were comments and recommendations of both reviewers, Bohumil Vykypěl (Czech Academy of Sciences) and Ilja Lemeškin (Charles University). I would like to mention that my interest in Baltic linguistics was initiated by Adolf Erhart and Wojciech Smoczyński, later also by Bonifacas Stundžia and Steven Young. It was Grasilda Blažienė, who revealed to me the charm of Baltic onomastics. My guides in Baltic mythology in the Indo-European context were especially Vjačeslav V. Ivanov, Ilja Lemeškin, Vladimir N. Toporov and Jaan Puhvel, and in comparative mythology in general Michael Janda, Krzysztof T. Witczak, and Michael Witzel. But I would also like to express my gratitude to other linguists, whose opinions, articulated either directly in mutual communication or mediated by their publications, formed my competences in the field of etymology, and consequently influenced the final shape of the present monograph, namely Robert Beekes, Bela Brogyanyi, Heiner Eichner, Eric P. Hamp, Eva Havlová, Eugene Helimski, Ilona Janyšková, Helena Karlíková, Johann Knobloch, Frederik Kortlandt, Alexander Lubotsky, James Mallory, Tom Markey, Mannfred Mayrhofer, Craig Melchert, Robert Nedoma, Norbert Oettinger, Jiří Rejzek, Karl H. Schmidt, Oswald Szemerényi, Radoslav Večerka, Calvert Watkins, Stefan Zimmer and others. With more difficult translations we were helped by Zuzana Handlová (German) and my father Václav Blažek (Latin). The final revision of the English translation was realized by John D. Bengtson. And without endless patience of my wife Marcela Blažková and two faithful supporters, tommycats Mulísek and his follower Tulísek, we would not have originated anything.

The Czech original was written in Příbram, Brno, Vienna, Regensburg, Freiburg, Leiden, Riga, Vilnius and Los Angeles in 2008–2012. The English translation originated simultaneously in Prague and Příbram in 2014–2021. Quite fundamental was the finacial support of its publication in Winter-Verlag from the Dean and Vice Dean of Faculty of Arts of Masaryk University, Milan Pol and Petr Kyloušek respectively, preceded by recommendations of Jadranka Gvozdanović and Michael Witzel, plus the help of Ondřej Šefčík, the head of the Department of Linguistics & Baltic Studies, who supported the typesetting realized by Dan Šlosar.

Václav Blažek

The greatest thanks belong to my family, which supported me for several years, when I studied in libraries and archives of Vilnius and Riga. I am also grateful to Almis Grybauskas, Ilja Lemeškin, Aldis Pūtelis, Janīna Kursīte, Svetlana Ryžakova and Dagmar Váňová for valuable consultations and to Pavel Štoll for checking and correction of my entries. Further I would like to express my thanks to Petra Butzke for her master's thesis about grass-snakes in Baltic mythology, and to colleagues from the Department of Linguistics and Baltic Studies of Masaryk University, namely Ondřej Šefčík, Vaidas Šeferis and Petra Hebedová for their comments and support, besides Ariadna Žilevičienė for her help during my stays in Vilnius. My sincere thanks further belong to my grandmother Marta Janoušková and sister Hana Běťáková for their patient reading of my entries, Ingūna Camrdová for information about Latvian folklore groups and finally to numerous Latvian friends: Indra Strīķe-Bozkuše, who taught me Latvian and helped me with Latvian texts, to inhabitants of the Lutheran parish in Saulkrasti, Solvita Pavloviče, Līza Kupče, Pēteris Kazeks, Jānis Paurnietis, Ģirt Blekte, and Ivo Pavlovičs, who mediated me the daina about Dievs. My sister Hana also helped me with the English translation.

Marta Eva Běťakova

Lexicon of baltic mythology

áit(i)varas, also **áičvaras, éit(i)varas**, in some dialects merely **áitas**; **óitas** in the East of Lithuania – Lith. "elf, flying spectre, goblin, paper kite, mare, pony-tail" (Latv. → *pūķis)*. Á.'s various forms and activities bear some level of resemblance to all of these words. The first mention of his name can be found in the first printed Lithuanian catechism, published by Martin Mosvidius (Lithuanian Martynas Mažvydas) in 1547. He mentions not only the name Aithwars[1] but also its Latin variant Eithuarus.[2] Á. was a household spirit. According to Lithuanian and Prussian tales, he usually lived at a farm and served the landlord. Sometimes, there were two á.s in one household. Á. is roughly an analogy to the English *hob* and the Czech *plivník*. He can fly, he can spit fire and his duty is to provide the landlord with money, grain, flour, smoked meat and dairy products, stolen from other farmers. However, the landlord's life was tied to á. forever: he had to feed him regularly and show him respect. If he did not, á. set his house on fire. In some Lithuanian tales, á. cooperates with the devil and so his landlord's soul goes to hell after death. Matthaeus Praetorius, a 17th century Prussian priest, says in his chronicle *Deliciae Prussicae* that owners of á.s are disliked by other villagers. We can see that á. is a being that ensures riches at the cost of losing one's friends or even one's soul. But he is also a being with many interesting traits; so, let us explore him more closely. To obtain á. was one's voluntary decision. There were many ways to do so: a) one could buy him in Rīga, Königsberg or Klaipėda from a "little German chap" (that was one of the forms the devil liked to take on; see →Velinas), from a "roaming Hungarian" or from a sorcerer; b) hatch him from an egg laid by a 3–, 7–, 9–, 12– or even 100–year-old rooster. The hatching is not easy: in most of the tales it must be done by carrying the egg in one's armpit around the clock, but it can also be hatched by a rooster, a cat or an old woman, with the egg

---

[1] *Aithwars ir deiwes to negal padariti* (i.e. Aitvaras and Deives cannot do that).
[2] *Qui ad malas artes adjiciunt animum, Eithuaros et Caucos Deos profitentur suos.* (They make it known to their gods Eithuaros and Caucos, who to evil deeds his soul commits.)

lying in a mug filled with fine down. It is also possible to c) find á. d) catch á. – on seeing a flying á. one must tie a knot on one's handkerchief or a rosary, alternately to thrust one's knife into the ground; e) to allure á., usually with the help of a meal put on a roof ridge together with a written note asking á. to bring a specific thing to a specific place. In some cases, á. f) offers his services by bringing a heap of coal, peas or something similar, of low value, to the house at night. If the landlord accepts it, á. starts bringing more valuable things. The tales pay great attention to á.'s appearance. It is characteristic of á. to change his form completely according to the circumstances: he takes on certain forms when being bought, a different form when letting himself get found, and yet another form when at home. Some sources even claim that a flying á.'s appearance changes in accordance with the cargo he is carrying. Let us now describe his appearance in individual situations. Á. is usually bought in the form of a piece of coal or resin. It is found as a curry-comb or a rope for tying horses'legs. At home, he usually takes on the form of a black animal: a tomcat, rooster, crow or a magpie. Sometimes also the appearance of the "little German chap" – then he is called Velnias, "the devil", in the story. A flying á. is most interesting and his appearance varies the most. Frequently, he is of longish shape, of black or red colour, glowing, sparkling, sometimes even burning, with the front part broader than the rear part. The tales often mention that he moves like a crawling snake: he contracts and stretches himself, or he wriggles. "… and an áitvaras flew out of the barn over the roof ridge, looking like a black poker, only his head was red, he was contracting and again stretching himself, and so he flew away and disappeared".[3] The flying á. is most often compared to a poker; in many cases also to a stake around which hay stacks were piled on meadows, to a snake, a sleeve, a ribbon or a log. In some tales, he is also compared to a flying worm or to a bird with fire sparkling from under his wings. In one tale, he is described as a "light horrible to look at", and in another, quite mysteriously, as a "sort of a creature, neither a tomcat, nor a bird, more similar to a fish actually, longish and wriggling like an adder".[4] When á. is not carrying anything, he is light with a dark tail, white or light red; while bringing food to his master, he is blue, dark red

---

[3]   … iš tokios klėties išlėkęs aitvaras per šelmenį, toks kaip pagaikštis juodas, tik galva raudona, ir driūkai driūkai taip driūkuodamas nulėkęs ir prapuolęs.

[4]   kažin koks padaras, nei katinas nei paukštis, labiau panašus į žuvį, pailgas ir vingiuojasi kaip gyvatė.

or black. Some tales mention his colour varying according to the cargo: an á. carrying money is red, while an á. bringing grain is blue, black or yellow. Having brought the cargo to the denoted spot, he "throws it up". To keep á. satisfied and to make him serve well, one must feed him regularly with fried eggs (in Aukšaitija, i.e. eastern Lithuania) or with gruel (in Žemaitija, i.e. western Lithuania). In some tales, á. demands very specific meals, e.g. herring heads or nearly hatched eggs. Á. is easy to offend, if he is not fed regularly, or when he gets to eat a meal that has already been tasted by someone, or when someone utters the name of God in front of him, when someone sprinkles him with holy water, or when someone eats his meal and then uses his plate as a toilet. The last mentioned offence is often committed by the farm's grooms who especially dislike á. This is caused by á. bringing so much grain that they have much more work to do than before. Grooms sometimes even beat á. These are also ways of getting rid of á., but definitely not very safe ones, as the offended á. simply leaves the house in some cases, but in most, he sets it on fire before leaving.

Á. is a popular being amongst Lithuanian mythologists. His association with several animals (rooster, snake, horse) and elements (fire, air) has inspired many theories of his connection with various mythological phenomena, both Lithuanian and Indo-European. Let us look at M. Gimbutienė (who also used the name M. Gimbutas) first: she considers á. to be a servant of the goddess of destiny → Laima, and given his association with eggs and birds, she connects him with her reconstructed Bird Goddess (Deivė-Paukštė). N. Vėlius is of the opinion that his popularity among peasants was caused by the absence of any other household spirit in Lithuania (unlike Latvia, where → Mājas kungs was known), making á. a being fulfilling all household spirits' functions. Vėlius agrees with the Latv. mythologist L. Adamovičs who claims that á. used to be a household spirit who protected the house and whose mere residence in it made it prosperous. Later, partly because of the influence of Christianity, his image changed to more negative, for his presence was beneficial to a very limited number of people. Vėlius focuses on his form of a rope for tying horses'legs and of a curry-comb. He discovered some Lithuanian tales from the area of today's Belarus mentioning an á. found in the form of two grains grown together. Vėlius deduces from this association with horses and double objects that the cult of á. developed from the Indo-European twin cult (cf. Vedic Aśvins, Greek Dioskuros and Latv. → Dieva dēli). Vėlius supports this hypothesis with a number of reasons: e.g. Indo-Eu-

ropean twins are associated with horses too, they were asked by people
to provide abundance of food, one of them hatched from an egg, and they
made themselves visible to people and sacrifices were brought to them
just before dawn and during sunset – that is, exactly at the times when
also á. is fed and makes himself visible. Hence, Vėlius' etymology of the
word á.: the first component can be associated with Lith. *aitrà* "heat",
while the second one with Lith. *vãras* "cross-bar" – and it was a cross-
bar that symbolized the mythical twins with the Indo-European nations.
It connected the top parts of two wooden poles that the twins used to lit
a fire. A. J. Greimas, however, puts á. in opposition to the horse. Also, he
notes that an etiological myth exists parallel to the tales about á. In this
myth, á. is pursued by the thunder god → Perkūnas and as a result of this
chase, a wind rises to form the landscape. For Greimas then, á. is one of
the oldest Baltic gods and an adversary of Perkūnas. Similarly to Velnias,
he loses to Perkūnas in the end and thus helps create the present world
order. Other etymologists connect the first component with the word *aeteis*
"parts" from the language of Oscans, the inhabitants of ancient southern
Italy, and with Greek αἴσα "part; destiny" < *aitia*. The second component could then be associated with Lith. *vãras* "force; violence", derived
from *varýti* "to propel, to drive", Latv. *vert* "to run". Cf. Russ. *vor* "thief".
That would make á. a being that enforces the destiny. The Polish Baltic scholar Smoczyński considered the possibility that the original form
was *ati-varas* – a prefixed verb derivate of *ati-varýti* "to chase away".
However, his solution relies on the irregular change of *ati-* to +aiti- that
has no analogy in any of the forms using this prefix. The etymologies proposed so far, strangely enough, do not take the initial *e-* into account, even
though it is contained in the Latin form *Eithuarus* in the oldest mention
of the being and also in some dialectal variants of the name. The composite *eiti-varas* or *eiti-tvaras* presents a promising explanation. It is
composed of Lith. *eitìs*, more frequently prefixed: *ateitìs* "future; the side
someone comes from", with a different prefix *išeitìs* "way out, solution";
plus *vãras* "force; violence". Then, the compound word *eiti-varas* could
have denoted a being that uses violence slyly, attacking not face to face,
but from the side. Alternatively, we could consider the composite *eiti-
tvaras*, where the second component – *tvaras* – is known from e.g. the
word *sùtvaras* "creator; creation" (cf. the cattle deity *Sotwaros* by Stryjkowski), which is derived from the prefixed verb *sutvérti* "to create". The
second component, then, would have a meaning similar to the Czech *tvor*
"creature", *stvůra* "monster" or *stvoření* "creation"– all of these words

have numerous parallels in other Slavic languages, and those parallels
are related to the Lith. words. On the Lithuanian shores of the Baltic sea
and in northern Lithuania, á. was called *pūkys*; in Latvia, *pūķis* (from
German *Puck* "hob") or → vilce. Unlike Lithuanian mythologists, the
Latvian ones consider the pūķis to be a relatively new fairy-tale character rather than an ancient part of the Baltic mythology. It is possible that
Latvians borrowed this household spirit from the Germans. The Latvian
pūķis is quite similar to the Lith. á., though there are some differences
between them. For example, the Latvian pūķis can be bought in Rīga of
course, and apart from taking on the forms mentioned with á., he also lets
himself be bought in the form of a mole. Some Latvian tales claim that
a flying pūķis has all the colours of the rainbow. It is said in Latvia that
one can obtain pūķis from the devil. One must give him several coins and
the devil throws them into a fire. Then, one must endure the sight of the
coins melting in the fire and the image in one's head of one's soul burning
in hell like the coins. Having brought pūķis home, the landlord must say
to his wife: "Devil in your heart, devil in mine, too!" One tale tells a story
of a farmer who did not take the incantation seriously and having come
home with pūķis, he said to his wife: "Devil in your buttocks, devil in
mine, too!" And when he woke up the next morning, pūķis was gone and
the whole entrance room was full of horse droppings.

Bibl.: BRMŠ II, 184, 186 > Mosv; BRMŠ III, 256, 258–260 > Prae; DLKŽ 6,
915; Fraenkel I, 4; II, 1152; 1149–1150; Gimbutienė 2002, 52–55; Greimas 2005,
86–122; Kregždys 2018a; LPG 280, LPG 536, 543, 330, 339; ME III, 446, IV,
542; Smoczyński 2007, 5, 144, 698 & 2018, 9; Vėlius 1977, 130–181.

Alabatis – Lith. deity, mentioned by Jan Łasicki in his book *De Diis
Samagitarum Caeteromque Sarmatarum et falsorum Christianorum. Item
de Religione Armeniorum* (abbreviated as "*De Diis* 1580" from now on
in this book) which was probably finished by 1580 but was not published
until 1615: "Alabatis, called to help by flax hacklers."[5] At the end of the
19th century, Mierzyński proposed the emendation *a la batis* "oh father",
supported by these two verses from a folk song:

Ey batti, batti, batuže mano,	Hey father, father, my daddy,
Perlejsk man ta mergyta.	let me have the girl.

---

[5]   *Alabathis, quem linum pexuri in auxilium vocant.*

However, it is a more promising theory to identify the first part of the
name with Lith. *ãlas* "bald; exhausted"; that, combined with Lith. *bàtis*
"friend, fellow; father", could have denoted one of the phases of flax harvesting ("the bald fellow"?). When we realize that flax harvesting consisted of several phases and one of them was flax retting we can speculate
that the name of this deity is actually the corrupt sentence *alė(k)[6] bàti*
"stand under water, friend", consisting of the words *alėti,-ėju* "to stand
under water" and *bàtis* "friend, fellow; father".

Bibl.: Kurschat I, 27, 279; LKŽ I, 91; LPG 357, 393; Smoczyński 2018, 17.

Algis – Lith. 'messenger of gods'(?). Information about this Žemaitian
(Samogitian; Western Lithuanian) deity can be found in J. Łasicki, *De
Diis* 1580: *Algis angelus est summorum deorum* "Algis is the messenger
of the highest gods". S. Stanevičius interpreted this theonym as the Lith.
word *algis* "groom; help hired at an agreed price". We cannot be sure that
this word actually existed, though, because it is not listed in any Lithuanian dictionary. German mythologist W. Mannhardt proposes a different
interpretation: Knowing that the word denotes a spokesman of gods, we
can assume that the name is a *nomen agentis* derived from Lith. *algti* "to
call up", *algóti* "to say, call, call by name". A. would then be a middleman
called by people when they needed help of the major gods. This theory is
supported by a number of scholars, e.g. V. Jackevičius, J. Jurginis and R. Balsys. The latter adds that in Algis' name "there might be some connection
to the Lithuanian custom of shouting and making noise during both family
and calendar festivals. So far, this custom has been explained as a reliable
way of chasing away evil spirits. We can speculate, though, that dangerous
spirits were neutralized by calling up [Lith. *algóti*] protective gods".

Bibl.: Fraenkel I, 7; LPG 356, 375; RB 384–385; RB 384 > Stanevičius 1967,
297; Smoczyński 2018, 18.

analogical magic – a type of magic that achieves the desired result by
imitation. Usually, that means an activity that is visually or symbolically
similar to the activity that needs to be done but cannot be carried out by
a human. For example, many Indo-European nations would sow their grain
when the moon was waxing. During this period, the moon gradually grows

---

[6]   Imperative forms without -*k* ending do exist in some Lithuanian dialects. See
      Zinkevičius, Z.: *Lietuvių dialektologija*, Vilnius: Mintis 1966, 370–373.

into a full moon, and there was a belief that this would ensure good growth of the grain. A. m. also denotes the belief that certain two objects are related by similarity of appearance or name, and therefore one of them must be treated in a certain way because this treatment automatically influences the other object. As documented by collected folk beliefs (or, as the collections' authors sometimes call them, "superstitions") and historical sources, the Baltic nations were no exception when it came to usage of a.m. They not only believed that it was used by witches and wizards to harm people, but they used it in everyday life, too. For example, Latvians believed that on the day of the Holy Cross it is not advisable to plough your field if you do not want it destroyed by hail. This sounds illogical to non-Latvian ears but it makes sense once you realize that the Latvian word for the "cross" is *krusts* and the one for "hail" *krusa*. Let us look at some more beliefs: Both Lithuanians and Latvians believed that cows will give more milk if they graze on a meadow where dandelions grow. This belief is inspired by the fact that Lith. *pienė* and Lat. *pienene* "dandelion" are similar to Lith. *pienas* and Lat. *piens* "milk". Latvian parents who wanted their little daughter to grow up to be as slender as a willow would hang her crib on a willow tree[7] whenever they went out to work in the field in summer. The oak and the birch were symbols of healthy men, and therefore when a Latvian woman cut birch branches, she was careful to leave the upper part of the tree untouched:

Smuidru griezu bērza rīksti,	Thin wand I cut from a birch
Kupl'atstāju virsunīti,	But the top I left dense;
Lai aug mans arājiņš	May my plougher grow up
Sprogainiem matiņiem.	To have curly hair. (LD 10711)

Water symbolised tears in a.m., and so witches would pour or sprinkle water around to cause sorrow. But a.m. was also used to cure. There is a Prussian record of the trial against Kotryna Gailiuvienė who was accused of witchcraft in 1560: "She voluntarily admitted to having helped and cured blind people. And that she always did in this manner – she took a piece of hazel or birch bark torn by wind from a fence, she laid it on the blind man's eyes and spoke so: 'Thou, eternal Lord, like the wind blows or tears bark from a fence, please tear the web from the eyes of this man.'" Bibl.: NarkGail; PŠ 14, 142, 214, 216, 223.

---

[7]   Willow trees in Latvia often grew near houses or in gardens.

Antrimpus – Pruss. 'god of seas and waters'. His connection with water and seas is unambiguously determined by statements such as *Antrimpus sal sein Gott des Meers vnd der See* "Antrimpus must be the god of sea and surf"; *Antrimpum, deum maris* "Antrimpus – the god of sea"; *Wasser-Götter Antrimpus* "water deities – Antrimpus"; *Antrympus Neptunus*. For more information on Antrimpus, see Balt. → *Trimpas.

Apidome – Lith. deity. J. Łasicki in *De Diis* 1580 remarks: *Habentque Apidome mutati domicilii deum*, "and they have a deity called Apidome for moving their dwellings". The name can be interpreted as a compound of the Lith. preposition *apì, apeĩ, apiẽ* "around" and the noun *dėmi* "spot; sign; stain", with the overall meaning "living around a certain spot". In the Žemaitian (Samogitian) dialect, *apideme* means "habitation". In modern orthography, *apýdėmė, apìdėmė*, besides *apydamė* or *apidamė* – "a small area in between buildings of a farm or at its edge" (Kurschat). The variant with *o* Łasicki recorded was probably influenced by the Pol. *dom* "house" or the Latin equivalent *domus* (rather than by Lith. *domẽ* "attention, interest"). Smoczyński (2018, 35) offers the most promising solution: Širvydas' *hapax legomenon* <apidame> may be considered an archaism retaining the lexeme *dam-* 'home' in its inherited form (cf. the Common Slavic form *domъ* "home" etc.), not assimilated to *namaĩ* "house").

Bibl.: LPG 357, 379 with reference to Prekier; Fraenkel I, 12, 92; Smoczyński 2018, 35.

Aspelenie – Lith. deity. J. Łasicki in *De Diis* 1580 describes it with the Lat. word *angularis* "having corners". Etymologically, its name can be interpreted as the compound *až-pelene* "behind the hearth", cf. Lith. *pėlenas* "hearth", Latv. *pęlns* id., Pruss. *pelanne* "ashes". Cf. *Pelengabija*.

Bibl.: Fraenkel I, 566; LPG 357, 373.

Ašgalvis – Latv. 'household spirit with a pointed head'; the name can also be interpreted as "having sharp wits". One of the regional variants of the household spirit (→ Mājas kungs). He is one of the topics in the 1740 report by H. von Hagemeister on the parish of Drusti[8]: "In Drusti, as I was told, there was a tree, which had 13 stone idols standing beneath it; some of them were created from several stones put on top of one another,

[8]   A town in northern Latvia, which lies between the towns of Cēsis and Gulbene.

and one of them was called *Spitzkopff*. Peasant Jānis Vīlums used to offer here a bit of every meal before he ate and of every drink before he drank. Last winter, when the abovementioned peasant was burning his offering beneath the tree, it fell on him and his sons, who were 6 and 12 years of age. The fellow himself lived for 4 more days, but he did neither perceive nor say anything; the 2 sons were dead on the spot. Inspector [...] reports the stones still being in their places." In the original German text, there is only the name *Spitzkopff*; its Latv. translation *Ašgalvis* can only be found in modern historiographical and mythographical resources. The name is composed of Latv. *ass* "sharp" and *gaḷva* "head". Dainius Razauskas is of the opinion that the name means "having sharp wits", but it is equally possible that it was merely a nickname for an idol with a pointed top part. *Ašgalvis* even found its way to Latvian fiction – Visvaldis Lāms published a novel in 1982 called *Pavarda kungs Ašgalvis* "Ašgalvis, the lord of the hearth".
Bibl.: BRMŠ IV, 154, 157; ME I, 144, 596; PŠ 55.

Atlaibos – Lith. deity. It can be found in J. Łasicki's *De Diis...* (1584/1615), in a list of deities that are not further specified. The basis of the word is probably Lith. *láibas* "slim, thin" and it might be somehow related to the plant name *atlaiba* "Eupatorium"; or, it could be an incorrect record of the Lith. word *ātlaipas* "echo".
Bibl.: Fraenkel I, 329; Kregždys 2011b; LKŽ I, 317; LPG 357.

Audėtoja – one of the seven Lith. goddesses of → fate. The word is most probably derived from the Lith. verb *áusti : áudžiu* "to weave"; hence, *audà* "woven fabric, spinning material", *audėjas & audėja* m. & f. "weaver". *Audétoja*, then, is a goddess or a spirit who "weaves" the fate or who holds the "warp" of fate in her hands.
Bibl.: RB 18.

Audros (dievas) – Lith. 'god of storm'. J. Łasicki in *De Diis* 1584 describes him as follows: "Audras – dedicated to the care becoming a god of sea and other waters"[9] This function can be specified as a 'god of storm' with the help of etymological identification with Lith. *áudra* "storm", *áudenis* "North-East", Latv. *audeniski* "quickly", *aũdrums* "naughty child".
Bibl.: RB 272, 292; Fraenkel I, 6–7; LPG 356.

---

[9]   *Audros deo maris caeterarumque aquarum cura incumbit.*

Augstlēcīte, zemlēcīte; also **Augsttecīte, zemtecīte** – Latv. metaphorical address of a frog, meaning "High-Jumper, Low-Jumper". According to Latv. mythologist Janīna Kursīte, it was a taboo name that was used to avoid addressing Mother of Abundance (Gausu Māte) by her real name. Mother of Abundance was known to show herself to people in the form of a frog. For further information on Mother of Abundance, see → Gausu māte and → Mātes. Other resources, though, claim that the frog was a form → Veļu māte would take on when visiting people. They would invite her to take part in the feast of veļi (→ *velijā) with these words:

Augstlēcīte, zemlēcīte,	"High-Jumper, Low-Jumper,
Nāc pa logu istabā;	Come through the window into the room,
Sēdies meldru krēsliņā,	Sit down in the chair of reed,
Velies vilnas groziņā.	Roll into the wool basket." (TDz 55097)

Bibl.: KL 313; Kursīte 1996, 325.

Ausca – Lith. goddess. J. Łasicki in *De Diis* 1584 describes her as follows: "Ausca – the goddess she is of rays of the sun when it either sets, or rises above the horizon."[10] Her name can be interpreted as the impersonal verb form *aũšta* "it is dawning", with the infinitive form being *aũšti*.

Bibl.: LPG 356, 380; Fraenkel I, 27; Smoczyński 2018, 76.

Auseklis, also **Auseklītis** m., **Auseliņš** m., **Auseklīte** f. – Latv. 'Morning Star'. Planet Venus, which can be seen about 2 to 3 hours before dawn in Latvia, and that is why it is called Morning Star. The Baltic tribes could not have known, of course, that it is a planet, not a star, and so it happened that A. is always mentioned together with stars. In Latvian folklore, he can only be found in folk songs and in one legend, and in those, he is always perceived as a positive character. In the songs, he is mentioned in connection with practical matters (he helps people determine the time) and in poetic context: he is compared to something beautiful, e.g. a wreath on a maiden's head, or a sweetheart, or the only brother. In songs, he is sometimes non-anthropomorphic (he is the golden rooster[11]

---

[10] *Ausca dea est radiorum solis vel occumbentis, vel supra horizontem ascendentis.*

[11] Haralds Biezais was the first one to realize that the golden rooster might be a metaphor for *Auseklis.*

that wakes the sky inhabitants in the morning); but, much more frequently, anthropomorphic – a sky deity. In spite of the fact that only one
type of songs deals with him – the so called cosmological songs – he is the
third most frequent character in them. One of such cosmological songs
was recorded by Gotthard Friedrich Stender, a Lutheran priest in Selburg
(today's Sēlpils in Latvia). In his work *Lettische Grammatik* ("Latvian
Grammar", Mitau 1783), he dedicated one chapter to Latvian mythology.
The cosmological song he recorded there follows, transcribed to modern
Latvian orthography:

Saule Mēnesi sacirta	Sun cut Moon in half
ar asajo zobeni,	With a sharp sword,
kam paņēma Ausekļam	Why he took from Morning Star
saderētu līgaviņ.	His bride betrothed.

In this song, A. is an innocent victim of Moon. Haralds Biezais explains
the fact by claiming that Morning Star is the smallest of all the sky inhabitants in Latv. dainas. He is, in a way, the baby of the family. That is
why he not only plays mostly passive roles in dainas and sometimes even
becomes a victim of the others, but he is also the most playful one and not
grown-up enough to work together with them, let alone to have children.
In most songs, you will see A. take part in games. But there are exceptions
– several songs say something like this:

Mēnestiņš zvaigznes skaita,	Moon is counting the stars,
Vai ir visas vakarā.	Are there all of them in the evening?
Visas bija vakarā,	All of them are there in the evening,
Ausekliņa vien nebij.	Only Auseklis is gone.
Ausekliņš jūrmalā	Auseklis is on the sea shore,
Brūnus svārkus šūdināja.	Sewing himself a brown coat.

(LD 33858,2)

Songs of this type were probably meant to explain what Morning Star
does when he cannot be seen in the sky. This particular song's topic is
partly similar to many so called sky wedding dainas (→ sky inhabitants,
wedding). A. also takes part in the games and washing procedures in the
sky sauna (→ sky inhabitants, sauna). This particular song and other Latvian dainas, too, make it clear that all stars are subjected to Moon with the
exception of A., who is partly independent: he acts on his own from time

to time, he has a relationship with the Sun's Daughter and, like all major sky inhabitants, his own horse to ride the sky mountain. He buys this horse himself, or, in some dainas, it is bought for him by Sun.

As for possible existence of A.'s cult – invocations or offerings – there is no evidence for it. (That is true for all inhabitants of Latvian mythic sky, with the exception of several addresses of Moon and Sun that might have been invocations.) There are probably two reasons for that: 1) Although A. is the third most popular sky inhabitant in Latvian cosmological dainas, as stated above, the actual number of dainas dealing with him is not very high. 2) It might be simply because the Morning Star was of no great practical importance to the Latvian peasant.

Bibl.: SLDDĢ 25, 26, 28; Kokare 1999, 48; ME II 177.

*Aušautis, also ***Auskautis** – Pruss. 'god-curer'. The first ones to record the theonym *Ausschauts*[12] with its Roman equivalent *Aesculapius* were the Lutheran bishop of the Sambian diocese Georg von Polenz (1478–1550) and the preacher at the court in Königsberg Paul Speratus (1489–1551). The book *Sudauerbüchlein...*[13] offers German interpretation of the name: "Aušauts – god of faults [of the flesh], of ailments and of sins."[14] The variant *Auschlauis* in the Sudauerbüchlein's so called "A" print is, without doubt, a printing error – instead of *l,* there should have been *t*, and not before, but after *au*. Johannes Maeletius [Jan Malecki] recorded in 1551: "... in what gods they themselves believe, namely ... in Auscutus – god of good health and also of illness".[15] J. Łasicki supplies his readers with a very similar, though briefer information: "[they honour] Auscutus of good health and also of illness."[16] As to etymology of the theonym, it is usually interpreted as the compound of *au-* prefix with a verb similar to Lith. *šáuti*, praes. *šáuju*, praet. *šóviau* "to shoot, to run fast, to move". The compound would then

---

[12]   In the work *Episcoporum Prussie Pomesaniensis atque Sambiensis Constitutiones Synodales* from 1530.

[13]   *"Sudauerbüchlein – Der vnglaubigen Sudauen ihrer bockheiligung mit sambt andern Ceremonien, so sie tzu brauchen gepflegeth"*; the text is preserved in several 16th century manuscripts.

[14]   *Auschauts – der Gott der Gebrechen Kranken und Sunden.*

[15]   *...quos ipsi Deos esse credunt, uidelicet: ... Auscautum, deum incolumitatis et aegritudinis* (see *De Sacrificiis Et Idolatria Vetervm Borvssorvm, Liuonum, aliarumque uicinarum gentium*, 1551).

[16]   *Auscūtum incolumnitatis et aegritudinis* (see *De Diis* 1584).

mean "the one that moves aside [the illness]". Toporov, on the other hand, drew the researchers' attention to the Lithuanian verb *kùsti* : *kuntù* : *atkutaũ* "to get better, get stronger", supposing it has a variant with *s*-mobile. The source compound **au-skaut-* would then mean "healer".

Bibl.: Fraenkel I, 322; II, 968; Kregždys 2018b; LPG 233, 245–246, 295, 362; Smoczyński 2018, 643, 1358–59; Toporov, *Prusskij jazyk* I, 166.

Austheia – Lith. 'goddess of bees'. J. Łasicki in *De Diis* 1584 recorded: "There are also goddesses of earth Žemina and of bees Austheia; they believe about both of them that they can influence the offspring, as well as encourage the bees to bring many more to the bee-hive and to keep the drones away from them, if asked."[17] The theonym is, presumably, derived from a verb like Lith. *áuščioti* "to chat, to talk" or *õšti* "to rustle, to whirr" = *aušti* "to hum, to rustle, to whirr, to bumble, to buzz, to swish". It would then mean something like "speaker" or "bumbler". A different interpretation is also possible, based on the Lith. verb *áusti* : *áudžiu* "to weave", which, according to Grienberger, might have provided the basis for the unrecorded noun **austa* (< **aud-stā*) "bee-hive", and that, in turn, the basis for the theonym **Austajā* "the one that lives in a bee-hive".

Bibl.: Fraenkel I, 26–27, 518; LPG 357, 368; Smoczyński 2018, 73.

*Auštrā (East Balt.) > Lith. *Aušrà*, *Aušrìnė* (Stryjkowski, Rhesa), Latv. *Auštra*; Lith. *aušrà*, in the Dzūkian dialect *auštrà* – which means "dawn, red morning sky". The Latv. equivalent is *àustra*. Cf. also related Latvian words *austra vējš* "Eastern wind", *àustrums* "East", *àusma* "dawn", *àust* "to dawn". There are siginificant parallels outside the Balt. languages: OCS *za ustra* "early in the morning", Ved. *uṣrā́* "morning light, morning", Avest. *ušrah-* "red morning sky", Gr. αὔριον "morning"; without the extending -r- Ved. *uṣás-*, Gr. ἠώς, Aeolic αὔως, Lat. *aurora* (**ausōsā*) "red morning sky" and also "goddess of red morning sky".

Bibl.: Fraenkel I, 27; Smoczyński 2018, 74–75.

---

[17] *Sunt etiam deae Zemina terrestris, Austheia apum, utraeque incrementa facere creduntur, ac cum examinantur apes, quo plures in alves aliunde adducant, et fucos ab eis arceant, rogantur.*

Autrympus – Pruss. 'god of sea and tidal waves'. *Autrimpus der Gott des Mehres vnd der grossen Sehe* "Autrimpus, the god of sea and great tidal waves". See → *Trimpas etc.

Auxtheias Vissagistis – Lith. god. J. Łasicki in *De Diis* 1584 describes him as follows: "You see, next to him who is for them god *Auxtheias Vissagistis*, the omnipotent and also the supreme god, those who have never known the one and only Christian God also revere many and many *Zemopacios*, that is, the earthly ones."[18] The theonym should probably have been recorded as *aukštiejas visogaļisis* "high (supreme) + omnipotent", as Mannhardt correctly deduced. Cf. Lith. *aukštiejas* "high; tall", *vìsas* "whole", in pl. form "everyone", *vìs* "everything", *galiñčius* "the mighty one", *galià* "power": *galéti* "to be able".

Bibl.: Fraenkel I, 25, 131; II, 1264; LPG 372; Smoczyński 2018, 70, 307–08, 1682.

Bāba, also **Bomba; Bubulis, Būzēlis** – Latv. 'hag, bogey; water spirit'. Latv. water spirits lacking concrete features, who would at the transition times of the day (i.e. noon, sunset, midnight) drag down into water people and especially children that were not careful enough to leave the bank of the river or to stop swimming at those times of the day. The name *Bāba*, which means "old woman, hag", suggests that this spirit liked to show itself to people in the form of an old woman. *Bomba* is a water spirit from Latgale (the eastern part of Latvia), about which mythologist Janīna Kursīte heard in her birthplace as a child, and the name of which she considers to be a variant of the name Bāba.

Bibl.: Kursīte 1996, 331–332.

Baltā mātīte – Latv. spectre "Little White Mother". A spectre in the form of a woman dressed in white that Latvians borrowed from Germans (Germ. *die weisse Weib*). It liked to show itself to people near roads or swamps, in forests or even near houses, and it would scare people. Sometimes it even lured their cows or horses away. Latv. *baltā* f. means "white" (*baĨts* m. "white"); *mātīte* is a diminutive form of *māte* "mother".

Bibl.: BMRT 162; LTT 1802; LPT XIII; ME I, 258; II, 587.

---

[18]   *Nam praeter eum, qui illis est Deus Auxtheias Vissagistis, Deus omnipotens atque summus, permultos Zemopacios, id est, terrestres ii venerantur, qui nondum verum Deum Christianorum cognoverunt.* See *De Diis* 1584.

*Bangputīs – Balt. 'god of storm and sea'. The theonym is recorded in both Lith. and Pruss. tradition. The first one to mention his name was Matthaeus Praetorius in *Idolatria veterum Prussorum*, which is the 4th volume of his *Deliciae Prussicae*, finished in 1703. Praetorius writes in Chapter IX: "*Bangputtys* is a god of storm. To honour him, they steal a spoon, which they later burn. […] Next to these gods, also fire and water are greatly respected; the former as a masculine, the latter as a feminine. The former is adored under the name of *Bangputtis*, the latter under the name of *Ponyke*."[19] In the tradition recorded in Lith., the theonym is mentioned by two 18th century lexicographers – although it is not clear to what extent they were inspired by Praetorius. The first one is a manuscript of a great Lith. dictionary (*Lexicon Germanico-Lithvanicvm et Lithvan-ico-Germanicvm*) by Jacob Brodowski (*1694–?), finished probably in 1740 and later discovered in the state archive in Königsberg (today's Kaliningrad). The second one is *Littauisch-Deutschen und Deutsch-Lit-tauischen Lexicon*, published in Königsberg in the year 1747 by the priest of Walterkehmen Philipp Ruhig (*1675–?). The information in both these dictionaries is almost identical. Brodowski has recorded *Neptunus Bangputtis – Gott des Meeres* "Neptunus Bangputtis – god of the sea", while Ruhig says *Bang-Puttys – der Seegott Neptunus*, i.e. "Bang-Puttys – god of the sea Neptunus". Etymologically, the name can be interpreted as "blowing into waves", cf. Lith. *bangà* "wave" and *pũsti*, *pūtúoti* "to blow"; cf. also Latv. *bañga* and *pùst* id. For further information on seas see →world.

Bibl: Fraenkel I, 34; II, 678; LPG 545–546; 609–612; ME I, 262; Smoczyński 2018, 96, 1044.

Bangu māte – Latv. 'Mother of Waves'. One of about a hundred Latv. goddesses and spirits called Mothers (→ Mātes). Latv. mythologist Pēteris Šmits considers her to be an original folk creation, but quite a new one, inspired by Mothers like Mother of Wind, Mother of Earth etc. She is, then, a newer, somewhat poetic variant of Mother of Waters and Mother of Sea. She is mentioned in this daina:

---

[19] *Bangputtys ist ein Gott des Sturms, dem sie zu Ehren einen Löffel stehlen und hernach verbrennen* [§23] …. *Nach diesen Göttern sind in grosser Consider-ation gewesen das Wasser und das Fewer. Jenes ist als ein Masculus, dieses als eine Femina verehret worden; jenes unter dem Namen Bangputtis, dieses unter dem Namen Ponyke angebetet worden* [§26].

Tais', tētiņ, oša laivu,   Build me an ash boat, daddy,
aud, māmiņ, zēģelīti: Weave me a sail, mommy:
Es lidošu jūriņā,   I will fly to the sea,
Bangu mātes klēpītī.   Into Mother of Waves' embrace.

(LD 30865)

The comparatively recent creation of this deity is confirmed by the Latvian word *bañga* "wave; downpour" itself, as it is not an original Latv.
word but an adaptation from Lith. or from the extinct Curonian language
that partly integrated into Latvian dialects. Latvian equivalent can be
found in the word *buoga* "huge number", which probably primarily meant
"flood". For further information on sea → world.

Bibl.: ME I, 262; PŠ 130.

*Bardait(a)s or ***Bardāt(a)s** – Pruss. sobriquet "the bearded one" (originally, probably an attribute of god Patollus). The authors of the earliest
mention of this name *Potrympos, Bardoayts ... Castor et Pollux* are the
Lutheran bishop of the Sambian diocese Georg von Polenz (1478–1550)
and the preacher at the court in Königsberg Paul Speratus (1489–1551),
in their work *Episcoporum Prussie Pomesaniensis atque Sambiensis
Constitutiones Synodales* (1530). In later resources, this deity is mostly
associated with ships: *Bardoayts der Schiffe Gott* (in the text titled *Sudauerbüchlein – Der vnglaubigen Sudauen ihrer bockheiligung mit sambt
andern Ceremonien, so sie tzu brauchen gepflegeth* that is preserved in
several 16th century manuscripts); *Bardoaits ... Ein Gott vber die Schiffe*
(in *Chronicon des Landes Preussen* collogirt durch Joannem Bretkium
Pfahrern zu Labiau, 1588). In resources newer yet, we discover several records of this name that begin with *P-*: *Perdoytus Aeolus* (Waissel, 1599); *Perdoytus* (Praetorius, 1703); *Perdoytus, Pardůtas – Gott des
Handelsleute* "god of merchants" (Ostmayer, 1775). The origin of this
p- is not clear; it could have appeared there due to the Upper German
ethnicity of the scribes or due to their knowledge of the Roman theonym *Portūnus*. There are also variants with initial *G-*; we dedicate the
symmetrical entry → Gardait(a)s or *Gardāt(a)s to them here. Etymologically, the theonym **Bardait(a)s* or **Bardāt(a)s* is usually interpreted
as adj. "bearded", cf. Lith. *barzdótas*, Latv. *bàrdaîns*; also cf. the Pruss.
noun *bordus*, Lith. *barzdà*, Latv. *bãr(z)da* "beard". This, however, does
not explain the association with divine twins Castor and Pollux, nor does
it make clear the connection with ships. The connotation with sailing can

be explained by the proximity of gods → Autrimpus and → Potrympus, who were associated with ships. Also, certain similarity of the name of the Roman god of ports and navigation might have played a significant part here. There is, though, nowhere in Baltic or Roman resources any information about his being bearded. There is, on the other hand, the explicit information by Simon Grunau about the "beardedness" of the god most old → Patulas and its absence in his young counterpart Potrympus, as depicted on Widewuto's banner: "One of them was [captured] as a man of a young constitution, without beard, crowned with a bunch of grain spikes ... and that was the god of grain and he was called Potrimppo. ... The third picture was an old man with a long green beard on his chin, his skin the colour of a deceased man, he was crowned with a piece of white linen in the form of a turban ... and he was called by the name of Patollo."[20] It is, therefore, possible to conclude that "beardedness" was originally the epithet of god Patols. However, as the list of gods grew larger, the attribute "bearded" moved to the proximity of god Potrympus. There, it was part of the opposition "beardless" : "bearded" at first, paralelly to the ancient gemini Castor and Pollux. Later on, *Bardaits was moved to the proximity of "water gods" and as a result, he was assigned a similar function – which was, apparently, once again an ancient Roman inspiration (Portūnas).

Bibl.: Kregždys 2008b; LPG 195, 243, 245–246, 615; MV 84; Toporov, *Prusskij jazyk* I, 194–197.

Barzdukai – Pruss. 'long-bearded dwarfs that live under the ground' (→ underworld). 16th and 17th century resources provide us with several descriptions:

"Barstucke – very small men"[21] (a text called *Sudauerbüchlein – Der vnglaubigen Sudauen ihrer bockheiligung mit sambt andern Ceremonien, so sie tzu brauchen gepflegeth* which is preserved in several 16th century manuscripts).

---

[20]   *eine war wie ein man junger gestalt ane bardt, gekronett mit saugelen ... und der gott vom getreide und hies Potrimppo ... das dritte bilde war ein alter mahn mit einem langen groen bardt und seine farbe gantz totlich, war gekronet mit einem weissen Tuche wie ein morbant ... unde his Patollo mit namen.*

[21]   *Barstucke – die kleinen Mennichen ... Parstucken – die kleinen menlin.*

"Barstucke – very small men whom we call 'underground men' or 'Wichtole'."[22] (the so-called 'A' print of *Sudauerbüchlein*).

"Barstuccas, called 'earthmen' by Germans, i.e. 'underground men' … however much they may pretend to be Barstuccae, who are called 'underground men' (as stated above)."[23] (Johannes Maeletius [Jan Malecki]: *De Sacrificiis Et Idolatria Vetervm Borvssorvm, Liuonum, aliarumque uicinarum gentium*).

"Barstucke are supposed to be very small men, servants of Puškaitis, the ones we call Wicholts."[24] (*Chronicon des Landes Preussen* collogirt durch Joannem Bretkium Pfahrern zu Labiau, 1588).

"Deities of luck, such as *Kaukuczei, Barzdukkai, Markopete*"[25] (Praetorius, *Deliciae Prussicae* 1684).

Praetorius goes on to tell his readers about the belief that was still alive in Nadrawia in his time, that these small people who serve god Puškaitis (→*Puš(k)aitis) live under the ground where elder trees grow. They are famous for their long beards that reach down to their knees. Praetorius even ventures to interpret their name etymologically, and his interpretation can be accepted even today: "Some people may call these [under]ground men [by the name] *Barsdukkas* because of their large beards. For [the word] *barzda* denotes "beard on chin" and Nadrawians call 'large beard' *Barsdukkas*."[26] The Prussian word *bordus* meaning "beard on chin" is recorded in the 14th century *Elbing Vocabulary* that reflects the West Prussian dialects. In Nadrawia, which is situated more to the East, the Prussian dialect could have been closer to Lithuanian; cf. Lith. *barzdà* "beard on chin". This difference between Eastern and Western dialects of Prussian can be traced in onomastics, as proven by the contrast between the toponym *Barduny* and the personal name *Barsde*. These names seem to be of the same origin.

Bibl.: Kregždys 2016; LPG 245–246, 252, 295, 299, 532; Toporov, *Prusskij jazyk* I, 198–199, 242.

---

[22] *Barstucke – die kleinen Menlin, die wir die Erdmenlin oder Wichtole nennen.*
[23] *Barstuccas, quos Germani Erdmenlen, hoc est, subterraneos uocant … utque sibi mittantur Barstuccae, qui (ut supra dictum est) subterranei uocantur.*
[24] *Barstucke – solten sein kleÿne menlein des Pußkaiten diener die wir Wicholt nennen.*
[25] *Glücksgötter als Kaukuczei, Barzdukkai, Markopete.*
[26] *Diese kleine Erdleute mögen auch wohl einige wegen ihres langen Bartes Barsdukkas genennt haben. Denn barzda heisst ein Bart und der einen grossen Bart hat nennen die Nadrawer auch noch Barsdukkas.*

Bauba, Baubutis, Būkas – Lith. names for → velnias, the devil (→ underworld). They were created in the process of degradation of the cattle god → Baubis, whose name is related to the name of bittern (Lith. *baublỹs*).
Bibl.: RB 164–165.

Baubas, Babaušis, Babaužis, Baubaušis – varieties of the Lith. word that denotes a bogey. These Lith. names of bogeys and spectres were created during the last few centuries in the process of degradation and demonization of the cattle god → Baubis (similarly to → bauba).
Bibl.: RB 165.

Baubis – Pruss. and Lith. 'cattle god'. Praetorius, at the end of the 17th century (*Deliciae Prussicae* 1684), recorded: "Baubis – God of cattle, who takes care of their cattle."[27] Further on, we find the information that "… In the times of our fathers [with the name] *Bunbis* they called the god of cows and oxen."[28] Another mention of the same name, though without any closer description, is brought to us by Wilhelm Martini in his *Ad plebem Lituanicam* (1666): *Absint Perkunas, Lituans, Babilasque Gabartai | Nec non Gabjaukurs Baubeque żemepati*. "Abandoned are Perkūnas, Lituanus, Babilis and Gabartai, also for sure Gabjaukurs and Baube, the lord of the earth." The theonym is etymologically derived from the onomatopoeic verb "to moo", which is documented by Lith. *baũbti* and Latv. *baubt*.
Bibl.: Fraenkel I, 37; LPG 513, 545, 582; Smoczyński 2018, 102; Toporov, *Prusskij jazyk* I, 201.

bear (Lith. *lokỹs*, Latv. *lâcis*, Pruss. *clokis*) – the mightiest beast of mediaeval Europe, also, the second most important animal character not only in the Balt. mythology (after the → wolf). For the most well-known characters and stories related to it, see entries → Lāčadēls, → Lāčausis, → Lāčplēsis, → Lāču Jānis, → Mežauckus, → Medžiojma, → Spalvaînis. A heroic figure very similar to the strongman Lāčplēsis can be found in the mythological systems of many European nations, and the principal motifs of the story (i.e. a mythical ancestor kidnaps a woman and they

[27]   *Baubis der Viehgott der ihr Vieh in Acht nimmt.*
[28]   *Zu unserer Väter Zeiten haben sie den Bunbis, den Kuh- und Ochsengott angerufen.*

produce an offspring – a strongman who later kills his father the bear and
frees his mother) have exact parallels in the myths of the Nordic people.
This proves that people dealt with the strongest animal of Europe not only
by referring to it with the help of taboo names but also by including it in
stories with totemic elements. Taboo names are alternative or descriptive sobriquets – e.g. Slavs referred to the b. by the descriptive sobriquet
*medъ-jedъ "the honey-eating one" in order not to summon the animal by
using its real name. The b. was nearly extinct in the Baltic countries in the
19th century but since after WWII b.'s from the continental population in
Russia have started to return there.

Bibl.: Blažek 2000 & 2017; Pilāts & Ozoliņš 2003; Pastoureau 2011.

Beaukuris – Lith. deity 'guard of the crop'. The theonym was first
recorded in 1611 by members of the Jesuit college in Vilnius. It is probably a compound of *bè* "without" and *aūkuras* "sacrificial stone; altar", cf.
aukà "offering; victim".

Bibl.: Balsys 2006, 42, 106–107; Fraenkel I, 24–25, 38.

Bēlis – one of the Latv. regional names for the household spirits of the →
Mājas kungs category.

Bibl.: MEnc II, 207.

Bentis (**Bendys?*) – Lith. deity. J. Łasicki is, unfortunately, very brief
in *De Diis* 1584: "… they believe about Bentis that he causes that two or
many set out on a journey."[29] Mannhardt proposes +*Bendys* as a source
form of the word. This form is based on Lith. *beñdras* "public, common;
fellow, mate, participant, associate", with an exact parallel in Latv. *biedrs*
"mate, associate". Let us also add Lith. *bañdžius* "participant, associate,
partner, friend". All these words are derived from the IE root **bʰendʰ-* "to
connect, to tie together".

Bibl.: Fraenkel I, 39; LPG 256–257, 375.

*Beržulis, ***Biržulis** (recorded in the form *Birzulis*) – Lith. 'god of birch-
trees, birch leaves and birch juice'; 'god – protector of lot borders'. He can
be found in two historical resources: for the first time, in J. Łasicki's *De Diis*
1584, in the section called "Of Žemaitian Gods" (i.e. Western Lithuanian

[29]   *Bentis is creditur, qui efficit, ut duo vel plures simul iter aliquo instituant.*

gods). "What Salaus, Szlotrazis, Tiklis, Birzulis, Siriczus (…) and other
similar gods do, they only reveal to Christians very unwillingly. They say
they assist people, and therefore they are to be turned to for help."[30] For
the second time, this god is mentioned one hundred years later in the work
of Pruss. priest M. Praetorius *Deliciae Prussicae* 1684 in a similar list of
gods, where Birzulis is described as a god of "birch-trees, birch leaves and
birch juice"[31]. W. Mannhardt agrees with Praetorius: "Here I deduce that
Praetorius, with Łasicki in hand, conducted his own research and perhaps
came across real cults of demons with similar names. Therefore, it is very
probable that (…) *Berzules*, i.e. Little Birch-Tree, the deified birch-tree,
existed". If this is true, then Žemaitians turned to B. with requests for
abundance of birch juice. On the other hand, there is Lith. mythologist
R. Balsys who claims that "Praetorius assigned functions to various gods
whom Łasicki mentions but does not describe in detail. These functions
were based on hypotheses he created about the origins of their names".
The theonym B. might be coined from the Lith. *béržas* "birch-tree", or perhaps from its derivations *biržè* "birch grove" (cf. Latv. *bę̃rzs* "birch-tree",
bìrzis "birch grove"; Pruss. merely *berse* "birch-tree"). However, Balsys
notices that (with the exception of the hazel-tree goddess Lazdona) there
are no records of Lithuanians ever having other specific tree gods, and
deduces that this theonym is more probably derived from the word *biržè*.
That denotes "bunch of twigs stuck into the ground to mark the border
of a sown field, or a branch stuck into the ground that marks the border
between two neighbours' meadows, or a clearing in a forest or a part of the
forest that has been designated for cutting down". In that case, B. would
not have been a god of birch-trees but a god of lots and Žemaitians would
ask him to protect the borders of their fields, meadows and forests. For
more information on the birch-tree, see also → world.
Bibl.: BRMŠ III, 148, 251 > Prae 1684, Chap. IX, §24; Fraenkel I, 40, 44; Las
1619, 49; LKŽ I, 850–852; LPG 522; MV 75; RB 349, 390.

[30] *Caeterum quid agant Salaus, Szlotrazis, Tiklis, Birzulis, Siriczus (…) alijque
eius generis, non libenter id Christianis aperiunt. Opitulatores illos hominum
esse, ideoque invocandos persuasum habent.*
[31] What Praetorius has in mind here is the sap bottled every spring from little
holes drilled in birch-trees. For 7–14 days in April, it has a pleasant sweet-
sour taste and strong healing properties. It is also used to make syrup, tea,
poultices etc. It has probably been a popular remedy with the Baltic nations
for many centuries.

Bezlea – Lith. 'goddess of dusk'(?). J. Łasicki in *De Diis* 1584 recorded: *Bezlea dea vespertina* i.e. "Bezlea – an evening goddess." Her name can only be explained in relation with the impersonal Lith. *blṭsta* "the night is falling", cf. *prýblindė* "nightfall, dusk".

Bibl.: Fraenkel I, 47; LPG 356, 380.

*Bičbirbis, *Bičių birbulis, *Birbulis – Pruss. 'bee god'. The name *Biczbirbius* is listed among deities that are related to various kinds of animals in the 4th book of Praetorius' *Preussische Schaubühne* 1684. The worship of bees is described in detail in Chapter V of the 6th book: "Some of them, especially those who live in wilderness, still maintain the custom of worshipping *Birbulis* as Bee God. He is sometimes also called *Bičių birbulis*. They invoke him so that he can give them happiness."[32] The name of this god is derived from the onomatopoetic Lith. verb *bir̃bti* "to hum, to rustle, to whirr, to bumble, to buzz", cf. *bir̃binas* "blue-bottle fly" (by the way, the Old Ind. word *bambhara-* "bee" also is of onomatopoetic origin). The first component of the two-component name is the Lithuanian (and Baltic in general) word for the bee: Lith. *bìtė & bitìs*, Latv. *bite & bitis*, Pruss. *bitte*.

Bibl.: Fraenkel I, 43–45; LPG 532, 585; ME I, 300–301; MV 81; Toporov, *Prusskij jazyk* I, 233.

Bišu māte – Latv. "Mother of Bees". One of the numerous (about a hundred) Latv. "Mothers". Latv. *bite*, gen. *bišu* "bee" (~ Lith. *bitė*, Pruss. *bitte*). For more information on Mothers see → Mātes.

Bibl.: ME I, 300–301; MV 81; PŠ 43, 50, 53, 68–69, 75, 83, 134–135, 147, 163, 197.

Blizgulis – Pruss. 'deity of snow'. The theonym was recorded in the first half of the18th century by J. Brodowski in the German-Lithuanian part of the manuscript of his great Lithuanian dictionary. It is derived from the Lith. verb *blizgéti* "to glow, to sparkle".

Bibl.: Fraenkel I, 46; LPG 611, 613; Smoczyński 2018, 133.

---

[32] *Einige, insonderheit die in der Wildnis wohnen, halten noch den Birbullis, der sonsten auch Bicziû birbullis genennt wird, vor den Bienen Gott und rufen ihn an, dass er ihnen Glück geben möge.*

Blūds – Latgalian spectre. Eastern Latvian (Latgalian) name of a spectre that belongs to the → Vadātājs category and causes people to get lost in forests. The theonym is analogical to standard Latv. *bluods* "someone who is casting one's eyes down"; cf. *bluôdîties* "to wander around aimlessly; to have no prospects due to one's bad conscience; to feel ashamed", *blènzt* "to stare, to not see properly, to hardly be aware of one's surrounding", Lith. *blandýti(s)* "to get dark; to cast one's eyes down; to feel ashamed"; also Old Church Slavonic *blǫždǫ*, *blǫditi* "to go the wrong way, roam (around); make a mistake; live a life of debauchery", *blęsti* "to wander around in a confused way; to be lost", Goth. *blinds* "blind".

Bibl.: Fraenkel I, 47–48; ME I, 313, 319; Smoczyński 2018, 126–27.

Blukku dievs – Latvian deity whose function is not known. A ritual to worship him was described as early as 1717 by pastor Baerent from Ronneburg[33]: "Inn-keeper Wohgul, late in the evening, lit four fires at some distance from the four corners of the barn [a building that was used to dry and thresh grain], he locked the door and barred the windows, and on the table in the barn he put a bunch of hay, a loaf of bread and a lamp, singing and praying with his people. When asked, he explained that it happens to honour the 'Blukku' deity."[34] This theonym is perhaps derived from Latv. *blukis* "log", which is, together with Lith. *blùkis*, an adaptation of Middle Upper Germ. *block*. However, the possible relation to Latv. *bluka* "ugly large face" must also be taken into consideration; cf. *bluka kâ mēnesis* "large round face like that of the Moon".

It is significant that this ritual was recorded on 24th December. If the theonym really is derived from Latv. *blukis* "log", there could be some relation to the Baltic custom of dragging a decorated log around the village and to individual houses on Christmas Eve, and to burn it in the end. This was usually accompanied by games, singing, riddles, providing refreshments and drinks, wild merriment etc., which was all meant to express the joy of the end of the old year. This custom was observed in

---

[33]   Today's Rauna in Northern Latvia.

[34]   *1717 d. 3 Nov. hat der Wohgul Wirth etwas entfernt von der Riege (Gebäude für Korndarre und Dreschtenne) auf deren vier Ecken bei spätem Abend Feuer angemacht, in der Riege aber bei vermachten Türen und Fenstern ein Schoss voll Heu auf dem Tisch liegen gehalt und Brod und Licht dabei, selbst aber mit den Seinigen gebetet und gesungen. Gefragt, hat er erklärt, es geschehe dem Blukku-dievam zu Ehren.*

both Latvia and Lithuania, although it differed significantly from region
to region. In some parts of Lithuania, for example, it was not observed
on Christmas Eve but on the last day of the year or during the Shrovetide
period. In Eastern Latvia, people would not burn the log in the end; in
Northern Latvia, they would "give it something to drink": it had a hole
in it into which drinks were poured. In Lithuania, good relationships
between neighbours were emphasized in this custom: the "log-pullers"
would, on entering a house, greet its master very politely, eloquently
praise his piousness and kind-heartedness, and then they would sit down
with the household members and have something to eat and drink. In the
20th century, however, this custom was already limited to visiting one's
neighbours. Three facts – a) that the term B. d. "Log God" was used as
late as the 18th century, b) in North Latvian town of Allaži, every household had a log which it treated with respect, and c) in some areas, the log
had human features carved in it – support the theory of J. Endzelīns and
also A. J. Greimas which claims that this log was originally a symbol of
a god. Unfortunately, there seems to be no way of finding out what kind
of a god it was, nor what his function was.

Bibl.: ME I, 317; LPG 503; Kudirka 1993, 234–242.

*Brēķina – Latv. household sorceress "Bawler"(?). G. F. Stender, pastor
from Selburg[35], included a chapter on Latvian Mythology in his *Lettische
Grammatik* (Mitau 1783). There, he mentions that "Brehķina Bawler
was an old woman in the house, who, as a protector of the household's
snakes and toads yelled at everyone coming not to step on her *Pēnu Mātes*
'Mother of Milk' or 'wet nurse'".[36] Stender interprets the name of this
character as derived from the verb *brehkt*, i.e. Latv. *brèkt* "to cry, to yell".
Salomon Henning, in the preface to his *Warhafftige Bericht* ("Truthful
Report") of 1570, tells us more about snakes and toads: "They are said to
have prayed to snakes and evil toads, from whose bodies, when crushed,
large amount of milk pours out. Because the old sorceresses Breckin,

---

[35]   Today's Sēlpils in South-Eastern Latvia.
[36]   *Brehķina Schreyerin, war eine alte Fummel im Hause, die als Beschützerin
       der Hausschlangen und Kröten jedem Ankommenden zuschrie, er möchte
       nicht ihre Peenu mahtes oder Milchmutter zertreten.*

whenever they came together, they would perform evil magic and cry [in Latvian]: *Man pane Math!* "Oh, my wet nurse!"[37]

One of the reasons these women protected toads and snakes might have been the belief that the Mother of Milk (*Piena māte* in modern Latv. orthography) is a goddess that takes care of cows. Mother of Milk is one of the many Mothers (→ Mātes) and she takes on the form of a toad (→ frog) or a snake (→ grass-snake). In the 20th century, however, this name was only used to denote a good milking cow. The Latv. *Mitoloģijas enciklopēdija* says: "Grass-snakes were considered by ancient Latvians to protect cows, and *Piena māte* ['Mother of Milk'] herself appeared from time to time in the form of a grass-snake, or occasionally, in the form of a wagtail. The grass-snake hunts for mice and the wagtail catches flies in the vicinity of cow-sheds, and that is probably why they were associated with the protector of cows – Mother of Milk."

Bibl.: LPG 414, 624; ME I, 330; MEnc II, 179–180.

Breksta (*Brėkšta) – Lith. 'deity of nightfall [and also of dawn?]'. The name is recorded by J. Łasicki in *De Diis* 1584: "*Bezlea* – goddess of evening", *Brėkšta* – "[goddess] of darkness".[38] The theonym is the impersonal form of the Lith. verb *brėkšti* "to come down (about dawn and dusk)".

Bibl.: Fraenkel I, 55; LPG 356, 380; Smoczyński 2018, 144.

Briežu māte – Latv. "Mother of stags". The first component is Latv. *briêdis* "stag" (~ Lith. *bríedis* "elk / moose", Pruss. *braydis*). For more information on Mothers see → Mātes.

Bibl.: ME I, 337; MV 86.

Bruteno – 'one of the two brothers that are said to have been the religious reformers of ancient Prussians'. This legend was put down by the Dominican monk Simon Grunau in the small town of Tolkemit, not far from Frauenburg (today's Fombork in North-Eastern Poland), in his *Cronica und beschreibung allerlüstlichenn, nützlichsten und waren historien des namkundigenn landes zu Prewseen*. This chronicle was written in the

---

[37] *Sie hätten Schlangen angebetet und böse Kröten, aus deren Leibe, wenn man sie zerschmettert, ein Haufen Milch geflossen, darüber denn die alten Zauberische Breckin, zumasse kommen, sich vbel gehat vnd geschrien Man pane Math!*

[38] *Bezlea dea vespertina, Breksta tenebrarum* (in *De Diis*, op. cit.).

years 1517–1521 and then 1529, but it was first published only in 1876–1889 in Leipzig (as *Preussische Chronik*). Grunau tells his readers about the expulsion of Goths from Italy, orchestrated by Narses, the war-leader of the Byzantian emperor Justinianus – without making a difference between real historical and his own fictitious events, the latter more often than not basing on naïve etymological interpretations: "Chased out of Italy by Narses, the Goths fled to the North. After having spent some time near Göttingen in Westphalia, they prepared to raid Denmark. The Danish king, to keep them at a safe distance from his empire, offered the island of Cimbria to them. There, a Swedish tribe lived in peace, called Cimbrians or Scandinavians [*Cimbri oder Scandianer*]. This tribe was as powerful as to demand regular taxes from the Danes; they did not feel strong enough to face the Goths, though, and they left the island on their own free will. The Goths took over immediately and called the island Gotland, while the capital got the name of Wisby after their duke Wisboo. The Cimbrians drew off over the sea, taking all their women and children with them, alltogether 46,000 souls, led by two brothers by the names of B. a Videwuto. They reached their destination in the area between the river Cronus [Germ. *Pregel*, Russ. *Pregolja*], the Haillibo bay [Germ. *Frisches Haff*, Pol. *Zalew Wiślany*], the river Wisła and the land of *Ulmiganea* or *Culmigeria*. Here, they subjugated the primitive original inhabitants and built numerous castles. In the year 521, the brothers called together the wisest men of the nation and made clear to them their intention to introduce their own [i.e. Cimbrian] gods, to be the only gods for the local people to worship and make offerings to. They intended for Videwuto to become the king and for B. to stand beside him as the high priest, to whom his brother listens as to a mediator of the gods, without whose consent nothing significant can be done and after whom the country bears the name *Brutenia*. And everything was done as they said. Videwuto built for himself a royal castle in Noytto, B., who took the title of *Crywo Cyrwaito*, had a seat built near Rikoyto for himself and his gods → Patollo, → Patrimpo and → Perkuno. There, he settled together with the priests that were subjected to him, called Waidolotts [Germ. Dat. pl. *den Waidolotten*]. In the year 523, they convened an assembly at a place called *Honeda*, where they announced the last words of gods' will."[39] Simon Grunau also … dra-

<hr>

[39] *Von Narses aus Italien vertrieben, flüchteten die Goten nach Norden, und nach einem längeren Aufenthalt zu Göttingen in Westfalen rüsteten sie sich, in Dänemark einzufallen, dessen König um sie von seinem Reiche abzulenken,*

matically depicts their voluntary departure from this world: "Then they commanded a great fire to be lit in front of the large idol of Perkuno, they reminded all people not to forget to respect their gods and the high priest Kirwait, and announced that gods had invited them both to join them. They wanted to sacrifice themselves for their beloved nation to become their advocates with the gods, to be able to ask them for mercy and help for their people. In their best attire, but Bruteno having left behind the trappings of his office, singing, the brothers went to make their sacrifice, to be consumed by the flames. The sky accepted their sacrifice with terrible weather, with thunder and lightning. The onlookers cried with prayer on their lips. Wooden idols were then built in various places that were dedicated to Videwuto and Bruteno and worshipped as gods. They were called *Worskaito* [*Wurskait, Wurschaite*] and *Iszwambrato*. The former was dedicated to Videwuto, the latter to Bruteno. When someone in need

ihnen ein Recht auf die Insel Cimbria zusprach. Ein schwedischer Stamm, die Cimbri oder Scandianer, lebte hier in Frieden und fand sich stark genug, den Dänen den beanspruchten Zins zu verweigern. Doch zum Widerstande gegen die Goten fühlte er sich zu schwach und räumte freiwillig die Insel, welche die Goten sofort in Besitz nahmen und nach sich selbst Gotland, wie die Hauptstadt nach ihrem Fürsten Wisboo Wisby benannt. Die Cimbri zogen mit Weib und Kind bei 46,000 Seelen unter Anführung der beiden Brüder Bruteno und Vidowuto über das Meer und gelangten durch den Cronus (Pregel) und das Wasser Haillibo (das Frische Haff) an die Weichsel nach Ulmiganea oder Culmigeria, untewarfen sich hier das unerfahrene Urvolk und erbauten mehrere Burgen. Im Jahre 521 riefen die beiden Brüder die klügsten Männer zusammen und eröffneten ihnen als den Willen ihrer vaterländischen Götter, dass das Volk keinen anderen Gottheiten diene und opferte als ihnen. Sie wollten, dass Videwuto zum Könige gekoren werde, Bruteno aber solle neben ihm stehen als priesterlicher Oberherr, ihm solle als dem Vermittler mit den Göttern gleich diesen gehorcht werden, ohne seinen Willen dürfe niemand etwas Wichtiges unternehmen und das Land solle nach ihm den Namen Brutenia tragen. So geschah es. Vidowuto errichtete seine Königsburg in Noytto, Bruteno aber, der den Titel Crywo Cyrwaito annahm, liess für sich und seine Götter Patollo, Patrimpo, Perkuno eine Wohnung zu Rikoyto aufrichten. Dort schlug er mit seinen Unterpriestern, den Waidolotten, den Sitz auf. Im Jahre 523 hielten Witowudo und der Krywe Kirwaito Brutteno einen reichstag zu Honeda, auf welchem letzterer verschiedene göttliche Willensäusserungen verkündete.

asked them for help, it would be given to him."[40] It is generally believed
that the name *Iszwambrato* is a distorted variant of Pruss. *swais brati* "his
brother". Toporov draws attention to the name of the village *Brutnino,*
which lies to the West from Wisła, between Pollenszin and Turmberg.
This name was recorded as early as 1255, when Pomeranian duke Sambor
II. presented the village as a gift to the monastery in Lekno. The hypothesis of its association with the mythological name is supported by the
proximity of a town called *Patull* – this name cannot but remind us of the
Prussian god of → underworld. The name of brother B. and of the country
Brutenia could be the distorted source word **Prutenia* "Prussia". **Prute-
nis* or **Prutenas* would then be a derived artificial name of a cultural hero
(in scholarly texts, this term is usually referred to as an *eponym*).

Bibl.: LPG 192, 194–195; Toporov, *Prusskij jazyk* V, 423; Vėlius 1989, 257–258.

Bubilos – Lith. 'god of honey and bees'. The report about his cult can
be found in the chronicle of Matys Stryjkowski (*Kronika polska, litewska, żmudska i wszystkiej Rusi kijowskiej, moskowiewskiej, siewierskiej,
wolyńskiej, podgórskiej etc. w Królewcu u Jerżego Osterbergera*, printed
edition in 1582, Latin version in 1650–1699). His name is probably an
onomatopoeic word for the bumble-bee, derived from the Lith. verb
baũbti "to moo", *baublỹs*, *būblỹs* "the one who moos". Apart from the
variant B., there is also a record of the variant *Babilas* by W. Martini in
his *Ad plebem Lituanicum* (1666): *Absint Perkunas, Lituans, Babilasque
Gabartai.* "Abandoned are Perkūnas, Lituanus, Babilis and Gabartai."

Bibl.: Fraenkel I, 37; LPG 331, 376, 513.

---

40   *Dann hiessen sie vor Perkuno, dem Abgott, ein grosses Feuer bereiten, ermahnten
     alles Volk, immerdar die Götter und den Kirwaiten zu würdigen, und verkündeten,
     dass die Götter sie zu sich geladen hätten. Sie wollten sich also für ihr geliebtes
     Preussenvolk opfern, damit sie durch ihre Gegenwärtigkeit die Ihrigen bei den
     Göttern vertreten und dieselben zu jeder Art von Hilfe und Gnade bewegen
     könnten. In ihrer besten Kleidung, Bruteno aber ohne den Amtschmuck, gingen
     die Brüder nach feierlichem Opfer mit Gesang in das Feuer und verbrannten,
     während vom Himmel her ein mächtiges Wetter mit Donner und Blitz sich
     vornehme liess. Die Zuschauer weinten vor Andacht. An vielen Stellen stellte
     man die Bildsäulen des Widewuto und Bruteno auf und verehrte sie als Götter,
     also solche nannte man den ersteren Worskaito, den letzteren Iszwambrato;
     wer sie in Not seines Volkes anrief, dem war geholfen.*

*Budintoja/*Budintojas – Lith. 'god/dess of awakening'. J. Łasicki in *De Diis* 1584 characterises this god/dess in these words: "Budintaia awakens sleeping people."[41] M. Praetorius (in *Idolatria veterum Prussorum*, which is the 4th part of his book *Preussische Schaubühne* 1684) says: "Budentoys – the god of vigilance, more precisely, the awakening one."[42] Both these theonyms are *nomina agentis bùdintoja & bùdintojas* "the one who awakens or reminds", derived from the Lith. verb *bùdinti* "to awaken", cf. *budéti* "to wake".

Bibl.: Fraenkel I, 62; LPG 357, 367, 374, 545; Smoczyński 2018, 159.

būrė̃jas,-ėjà – Lith. "male/female fortune teller". These terms with problematic etymologies are perhaps formed from *būrỹs* "flock, swarm, crowd", *būrỹs žąsių̃* "flight of wild geese", hence "seer of the flight of wild birds" or "that who foretells weather"; cf. also *ledų̃ būrỹs* "hail(storm)", *lietaũs būrỹs* "heavy rain, downpour".

Bibl.: Fraenkel I, 66; Kurschat I, 356–357.

bùrtvis,-ė (Lith.), **bùrvis,-e** (Latv). – "sorcerer; enchantress". These words are coined with the root that can be found in the modern Lith. verb *bùrti* "to conjure, to soothsay", Latv. *bur̃t* "to enchant". Also Lith. *burtójas* and *bùrtininkas* "sorcerer, soothsayer, fortune-teller", *bùrtas* "destiny", pl. *bùrtai* "magic, prophecy"; Latv. *bur̃ts* "sign made while performing magic; omen, portent; letter", *bur̃tnieks* "sorcerer, interpreter of signs" are of the same origin. There are some interesting external parallels. In ancient Italy, two goddesses were worshipped that were called *Fors* and *Fortūna*. In many cases, though, it is difficult to distinguish whether these two names referred to two deities or one and the same. These words have the meaning "blind chance" and "accident, destiny, luck", but also "bad luck". A temple dedicated to *Fors/Fortūna* was said to have been built in Rome by the third legendary king, Tullus Hostilius.[43] The cult of this goddess existed outside Rome as well: in Praeneste and among Sabines. The names *Fors, -tis*, abl. *Forte* (= Paelignian *forte* "fortunae") & *Fortūna* have their origin in *i*- & *u*-stems *$b^hr̥ti$*- & *$b^hr̥tu$*-. Formally analogical *i*-stems can be found e.g. in Ved. *bhr̥tí-* (RV) & *bhŕ̥ti-* (ŚB) "support, care, feeding, food", primarily, "carrying, bringing", Avest. *hąm.bərəti-*

---

[41]   *Budintaia hominem dormientem excitat.*
[42]   *Budentoys ein Wachgott, ist eigentlich der Aufwäcker.*
[43]   Livius X 46; Ovidius, *Fasti* VI 773f.

"gathering, collecting", in the Digor dialect of Ossetic: æn-burd "gathering", and in Old Saxon *giburd* "birth; destiny"; the *u*-stem can be identified in Welsh *bryd*, Cornish *brys* "idea, thought"; all tracing their origin to the IE root **bʰer-* "to carry". For mythological content of these words, see entries → priests, → soothsayer and → witch.

Bibl.: Blažek 2001, 257–259; Fraenkel I, 67; LPG 549–550, 556; ME I, 354–355; Pokorny 1959, 128–132; Smoczyński 2018, 168–69; Walde & Hofmann I, 534.

bužỹs and babaū̃žė̇ – Lith. "bogey, spectre, clown/jester" and **būzis** – Latv. "bogey, clown/jester; groom, stable-boy". Both these words might somehow be connected to Old Norse *púki* "devil", Old Eng. *pūca* "goblin, gnome"; or, more likely, they were borrowed from a closer source, i.e. Swed. *buse* "bogey".

Bibl.: Fraenkel I, 29; ME I, 360; Smoczyński 2018, 174.

Ceļa māte – Latv. "Mother of Path / Journey". One of the hundred Latvian Mothers (for further reference, see → Mātes). Like most other Mothers, she is not anthropomorphic, or at least there is no information on what she looked like. The first one to mention her name was the superintendent of Curonian dukes Paul Einhorn († 1655) in his treatises *Wiederlegunge der Abgötterey* (1627) and *Historia Lettica* (1649): "Latvians worshipped the sun, the moon, the thunder, the lightning and the winds, and apart from those, they also had other gods and goddesses, e.g. Mother of Sea, whom fishermen called to help, (…) and Mother of Path, whom travellers called to help". Elsewhere in the book, he says: "[Latvians] still call to their gods for help, which can be seen particularly in their songs: they sing them in their own language and they are real hymns to honour their gods; I myself have heard several times hunters to call to Mother of Forest and travellers to Mother of Paths…"

250 years later, Latvian revivalist Krišjānis Barons collected numerous such songs (called dainas) and published them in the collection *Latvju dainas*. These songs do not strike one as hymns to honour gods; several of them, though, praise Mother of Path as a protector of travellers who never goes to sleep (LD 6705, 31790) and is very rich, as she has access (though in a very specific way – see the song below) to a large amount of metal and large number of horses, carriages etc.:

Lai bagāta, kas bagāta,	This one is rich, that one is rich,
Ceļa māte, tā bagāta:	Mother of Path is the richest one:

Tur tecēja dien' un nakti	Day and night, there run
Dzelžu kalti ritentiņi,	Iron-sheathed wheels,
Dzelžu kalti ritentiņi,	Iron-sheathed wheels
Pakavoti kumeliņi.	And shod horses. (LD 34058)

How is it possible that Einhorn used as classic a term as "hymns to honour gods" in reference to short, simple dainas such as this one? Latvian mythologist Elza Kokare finds some interesting answers several centuries later (in 1999, to be precise): 1) Einhorn could not have meant this type of songs as they were recorded in Northern Latvia that was then divided from Curonia (today, Western and Southern Latvia) by a political border. It is therefore possible that the Curonian songs, heard by Einhorn, were longer and more festive, but none of them had been preserved in the 19th century, and thus Barons could not have recorded them.

2) In Einhorn's time, the cult of Mother of Path could have still been preserved in its more or less original form, unlike the 19th century Northern Latvia. The Mother of Path of this cult might have been much more than a mere personification of the road in a folklore genre that is purely narrative and poetic (as seen in the daina above). She might have been an important goddess that had the function of both a protector of travellers and a healer of sick. Her duty was to "lead the ailment away along the path", usually from a person who was about to set on a long journey. As a collection of Latv. incantations informs us, a woman was accused of witchcraft in 1699 because she did some magic with goat meat broth and then had it poured out on a crossroads with the words "Mother of Path should take Mother of Lying [i.e. illness] far away to Russia."[44] There is also a record of a long and complicated healing incantation that starts off with the theme of journey: "The one who runs without hands, without legs, let them run to the sea, to the seashore, let them sprinkle small eggs / pebbles, small stones. God the Father, Father of Path, Mother of Path, Sun Path, give back health…"[45] But this incantation is not a "hymn to honour gods" either.

There is also the possibility that 3) Paul Einhorn was educated in the Classics and liked to use the terminology even when there was no relation whatsoever to Ancient Greek or Roman practice.

---

[44] *Ceļa mātei vajag Guļas māti aizvest prom uz Krievzemi.*

[45] *Kas bez kājām, rokām skrej, lai tie skrej uz jūru, jūrmalu, lai sijā sīkas olas, akmeņus. Dievs Tēvs, ceļa tēvs, ceļa māte, saules teka, atdod veselību…,*

The first component of Mother of Path's Latvian name is the Latvian word *ceļš* "path, road; journey"; it has a parallel in Lith. *kẽlias* id.

Bibl.: BRMŠ III, 621 > Einhorn 1649, 17; Kokare 1999, 184–185; LPG 399, 460–465, 469; ME I, 371; PŠ 20, 76; Straubergs I, 112, 425.

Cēlis – one of the Latv. regional names for the household spirit of the → Mājas kungs category. According to P. Šmits and J. Kursīte, he was known to the inhabitants of the region east of the Northern Latvian town Valmiera. For example, in the village of Vijciems, it was said that "… Lielais Skripsts kept Cēlis in a linden-tree and fed him". Cf. Latv. *cêlējs* "the one who lifts up; builder", *ceĺt* "to lift up, to build".

Bibl.: Kursīte 1996, 321; ME I 369, 376; PŠ 55.

Cepļa dievs – Latv. "god of the stove". One of the Latvian regional names for the household spirit of the → Mājas kungs category. Latv. *ceplis* "stove" is derived from the verb *cept* = Lith. *kèpti* "to bake, to roast, to fry".

Bibl.: ME I, 373; II, 207.

Cereklicing, also **Cerekling**, **Ceroklis** – Latv. 'god of fields'. Joannis Stribingius recorded this information in his description of the mission to Eastern Latvia of the year 1606: "In certain times of the year, they sacrifice in forests a black bull, a black hen, a black sucking pig to the god of fields and grain whom they call *Dewing Cereklicing*, together with several tons of beer, sometimes more, sometimes less, depending on how cheerful god Cerekling makes them. Similar gifts are presented in similar way to the trees."[46] Another report of a Jesuit mission of 1618, *Annales Residentiae Vendensis,* recorded a shorter form of the theonym – *Ceroklis*: "Apart from other sacred things, they honour trees. They offer to them their gifts: men a black rooster under an oak tree, women a black hen under a linden tree. They also sacrifice the first bit of every meal and first draught of every drink to a god called Cerroklis."[47]

---

[46] *Deo Agrorum frumentorumque, quem vocant Dewing Cereklicing certis temporibus Bouem nigrum, Gallinam nigram, Porcellum nigrum, etc. aliquot tonnas Cereuisiae, pro ut illos deus Cerekling iuuerit, plus vel minus, offerunt in sylvis. Haec dona hoc modo offeruntur Arboribus.*

[47] *Arbores quoque tanquam sacras in honore habent, quibus dona sua offerunt: masculi offerunt quercui gallum, foeminae vero tiliae gallinam. Unum Deum*

Taking the deity's relation to vegetation into account, we can speculate that its name is derived from the stem that can be found in Latv. *cerēklis* "place overgrown with bushes"; cf. also *cęrs* "bush" and Lith. *kẽras* "tree stump, leafless stem", *keréti* "to grow wider and thicker". Surprisingly, there is also Lith. homonym *kẽras* that means "magic, enchantment".

Bibl.: Fraenkel I, 241; LPG 442, 445, 452, 455–456; ME I, 374–375; Smoczyński 2018, 526.

Chaurirari – Lith. "horse god". This deity is described in Matys Stryj-kowski's 1582 chronicle: "*Chaurirari* – horse god; they sacrificed mature hens and strong roosters of various colours to him in order to ensure horses' fecundity; and when they were asking him for peace (as they took him to be a god of war as well), like ancient Greeks and Romans asked Mars, they were sitting on saddles behind furnaces, sacrificed to him and prayed to him."[48] From several etymological interpretations available, the one of Vladimir Toporov seems to be the most promising. Toporov explains the horse god's name as derived from the Lith. word *kaũras*, which means either "hair" or "mould". The horse mane or colour could be the motivation behind the theonym; cf. Germ. *Schimmel* "mould", later also "white horse". The initial *ch* instead of *k does not pose a problem, seeing as e.g. the name of the Pruss. deity → *Kurke/*Kurko was recorded as *Curche* (1249) or *Gurcho* (1703).

Bibl.: Kregždys 2010; LPG 330, 339; Toporov 2000a, 172–178.

Christmas see → **Bluķķu dievs** (Latv.)

Ciemnieks – Latv. 'patron of guests', literally "belonging to the village"; typologically, a deity of the → Mājas kungs category. Cf. Latv. *ciems*

---

quendam colunt, dictum Cerroklis, cui ex omnibus comestibilibus primum bolum, et ex potabilibus primum haustum offerunt.

[48] *Chaurirari – koński bóg; temu pietuchy rosłe, cerstwe, różnej farby ofiarovali, aby się też konie kakie mnożyły, a kiedy go o pokój prosili od ich nieprzyjaciół (bo go też mieli za boga wojny), jak Grekowie i Rzymianie Marsa, tedy za piecem na siodłach siedząc ofiary i modły mu czynili.* (see *Kronika polska, litewska, żmudska i wszystkiej Rusi kijowskiej, moskowiewskiej, siewierskiej, wolyńskiej, podgórskiej etc. w Królewcu u Jerżego Osterbergera*, first published in 1582, Latin translation in 1650–1699).

"village, homestead", *cìemiņš* "guest from neighbourhood"; also Lith. *kiẽmas* "yard", *kaimýnas* "neighbour".

Bibl.: Fraenkel I, 251; ME I, 393–394; PŠ 56.

*dainā – East Balt. "folk song". Lith. *dainà* "(secular, i.e. non-religious) song", Latv. *daĩņa* "folk song". This term is usually associated with Lith. *dejà* "woe", *dejúoti* "to lament", or with Latv. *diêt* "to dance; to sing", *deja* "dance", *deinis* "dancer, jumper". The closest parallel can be found in Romanian *doină*, which means "elegiac, doleful song" and is generally considered to be of Dacian origin. The Balt. terms might be Dacian-mediated adaptations of a word that is originally Iranian and can be identified in words like Avestan *daēnā-* "religion, faith", Sogdian *δyn*, Parthian, Middle Pers. *dēn*, Pers., Kurdish and Ossetic *dīn* id.

Bibl.: ESIJ II, 297–299; EWAI I, 777; Fraenkel I, 80; KEWA II, 113; ME I, 432; Smoczyński 2018, 192; Trubačev 1967, 20.

Dalia – one of Lith. 'goddesses of destiny' (→ destiny). Lith. word *dalià & dalìs* "part; destiny, fate" is related to Latv. *daļa & dalis* "part", Russ. *dolja* "part; destiny", etc. All of them are probably derived from a verb such as Lith. *dalýti* "to divide", Latv. *dalît* id., or similar.

Bibl.: Fraenkel I, 81; Smoczyński 2018, 193–94.

Dārza māte – Latv. "Mother of Cattle Pound". One of the hundred Latv. "Mothers". Latv. *dā̀rzs* means "garden; cattle pound" (~ Lith. *dařžas* "garden"). For more information on Latv. Mothers, see → Mātes.

Bibl.: ME I, 448–449.

Daughters of Sun, also **Sun's Daughters** see **Saules meitas**

Debess bungotājs – Latv. "Sky Drummer". In the Latv.-Germ. dictionary *Lettisches Lexikon* (1789) by G. F. Stender (called *Vecais Stenders* – Stender Sr. – by Latvians), this phrase is translated as "god of thunder" or merely "thunder". As there was only one god of thunder known in all of Latvia, → Pērkons (see also → sky), it does not seem likely that D. b. was the name of a different, "competition" god. It was probably Pērkons' sobriquet. Latv. *debess* is both nom. and gen. sg. of the word, meaning "sky". Cf. related Lith. *debesìs* "cloud". The second word, *bungotājs/bun-*

guôtājs "drummer", is derived from the word *buñga* "drum", which is an adaptation of Middle Germ. *bunge* id.

Bibl.: BRMŠ IV, 212 > Stender 1789; ME I, 351–352, 449–450; Smoczyński 2018, 203.

Debess māte – Latv. "Mother of Sky". Latv. *debess* is both nom. and gen. sg. of the word, meaning "sky". Cf. related Lith. *debesìs* "cloud". For more information on Latv. Mothers, see → Mātes.

Debesstēvs – Latv. "Father of Sky". Latv. *debess* is both nom. and gen. sg. of the word, meaning "sky". Cf. related Lith. *debesìs* "cloud". The expression "father of sky" can be found in numerous IE languages, cf. Vedic *dyáuṣ pitá̄*, Gr. Ζεὺς πατήρ, Lat. *Iūpiter*, Luwian *tātis tiwaz*, and others. For more detail, see → *Deivas.

Bibl.: EIEC 230–231.

*Dēivas – 'the supreme god of the Balt. pantheon'; also, literally, "god". This theonym is recorded in a number of variants: Lith. *Diẽvas* (in earlier orthography, also *Dëwas*), Old Lith. *deivas* (Bretkūnas), Latv. *Dìevs* (in earlier orthography *Deews*) 'god of sky, light, justice, destiny, and field fertility', Pruss. *deiwas* & *Deiws* (Enchiridion), *deywis* (Elbing Vocabulary) "god" (see also → sky). Pruss. theonym → *Ukapirmas (recorded in variants *Occopirmus* and similar), i.e. "the first and foremost one", is probably a sobriquet or a second name of the same supreme god. It is, therefore, possible to reconstruct the original Baltic form *Ukapirmas Deivas "the first god", the first part of which was preserved in West Baltic languages, while the second part in East Balt. languages. Some mythologists also consider the theonyms *Andajь* (**An(t)-deivas*) and *Nъnadějь* (*Numa-deivas) to be his other names or hypostases. The Balt. name of the supreme being *D. is an inherited IE word for "god", which is preserved (with the same meaning) in Vedic *devá-*, Lat. *deus*, Old Lat. *deiuos*, Old Irish. *día*, Welsh *duw*, Old Norse pl. *tívar*. The original protoform is IE **deiu̯os* = **deiu̯os*, derived from **di̯eu̯-* "sky" – a form reconstructed on the basis of Vedic *dyáuṣ* "sky" and the name of the supreme god in Gr. mythology Ζεύς. All in all, these forms denote the concept of "god" = "the sky inhabitant". Also Fin. *taivas* and Est. *taevas* "sky" might be of Baltic origin, although Indo-Iranian origin is possible as well.

According to Lithuanian-American archaeologist Marija Gimbutas, D. was the supreme god of Indo-Europeans; she does not express any opinion as to his supremacy within the Baltic myth. system. Both she and Lith. mythologist Gintaras Beresnevičius regard him as a member of the supreme Lithuanian divine trinity: as Prussians worshipped the trinity → Patrimpo; → Perkuno; → Patollo, it is not entirely impossible that Lithuanians worshipped a similar trinity: D. → Perkūnas; → *Velinas/Velnias. G. Beresnevičius does not assign the supreme position to any of them, either. Latvian mythologist Haralds Biezais is convinced that D. was simply one of the inhabitants of Latvian mythic sky (see → sky; → sky inhabitants; → sky wedding), but a deity with substantial power over the world as well. There is one thing virtually all treatises on Balt. mythology have in common, though: D. is usually discussed as first.

There are no unambiguous reports of Baltic gods having observed a complicated hierarchy in the way Greek gods did and of D. being the supreme god; nevertheless, the Baltic pantheon was not entirely devoid of relations. D. had a significant place in it and also certain influence over the thunder god Perkūnas. Most of his power, though, was over the non-divine sphere of the world, i.e. nature and people. His particular domains were justice, growth of crop and vegetation in general; he helped peasants with field and house work and he knew every person's destiny. Apart from that, he took part in the events in the sky. Taking all these facts into account, we can assume that D. was one of the most important and powerful Baltic gods. In mediaeval Lithuania, though, his cult was overshadowed by that of thunder god Perkūnas. The reason might have been D. being too similar to the God of the enemy Christians, while P. being the god of the ruling class of warriors. That is also probably the reason why the chief / main sanctuary of the Lithuanian Grand Duchy was dedicated to Perkūnas. In Lithuanian folklore, D. is mentioned most frequently of all the gods – but that is probably caused by the popularity of the Christian God, which is of much later date. In some instances, it is even impossible to state whether the author of the song or the saying had the pagan D. in mind, or the Christian God. E.g. the saying *Kas Dievo žadėta, bus ištesėta* "What God promised he will fulfil" does not make it clear whether "Dievas" means the pagan god or the Christian God. As paganism was dispersing in Christianity, Dievas took on more and more traits of Christian God, and vice versa. D. became the father of one son and started to be associated with churches, while expressions used in folklore to describe Dievas were also used to describe God. Similar process was going on in Latvia, of course. The language of folk songs is so deeply rooted in the nation's subconscious that it is used even today by poets, popular song lyricists etc. And this fusion of two traditions and religions culminates in a recently written poem-confession by Lutheran priest Ivo Pavlovičs. The style used is that of folk songs *dainas*, but the plot changes gradually from the plot of a traditional folk song about D. to a personal confession of Christian faith:

[...] Lēni, lēni Dieviņš nāca	[...] Slowly, slowly[49] Dievs was coming
No kalniņa lejiņā,	Down from the hill;
Nemaitāja ievas ziedus,	no bird-cherry blossoms he crushed,
Ne arāja sējumiņ.	Nor any sown fields.
Lēni, lēni Dievs atrada	Slowly, slowly Dievs found me
Mani kalna lejiņā,	At the foot of the hill,
Nesacīja bargu vārdu,	He did not say one strict word,
Ne man' gauži biedināj'.	Nor one that would make me sad.
Lēni, lēni es atradu	Slowly, slowly I found my path
Savu ceļu pie Dieviņ,	To walk towards God,
Nu ir mana dvēselīte	My little soul is now
Dieva dēla rociņā.	In the hands of God's son.

In all other entries we include names of the resources (chronicles, dictionaries etc.) that mention the theonyms. In case of D., the situation is much more complex. "Chronicles like to emphasize that Baltic nations worship the Devil.[...] And as *Dievs* seemed to be similar to Christian God, chronicles keep silent about him," wrote Latvian mythologist Pēteris Šmits in 1926. That is only partly true: there really is no report of a cult of the powerful and caring god called *Dievs/Dievas*, but on closer look, we find some fragments of information: cardinal Valenti composed a report about Latvian pagan religion in 1604, including a supreme god by the name *Tebo Deves*. This theonym is probably the distorted Latvian expression *Debess dievs* "God of Sky / Sky God". Superintendent of Curonian dukes Paul Einhorn published a list of Latvian gods in 1636, with a nameless "god of sky" at the top. Lutheran priest A. W. Hupel mentioned in 18th century that the word *Dievs* in Latvian does not only denote one of the old pagan gods, but also the supreme God. The predecessor of Latv. national

---

[49] *Lēni, lēni* is an expression used frequently in connection with Dievs in Latvian folklore. It can be translated as "slowly, slowly", "lightly, lightly" or "carefully, carefully".

revival G. F. Stender even lists D. as a pagan god, but also adds the incorrect note that claims that one of his names was *Velns*, i.e. god of *veļi*, souls of the dead (→ **velijā*). As to folklore, D. can be found in all its genres. His image in Lithuanian and Latvian folklore resources is quite homogenous. In both mythological systems, he is a powerful god that maintains world order:

Es redzēju zvaigžņu sietu,	I saw a cluster of stars
Gaisa vidū līgojot:	Swinging in the middle of the air:
Dieviņ, tavu likumiņu,	What a wonderful arrangement, Dievs,
Ka zemēi nenokrita.	It does not fall to the ground. (LD 33780, 1)

Together with *Laima* and other deities, he determines (in earlier beliefs, merely knows) individual people's destiny:

Tai Dievo duota, Laimužės, lemta	It was stated by Dievas, decided by Laima
kad per laukelį bernužis auga.	That the boy grew up over the field.
Dievam dieniņa aizgāja,	Dievs spent the day
Ar Laimiņu runājot,	Talking to Laima,
Kam būs mirt, kam dzīvot	Who is to die, who is to live
Šai baltā saulītē.	In this lovely world. (LD 27684)

He is not an omnipotent ruler of the world, though – he himself is subject to its fixed order. Even animals that are under his special protection sometimes fall victims to birds of prey:

Dievins koši gavilēja	Dievs was singing loudly,
Baltus gaiļus ganīdams.	Keeping white roosters out at grass.
Vai gavil, negavil,	He can sing as much as he wants,
viens jādod vanagam.	One rooster belongs to a hawk.
	(LD 30622, 1)

As to his activities described in folklore resources, great attention is paid to the means of transport he uses. In more recent beliefs, he uses a carriage; but mostly, he rides on a sledge. For example, in the songs that inspired Ivo Pavlovičs' poem, he is always pictured as going downhill on a sledge, and the songs seem to draw special attention to the fact that

D. does not destroy any leaves, blossoms or sown fields. H. Biezais is convinced that this activity is in some relation to D.'s power over fields and vegetation in general. D. always goes down from the sky hill towards earthly fields in spring, while bird-cherry is in blossom, and thus perhaps "blesses" the fields and enables vegetation to grow. The songs perhaps also stress his endeavour not to crush any plants because he is their creator and / or protector and therefore does not want to destroy his own work. One need not wonder why D. uses sledge in spring, as up till the beginning of the 20th century, light "summer sledge" was used to transport hay and grain from fields in Latvia.

D. is most frequently mentioned in connection with horses, though. He rides the sky vault on his own horse. He also helps people take care of their horses:

Dievs iemauktus šķindināja	The bridle was ringing
Mana staļļa dibenā,	In my stable,
Sukādams, glaudīdams	When Dievs was grooming and stroking
Manus bērus kumeliņus.	My brown horses. (LD 30055)

and he also helps keep horses out in the forest at night:

Te gulēj'ši pieguļnieki,	Here is where the herdsmen lay,
Te kūruši uguntiņu,	Here is where their fire burned.
Te Dieviņš sildījies,	Here Dievs warmed himself,
Te palicis mētelītis.	Here he forgot his coat. (LD 30074)

Another of D.'s duties is to take care of vegetation. As described above, he ensures good crop by ritual descent on the earth and walking around fields. His power over crops is described in this Lithuanian daina:

Oi tu Dievužėli,	Oh great Dievas,
didis sėjužėli,	great sower,
dovanok pėdelį,	give us sheaf
o atstumk vargelį.	and push poverty away.
Užaugink javelius	Make grains grow
ant pūstų laukelių,	on our wind-blown fields,
išbarstyk sėkleles	sprinkle seeds
ant žalių lankelių.	over green meadows.
[...]Pašersiu žirgelį,	I'll feed my horse

O ir avinėlį,	And also my lamb,
atnešiu glėbelį	I'll bring an armful
Dievui dovanėlę.	To Dievas as a gift. (Trinkūnas 2009, 172)

It transpires that in Lithuania, hay and grains were sacrificed to D. and he was asked to make it grow well next year. In Latvia, on the other hand, it was more usual to offer him hens in return for an abundance of calves.

Like other supernatural beings, D. was most powerful during so-called transition times of the day and of the year, especially during solstices. That is probably why it was recommended to let horses out to graze at Midsummer Night (in the evening of 23rd June). If a horse got lost, its life was fully in D.'s hands:

Tumša nakts, zaļa zāle,	Dark night, green grass,
Laukā laižu kumeliņu.	I let my horse out.
Nu, Dieviņi, tava vaļa,	Now he's in your power, Dievs,
Nu tavā rociņā.	He is in your hands now. (LD 30201)

D. would also visit people's households, and the landlord usually let him sit in his place at the table out of respect:

Klusat jauni, klusat veci,	Silence, young ones, silence, old ones,
Dievs ienāca istabā,	Dievs has entered the room,
Dievs ienāca istabā,	Dievs has entered the room,
Vaicā nama saimenieku.	He asks who the landlord is.
Tas bij nama saimenieks,	The landlord is the one
Kas sēd galda galiņā,	Sitting at the end of the table
Alus kanna rociņā.	Drinking beer from a tankard. (LD 33271, 1)

D. also helps people with various household chores:

Labāk malu timsiņāi,	I like to grind flour in the dark,
Timsā Dievs palīdzēja;	In the dark, that's when Dievs helps,
Timsā sēd mīļa Laime	In the dark, that's when Laima sits
Dzirnu galda galiņā.	behind the grain grinder. (LD 8249)

As to his traits, D. is described in Lithuanian and Latvian folklore as considerate, wise and just. Latvian folk songs do not mention anything about his countenance, though. We must, therefore, rely on the theory of M. Gimbutienė that Lithuanian D. took on the form of a young man. According to M. Gimbutienė, just like the Prussian supreme divine trinity consisted of young Patrimpo, middle-aged Perkuno and old Patollo, the Lithuanian supreme trinity was young D., middle-aged Perkūnas and old Velinas/Velnias. As to his clothes and accessories, Baltic folklore resources picture him as a strong, dignified man, wearing a long gray, silver or green coat with the traditional Baltic woven belt called *juosta* (Lith.) / *josta* (Latv.). He has a sword by his side and his horse is covered with "starry blanket" (the Latv. expression *zvaigžņu deķis* does not make it clear whether the blanket is woven with stars' rays or merely decorated with stars). But whenever D. descends on the earth and walks around a field, he wears a gray coat and a cap made of rye ears.

Latvian folklore material provides us with abundance of information on D.'s life in the sky. Just like other sky inhabitants, he engages in activities similar to those of Latvian peasants: he keeps his horses out at pasture, brews beer, sows fields, and even has two grooms who are in the habit of getting up too late and forgetting to mow D.'s meadow. The number of these activities is smaller than with e.g. Sun's Daughters, though. In contrast to the commonness of said activities, all objects used in them are more exquisite, more precious and beautiful than their earthly counterparts – they are golden, silver, made with diamonds and expensive materials:

Dieviņš medīti aizgāja	Dievs went hunting
Ar sudraba sunīšiem;	With silver hounds,
Divi zelta vāverītes	Two golden squirrels
Pār kalniņu pārtecēja.	Ran over a hill. (LD 33825, 1)

Also, just like other inhabitants of Latvian myth. sky, D. has his own house. Right next to it, there is a forest – oak forest in some dainas, in others linden forest, pine, spruce or birch forest. There are also springs and rivers, silken meadows and golden mountains, even sea in one daina. Latvian folklore does not describe the house itself, though. It is only known that it has a yard in the centre with three springs, and that it stands on a hill or beyond a hill. Mother of Wind (→ Vēja māte) sweeps the dust in the house. The songs pay great attention to the house's gate. Sun's Daughters' carriage stops by it, and folk song authors sing about hanging their shawls and caps on the hook by the gate. According to L. Adamovičs and H. Biezais, "the gate of the house" is in these cases a mere metaphor for a place in the sky that has some kind of contact with the earth and where D. accepts guests, among them also mortal people.

D. also takes part in the events in the sky and relationships among sky inhabitants. For example, he is angry for three days and three nights with Sun because she complained to him that his sons turned over her daughter's sledge, alternately, that they pulled her golden ring from her finger or took the wreath from her head. D. also takes part in the sky inhabitants' wedding as Sun's or Sun's Daughter's bridegroom; sometimes only as the father-in-law or the patriarch of the family (→ sky inhabitants, wedding). What causes problems to Baltic mythology researchers is the contradiction between dainas that mention D.'s sons (*Dievo sūneliai*, → *Dieva dēli*) and D.'s mother (*Dieva māte*), and dainas similar to this one:

Kur, Dieviņ, tu paliksi,	What will become of you, Dievs,
Kad mēs visi nomirsim?	When we'll all have died?
Ne tev sievas, ne tev bērnu,	You've no wife, you've no children
Kas tev vecam maizi dos?	Who will feed you when you're old?

(LD 33678)

According to H. Biezais, the fact that D. can be encountered both as having and not having sons, cannot be explained within one period of time. The daina that claims D. has no family was composed in a different period than the ones where he has sons – probably in the time when the image of D. was already corrupted by the influence of Christianity – and the author of this and similar dainas were "rationalists" for whom images of Latv. gods were not an unquestionable axiom, and who preferred to look at them from a purely practical point of view. Here, we dedicate an entry to Dievs's sons (→ Dieva dēli). Dievs' Mother is not mentioned frequently in Balt. folklore, and in most cases, it is in reference to Virgin Mary. In the remaining cases, it is virtually impossible to state whether the author had Dievs's mother or Virgin Mary in mind. Even the daina, in which God's Mother (Dieva māte) fights → Velna Māte, "Devil's Mother" (LD 34054), might have been composed or later altered under the influence of traditional images of Jesus' mother. There is nothing whatsoever said about D.'s wife in Balt. folklore, and yet there must have been one, as D. has sons. Some mythologists are of the opinion that "Mother of Earth" (→ Zemes māte) was his wife. This opinion is based on the fact that at the centre of other IE mythological systems, there was the couple Sky God – Earth Mother.

Lith. D. has a special relationship with the other two members of the supreme divine trinity. G. Beresnevičius notices that Perkūnas is almost equal to him, but pursues Velinas "in D.'s service". This could mean that Perkūnas is D.'s son. As to Velinas, D. competes with him in the myths where they both create the world and then they both farm on the land they created. In other myths and tales, their competition is less obvious and Perkūnas takes on the role of Velinas' competitor. D. never pursues Velinas himself. Beresnevičius deduces that Velinas is D.'s brother.

There is one noteworthy difference between Balt. D. and Christian God: Balt. D.'s power is limited to only several spheres of the world – the sky, the vegetation, people's destiny. There are some places we never find him in – for example, the realm of veļi / vėlės (→ *velijā) and the sky inhabitants' sauna – which is surprising, considering his important role in the sky inhabitants' wedding. Also, D.'s power over the sea is fairly limited. This might be caused by the fact that he came to the Baltics from the south, with agricultural Indo-Europeans.

Before the Christianisation of the Baltics, local nations adopted a number of IE etiological myths. In these myths, D. is the chief protagonist and creator of the universe: he creates the Earth, models man out of clay and breathes life into his nostrils. According to a different, Lith., myth, however, man came to be when D. was washing himself and one drop of water fell on the ground. In other myths, D. co-operated with Velnias / Velns to create the world. As it is not possible to list all motifs of all these etiological myths here, let us at least tell one of them in full (a Latv. one):

'When the Earth was created, it was too big to fit under the sky vault. What to do with such a huge disc? Here comes the hedgehog, just in time, and asks, what's the trouble here? You see, it's like this: the Earth is created, but it won't fit under the sky vault and it'd be wasting D.'s work to break a piece of it off. "Oh, that's easy", says the hedgehog,, "just press the disc at the edges, it'll get smaller and will fit under the sky." All right, then. D. pressed the Earth disc at the edges and slipped it easily under the sky. The only trouble was, as he was pressing it, it got wrinkled at some places – those are hills and valleys. And he gave the hedgehog a strong coat made of real needles, so that nobody dares to attack him.'

D. is not a good and omnipotent Demiurge in these myths, unlike God in Judaism, Christianity and Islam. He is powerful, but there are moments when he is at a loss what to do, as we just saw. In spite of that, he often appears in such myths as a rich farmer and neighbour of Velinas / Velns, who differs from him not by greater kindness or power, but cunning. He agrees with Velinas / Velns that they will work in a field together, and when the crop time comes, he will get what is under the ground and Velinas / Velns what is above it. D. then plants potatoes and has plenty to eat during winter, while all Velinas / Velns gets is potato haulm. According to the author of web pages *Latviešu folklora*, the story was not meant to suggest that D. is treacherous or malevolent. He is simply cunning, and cunning was considered to be a sign of intelligence. This myth is fairly new, or it was recently adapted, as potatoes spread in Europe only in the 18th century.

Probably even more recently created are the tales where D. appears as an old, grey-haired beggar. His age suggests that he is the oldest being in the world, because he created it. A poor man usually takes pity on this beggar and D. rewards him. These tales are popular especially in Lithuania and they emphasize D.'s justness and strictness: when someone does not treat the beggar well, D. transforms him into an animal and it is not possible to revert this transformation. Similar tales are also known in other parts of Europe.

In Latvian folk ornamentics, the sign for D. is a semi-circle with its ends facing down. This sign also denotes the sky and a hill.

Bibl.: Beresnevičius 2004, 151–155, 158–160; Biezais 2008; BRMŠ III, 601, 612 > EinhRef kap. I, §2; BRMŠ IV, 203 > Stend; EWAI I, 742–743, 750–751; Gimbutienė 2002, 83–91; Kokare 1999, 65–89; Kraukle 2008, 71; LKŽ 135; LPG 469, LPG 509 > Hup 1789, LPG 626, ME I, 485; Mitologijos enciklopedija II, 277–278; MV 114–15; Pavlovičs (p.c.); Pokorny 1959, 184–185; PŠ 15, 21–26, 165; Smoczyński 2018, 224–25; Toporov, *Prusskij jazyk* I, 321–324.

Dēkla – one of the three Latvian 'chief goddesses of fate'. The first mention of this theonym is probably in *Historia Lettica, das ist Beschreibung der Lettischen Nation* by Paul Einhorn (Dorpt in Liefland (today's Tartu in Estonia) 1649; Chapter VII, §27): "Beside this [goddess Laima], they have a goddess that they call *Dēkla*; she, when a child is born, rocks them, for it is her duty, to rock and to protect little children. When these [children] were born, they were given names; it is impossible, though, to state when this [childbirth] happened."[50] Ch. Kelch recorded her name as *Dähkla* in his *Liefländische Historia* (Frankfurt und Leipzig, 1695).

---

[50] *Neben dieser* [= *Laima*] *haben sie noch eine Göttin gehabt, die **Däckla** genant; dieselbe hat die Kinder, wenn sie gebohren, eingewiegt, denn das ist jhr Ampt gewesen, die kleinen Kinder einwiegen und derselben warten. Wann nu dieselben gebohren, haben sie jhnen Namen gegeben; wann aber dasselbe geschehen, kann man eigendlich nicht anzeigen.*

The first attempt at etymological interpretation of the name D. was made by Wilhelm Hupel in *Topographische Nachrichten von Lief- und Ehstland*, published in Rīga in 1774–1777. Hupel says: "Several goddesses can be counted. *Dēwekla*, or, in short form, Dēkla, is generally their name for the goddess of women in childbed, under whose beneficial influence newborn children are said to sleep and grow well. Other people ascribe this influence to *Tikla* or *Tiklis*. *Dēkla*, though, whose name is derived from the Latvian *dēt* 'to suck', guards sucklings…"[51] All the information about the goddess given here inspired various etymology proposals, all of which have their supporters amongst mythologists. (1) It is the name of St. Thecla transformed by popular etymology (Biezais; Pogodin). (2) The theonym is derived from the IE root $d^heH_1(i)$- "to suck; to breast-feed" (Ivanov & Toporov; Polomé). (3) Stender in *Lettische Grammatik* added the third etymological interpretation, associating the theonym with the Latv. verb *dēt* "to put; to wait; to take care of" < IE $*d^heH_1$- "to put", cf. Latv. *pupu* dēt "to give breast", *pa-dēkls* "nest-egg".

(4) Another etymology is inspired by the comparison with the names of two ancient goddesses of Southern Italy. The nation of Volsci, which lived south of Rome, worshipped a goddess by the name *Dekluna*; the neighbouring nation, Osci, who lived in a land-locked region of Southern Italy, knew a goddess called *Tekliia /Deklija/*. The initial *d-* eliminates $*d^h$- as the original IE consonant, because this sound of the IE proto-language transformed into *f-* in Osco-Umbrian languages. There are no reports as to what the function of this ancient Italian goddess was, and so the etymological intepretation of this theonym is usually based on mere comparative analysis of the word.

One of the possibilities is to focus on Hupel's record of the Latv. theonym *Deewekla*. If it is not Hupel's own creation inspired by the word → Dievs 'the supreme god', which he recorded as *Deews*, but an abbreviation of the proto-form *Dievekla*, as Hupel himself suggests, then it is possible to find a similar sound change in ancient Italy. The name of the Roman goddess of women, childbirth and the moon *Dīāna* is actually the

---

[51] *Göttinnen zählt man auch etliche*: *Deewekla heisst überhaupt die Göttin, zusammengezogen Dehkla*; *das letzte soll eine Göttin der Wöchnerinnen bezeichnen, durch deren wohlthätigen Einfluss die neugeborenen Kinder Schlaf und gut Gedeyen erhalten sollten*; *andre legen solche Wirkungen einer Tikkla oder Tikls bey*; *der Dehkla aber, die sie von dem lettischen Wort Deht saugen, Dehjkla schreiben, die Aufsicht über die Säugenden…*

contracted proto-form *Diviāna* (Walde & Hofmann I, 347). The other
part of the word is reminiscent of the suffix typical of *nomina instrumenti*,
known in both Baltic and Italic languages[52]. This suffix usually appears
with verbal stems, though, and this is not the case. Thus, it is more promising to analyze the theonym as a compound name, the second component
of which can be identified as IE root $*kleH_I–$ > Lat. *calō, -āre* "to call
together", Pruss. *kelsāi* "they are calling", Lith. *kalbà* "language, speech".
Primarily "god's spokesperson", then? That would be a fitting name for
a goddess that informs parents of a child's fate.

Beside the interpretation based on the form *Deewekla*, another solution is possiblese: prefix *dĕ-*, meaning "away", plus the already mentioned verbal root $*kleH_I–$. The compound would then describe someone
who wards off the effects of evil chants. This, too, is one of the duties of
a good goddess of fate.

Bibl.: Biezais 1975, 366 > Pogodin; Blažek 2001; Holthausen 1916, 308; Ivanov
& Toporov 1987, 364; LIV2 361; LPG 482–483, 509–510, 620; Meiser 1986, 21;
MV 349–50; Pokorny 1959, 182, 184, 548–549; Polomé 1995, 38; Radke 1965,
103, 223–224; Untermann 2000, 164, 740.

Derfintos (**Derfintois* < **Der(p)intojas*) – Lith. 'god that provides
peace'. This Žemaitian god is described by J. Łasicki in *De Diis* 1584:
Derfintos pacem conciliat, "Derfintos negotiates peace". This is also the
only information preserved.

The theonym D. is not transparent, and so it has inspired several different interpretations. For example, Lith. mythologist Gintaras
Beresnevičius sees it as a compound of two word stems. The first one is
derýbos "negotiation, haggling" or *dẽrinti* "to adapt, to tune". The second
one is *pìnti* "to tie, to knit" (supposing the original *p* was later changed to
f). The compound **der-pintojas* would then mean "the one who ties people together and makes them negotiate peace". Other researchers consider
this theonym to be an incorrect record of the word *derrintos*, because the
letters "r" and "f" look similar to each other in print. Thus corrected, the
theonym could be transcribed to modern Lithuanian as *derintojas* and
translated as "negotiator".

Rimantas Balsys draws attention to the fact that the role of peace-
maker and judge is usually taken on by → Deivas himself in Lith. folk-

---

[52]   Cf. Lat. *ob-stāculum* "obstacle" and Lith. *stãklès* pl. "weaver's loom" < **stā-
tlo-* (Brugmann II.1, 340–341).

lore; sometimes also → Perkūnas. Considering that, he does not exclude the possibility of *Derintojas* and → *Ligyčius* being actually sobriquets or euphemisms referring to a member of the supreme divine trinity.

Bibl.: BRMŠ II, 581, 594; Jaskiewicz 1952, 79; LPG 356, 370; RB 385–386 > Beresnevičius; Smoczyński 2018, 213.

Dieva dēli – Latv. "Dievs' Sons", can also be translated as "God's sons". They are a pair (or more) of young men, usually twins, of divine pedigree, that chase young beauteous girls, who also are of divine ancestry (→ sky). This pair can be encountered in several other IE traditions, too: Ved. *Divo nápātā* "offspring [of the god] of Sky"; Gr. Διόσκουροι "Zeus' sons"; Lith. *Diẽvo sūnėliai* "sons of God/Dievas", and others. In the Baltic traditions, D. d. are best described in Latv. dainas; however, these dainas often mention only one son. The first daina about D. d. to be recorded was this one – in the chapter *Lettische Mythologie* of *Lettische Grammatik* (Mitau, 1783) by G. F. Stender:

Kur palike Dieva zirgi?	Where are Dievs' horses?
Dieva dēls jādīja.	Dievs' son is riding them.
Kur aizjāje Dieva dēli?	Where have Dievs's sons gone to?
Saules meitas raudzitiês.	To choose Sun's daughters as their brides.
Pati Saule atbildēja:	Sun herself answered them:
Mazi mani bērniņi	Small are my children,
Mazas manas dāvanas.	Small are my presents. (LPG 623)

As we can see in this daina, not only horses, but also roosters support the divine twins:

Sudrabiņa gaiļi dzied	Silver roosters are singing
Zeltupītes maliņā;	At the bank of a golden river;
Tie piecēla Dieva dēlus,	They woke up Dievs' sons,
Saules meitas preciniekus.	suitors of Sun's daughters. (LD 34008)

Dainas only rarely mention explicitly that Dievs has two sons:

Dievīnam dui dēlīni,	Dievs has two sons,
Saules meitas precinieki.	Sun's daughters' suitors.
Saule pate, meitu māte,	Sun herself, mother of adult daughters,
Pušķo meitu kambarīti,	Decorates the daughters' room,

Ik rītiņa uzlēkdama,   Rising every morning,
Puķu ziedus kaisīdama.   Sprinkling flower blossoms. (LD 33766)

More often, one Dievs' son takes place of the twins – perhaps Christianity had its say here. But this only son, too, woos the Sun's daughter:

Kam tie sirmi zirgi stāv   Why are the gray horses
Pie Saulītes nama durīm?   Standing at the door of Sun's house?
Dieva dēla sirmi zirgi,   They are horses of Dievs' son,
Saules meitas precenieka.   The suitor of Sun's daughter. (LD 33801)

Another daina pictures Dievs' son in the middle of voyeuristic observation of the bathing Sun's daughter:

Saules meita mazgājās   Sun's daughter was washing herself
Straujupītes līkumā;   In the crook of a fast river;
Dieva dēls lūkojās   Dievs's son was watching her,
Zelta kārklu krūmiņā.   From behind a golden willow bush.
                               (LD 33974)

Dainas also suggest that Sun's daughter celebrates the long-expected wedding with Dievs' son in the end (see also → sky inhabitants, wedding) – the sky black-smith works on gifts for both the bride and the groom:

Kalējs kala debesīs,   The black-smith was forging in the sky,
Ogles bira Daugavā;   Cinders were pouring into Daugava;
Saules meitas saktu kala,   He was making a brooch for Sun's daughter,
Dieva dēla zobentiņu.   A sword for Dievs' son. (LD 33728)

Unexpectedly, though, in the middle of the wedding feast, Moon appears and exchanges the rings with Sun's daughter:

Dieva dēli, Saules meita   Dievs' sons, Sun's daughters
Vidū gaisa kāzas dzēra;   Were getting married in the air;
Mēnestiņš tecēdams,   Moon came in haste,
Tas pārmija gredzeniņus.   He exchanged the rings. (LD 33763)

In the inexhaustible Latvian folklore resources, there can be found numerous other variants of stories of Baltic Dioscuri courtship. The plot line we present here, composed of individual fragments, paints a representative enough picture, though.

Latv. *dêls*, pl. *dēli* means "son". Cf. related Lith. *pirmdėlỹs* "just born (child, suckling)", Ved. *dhārú-* "sucking infant" and others; all of these are derived from IE root *dʰeH₁(i̯)-* "to suck; to breast-feed".

Bibl.: Ivanov 1986, 3; Jonval 1929, 95/396; 96/č. 405; 97/č. 413, 415; 104/455; LIV 138–139; LPG 623, 625; ME I, 463; Pokorny 1959, 242.

Dievo dukrytės "Dievas' daughters" → **Saules meitas**

Dievs / Dievas → ***Deivas**

*Dievų-rikis – Lith. "lord of gods". The only record of this theonym is provided by *Galician-Volhynian Chronicle* in the description of the year 1252: "His baptism was a mere artifice and he continued to offer sacrifices to his gods in secret: to *Nonadej*, *Teljavel*, *Diverikis*, to the hare god (and) *Mejdejn*. Whenever he rode into a field and saw a hare running into it, he felt he was not allowed to step into a forest, let alone break a branch there. He sacrificed to his gods, cremated his dead and openly practised paganism."[53] The manuscripts of the chronicle use two different graphic forms of the theonym D. in dat.pl.: *Diverikъzu & Diviriksu*. There is also the Ermolaev transcription of the manuscript that uses the variant *Devikzъ*, omitting the syllable *ri*, but this is most probably an error on the scribe's part. The reconstructed form **Dievų-rikis* that we use as the source for etymological interpretation is based on the premise that the first component is gen.pl. of Lith. *diẽvas* "god" and the second one **rikis* "lord" – a reconstruction based on Pruss. *rikijs* "lord", probably adopted from Gothic *reiks* "ruler". The Lithuanian equivalent *rỹkis*, *rykỹs* "ruler, king" is probably a recent creation of Lithuanian lexicologist and historian Simonas Daukantas, formed after the Prussian word.

Bibl.: Fraenkel II, 733; LPG 51, 54; Smoczyński 2018, 1094–95.

---

[53] *Kreščenie že ego lьstivo byst: žrjaše bogomъ svoimъ vtaině, pervomu Nьnadějevi, i Teljaveli i Diverikъzu, zaejačemu bogu₍ᵢ₎, Mějdějnu: egda vyěxaše na pole i vyběgnjaše zajacь na pole, v lěsъ roščenija ne voxožaše vnu i ne smějaše ni rozgy ulomiti, i bogomъ svoimъ žrjaše, i mertvyxъ telesa sožigaše, i poganьstvo svoe javě tvorjaše.*

*Dimstipatis – Lith. 'god of house'. The theonym can be found in reports of Jesuit missions from the year 1701: "They have one household god, they call him Dimstapatis in their language and imagine him each in a different way. Some of them say that this god is fire and he protects houses from fire, and sacrifice roosters to him …"[54] There is also an older report of the existence of this theonym, though in distorted form, this time by priest Stanislaw Rostowski from 1583: "… whom we call Larus, the pagans [call] *Dimstipa[ti]s*"[55]. The first component is the Old Lith. word *dimstis* "yard, court, mansion" < **dm̥-stH₂-i-*.

Bibl.: Fraenkel I, 95; LPG 432; Smoczyński 2018, 230.

Drebkullis – Pruss. 'god of → underworld endowed with the power to move the earth'. The theonym was recorded in the 17th century by M. Praetorius: "Drebkulis is the aide of Pykullis and they ascribe to him the power to move the earth".[56] Mannhardt interprets the name as a compound, with the first component being derived from the verb *drebéti* "to shake" (cf. *drebùs* "shaking", *drebulẽ* "aspen-tree"). The second component, according to Mannhardt, is nomen agentis *kulỹs*, of the verb *kùlti* "to beat" – so, D. can be translated roughly as "shaker-beater". See also entries → world, → underworld.

Bibl.: LPG 523, 545; Smoczyński 2018, 243.

Dundulis, Dundutis, Dudutis, Dūdų senis – Lith. sobriquets of thunder-god → Perkūnas. The Lithuanian word *dundùlis* "thunder" is derived from the onomatopoetic verb *dundéti* "to boom, to rumble, to resound"; cf. Sanskrit *dhvana-* "sound, tone, noise, thunder" and other similar IE words.

Bibl.: Fraenkel I, 110–111; Smoczyński 2018, 264.

---

[54] *Unum enim Deum domesticum habent, quem ipsi lingua sua Dimstapatis vocant, de quo diverse opinantur. Alii dicunt eum Deum esse ignis, qui domos ab igne custodit, et huic offerunt gallum …* (see *Annuae Litterae Societatis Jesu ad Patres et Fratres ejusdem Societatis*, Tom XXI, 1604).

[55] *… quos diximus Larem pagani Dimstipam …*

[56] *Drebkullis ist des Pykullis Diener, dem sie die Macht, die Erde zu bewegen, zuschreiben.* (see *Idolatria veterum Prussorum* – the 4th volume of his *Deliciae Prussicae*; published in 1703).

Dzelzspuika – Latv. "Iron Lad" or "Iron Youth". In some tales, this is the name of the Latv. mythical strongman who is more frequently referred to as → Lāčplēsis or → Lāčausis.

eagle-owl see **Ievulis**

Ēglė – Lith. "spruce/fir tree" & the name of 'queen of grass-snakes'. She is the heroine of one of the most well-known and popular Lith. folk tales. The tale was first published in M. Jasevičius' 1837 almanac *Biruta*. It tells this beautiful but sad story, including several variants:

E. was a young, beautiful village girl, who bathed with her sisters in a lake / in the sea one day. When she wanted to dress again, in the sleeve of her chemise she found a grass-snake who talked with a human voice and persuaded her to marry him, otherwise she would not get her chemise back. E. promised marriage to the snake and went back home. After a time, a whole procession of grass-snakes crawled through the village to her house and asked for the promised bride. E.'s family did not want to give E. away, and so they gave the grass-snakes a succession of white female animals instead, but a cuckoo always told the snakes that it was not the right bride. In the end, the family agreed to give away E. herself. She was met at the lake / sea shore by a handsome young man, who told her that he was the king of the grass-snakes who lived at the bottom of the lake /sea (some variants say that he has a crystal castle) and put on a human form for her sake. E. married him and they lived happily at the bottom of the lake /sea and had 3 (or 4) children: 3 (sometimes only 2) boys and 1 girl. The boys were named Ąžuolas "Oak", Úosis "Ash" and *Béržas* "Birch"; the girl was called *Ẽpušė* / *Drebulẽ* "Aspen".

E. was happy with her husband in the underwater kingdom, but she began to miss her old home. Her husband, however, did not want to let her go. In the end, he relented, but he told her that she had to return in 9 days, and that she could not possibly come to visit home without a "hare's cake / pirog", which is a traditional name for any sort of a gift from a journey, claimed to have been "given by a hare". E. decided to bake a cake for her family, but her husband hid all her kitchen utensils. In the end she still managed to bake the cake and with her children, she visited her family on earth. Her 12 brothers did not like the idea of E. going back to live in a different world among animals, and so they tried to learn from the children what their father's name was and how he could be made to step ashore. The sons did not tell anything, but the daughter *Drebulė,* threatened with beating, revealed that her father's name was *Žilvinas* and that he would come ashore after this calling:

Žilvine, Žilvinėli,	Žilvinas, dear Žilvinas,
jei tu gyvas – atplauk pieno	If you are alive – come with milky foam,
puta,	
jei negyvas – kraujo puta!	If dead – with bloody foam!

The brothers then went to the lake / sea, called Žilvinas and then killed him with their scythes. When E. with her children came back to the shore and called her husband, waves topped with foam red as blood rose on the water and her husband's voice told her what had happened. In despair over the loss of her husband and her daughter's betrayal, E. cursed both herself and her children. The sons, who had kept their word, she turned into fine, strong trees – oak, ash and birch; the daughter, who had betrayed her father, she turned into the ever trembling aspen. Herself, then, she turned into a spruce or fir tree (the Lith. word *ėglė* designates both kinds of tree). In some variants, Sun then mourns the dead Žilvinas. Variants told in northern Poland, in the former territory of the Baltic Yotvingian tribe, also add that the 12 brothers were punished by the thunder god → Perkūnas for their horrible deed.

Russian Baltic scholar S. Ryžakova says that the sujet of this tale is one-of-a-kind. Similar ones can be found with neighbouring nations, but these tales are not so well thought-out. She thinks it noteworthy that every character in this particular tale is correct in their own way and has their own story that leads to a final end. The syuzhet is so complete that it gave rise to many theories trying to explain its origins and meaning. One evident fact is that it mirrors the important role played by → grass-snake in Balt. mythology. All the theories also explain the tale as interaction between two different worlds. For example, mythologist A. Greimaitė-Zemp explains the tale as an etiological myth: before the creation of the world, there was no clear distinction between earth and water and only the conflict between E.'s family and the underwater king cause these two spheres to forever divide and close themselves to each other. The tale also describes the creation of trees. Lith. culturologist and mythologist G. Beresnevičius argues that it is also a Lithuanian theogonic myth. Historian and philosopher J. A. Krikštopaitis interprets the tale as the result of an exogamic marriage between two worlds. At the end of the tale, trees are created; because trees symbolise ever-refreshing life, harmony is restored. And Donatas Sauka focuses on Sun's mourning over Žilvinas' death and links it to Lith. songs of mourning over a soldier's death.

Bibl.: DLKŽ 59, 76, 148, 170, 177, 889; MV 9; Ryžakova 2009; Smoczyński 2018, 281.

*Ežerinis – Lith. 'lake god'. This deity was briefly described by J. Łasicki at the end of the 16th century: "… they honour **Ezerinis*, god of lakes".[57] Mannhardt supposes that acc. *Ezernim* is a shortened form of **Ežerinim*, the nom. sg. of which would be **Ežerinis* (the recorded form with *z* instead of *ž* is caused by the absence of this sound in Lat. consonantism). Lith. *ežerìnis* "of lake" is derived from *ẽžeras* "lake" (~ Latv. *ę̃zęrs*, Pruss. *assaran*; Russ. *ozero*). There is a noteworthy similarity, perhaps even relation to the name of the Roman nymph *Egeria*, who, according to Ovidius and Vergilius, guarded a spring of the same name and a lake called *Lacus Nemorensis* in Ariccia. See also → world.

Bibl.: Blažek 2003b, 243–257; Fraenkel I, 125; LPG 356, 369–370; Prosdocimi 1969, 130–142; Smoczyński 2018, 295.

*Ežiagulys – Lith. 'god of death'(?). According to the testimony of J. Łasicki in *De Diis* 1584, this deity is identical to *Veliuonà* (recorded by Łasicki as *Vielona*). He was usually invoked at pig-slaughtering. However, etymology does not support this characterisation. The first component of the theonym could be Lith. *eži, ežià*, dial. *ažià* "furrow, boundary between fields, edge, border" (~ Latv. *eža* "flower-bed; boundary between fields", Pruss. *asy* "boundary between fields"); the second one Lith. *gulỹs* "lying", i.e. *nomen agentis* of the verb *gulḗti* "to lie", i.e. "the one lying on the boundary" (perhaps the slaughtered pig?), cf. *žemgulỹs* "the one lying on the ground".

Bibl.: Blažek 2003b, 243–257; Fraenkel I, 125, 175–176; LPG 359, 386–387; MV 49; Smoczyński 2018, 295, 406.

fate – F. played an important role in the world view [*Weltanschauung*] among the Baltic people in the past. There were even 12 Lithuanian deities, namely Andaj (→ **An(t)-deivas*); → Dalia; → Dievas; → Janda; → Laima; → Verpiančioji; → Metančioji; → Audėtoja; → Gadintoja; → Sergėtoja; → Nukirptoja; and → Išskalbtoja; and 6 lotyšských božstev →

---

[57] *colunt … Ezernim lacuum Deum* (see *De Diis* 1584).

Dēkla; → Dievs; → Laima; → Kārta; → Rīšu māte; → Vīkala, which were connected with the phenomenon of f. in local traditions. Two of the most significant Baltic deities, Lithuanian Dievas (~ Latvian Dievs) and Laima, were characterized by their ability to know a person's fate. Together they belong to the divine minority, which is common for both the Lithuanian and Latvian traditions. F. also appeared in a lot of folk tales and songs. All these facts imply that the cult of the Fate deities has deep roots in the past. In the lives of Baltic people fate always played an important role, judging from the observation of Lithuanian and Latvian exponents of resurrection. E.g. G.F. Stender in his book *Lettische Grammatik* (1783) wrote: "*Liktens* – 'fate'. If early Latvians adhered to any philosophy, fate undoubtedly formed its base. Till the present time the Latvians are absorbed by this point of view on the world. Everywhere it is possible to hear : *tas jau bija viņam likts* 'It was his fate.'" The meanings of the verbs used in Lithuanian in connection with fate bear witness to the belief that gods know the fates of people, but they do not determine them. E.g. the verb *lémti* means "to fate, foretell, determine sth", but also "to ordain, make sth happen, decide about sth, suppose, presume; draw, cast (lots)". Concerning fate the Latvians use the verbs *laîst* and *likt*, whose primary meanings are passive: "to let", "to release", "to remain". Besides these verbs Latvian also uses others mentioned in the lemmas → Kārta and → Laima. The name of the latter goddess also served as the appellative "fate": Lithuanian *láimė*, Latvian *laĩme*. Lith. *likìma*s and Latvian *liktenis* "fate" are more recent formations. Lithuanian also knows the word *dalià* "destiny, lot". It is also necessary to stress that none of the fate-deities is specialized only on this function. E.g. *Deivas has a lot of other functions, Laima and Kārta frequently offer help to women. Dalia and seven Lithuanian goddesses of fate are recent artificial creations (see below) and → Rīšu māte and → Vīkala are connected with f. only indirectly: they appear at the moment of human death. A remarkable company of the seven fate-goddesses called ìndėvės consists of: Verpiančioji, Metančioji, Audėtoja, Gadintoja, Sergėtoja, Nukirptoja, Išskalbtoja. These goddesses had to rule human lives. They first appeared in one West Lithuanian legend recorded by A. L. Jucevičius in the 19th cent. Later they are mentioned by Simonas Daukantas and added two others. Apparently they represent a product of imagination of both the authors, since the incredibly rich Baltic folklore does not know them. The names of the goddesses indicate their functions: *Verpiančioji* spins flax, *Metančioji* threads yarn onto a weaving loom, *Audėtoja* weaves linen, *Gadintoja* spoils it, *Sergė-toja* guards it, *Nukirptoja* cuts it and *Išskalbtoja* washes it.

Bibl.: BRMŠ IV, 197, 205 > Stend 1783; Greimas 2005, 195–196; LKŽ 403, 416; ME 407, 411; RB 17–19, 85.

frog – besides frog designated also other amphibia, frequently toad. Their form was taken by various house-spirits and chthonic goddesses, later degraded to witches. See also → witch; → Gausu māte; → Mājas kungs; → Mātes.

*Gabija – Lith. 'goddess of fire in the household'. J. Łasicki in *De Diis* 1584 notes: "Only then the deity called Gabie is supposed to be asked with these words … Lift the flame so as not to let the sparkles fall."[58] He also records the last sentence in Lith., in contemporary orthography: "Fire, divine daughter, lift the steam/smoke, do not let the sparkles out."[59] It could be said, then, that an analogy to the theonym is Lat. *flamma* "flame". Lith. writer and linguist M. Akelaitis (a.k.a. Akielewicz; 1829–1887) recorded: "In Lithuanian, fire is called *gabija* or šventa gabija in festive language."[60] Further on in the book, "Fire is called *ugnìs* in colloquial language, *gabija* in festive language."[61] Akelaitis also recorded the form *gubija*, which is a Žemaitian dialectism. Baltic scholar Antoni Mierzyński from Poland added this brief prayer, sent to him by his Žemaitian correspondents and said to be chanted by housewives while walking around the hearth: "Saint Gabėta, live with us cheerfully."[62]

Lith. *gabijà* means "hand-made candle". The word is put in connection with Lith. *gabanà* "armful; heap of hay", *gebéti* "to take care, to be used to sth, to be able to do sth" and other related words. Goddess *G. is obviously related to fire, and the same is true of the candle. The other Lith. parallels are too remote in terms of meaning. Let us search for other expressions that are related to the phenomenon of fire, then: see, for example, the Celtic

[58] *Tum vero precandus est hisce verbis Gabie deus. … Flammam eleva, at ne demittas scintillas* (see *De Diis* 1584).
[59] *Gabie deuaite pokielki garanuleiski kirbixstu.* Mannhardt attempted to transcribe this sentence to an intelligible form: *Gabė dieváitė pokèlki garą, ne leĩski kibirkštų* (LPG 389).
[60] *Ogien w mowie uroczystej nazywa się po litewsku gabija albo szwenta gabija.*
[61] *Ogien w pospolitej mowie zowie się ugnis, a w uroczystej gabija.*
[62] *Szwenta Gabieta, givenk su mumis linksmaj.*

words denoting a blacksmith – Old Irish *gobae*, Welsh and Breton *gof*, Gaelic inst.pl. form *gobedbi*, cf. divine blacksmith *Goibniu* of the Middle Irish Gaulish text *Lebor Gabála* – or the craftsman who works with fire.

The word *G. is also a component in some compound theonyms recorded by Łasicki: (a) "*Pelengabija is a goddess believed to take care of the hearth and makes sure that it always shines"[63] The first component of the theonym is Lith. *pēlenas* "open furnace" (~ Latv. *pęlns* "hearth", Pruss. *pelanne* "ashes"). (b) "A cake made by a woman is sacrificed to *Matergabia* … It is baked in the furnace …"[64] In this case, the first component is a Latinized version of Lith. *mótė* "woman, wife", which has retained the meaning "mother" in some dialects.

Bibl.: Blažek 2010, 40–41, 45–47; Fraenkel I, 126–127, 566, 465; LPG 352, 357–358, 372–373, 389.

Gabikis – in modern Lith., a non-specified evil spirit or devil. This name might be related to theonyms *Gabjauja* and *Gabvartai*, if they are derived from a verb similar to *gabénti* "to transport, to bring". There is a related word in Latv.: *gãbiķis* "niggard". The Lith. word G. probably became a synonym of "evil spirit" during the process of degradation and demonization of Lith. polytheism.

Bibl.: Fraenkel I, 127.

Gabjaujis & Gabjauja – Pruss. 'deities of agriculture and riches'. Praetorius lists the god called *Gabjaujis* (recorded as *Gabjaugis*) among 'gods of work' (Arbeitsgötter), somewhat surprisingly, together with the god of nature *Pergrubrius*. At another place of his book, he mentions his female counterpart: "Gabjauja is the deity in charge of grains and barns; to honour her, a rooster's neck must be slit".[65] Lexicographer Philipp Ruhig in his 1747 glossary adds "Gabjauja – goddess of riches."[66] The Lith. word *gabjáuja* means "minor feast to mark end of work in fields". The second component *jáuja* denotes "building where flax or grains are dried", the first component is derived from the verb *gebéti* "to take care, to be able",

---

[63]   *Polengabia diva est, cui foci lucentis administratio creditur.*
[64]   *Matergabiae deae offertur a foemina ea placenta, … In furno coquitur …*
[65]   *Gabjauja ist ein Gott über das Getreydigt und dessen Gebäude und dem zu Ehren muss ein Hahn geschlachtet werden…*
[66]   *Gabjauja – Göttin des Reichtums.*

cf. *gebùs* "diligent", *gobìnti* "to bring home", *gabénti* "to transport" and others.

Bibl.: Fraenkel I, 126–127; LPG 532, 611.

*Gabjaukurys – Lith. 'god that maintains the sacred sacrificial fire'(?). The deity is mentioned without any detailed description by priest Wilhelm Martini from Werden, which lies in the vicinity of today's Lith. town Klaipėda, in the Lat. foreword to his 1666 songbook, as *Gabjaukurs*. Mannhardt attempted to interpret the god as an evil spirit that sets fire to … in barns. This interpretation was based on the … that the second component of the theonym is derived from the verb *kùrti* "to lit fire", while the first component is actually the theonym *Gabjauja*. Instead of this rather forceful solution, we propose a different etymology: the compound **gabija* "sacred fire" (→ *Gabija), plus *aukurỹs* "the one who lits the sacrifice" (LKŽ), with the possible meaning "the god that lits the sacred sacrificial fire".

Bibl.: LPG 513.

*Gabvartas – Lith. 'guard of crops or riches'(?). Priest Theophil Schulz mentions this theonym in his *Compendium Grammaticae Lituanicae* (1673). It is in the chapter where he lists some examples of Lith. masc. nouns together with the names of three ancient deities, and he does not elaborate on what sort of a god G. was. Another form of this theonym, *Gabartai*, can be found in his colleague Wilhelm Martini's (of Werden, not far from today's Klaipėda) Latin foreword to the 1666 songbook. Mannhardt suggested that the theonym be interpreted as "the one who turns over fire", where the first component is Lith. dial. *gabė* "fire" and the second component is derived from the verb *vartýti* "to turn (over)". That seems rather forceful, though. It is more pragmatic to see the second component as the Lith. word *var̃tas* "guard, warden, gamekeeper", which is an adapatation of Eastern Prussian Germ. *Wart*. If the first component is the word *gabė* "fire", the meaning of the compound word is "guard of fire". If, on the other hand, the first component is related to the theonym *Gabjauja*, then G. is "guard of crops or riches".

Bibl.: Fraenkel II, 1204; LPG 513.

Gaisa māte – Latv. "Mother of Air". Latv. *gàiss* means "air" and is related to Lith. *gaĩsas* "light in the sky". For further reference see → Mātes.

Bibl.: ME I, 587; Smoczyński 2018, 302.

gàišreģis – Latv. "soothsayer". A compound with the first component being Latv. *gàišs* "light, bright, shining", cf. Lith. *gaĩsas* "light on horizon", and the second component derived from Latv. *redzêt* "to see", Lith. *regéti* id. For more information on soothsaying practice in the Baltics see entries → priests, → soothsayer.

Bibl.: Fraenkel II, 712; ME I, 588; III, 502.

*Gardait(a)s or ***Gardāt(a)s** – Pruss. 'god of ships'(?). Most scholars doubt whether this is really an original Pruss. deity, and rightfully so, in spite of the fact that its name is recorded in the works of the most renowned 16th century chroniclers. There, we encounter several different variants of this theonym:

Gardoayts – der Schiff Gott "the ship god" in the so-called A print of *Sudauerbüchlein – Der vnglaubigen Sudauen ihrer bockheiligung mit sambt andern Ceremonien, so sie tzu brauchen gepflegeth*;

Gardoaeten – deum nautarum, qualis olim apud Romanos fuit Portunnus "god of sailors, who was Portunnus for the ancient Romans" according to J. Maeletius/Malecki's *De Sacrificiis* 1551. Let us now look at *Preussische Chronik* (written in approx. in 1575, published in 1812–1817 in Königsberg), by Lucas David, who is much more eloquent when this deity is concerned: "Also, we would like to inform the readers how the sailors (in the towns or on the shores of the large sea that they called *Meherwirdt*), and also the people that lived on both shores of this sea, worshipped the god of sea *Gardoaits* and what they sacrificed to him when they were in distress. They also believed this god to be a big angel standing on the sea who blows away ships, water and everything with his wind. When he becomes angry, he tips over ships with his powerful breath, which is so strong that it makes everyone retreat; or, he forces them in unknown lands [places], where they [*alda* = probably meaning "all"] must suffer or even die. He also has power over all the fish of the sea and everything that is in waters."[67]

[67] *Wollen ferner nun auch antzeigen, wie die Sehefahrer, vnd so an den Staden oder Strande der grossen Sehe, das sunst das Meherwirdt genandt, auch die so an den beiden Haben gewonet, den Sehe Gott **Gardoaits** geehret, vnd was sie Ime zu Ihren oder in Iren Nothen geopfert haben. Dann sie haben gleubtt, dass dieser Gott sei ein grosser Engell, stehe auf dem Mehre, wohin er sich wendet, da blase er mit seinem Winde das Wasser, Schiffe vnd anders von sich. Wann er zornig werde, so sturtze er die Schiffe mit seinem starckem Odem,*

Gardoeten – [deum] nautarum, see J. Łasicki's *De Diis* 1584. Formally, the theonym *G. can be analysed as a patronym, i. e. "son of Gardas". There is, however, a record of the word *gárdas* meaning "ship"; but this record is only found with one author, namely, the Lith. writer Mikalojus Akelaitis (1829–1883). It is, therefore, possible that *G. is actually an incorrect spelling of the theonym *Bardaitas* (and similar variants) which secondarily led to the creation of the 'primary' apellative "ship".

Bibl.: Kregždys 2008b; LPG 295, 299, 322, 362; Toporov I, 194–197.

Gaujas māte – Latv. "Mother of River Gauja". One of about hundred representatives of the Latv. cult of Mothers (→ Mātes). She was "in charge" of a single particular geographic spot – the river Gauja, which flows through the North Latvian region of Vidzeme – and that is quite unusual with the Mothers. Gauja, unlike other rivers in Latvia, has a deep basin and steep rocky banks at some places, as it is the only river that returned to its original basin after the Ice Age. According to L. Adamovičs, originally, it was Mother of Water who was responsible for all water bodies (→ Ūdens māte) and Mother of Gauja and other Mothers of more specific kinds of waters appeared only later. Therefore, in his opinion, G.m. is a rather recent creation.

G. m. helped fishermen and folk songs refer to her as "rich" because she has an abundance of fish:

Ai, bagāta Gaujas māte,	Hey, rich Mother of Gauja,
Pildi manu ķeselīti!	Please fill my hand net!
Tu jau pati gan zināji,	You know very well yourself
Caur cepuri mati auga.	That my cap is worn out[68]. (LD 30685)

There is a note in the book by Lutheran priest and writer A. W. Hupel called *Topographische Nachrichten von Lief- und Ehstland*, written at the end of the 18th century, that might be associated with G. m.: "In some places, for example, in the Gaujiena parish, peasants wash themselves with the water of the river Gauja during certain festivals of the year to

das sie musten vorgehen, oder dringe vnd bringe die in vngelegene orthe, das sie alda mussen schaden leiden oder gantz vorterben. Auch habe er Gewalt vber die Fische des Mehres vnd was sunsten in Wassern ist.

[68] Literally "my hair grows through my cap", implying that the author of the song needs to sell the fish in order to buy new clothes.

ensure fecundity." Regardless of whether that was a ritual dedicated to
G. m. or not, it is clear that there existed some sort of water cult in the
immediate vicinity of the river Gauja. It is also perhaps worth mentioning
that G. m. inspired a book of poetry for children in the 1980's.[69]
The Latv. word *gauja* means "large number" and has an equivalent in Lith.
gaujà "crowd, flock, pack, cluster" and also Russ. dial. *gavez* "very large
number". It is also possible that the name of the river is actually a lettonised Livonian word *koiva* "birch-tree", seeing as it grows in large numbers on its banks, as the exhibition *Gaujas lībieši Latvijas kultūrvēsturē*
(Gauja Livonians in the cultural history of Latvia) in the Kuldīga castle
claims. For more information on water and birch-trees see → world.

Bibl.: Fraenkel I, 140; Hup IV, 1789, 408; ME I, 611; Adamovičs 1937.

Gausu māte – Latv. "Mother of Abundance". One of about a hundred
Latv. Mothers (see → Mātes), whose name might not be transparent to the
Latvians of today, as the word *gaûss* means "slow", while in the name G.
m. it is preserved in its original meaning – "abundant". To specify, G. m.
was a household spirit. She lived in the house and was said to ensure that
the household never ran out of food, especially grain and flour. In larger
farmsteads, she also made animals abundant, especially horses. She liked
to show herself to people in the form of a toad or a mouse. The housewives left meals aside for her and before every harvest and before leaving
to grind flour, they would lure her with these words: *Ļiku, ļeku, ļekainīti,
nāc uz balto vilnainīti!* "Hop, skip, jumper, come sit on the white woollen
shawl!" (Kursīte 1996, 325). A housewife that had G. m. to her aid could
sing merrily:

Malu, malu visu rītu,	Even though I was grinding all morning,
Siekam kaudzes nenomalu:	I didn't finish all the grain in the bushel:
Gausu māte ietupās	Mother of Abundance has squatted down
Mana sieka dibinā.	At the bottom of my bushel. (LD 8102)

G. m. can be found in several folk songs and tales, sometimes under the
name of *Gausībiņa*. There, in most cases, we encounter her as a frog
that jumps around a meal and thus makes it abundant and wholesome.
Her name was probably subject to some sort of taboo. The housewives

---

[69]   Bērza, Ilga. 1988. *Gaujas māte*. Rīga: Liesma .

almost never referred to her as G. m. or *krupis* "toad". Most frequently, they addressed her with these three taboo names: Ļekatu māte "Mother of Jumps", *Augsttecīte, zemtecīte* and *Augstlēcīte, zemlēcīte* (see → Augstlēcīte, zemlēcīte).

Bibl.: Kursīte 1996, 325; Lerhis – Puškaitis I, 325; MEnc II, 208.

Giltinẽ – Lith. 'goddess of death', who had an aide by the name of → Magyla. A deity called *Giltynė & Giltinė* is first mentioned as a goddess of misfortune (and of death at another place in the book) by M. Praetorius in *Idolatria veterum Prussorum*, which forms part IV of his book *Preussische Schaubühne*. (Praetorius was writing the book for several decades in the second half of the 17th century, but it was not published until 1703.) Cf. Latv. *ģiltene* "skeleton of corpse", which is derived from a verb such as Lith. *gélti* "to stab, to sting, to cause pain", Latv. *dzel̃t* "to stab, to sting; to burn". There is also a different derived word – Lith. *gãlas*, Latv. *gals* "end", Pruss. *gallan* "death".

Bibl.: Fraenkel I, 145; LPG 532, 544.

*Girstis, ***Giratis** (recorded as **Gyrstys**, **Girristis**) – Pruss. (Lith.?) 'god of forests' or 'god of listening'. Pruss., perhaps also Žemaitian deity of uncertain origin and function. It is mentioned by M. Praetorius in *Preussische Schaubühne* 1684: "… forest god who is more or less the same as Silvanus", i.e. ancient Roman god of forests.[70] In later centuries, G. is listed in Lith.-Germ.-Lith. dictionaries by 18th century Pruss. authors Jacob Brodowsky, Philipp Ruhig and Ch. G. Mielcke, who changed his name to *Girristis* and *Girrystis*. Mythographers' interpretations of G. vary profoundly. According to P. Skardžius and R. Balsys, the theonym was created by Praetorius himself on the basis of Łasicki's → Prigirstytis, i.e. the god or spirit that hears those who whisper. The theonym is derived from the verbal root **gerd-* with the derivational suffix *-st-*: Lith. *girdéti* "to hear", *išgir̃sti* "to overhear, to learn", Latv. *dzìrdêt* "to hear", *dzìrst* "to hear, to overhear", Pruss. *gerdaut* "to say". Skardžius is of the opinion that Praetorius wrongly assumed the mentioned verbal root to be that of the Lith. word *girià* "forest" which led to the conclusion that G. is a forest deity. Balsys expresses his approval of this interpretation and adds that everything suggests that the cult of G. was extinct in Preatorius'

---

[70] *Gyrotys, der Waldgott, ist soviel als ein Sylvanus.*

time, and so Praetorius' alteration is not based on reality but merely on his own understanding of the theonym. This theory is supported by the fact that Praetorius himself admitted having listed some of Łasicki's theonyms in a slightly different form that is based on his knowledge of spoken Lith. (see → Ligyčius). The second interpretation is to the effect that G. is not associated with Prigirstytis in any way and his name really is derived from the word *girià* "deep, thick forest". That is why W. Mannhardt alters this theonym to *Giratis*. N. Vėlius favours Brodowsky's and Mielcke's variant *Girristis*, as they wrote their dictionaries with excellent knowledge of Lith. language and of the customs of Pruss. Lithuanians: "It would seem that Brodowsky corrected the names and function of some of Praetorius' gods according to his knowledge about his Lith. contemporaries, and that his corrections are likely to be reliable." Apart from these two interpretations, there is the theory of mythologist and philosopher A. J. Greimas that merges them and divides them at the same time in a rather unexpected way. From the… *Akyli laukai, ausyli miškai* "Fields have sharp sight, forests have keen hearing" he deduces that forests are associated with listening in Lith. consciousness and therefore it is quite possible for a forest god to be named after hearing. Brodowsky's and Ruhig's *Girristis,* on the other hand, is a different deity according to Greimas and its name is derived from the word *girià* "forest". Balsys disagrees with this point: "J. Brodowsky and P. Ruhig used Praetorius as a source for their dictionaries, which, in turn, were used as a source by Ch. G. Mielcke a F. Kurschat. […] This means that the theonyms listed in all these dictionaries come from one source – M. Praetorius. There is, therefore, no reason to interpret said theonyms as derived from two different concepts ["forest" and "to hear"]." As the above discussion shows, the question of origin of the theonym Girristis and its variants remains unsolved.

Bibl.: BRMŠ III, 148, 260; IV, 19, 29, 41, 79; Fraenkel I, 153; Greimas 2005, 619–621; LPG 545; LM III, 95 apud RB 355; LPG 523; Prae 4, Chapter 9, §XXIII; RB 356.

Gov(j)u māte – Latv. "Mother of Cows". One of the hundred Latv. Mother spirits. The first component is Latv. *gùovs* "cow". Cf. Russ. *govjado* "cattle", Avest. *gāuš* and others. For further information on Mothers see → Mātes.

Bibl.: ME I, 692–693.

grass snake (Lith. *žaltỹs*, Latv. *zal̃ktis*) – one of the most important animals in Baltic mythology. Its importance is reflected in historical sources,
as well as invocations and prayers that have survived, but also in proverbs
and tales (→ Eglė). Historical sources, especially chronicles, give us an
interesting, though not always accurate, image of its cult.

In the entry → Brēķina, we cite two such historical records about g.
s. in Latvia. J. Malecki and J. Łasicki wrote about g. s in Lithuania. Jan
Malecki, a catholic priest in Prussia, says in his book *Epistola de sacrificiis et idolatria veterum Borussorum* (1551): "Latvians and Žemaitians
[Samogitians] keep snakes in their houses under the stove or in the corner
at the window, and these they worship as deities. At a certain time of the
year, sorcerers lure them to the table with prayers. The snakes crawl out,
climb on the tablecloth to the table, taste the meals and then crawl back
to their holes. When the snakes crawl away, the people start eating with
joy, believing that they will do well that year. If the snakes do not answer
the sorcerers' prayers and do not come out, or they do not taste the meals,
they believe they will meet with very bad luck that year."[71]

Polish historian J. Łasicki gives a detailed description in *De Diis*
1584: "As house gods, they keep black, thick four-legged snakes, whom
they call Giuoitos. Those they watch with awe and reverence when they
crawl out of their holes to the food, and having eaten, crawl back in.
When someone who keeps grass snakes at home meets with misfortune,
they believe they have treated them disrespectfully."[72] Although Łasicki
speaks of "black, thick four-legged snakes, whom they call Giuoitos"
(Lith. *gyvãtė* "adder"), in fact these were black g. s.'s. The idea of four

---

[71] *Praeterea Lituani et Samogitae in domibus sub fornace, uel in angulo uapo-
rarii, ubi mensa stat, serpentes fouent, quos numinis instar colentes, certo
anni tempore precibus sacrificuli euocant ad mensam. Hi uero exeuntes, per
mundum linteolum conscendunt, et super mensam assident. Ubi postquam
singula fercula delibarunt, rursus discedunt, seque abdunt in cauernis. Ser-
pentibus digressis, homines laeti fercula illa praegustata comedunt, ac sper-
ant illo anno omnia prospere sibi euentura. Quod si ad preces sacrificuli non
exierint serpentes, aut fercula super mensam posita non delibauerint, tum
credunt se anno illo subituros magnam calamitatem.*

[72] *Nutriunt etiam quasi deos penates, nigri coloris, obesos et quadrupedes quos-
dam serpentes Giuoitos vocatos. Hos timore perculsi, dum ex antrix aedium ad
pastum appositum prorepunt seque pasti in ea recipiunt, aspiciunt et colunt. Si
quid infortunii accidat cultori, serpentem male fuisse tractatum censent.*

legs could have its basis in the double penis of male g. s., and the word *gyvatė* is also used for g. s. in Žemaitija (Samogitia, western Lithuania).

Baltic scholar from the Czech Republic Petra Butzke argues that it is not certain whether Baltic nations really perceived g. s. as deities. It seems rather that they treated them as intermediaries between this world and the supernatural world. The key to understanding the Balts' perception of g. s. is this serpent's behaviour: one, g. s.'s lived near barns, because there were always many mice there, two, the g. s. is (beside adder) the only living creature in the region that can both crawl on earth, swim in water and also crawl under a stone; moreover, they change their skin regularly. This is why they were associated with the household and treated as protective household spirits, or as the appearance that deities of farm animals take on in front of humans. They were also associated with the middle and lowest levels of the world (→ world) and with the idea of eternal revival (because of their ability to "change skins", Balts sometimes believed g. s. to be immortal). They were also considered to be the intermediaries between earth and water, i.e. between the middle and lowest spheres of the world. This is where the idea that the underwater kingdom is ruled by g. s. (in the tale of → Eglė) springs from.

It will probably never be possible to reconstruct an exact and definite concept of the Balt. perception of g. s., because this perception changed depending on the era and the area. But it is beyond all doubt that there did exist a cult of g. s. with the Balt. nations. Another proof is this Lith. evening prayer that mixes the cult of g. s. with Christianity:

Dėkavojame tau, meilingas žalty,	Thank you, dear grass snake,
Už suteiktas gerybes ir dovanas.	For everything you gave us,
Dėkavojame tau, suklaupę ant kelių,	We thank you on our knees,
Dėkavojame tau, geras Dieveli.	Thank you, dear God,
Būk tu meilingas, suteik ir rytojui	Be merciful to us, give us tomorrow
Viso to, kiek davei šiandieną!	Everything you gave us today!
Prašome tave, duok ir kitą dieną!	We beg of you, give us everything tomorrow as well!

Žalty, žalty, suteik, suteik,	Grass snake, grass snake, give us
Ko prašom! Visa priduok!	What we beg of you! A plenty of
	everything!
Iš sunkaus vargo vaduok!	And free us of dire poverty! (Butzke)

Lithuanian proverbs provide us with another interesting fact. It is said: "If you kill a grass snake, bad luck will follow, because the other grass snakes will milk your cows."[73] G. s.'s are therefore benevolent, they benefit the animals as well as the house and its inhabitants, if they feed them and treat them well. If not, they can take revenge. In this, they are similar to → áitvaras and the Latvian household spirit called → Mājas kungs.

From the linguistic point of view, Lith. *žal(k)tỹs* and Latv. *zaĺ(k)tis* "grass snake" are derived from the Baltic word for green, which is the most usual skin colour of a grass snake (*Natrix natrix*): Lith. *žãlias*, Latv. *zaļš*, Pruss. *saligan /zalijan/*.

Bibl.: BRMŠ II, 584, 597 > Las; BRMŠ II, 204–205, 209 > JohMal; Butzke 2009, 20–67; DLKŽ 965; Fraenkel II, 1287–1288; LPG 296 > Mal; LPG 359 > Las; ME IV, 684; MEnc II, 179–180.

*Grubrius – Pruss. 'god of vegetation'. The most frequent form of this deity's name is *Pergrubrius* ("Sudauerbüchlein"; Bretke 1588) or the corresponding Latin accusative form *Pergrubrium* (Malecki 1551; Łasicki 1584). The variant *Pergrubius* (in "the A print") without the third *r* has been explained as the copyist's mistake. There is also a version of his name containing *a* instead of *e* in the first syllable *Pargrubius* ("Sudauerbüchlein") where the origin of the *a* is unclear. Bretkūnas (1588), in whose book *Pergrubrius* takes the second place, right after "the first and foremost one" *Okopirmus*, notes that he's a god of everything that grows; it is him who makes grass and leaves grow. Some of the other sources also mention his assistance to the growth of grass and leaves ("Sudauerbüchlein"; "the A print"), other sources describe him as a god of spring (Malecki 1551; Łasicki 1615).

Most information about this deity is contained in a 16th century source called "Sudauerbüchlein: Der vnglaubigen Sudauen ihrer bockheiligung mit sambt andern Ceremonien, so sie tzu brauchen gepflegeth". It describes the first important festival of the year: "Their first devotional

---

[73]   *Jeigu žaltį užmuši, tai bus blogai, nes kiti žalčiai išmelš karvę.*

feast takes place every time the plough goes out. They call this festival
the worshipping of Pargrubij".[74] Bretkūnas's report is more detailed: "The
Sudavs hold two festivities of their devotion every year, and that with
particular solemnity and ceremonies; they call the first one the festivity of
Pergrubrij and hold it every year in the time when the plough first comes
out…"[75] The description in "Sudauerbüchlein" goes on like this: "And
Wourschkaite lifts a goblet full of beer in his hand and asks: you, great
and mighty god *Pargrubrius*, chase winter out and give leaves and grass
to all lands, we ask of you, hope you can make our crops grow, too, and
water all weeds".[76] Elsewhere in "Sudauerbüchlein", we find a succession
of gods in accusative forms; surprisingly, one of the accusative forms is
in Latin and the other three are in German: *Grubrium, Parkunen, Swayx-
tixen und Pilniten* (LPG 249). This quotation provides us with excep-
tionally important information, that is, the name of the god appears here
without *Per-/Par-* at the beginning. This *Per-/Par-* is most probably a prefix analogical to Latin "ad-" or "pro-" (*perēit* "to come"). There is also
a variant *par-* (*parioth* "to come"). As a preposition, Prussian *per* means
"for; over", similarly Lith. *peȓ, paȓ* "over; by, at", *par-dúoti* "to sell", *par-
eĩti* "to come back". In a way similar to *Pergrubrius,* another designation
of a supernatural being was formed, *pērgimmans* "Creaturen", where the
second constituent is probably related to the verb **gimt*, Lithuanian *giᵐti*
"to be born". Thus the addition of the prefix *per-/par-* might have been in
some connection with the name of the festival that was held for *Grubrius*.
     The root **grub-* might come from the Baltic root **grāb-*, cf. Prus-
sian *mūti, muthi* "mother" < **mōtē* < **mātē(r)*. Also related to this word
might be the second constituent of the Prussian name for "spindle-wood"
wofigrabis < **(v)āzī-grabīs*, literally "goat's *grabis*", and Latv. toponym
Grobiṇa. Outside the Baltic region, as a possible relative, the Slavic name
for a "hornbeam" offers itself, which is recorded both with *r* and without

[74] *Das erste fest irer heiligung halten sie ehe wann der pflug ausgehet. Das Fest
      heissen sie die heiligung Pargrubij.*
[75] *Die Sudawen hielten iehrlich zwey grosse fest ihrer heiligung vnd solches mit
      sonderlicher sollemnitet vnd Ceremonien, als das erste heissen sie das Fest
      Pergrubrij vnd hieltens iehrlich im Fruling, ehe der pflug außging…*
[76] *vnd der Wourschkaite hebt eine Schalen voll Biers auff mit der hand vnd
      bittet: du grosser mechtiger Gott Pargrubrius du treibest den winter hinweg
      vnd gibst In allen landen laub vnd grass, wir bitten dich du wollest unser
      getreide auch wachsen lassen vnd dempffen alles vnkraut…"*

it: *grabrъ & *grabъ. It is tempting to add the Old Italic deity *Grābovius, recorded in so called Iguvian Tables in the Old Umbrian script in the dative form as Krapuvi, in the newer form of Umbrian, written in the Latin script, as Grabouie.

The theonym is sometimes interpreted as "oak deity."An interesting symmetry of forms with and without r for *grāb- stems (left) and *merk- stems (right) offers itself

suffix	*grāb-	*merk-
with -r-	Prussian Grubrium, Pergrubrius Slavic * grabrъ	Latin Mercurius Praeneste Mirc/qurios
without -r-	Prussian Pergrubius ["the A print"] Umbrian *Grābovius Slavic *grabъ	Faliscan Mercui, Oscan Mirikui Hittite Markwaya- Prussian Markopotis, Merkopete

To sum up, we can assume that Old Prussians worshipped a vegetation god called Grubrius (or merely Grubius), which seems to originally have been a name of a specific tree species, as the etymological analysis suggests. The Latin and German chronicles recorded his name together with the prefix per / par "for" that was part of the name of the festival dedicated to this god. For further information on trees in Baltic mythology, see → world.

Bibl.: Blažek & Běťáková 2014; Kregždys 2015; LPG 247, 249; Mažiulis III, 256–257; 262–263; IV 264–265; Pokorny 1959, 404; Toporov 1972, 295.

Igauņu māte – Latv. "Mother of Estonians". Latv. Igaŭnis & Iguonis "Estonian", Igaŭnija "Estonia" are an adaptation of the name of the historical part of Estonia Ugaunia, in which the initial u- was perceived as ü-. For further reference on Latv. Mothers, see → Mātes.

Bibl.: ME I, 702.

*Ievulis or ***Yvulis** (recorded as **Iwullis**) – Pruss./Lith. 'forest god', possibly "sacred bird-cherry tree" or "eagle owl". M. Praetorius in Preussische Schaubühne 1684 lists this deity among forest gods without elaborating on his function or on the meaning of his name, and thus providing room for scholars to create theories. For example, W. Mannhardt, H. Usener and J. Basanavičius consider the theonym to be a diminutive form of Lith.

(j)ievà "bird-cherry" (~ Latv. *iẽva*, Pruss. *iuwis* id.) and transcribe it as
Jvules či *Ievulis*. In that case, I. would be a sacred tree rather than a deity.
A. J. Greimas and R. Balsys, on the other hand, claim that the theonym is
a diminutive of Lith. ývas "eagle-owl". If that was so, I. would be a divin-
ised bird, or perhaps a mere set of superstitions related to it that Praetorius
interpreted incorrectly as a cult. There is no doubt that such superstitions
existed, as Praetorius himself mentions at another place of the book "…
eagle-owls are worshipped for the various tricks that the devil perpetrates
through them". Lucas David, in the 16th century, describes another superstition in his chronicle: "Prussians are convinced that when the large owl,
called eagle-owl, hoots for three nights on the roof of a house, then somebody dies in that house". The theory of I. being a mere set of superstitions
related to the eagle-owl is also supported by this text of Norbertas Vėlius':
"… [in Žemaitian mythology of the 16th century,] the boundaries between
gods, mythical beings of 'lower ranks' [protectors of fields, forests and
households] and various objects of worship [places, animals etc.] were
starting to blur. Łasicki [or, more precisely, his source Laskowski] did not
endeavour to make a distinction between these categories and referred to
all deities, mythical creatures and objects of worship as 'gods'". It is possible that numerous other chronicle authors, among them also Praetorius,
handled the provided mythological material in a similar way.

Bibl.: BRMŠ 576; Fraenkel I, 183, 189; Greimas 2005, 621; LPG 523; MV 321;
Prae Chapter IV, §3; RB 357; Smoczyński 2018, 417, 438–39.

ìndėvės – Lith. word (pl.), used by 19th century national revivalist Simonas
Daukantas in reference to Lith. goddesses that determine people's destiny
(→ destiny). Beside that, the word can be found in Lith. folklore; with
a different meaning, though: it denotes a spirit that has possessed a person or has some power over them. *Ko šauki, ar ne indėvė tave smau-
gia?* "Why are you crying, is *indėvė* smothering you?" This word was
probably formed by blending Lith. words ìndėvė "gift, present" and *deĩvė*
"goddess", or perhaps by compounding Lith. words į "into, in" and *deĩvė*
"goddess". Lithuanian mythologist and semiologist Algirdas J. Greimas
is of the opinion that the term denotes incarnation of initial divine essence
(both good and evil) into Man.

Bibl.: Daukantas I, 1976, 488–510; Fraenkel I, 94, 112; RB 18; Greimas 2005,
631–632; Smoczyński 2018, 424–25.

*Jaugabis (recorded as **Jagaubis**) – Lith. 'god that attends to fire and expands it' (?). Lexicographers Jakob Brodowski (1730) and Philipp Ruhig (1747) both identified this deity with Roman god *Vulcanus*. Mannhardt saw this name as an anagram of the theonym *Gabjaujis*; that is highly improbable, though. It is more promising to interpret the theonym as a deformed compound **Jau-gabis*, the first element of which is derived from the verb *jáuti* "to turn over, to throw in all directions, to stir", and the second element is related to Lith. *gabijà* "sacred fire", dial. *gabis*. The name would then mean "the one who expands the sacred fire". Note: The name of the Roman god *Vulcanus* was used e.g. by Caesar in *The Gallic Wars* [VI, 21.2] to denote the cult of fire that existed parallel to the Sun and Moon cult with Germanic tribes.

Bibl.: Fraenkel I, 191; LPG 610–611; Smoczyński 2007, 231 & 2018, 445.

Jawinne (***Javìnė**) – Pruss./Lith. 'goddess of grain'. Among historical sources, only the 1740 Germ.-Lith. dictionary by Pruss. preceptor J. Brodowski mentions her, and that in a brief entry: "Goddess of grain – Jawwine". This theonym is a feminine form of Lith. adj. *javìnis* "of grain" and is derived from Lith. *javaĩ* "grain", *javienà* "grain field" (hence Pol. *jownia*, Belorussian *jovn(i)a* id.), cf. Russ. archaic dial. *jevin*, later *ovin* "building for dehydrating grain", Avest. *yəuuīn-* "grain field" : *yauua-* "grain" and others. G. Beresnevičius claims that it is a recent creation, a merge of several previously worshipped deities of grains and fields. According to A. J. Greimas, J. actually is the same being as → Rugių boba (see → Rugių boba). R. Balsys agrees with Greimas, seeing as both these deities were Prussian.

Bibl.: BRMŠ IV, 29; Fraenkel I, 192; Greimas 2005, 485; LPG 611, 613; RB 134 > Beresnevičius; Smoczyński 2018, 446.

Jods [Juõds] – Latv. 'devil', 'demon' and one of the names of Latv. Velns (see → Velinas, → underworld), who is similar to European fairy tale devil in some aspects. That is probably why the first translator of the Bible to Latvian, priest E. Glück, chose this name to denote the biblical Satan in 1688. A century later, another Lutheran priest, G. F. Stender (also called Stender Senior), listed the name in his dictionary as "*Jods* – the devil of fields and forests". The origin of the word is not clear. In terms of sounds, it corresponds with Lith. *júodas* "black"; the Latv. word might be a taboo substitution, cf. Liv. *mustā-mies* "devil", literally "black man". Parallels found with northern neighbours of the Balt. nations who speak languages that belong to the Finno-Ugric (Uralic) language family – Est. *juudas* "devil, demon" and Finn. *juutas* "villain" – are not related to these words, as they are motivated by the name of Judas Iscariot. Some scholars claim that the word J. is related to Old Indian *yātú-* "wizardry, magic", which has several parallels in Iranian languages: Avest. *yātu-* "wizardry; wizard", Pers. *j̄ādū* "wizardry". This theory, however, does not take into account the fact the Balt. *-d-* does not correspond with the Indo-Iranian *-t-*.

The brief description of J. given above is not entirely precise: J. is not identical to Velns. As Latvian scholar Jāzeps Rudzītis noted, the name J. only appears in those tales about Velns that show his darkest and most dangerous side (although he is called Velns in some of these tales, too). No wonder that writer Andrejs Pumpurs chose J.'s and their leader → Līkcepure to be the second most dangerous enemy figures to his hero → Lāčplēsis. The hero fights them in two situations: first, when attempting to free the drowned castle from its enchantment, and then on an island in the northern sea. The latter situation is copied from Latv. fairy tales. In some of them, the hero's enemies are called Velns's, in others, they are referred to as J.'s. What might be of interest to non-Latvian readers is the fact that in these tales and the epic Lāčplēsis, the three J.'s in the second scene do not have one, but 3, 6 and 9 heads respectively. The nine-headed one is the most dangerous one; nine is a significant number in Baltic mythology and symbolizes a large amount (sometimes in the variant 3 × 9). That is perhaps why Lāčplēsis in the epic becomes worried for the first time when he realizes that he will be fighting a nine-headed adversary the next day. He gives his friends a bowl filled with water and asks them to come to his aid if the water starts turning into blood. This sign left with friends or parents for them to know how the hero is doing is a common motive in Latvian folklore.

Beside fighting heroes, J. acts as an adversary for gods, especially → Pērkons. For example, in western Latvia, there was a custom to say about a thunderstorm: *Pērkons jodus gaiņā* "Pērkons is pursuing demons". Unfortunately, almost no other information is preserved on this interesting topic.

Bibl.: APL 221–225; BRMŠ IV, 195, 203 > Stender; DLKŽ 292; Fraenkel I, 197; KL 289–290, 325–326; LKŽ 292; LPG 627; ME II, 125; PŠ 97–99; Pumpurs 1987, 37–38, 65–68; SKES 127; Thomsen 1890, 176.

Jumis – Latv. 'god of field fecundity'. This deity cannot be found in any historical sources but appears in a number of 19th century folk songs.

These songs e.g. ask J. to start a new vegetation period after the winter
that he spent sleeping under a stone:

Ej, Jumīti, nu uz lauku!	Go, Jumis, to the field now!
Garu ziemu izgulējis;	You slept through the long winter;
Sāci jaunu vasariņu,	Start a new summer,
Svētī mūsu labībiņu.	Bless our crops. (LD 28524)

Judging by the lyrics of other dainas, J.'s sleep could last the whole summer till the harvest:

Kur gulēji tu, Jumeiti,	Where were you sleeping, Jumis,
Vysu garu vasariņu?	All the long summer through?
Vai bruoliša mīžu dryvā,	In brother's barley field
Vai muosiņas lynu laukā.	Or in sister's flax field? (LD 50251)

J. was usually associated with some types of grain and other plants,
namely with rye, barley, wheat, oat, flax and others. The Latvian peasant
therefore endeavoured to "get in J.'s good books" by promises of material
gifts, in hope of increasing the fecundity of his fields:

Nāc, Jumīti, mūs mājās,	Come, Jumis, to our home,
Še būs laba dzīvošana.	You'll have a nice time here.
Došu maizi, došu zirņus,	I'll give you bread, I'll give you peas
Saldu alu nodzerties.	And plenty of sweet beer to drink.
	(TDz I, 1751)

This story bears a striking similarity to the Hymn 10 of the 10th Mandala
of *Ṛgveda*, where we encounter siblings by the names of Yama and Yamī.[77]
The similarity of the Old Indian and Latvian names is not coincidental, and
it is even supported by the similarity of meanings of their corresponding
apellatives. The Vedic word *yamá-*, as well as the Avestan word *yə̄ma-*,

[77] RV 10.10.7. *Yamásya mā Yamyàṃ kā́ma ā́gan samāné yónau sahaśéyyāya jā́yéva pátye tanvàṃ riricyāṃ ví cid vṛheva rát{}yeva cakrā́* "Desire for Yama has come to me, Yamī, to lie together in the same womb (/place). Like a wife to her husband I would yield my body. We would 'ler 'er rip' like two chariot wheels." (translation: Stephanie W. Jamison and Joel P. Brereton: *The Rigveda: The Earliest Religious Poetry of India*. Oxford: University Press 2013).

mean "twin" and reflect the IE starting point $*iem\acute{o}$- or $*immó$-. The Lat-vian form *jumis* refers to "two pieces of fruit grown into one, e.g. double apple, double nut, or double grain ear" or any other "double object or two connected objects". Inner reconctruction leads to the proto-form $*imio$-, to which also Vedic adj. *yamyà*- "of or belonging to gemini, twins" and Old Norse *Ymir*, the primordial bisexual giant capable of self-fertilization. The etymological correspondence in the mythological context make the Latvian word and theonym *jumis* an IE archaism *par excellence*.

Bibl.: Blažek 2016; Elizarenkova 1999, 125; EWAI II, 400–401; Ivanov 1986, 7–21; Ivanov & Toporov 1983, 140–175, especially 163; ME II, 117–118; Pokorny 1959, 505; Schmid 1979, 261–267.

Jupis – Latvian and Žemaitian 'devil, evil spirit'. Latvian and Western Lithuanian (= Žemaitian) name for a being of uncertain origin and character. Several 19th century writers deduced from its name and this daina

Jupis bija liels dieviņis	Jupis was a mighty god,
par visiem dieviņiem	the mightiest of gods

that J. was a "high-ranking" Baltic god, similar to Jupiter of ancient Romans. In the 1920's, though, mythologist Pēteris Šmits rejects this daina as a recent creation, claiming that its choice of expressions does not correspond to that of original dainas. And not only that – the word *dieviņis* "god" is used to denote a whole category of beings, while in original dainas, it only refers to one specific god, i.e. Dievs, also called Dieviņš, *Dieviņis* (see → *Deivas). Authors of a Latvian-German dictionary J. Endzelīns and K. Mühlenbach, also in the 1920's, claimed the word to be of Livonian origin, although their theory is supported only be the Est. word *jupe* "horrible, terrifying; dangerous". That would explain, though, the fact that J. is known chiefly along the Baltic coast – that is, in the area where Livonians used to live.

This theonym does not appear very frequently in Latvian folklore. It can merely be found in two kinds of context: first, in curses such as *Rauj tevi jupis!* ~ "May the devil carry you away!", and second, in this song:

Pērkons Jupi tik ilg' sita,	Pērkons kept beating Jupis
Līdz iesita zemītēi.	Till he beat him into the ground.

By the way, this song was rejected by P. Šmits as a recent creation as well; but in this case, he did not give any specific reasons. Seeing as the chief adversary of → Perkūnas was Velns (→ Velinas), it is not impossible that J. was another name for Velns – perhaps a taboo name – or J. was an evil spirit that was somehow related to Velns, and was very similar to him, or blended with him gradually.

Bibl.: BRMŠ IV, 196, 203 > Stender; LPG 627; ME II, 119–120; PŠ 13, 66, 99, 117, 119–120.

Jūras māte "Mother of Sea" see Ūdens māte "Mother of Water"

Jūratė – Lith. 'queen of sea nymphs and lover of Kastytis'. Romantic literary creation of T. → Narbutt.

Bibl.: RB 34, 273, 294–295.

kadars see **werewolf**

Kakta tēvs – Latv. "Father of Corner"; one of the names of Latv. "Father of Forest" (→ Meža tēvs). This compound consists of Latv. words *kakta* & *kakts* "corner" (~ Lith. *kãkts* "jump of the wall; oriel", *kaktà* "forehead") and *tẽvs* "father".

Bibl.: BRMT 256; Kregždys 2009c; LD 30489; ME II, 139; IV, 177; Smoczyński 2018, 470–71.

Kapu māte – Latv. mythical being "Mother of Graves". One of about a hundred Latv. "Mothers" (→ Mātes). Latv. word *kaps* means "grave, burial mound" (~ Lith. *kãpas*). For further reference, see → Rūšu māte.

Kaṛa māte (Kara māte in modern orthography) – Latv. "Mother of War". One of about a hundred Latv. "Mothers" (→ Mātes). The first component – Latvian word *kaṛš* "war; army" – is related to Lith. *kãrias* "war; army" and also Pruss. *kargis* /karjis/ "army", Goth. *harjis* "army" and others. For further reference, see → Mātes.

Bibl.: ME II, 166.

Kārta – Latv. 'goddess of fate'. Frequently mentioned in connection with other goddesses of → fate: Laima and Dēkla. Some mythologists suggest she might be a parallel of ancient Roman *Parcae*, others interpret the name K. as an attribute of Laima and Dēkla. Etymologically, the theonym is probably motivated by the verb *kãrt* "to hang" (~ Lith. *kárti* "to hang"), as shown in the phrase *mūžu kãrt* "to determine life" and the expression *Kārtiņ, tavu kārumiņu* "Kārta, what a hanging!".

Bibl.: Biezais 1975, 365–367; Fraenkel I, 224; Ivanov & Toporov, MNM 625; ME II, 199–201.

Kastytis – Lith. 'human lover of the queen of sea nymphs → *Jūratė*'; also romantic literary creation of T. → Narbutt.

Bibl.: RB 34.

*Kaukas – 'devil' or 'evil spirit' in Prussia and Lithuania (→ under-world). Pruss. word *cawx* is explained as 'Tufel', i.e. *Teufel* "devil" in the Elbing Vocabulary. It is listed immediately after the word *Pyculs* "hell". There is an abundance of the *kauk-* element in Balt. toponyms: e.g. *Kau-kalawke* "Devil's Field" (*laucks* "field"). The abovementioned Pruss. word has exact parallels in Eastern Baltic languages as well: Lith. *kaũkas* "troll, a spirit that takes on the form of a dwarf, goblin; mandrake", Latv. *kauks* "dwarf, goblin, troll".

In Lith. tradition, this name was recorded in 1547 in the first Lith. printed catechism by Martin Mosvidius (Lith. Martynas Mažvydas), in Lith. as *Kaukus* and in Latin (ACC pl.) as *Caucos* (LPG 280). Bretkūnas in his 1591 Lith. *Postilla* reports Lithuanians to "… pray to Žemepatis's [i.e. 'Lords of the Earth' and] Kaukas's".[78] This name also appears in Daukša's *Žemaitian* translation of Ledesma's catechism, published in print in 1595. When we look at the passage that deals with the question of who first transgressed the Decalogue, we find a number of mythological names. "Especially those who worship the fire, *Žemyna [the goddess of Earth], snakes, grass-snakes* [translator's note: in zoology, the word used here – žaltys – denotes the grass-snake, but historically, it also means "adder, poisonous snake"], Pẹrkûnas, trees, groves, Mẹdeina, Kaukas's and other demons; and then those who perform magic, incantations, brew potions, cast tin and wax, use foam and testicles to soothsay; also those who believe in all this: all those abandon God, accede to the Devil and

[78] *..meldessi Szemepaczus, Kaukus.*

behave as if they were equal to the Lord."[79] J. Łasicki in *De Diis* 1584 elaborates on this topic: "Kaukas's are the same spirits as those who Russians call *Vboze*."[80] Further on, he draws the reader's attention to the fact that the expression *kauko akmuo* "Kaukas's stone" denotes 'belemnite' (→ kaukaspenis, → laumės papas).

Russ. linguist and mythologist Vladimir Toporov looks beyond the borders of the Baltic area – to Bulgaria – to find a related word: Bulg. *kuk*, *kùker* 'supernatural beings similar to dryads'. He also notes the Lith. word *kaũkaras*, *kaũkuras* "mountain top; mountain", which, accidentally, even has a theonymical parallel in the word *Kaukuras*, recorded in the 18th century Prussia by Brodowski and Ruhig and translated as "Berggott" – "mountain god". This interpretation is supported by formal comparison with Germanic parallels such as Goth. *hauhs* "high", Old Norse *hár* id., *haugr* "hill" and others. There is also another apophonic variant: Latv. *kūķītis* "dwarf" plus Pruss. *kuke* "dwarf, goblin".

Bibl.: Fraenkel I, 230; Kregždys 2020, 76–88; LPG 280, 359, 402, 425; ME II, 173; MV 382–84; Toporov, *Prusskij jazyk* III, 295–97.

kaũkaspenis – Lith. "belemnite"; compound consisting of *kaũkas* "evil spirit; dwarf, goblin" (→*Kaukas) and *spenỹs* "nipple, teat". The beings called Kaukas's could be female as well as male. A belemnite is a narrow, hollow, pointed, about 1–5 cm long petrified shell that used to belong to an animal of the same name. The belemnites were similar to squids and inhabited Mesozoic oceans. Their shells can be found all over the world, frequently on the surface of the ground. Many a nation of the world became intrigued by their unusual form and created tales about their origin.

The first scholar to mention belemnites in mythological context was the Prussian priest Phillip Ruhig (Lith. Pilypas Ruigys) in his Lithuanian-German and German-Lithuanian Dictionary (*Littauisch-Deutsches und Deutsch-Littauisches Lexicon*, 1747): "Laumės papas a small, brown, somewhat hollow stone found usually on dunes". A dictionary of modern

---

[79] (in original orthography): *Szitie ipaczei, kurie gárbiną vgnį, żęmîną, giwatés źálczius, Pęrkûną, mędźiús, ałmíś, Mędeinés, kaukús ir kitús biéssus: ir anié, kurie żinauia búrę, nůdiią, ałwu yr waßkú łâia, ant'pútos ir ant pâuto wężdi: ir kurie tã tiki: ßitie wissi Diewo atsiźada, ir pristôia węlnóp ir vź Wießpaty sau ápturi.*

[80] *Kaukie sunt lemures, quos Russi Vboze appellunt.*

Lithuanian lists an example sentence recorded in the town of Jurbarkas
Po perkūnijos einam laumės papų rinkt "After a storm, we usually go out
to collect belemnites". And as Lith. poet Marcelijus Martinaitis recalls
in his book *We Lived: Biographic Notes*,[81] in western Lithuania in the
1940's, the children still liked to tell stories about these stones being left
on the hills following secret gatherings of witches, and it was a popular
pastime to look for them in the woods. In western Lithuania, belemnites
were called *laumės papas*, while in eastern Lithuania, they were referred
to as k.

   Laumės papas means "Laumė's nipple". Lith. word *laũmė* nowadays
means "fairy; witch" (~ Latv. *laũma* "flying sorceress or witch; soothsayer"; also described as "goddess of the underground and underworld of
pagan Latvians"), *pãpas* means "nipple". These stones were also sometimes called *Perkūno kulka* "Perkūnas' bullet". For more information on
the myths of their origin, see → Lauma and → Perkūnas.

Bibl.: Fraenkel I, 345, 538; LKŽ IX 1973, 350; LPG 612 > Ruh; Martinaitis 2009,
107; Vėlius 1977, 148.

Kaunis – Lith. 'god of love'; together with → Milda (and other characters – see → Kastytis, → Jūratė), a literary creation of T. → Narbutt.

Bibl.: PŠ 117–118.

kāvi – Latv. "northern lights". Its etymology is based on the verb *kaût*
"to beat" (~ Lith. *káuti*) and is motivated by the mythological notion that
northern lights are the souls of deceased soldiers who continue fighting in
the sky. For further reference, see → northern lights.

Bibl.: ME II, 205, 179–180.

*Kelių diẽvas – Lith. "god of paths and roads". His cult was first
described by Matys Stryjkowski in the book *Sarmatiae Europeae descriptio* (Kraków 1578): "**Kelių diẽvas* – god of travelling. They sacrificed
white roosters to him, holding walking sticks in their hands, while putting
on bast shoes…"[82] The first component of the theonym is derived from
Lith. *kẽlias* "way; path, road; journey" (~ Latv. *cęļš*); the second compo-

---

[81]   *Mes gyvenome: biografiniai užrašai.*
[82]   *Kielu Dziewos, der Reisegott. Diesem opferten sie weisse Hähne und hielten
       Stöcke in der Hand, indem sie Bastschuhe antaten…*

nent means "god" (see also → *Deivas). There is no clear relation to the being called → Kellukis 'patron of paths'.

Bibl.: Fraenkel I, 236; LPG 331, 340; Smoczyński 2018, 517–18.

Kellukis – Pruss. 'patron of paths'. M. Praetorius in *Idolatria veterum Prussorum*, which is a part of his comprehensive reference book on Pruss. history and mythology *Preussische Schaubühne* 1684, notes: "Kellukis who takes care of paths."[83] Lith. *kelùkas & keliùkas* are diminutive forms of the word *kēlias* "way; path, road; journey" (~ Latv. *cęĺš*).

Bibl.: Fraenkel I, 236–238; LPG 545; Smoczyński 2018, 517–18.

*Kerpyčius & ***Šilinyčius** (recorded as →**Kierpiczus & Siliniczus**) – Lith. 'deities of moss and lichen'. These plants were used by the Balt. nations to fill the spaces between logs in their cottages. The names of these two gods are mentioned by J. Łasicki in the book on Žemaitian (Samogitian, i.e. western Lithuanian) deities *De Diis* 1584: "*Kierpiczus* and his aide *Siliniczus* are deities of forest moss; [Žemaitians] use large amounts of moss in construction of their houses. They also offer sacrifices to this god while picking moss."[84] In Lithuanian mythologist R. Balsys's opinion, it is possible that these deities (or, one god and his aide, as Łasicki states) were really worshipped by Žemaitians, seeing as there was a custom observed up till the 20th century with Lithuanians to sacrifice bread or coins after finishing the building of the house, in order to ensure long life both for the house and for its inhabitants. Unlike other deities mentioned by Łasicki, it is rather easy to determine the functions and origins of the names K. and Š.: most mythologists support the theory that the theonym *Kierpiczus* can be transcribed to modern Lith. as *Kerpyčius and put in connection with Lithuanian words *kérpė* "lichen" (~ Latv. *cęŕpa* "small heap of soil or sand or grass; bush; tufty hair") and the verb *apkerpinti* "to cover with lichen"; if it was derived from the verb, the theonym was more likely pronounced as *Kerpintjus*; *Kerpintojas* in present-day Lithuanian. The theonym Š. is probably related to Lith. *šìlas* "evergreen, especially pine, forest; heath, heather" (~ Latv. *sils* "tall forest, pine forest; heath", Pruss. *sylo* "heath"). Balsys remarks: "the connection

---

[83] *Kellukis der auf die Wege Achtung hat.*
[84] *Kierpiczus huiusque adiutor Siliniczus, musci in syluis nascentis: cuius in aedificiis magnus apud illos est usus. huic etiam muscum lecturi sacrificant.*

of Šilinyčius with moss has not […] been looked into sufficiently. […] It
is in those [evergreen] forests that the kind of moss that was used in house
construction grows in abundance: wads of moss stuck into gaps between
logs in walls are called *samanójai*, the verb *samanóti* means 'to cover with
moss'. Lichen […] was also used in house construction".

Bibl.: BMRŠ II, 581; DLKŽ 332, 806; Fraenkel I, 244, 761, 982–983; Las 1619,
47; LPG 369; MV 848; RB 354; Smoczyński 2018, 528–29, 1379–80.

Ķēvesdēls see **Lāčausis**

Kiaulų Kruke – Lith. 'god of hogs' see **Krukis**

Kirnis – Lith. 'god of cherry trees and orchards' or 'god of moors overgrown with shrubs'. The only primary source that mentions this god is J.
Łasicki's *De Diis* 1584: "Kirnis takes care of the cherry trees that grow on
the lake shore. When they want to ask for his forgiveness, they slit throats
of several roosters and throw them between the cherry trees, as well as
stick burning candles into the ground. […] Besides, certain places as well
as noble families have their own deities. For example, along the sea coast,
Deuoitis is worshipped […], in Plateliai, *Kirnis* […]."[85] R. Balsys notes
that what Łasicki had in mind was the western Lith. village of Plateliai
that lies at the lake of the same name, to the north-east of Klaipėda, not
far from the town of Plungė.

   As can be seen in the title of this entry, scholars are not of one mind
when it comes to the function of this deity. One school of thought proposes that Łasicki's source can be trusted in this matter and the aforementioned sacrifices were made to the god of cherry trees K., just as Łasicki
says. IE scholars[86] claim that the name of this 'cherry' deity is related
to the Lat. word for "cherry" *cornus* (tree) & *cornum* (fruit) and to Gr.
κράνος & κράνον id. N. Vėlius approves of this theory and adds that there
is the word *kirnis* "sour cherry tree / *Prunus cerasus*" (LKŽ) in Lith.
Balsys, however, disagrees as there are no wild cherry trees in Lithuania, and cultivated cherry trees were only planted in the 16th century by

[85]   *Kirnis caerasos arcis alicuius secundum lacum sitae curat. in quos, placandi
eius causa, gallos mactatos inijciunt, caereosque accensos in eis figunt …
Praeterea, sunt certis agris, quemadmodum nobilioribus familiis, singulares
dei videlicet Deuoitis agri Poiurskij (…), Kirnis Plotelscij.*
[86]   Schrader & Nehring I, 589; Pokorny 1959, 572–573.

aristocracy in mansion gardens (as mansion inventories suggest). Balsys admits that it is possible that there were cherry trees growing in Plateliai in Łasicki's time but doubts that they were called *kirnis*. If there were no cherry trees in Lithuania, their name could hardly have been preserved. This theory is refuted by the existence of the word *kirnis* "sour cherry tree" – that is, assuming that it was not created by an overenthusiastic lexicographer after Łasicki's theonym.

Bibl.: Smoczyński 2018, 549–50.

*Krivė (Krivaitis ~ Kirvaitis) – Pruss. (Balt.?) 'title of a high priest'. The first mention of a Pruss. high priest comes from Peter von Dusburg and his work *Cronica Terre Prussie* in 1326: "In the middle of the area inhabited by this backward nation, in Nadrovia, there was a place called Romowe. Its name was transferred from the name of Rome. There lived someone whom they revered as if he were the Pope, because the same way His Holiness leads the church, Krive exerted power not only among the aforementioned [i.e. Prussian] tribes, but also among Lithuanians and other nations, living in Livonia. His authority was so great that not only him and his fellow tribesmen, but also his ambassadors with a staff or another well-known insignia, received the highest regard from the rulers and aristocracy, as well as the common folk."[87]

This information is supplemented by Simon Grunau in his chronicle[88], written in the years 1517–1521, with a continuation up to the year 1529: "In the year 521, both brothers summoned the wisest men and announced to them their intent to establish their [i.e. Cimbrian] gods, so that the local people would worship and make sacrifices to no other gods. They wanted Videwuto to become king and Bruteno to stand next to him as the

---

[87] *Fuit autem in medio nacionis hujus perverse, scilicet in Nadrowia, locus quidam dictus Romow, trahens nomen suum a Roma, in quo habitabat quidam dictus Criwe, quem colebant pro papa, quia sicut dominus papa regit universalem ecclesiam fidelium, ita ad istius nutum seu mandatum non solum gentes predicte, sed et Lethowini et alie naciones Lyvonie terre regebantur. Tante fuit autoritatis, quod non solum ipse vel aliquis de sanguine suo, verum eciam nuncius cum baculo suo vel alio signo noto transiens terminos infidelium predictorum a regibus et nobilibus et communi populo in magna reverencia haberetur.*

[88] *Cronica und beschreibung allerlüstlichenn, nützlichsten und waren historien des namkundigenn landes zu Prewssen.*

high priest, who would be listened to as an intermediary with the gods, without whom nothing of importance could be conducted, and the land would be called *Brutenia* after him. So it happened. Vidowuto built his royal castle in Noytto; Bruteno, who received the title *Crywo Cyrwaito*, had a seat built for himself and his gods *Patollo, Patrimpo, Perkuno* at Rikoyto. There he settled with his under-priests, Waidolottes [Ger. DAT pl. *den Waidolotten*]. In the year 523, they called an assembly in a place called *Honeda*, and there they announced the latest revelations of the gods' will."[89]

The *Chronicle of the Grand Duchy of Lithuania and Samogitia* and the Polish chronicler Matys Stryjkowski in *Chronicle of Poland, Lithuania, Samogitia and all of Ruthenia*[90] describe the role of a high priest with the same title during the establishment of the town of Vilnius, that means in Lith. tradition. Krivė-Krivaitis was supposed to be the priest of → Perkūnas and his seat was in the Šventaragis Valley (Svintorog's Valley) in the bend of the Vilnia River, near its confluence with the Neris River. The Neris was originally called Vilija; the name is nowadays only used for its upper reaches. A Krivė-Krivaitis named Lizdejko[91] entered the history of Lithuania when he interpreted a mysterious dream to Duke Gediminas. In the dream, the Duke had seen a wolf in metal armour who had howled as if there were a hundred wolves in it. Krivė-Krivaitis interpreted the dream as a sign for Gediminas to build a castle and a city in

---

[89] *Im Jahre 521 riefen die beiden Brüder die klügsten Männer zusammen und eröffneten ihnen als den Willen ihrer vaterländischen Götter, dass das Volk keinen anderen Gottheiten diene und opferte als ihnen. Sie wollten, dass Videwuto zum Könige gekoren werde, Bruteno aber solle neben ihm stehen als priesterlicher Oberherr, ihm solle als dem Vermittler mit den Göttern gleich diesen gehorcht werden, ohne seinen Willen dürfe niemand etwas Wichtiges unternehmen und das Land solle nach ihm den Namen Brutenia tragen. So geschah es. Vidowuto errichtete seine Königsburg in Noytto, Bruteno aber, der den Titel Crywo Cyrwaito annahm, liess für sich und seine Götter Patollo, Patrimpo, Perkuno eine Wohnung zu Rikoyto aufrichten. Dort schlug er mit seinen Unterpriestern, den Waidolotten, den Sitz auf. Im Jahre 523 hielten Witowudo und der Krywe Kirwaito Brutteno einen reichstag zu Honeda, auf welchem letzterer verschiedene göttliche Willensäusserungen verkündete.*

[90] *Która przedtem nigdy światła nie widziała, Kronika polska, litewska, żmudzka i wszystkicj Rusi kijowskiej, moskowiewskiej, siewierskiej, wołyńskiej, podgórskiej etc. w Królewcu u Jerżego Osterbergera* (1582).

[91] Formed from Lith. *lìzdas* "(bird's) nest" (Fraenkel I, 383).

the place where he had seen the armoured wolf in the dream. The hundred howling wolf voices meant the future renown of the city. Gediminas liked the interpretation and immediately began the construction of the upper and lower castles on the Vilnia River. The city of Vilnius grew around the castles; the name was chosen after the Vilnia River. In connection to the title of Krivė-Krivaitis, *Krzywa dolina* from the legend of the establishment of the city of Vilnius is also worth noting, as well as a later quarter of the city, called *Krzywogrod, Krivoj gorod* or *Curvum castrum*. For the Polish original of the aforementioned passages from Stryjkowski's chronicle and their translation see the Appendices.

Lithuanian linguist Kazimieras Būga (1879–1924) was of the opinion that the title *K. was used by the high priest from Romowe, while the derivative title *Krivaitis* applied to the high priest from Rikoyto. V. N. Toporov interpreted both titles as a parallel to the names of mythical twins *Remus & Romulus* from the Roman legend of the establishment of Rome or *Xsart & Xsærtæg* from the Ossetian *Nart saga*. In all three cases, the second name is interpreted as a diminutive of the first name and could apply to a younger brother. The etymology of the title can be based on Lith. *krìvis,-ė* "bent, crooked (person, tree etc.)", beside the more frequent *kreĩvas* "crooked, slanting". Most probably, this title was not related to the figure of the high priest, but rather to the symbol of his power (*baculum* "staff" in Dusburg's account), because one of the meanings of Lith. femininum *krìvė* is "crooked cane, crooked staff".

So far, authors of etymologies for this title interpret the name *Krivaitis* as a derivative of the first name *Krivė*, without explaining the fact that the sources record, quite consistently, the form *Kirvaitis*. Unless this is a scribal error, it is necessary to find another explanation. This could be found in the Lith. word *kir̃vis* "axe, hatchet; halberd" (~ Latv. *cìrvis*). The suffix -*aitis* is a diminutive and patronymic suffix in Lith. The hypothetical meaning "son of axe" seems odd, but it is meaningful, because the Lith. *Krivė/Kirvaitis* was supposed to be a priest of Perkūnas and the IE god of thunder used an axe or hammer as his thunderbolt. Lithuanian folklore has direct references to the function of axe (Lith. *kir̃vis*) as Perkūnas' weapon[92].

---

[92] *Perkūnas velnius tranko dėlto, kad velniai pavogė jo kirvį* "Perkūnas strikes Velniases (devils), because Velniases (devils) stole his axe." (Ivanov & Toporov 1974, 93; Toporov 2002, 84). The motif of stealing the thunder god's weapon has a parallel in Norse mythology, namely in *The Lay of Thrym* in

Bibl.: Dějiny Pobaltských zemí, 55; Fraenkel I, 259; Janyšková, ESJS 8, 483–484; LKŽ 6, 658; LPG 88, 192, 335; ME II, 627; MV 473–75; Pokorny 1959, 722; Téra 2009, 202–209; Toporov, *Prusskij jazyk* IV, 196–205; Toporov 1980, 3–71; Vaitkevičius 2004, 348–351; Váňa 1990, 71–72; WLS 526.

Krūminė Pradžiū̃ Varpū̃ – Lith. 'deity that provides all sorts of grain'. As Stryjkowski in his *Kronika*[93] commented, roosters with fat crests were sacrificed to it, while their meat was cut to small cubes and eaten. From the linguistic point of view, this theonym is rather unusual, especially when translated: *krūminė* is the feminine form of the adjective *krūminis* "of bushes", and it is followed by genitive plural forms of the words *pradžià* "beginning" and *várpa* "grain ear". Perhaps its symbol was a sheaf of green grain ears.

Bibl.: LPG 330, 338; Smoczyński 2018, 614.

Krūmu māte – Latv. "Mother of Bushes". One of roughly a hundred Latv. "Mothers". Latv. *krūms* means "bush, shrubbery" and is a parallel to Lith. *krúmas*. For further reference see → Mātes.

Bibl.: ME II, 292; Smoczyński 2018, 614.

Krukis – Lith. 'god of hogs'. In his book on Samogitian (Žemaitian) gods *De Diis* 1584, J. Łasicki says: *Krukis suum est deus* (K. is the god of hogs). A century later, Prussian priest Matthaeus Praetorius includes the same piece of information in his *Preussische Schaubühne* with the difference that the theonym is more specific: *Kiaulių Krukė* (recorded as *Kiauliû Kruke*) – *der Schweingott*. The name *Krukis, Krukė* is derived from the verb *kriũkti* "to grunt", *Kiaũlių* is a gen.pl. form of *kiaũlė* "pig".

Bibl.: Fraenkel I, 249, 300; LPG 357, 375, 545; Smoczyński 2018, 610.

Poetic Edda. Thor's famous hammer *Mjǫllnir* is notably paralleled by Latv. *milna* "Perkōns' hammer", compare *Pērkuons mẹt savu milnu* "Perkōns throws his hammer." It is also paralleled in Slavic languages by Russ. *molnija* "lightning", Old Slav. *mlьnii* etc. Both archaeological and ethnographic evidence suggest that the main weapon of the Slavic god of thunder was an axe as well.

[93] *"Która przedtem nigdy światła nie widziała, Kronika polska, litewska, żmudzka i wszystkiej Rusi kijowskiej, moskowiewskiej, siewierskiej, wołyńskiej, podgórskiej etc. w Królewcu u Jerżego Osterbergera"* (1582).

Kurbads – Latv. name of a mythical strongman. This particular hero is similar to → Lāčplēsis but unlike him, he is a son of a mare and does not have bear's ears. His name is probably a compound of Latv. *kurs* "hearth, fire", *kurt* "to lit fire", and *bads* "hunger" – "burning, fiery hunger"? Bibl.: ME I, 248; II, 325–26.

*Kurke, also ***Kurko** – Pruss. deity, first mentioned in the oldest known record of Old Pruss. pagan religion – the 7th Feb 1249 peace treaty signed by Prussians and the Order of the Teutonic Knights. The paragraph in question goes as follows: "They shall not sacrifice to the idol that they carve [of wood] once in a year so that they can worship it as a god called *Curche*, nor to other gods that have not created heaven nor earth and are called by various names."[94] The next one to mention K. is Simon Grunau in the chronicle written in 1517–1521, later extended to include the years up to 1529 (*Cronica und beschreibung* 1529): "Curche was the sixth god, they have borrowed him from Masurians. This god was a deity of food and therefore they demanded supplies of food and drink from him. That is why even now, in the vicinity of the village Heiligenbeil [today's Mamonovo in Kaliningrad Oblast], his image and oak are marked by fire, etc. Also, the first sheaves of grain were burned to honour him, and other similar customs were observed."[95] The most detailed information comes, surprisingly, from the latest "witness" – Matthaeus Praetorius. In the 4th book of the volume *Idolatria veterum Prussorum* of his book *Preussische Schaubühne* 1684, he first lists this deity among the gods of people (*Menschengötter*) *Auſzaitis*, *Gurcho*, *Pillwittus*. Then he goes on to describe the way it was worshipped: "And it was similar with Gurcho or Gurklio, who was often worshipped with fish bones and [animal] bones, as it still is common among some Žemaitians and their neighbours to burn the bones of the meat that was eaten to worship the god and to hide or bury the ashes to

[94] *Ydolo, quem semel in anno, collectis frugibus, consueverunt confingere et pro deo colere, cui nomen Curche imposuerunt, vel aliis diis, qui non fecerunt celum et terram, quibuscunque nominibus appellentur, de cetero non libabunt.*

[95] *Curche war der 6. gott, und diesen sie hetten von den Masuren genomen. Dieser gott war ein gott der speise von dem, das zu essen und trincken fochte. Darumb auff der stel itzundt Heiligenbeil genant sein bilt und eiche mit dem feuer war, und dergleichen. Diesem man auch vorbrandte zur ehren die ersten garben des getreides und solchir manirung vil.*

prevent witches and sorcerers from using them. [...] Next to the hearth, the first fruits, drinks and other sacrifices were burned. [...] Although not all the meals were burned, as it was a custom to sacrifice to Gurcho (who was called by a different name at these occasions) by throwing some food in the corner of the house and pouring drinks there. All that was usually afterwards eaten by rats and other vermin."[96]

Despite the fact that the theonym cannot be found in other Balt. languages, the Baltic adoption in Finn. *kurko*, *kurki* "evil spirit, devil, spectre" proves that the word was once generally Baltic. First and foremost, let us draw the attention to its possible relation to Latv. *ķurķi* "Kleinkorn" which seems quite plausible as the deity ensured abundance of food and grains were sacrificed to it. There is also the possibility of the word being related to Slav. *kъrčь* (< *kurki-) "bushes" and other similar meanings, cf. Ukrainian *korč*, Pol. *karcz*, Kashubian *kårč*, Cz. *krč*, Slovak *kŕč* and others, though what is the nature of this relation is not entirely clear.

Bibl.: Fraenkel I, 316; Kregždys 2009b; LPG 41, 539; ME II, 392; MV 491–93; Toporov, *Prusskij jazyk* IV, 314–21.

Lāčadēls – Latv. name of a mythical strongman. Literally, it means "son of bear". L. is a variant of → Lāčplēsis in some tales (see also → bear).

Lāčausis – name of a Latv. mythical strongman that means "the one with bear's ears". He is a variant of → Lāčplēsis in some folk tales (see also → bear).

Lāčplēsis – Latv. strongman. His name means The One That Tears Bears in Half. But he was given other sobriquets, too (see above, plus further on in this article).

---

[96] *Also ist auch diesem Gurcho oder Gurklio ergangen, den sie ofters mit Gräten und Knochen beehret haben, wie denn noch bey einigen Zamaiten und deren Grentznachbarn der Gebrauch ist, dass sie die Knochen der Speise, so sie zovor aufgegessen, ihrem Gott zu Ehren mit Feuer verbrennen, aber die Asche zur Zauberei verwahren oder vergraben. ... Nebst dem Feuer haben sie die Erstlinge der Früchte und allerhand Ehren und Trinkwaaren geopfert und verbrennt. ... Wiewol nicht alle Speiss sind verbrennet worden. Denn sie öfters auch dem Gurcho unter eines anderen Namen Speis und Trinken in den Winkel des Hauses geworfen und vergossen haben, welches von Ratzen und anderem Ungeziefer ist verzehret worden.*

Virtually every nation has its mythical hero or strongman. Latvian tales are no exception. The motif of a strongman was very popular there. Perhaps the reason is that L. was not only unusually strong, but friendly, imaginative and witty as well.

The Latvian strongman is always described as being a son of a man and a bear, or a man and a mare. The reason for this is not clear. One of the explanatory theories (proposed by Gatis Ozoliņš) claims that this plot originates in the time when the Balt. tribes believed the bear to be one of their totemic ancestors. The story of L. growing up to kill his father – the bear, according to Ozoliņš, refers to the victory of humans over the natural world and the end of totemic relations with animals.

The strongmen in Latvian tales have various names: → Lāčadēls ("Son of Bear"), Dzelzspuika ("Iron Boy"), Ķēvesdēls ("Son of Mare"), → Mežauckus ("The Forest One"), Spalvainis ("The Furry One") or mare's son → Kurbads. They are characters in various plotlines that are mostly shared by many IE traditions: the hero sets out to travel the world, finds a friend who is almost as strong as himself (in some variants of the tales, there are two such friends who later betray him), outwits the devil and rescues a princess. We find him interacting with specifically Latvian characters, too: for example, he wins fight against → Jods and outwits → Velna māte "Mother of Velns". In many cases, he has a characteristic feature: bear's ears.

Out of the many names of the Latvian strongman, L. has become most famous. No wonder – Andrejs Pumpurs chose it as the name of the main character of his national epic, as well as the name of the epic itself (1888).

It would take up half of this book to explain the historical context of the epic and to re-tell its plot. Briefly put, Andrejs Pumpurs set L.'s biography in the 13th century, used many motifs from various Latvian folk tales and added a description of the conquest of the Baltics by crusaders, with L. as the unifier of Latvian and Estonian tribes in the war against them. Pumpurs also created a bride for L. – the beautiful and wise Laimdota[97] added L.'s journey across the Arctic Ocean and the German crusader "Black Knight" who defeats L. because he finds out that the source of his strength is his bear's ears. In the epic, the reader will also find several mythical beings described in this lexicon: → Staburadze, Spīdala

---

[97] Her name means "provided by the goddess Laima".

(→ witch), Daughter of the Northern Wind → Ziemeļmeita, dog-headed people → sumpurņi and demons → Jodi. In the ever-occupied Latvia, these final verses rang loud and strong:

But still, the day will come, is sure,
When he the Black Knight will cast down:
In Staburags's raging maw,
His deadly foe alone will drown.
Then for the folk new times will dawn;
At last their freedom will be born.[98]

The epic has been translated to English and is available online as part of Project Gutenberg. The folk tales that inspired it, however, are numerous and only few of them have been translated. Here is the first part of a typical one:

"Once upon a time, there lived a peasant who had a daughter. One day, he sent her out on the field to collect flax. At noon, she was so tired that she lay down and fell asleep. Suddenly, a bear came out running from the nearby forest, grabbed the daughter in his paws and brought her to his cave. He lived there with her for almost a year. Then she gave birth to a lively boy. He looked just like a human boy, only his ears were those of a bear. So they called him Lāčausisem ("Bear's Ears"). When he was eight years old, he bragged that he could kill his father for not allowing him and his mother to leave the cave [the bear had blocked the entrance to the cave with a large stone]. But his mother talked him out of it. One day, the bear lay down outside the cave beneath a tall oak tree to have a rest and enjoy the sunshine. Lāčausis rolled the stone away, stepped out of the cave, grabbed the bear by his hind paws and threw him against the tree with such force that the brain sprinkled out. Then he had an iron cane made that weighed about 160 kilograms and set out to travel the world. But first, he went outside to see if the cane is strong enough. He threw it so high up into the air that one could not see it. While the cane was falling, he went back inside and had a drink. Finally, the cane came falling down again. When he saw it falling down, he stuck out his little finger. And the cane bent in two places when it fell on his little finger. So he had a stronger cane made and set out to travel the world.

[98]   Translation by Arthur Cropley, 2005.

He met two other remarkable wanderers on the way: Kalnulauzējs ['The One Who Breaks Hills'], a big and strong fellow; and another strongman, Mežabrāzējs ['The One Who Fells Forests'], who was so strong that he could break trees in halves with his bare hands, and then to chop them up to smaller pieces and pile them up like firewood. So the three of them set out to wander the world. They wandered and wandered, till they met a devil. L. suggested a competition to find out which of them is stronger. They agreed to drive wedges into a tree stump. Whoever drives the wedge deeper wins the competition.

First, it was the devil's turn. He drove his wedge really deep. He was very surprised at his own strength and sat down on the ground to see how deep the wedge went. But L. swiftly drove in his wedge and caught the devil's beard in the stump. The devil struggled to free himself with such vigour that his eyes almost fell out of their sockets, but the three strongmen just laughed and went on."

Bibl.: L; PL; APL; Pumpurs 1987; LPT I; Ozoliņš 282–286.

*Laima & ***Laimija** – Balt. 'goddess of fate, luck and successful childbirths.' The Latvian variant of the theonym is first mentioned by P. Einhorn in his work *Historia Lettica* (1649): "The womenfolk, especially pregnant women or women in childbed, particularly worship *Laima*, that is *Fortuna* or goddess of luck; she helps with complicated childbirths and is perhaps identical with *Iuno Lucina*..."[99]

In Lithuanian context, the first mention of the goddess comes from pastor Wilhelm Martini from Verden near Klaipeda, in his sermon *Ad plebem Lituanicam* ('To the Lithuanian Folk'; 1666): "Finally, you will abandon the countless imagined gods, / who rule the sea, the sky, the earth, / Perkunas, Litanus, Babilas and Gabartai will step back / and surely neither [will remain] *Gabjaukurs* nor *Baube*, *žemepati* [= lords of the earth], / what does *Laimele*, what Meletete offer you?"[100]

---

[99] *Insonderheit aber ist von den weiblichen Geschlecht, fürnemblich aber von den Schwangern und Kindbetterinnen geehrt und angeruffen die Laima, das ist die Fortuna oder Göttin des Glückes, denn dieselbe in Kindes-Nöthen den Gebährenden geholffen, und ist diese vielleicht gewesen die Iuno Lucina...*

[100] *Omittas tandem plures effingere Deos | Qui mare, qui coelum, qui moderentur humum, | Absint Perkunas, Lituans, Babilasque Gabartai | Nec non Gabjaukurs Baubeque žemepati: | Quid Laimelea tibi praestabit, quid Meletette?*

M. Praetorius in the 4th section *Idolatria veterum Prussorum* of his book
Preussische Schaubühne (1684) did not add much to this information:
"Sky deities include Okkopirnus, Laime, Perkunas." [101] … "Laimele is
the goddess of childbirth, who is invoked when a woman in childbed
or a child need to be healed." [102] There is a noteworthy record of continuous worship of L. that possibly evolved into the cult of Virgin Mary, as
described by Praetorius in *Consecrationes veterum Borussorum*, the 6th
section of his compendium: "Then the *pribuveje*, that means the old mid-
wife, takes a ladle, and praises Virgin Mary; some also praise Laima, for
whom they also pour aside [homemade liquor]."[103] "When the father has
prepared for the baptism and the godparents are coming, the godmother
comes to meet them with a ladle and gives drink to them all. Then the
godmother, carrying it on her left arm, gives the child to them and takes
a filled ladle in her left hand; she invokes the help of Virgin Mary (or
Laima), so that the child can receive baptism and its new name."[104] The
goddess' name also appears in early Lith. dictionaries from the 18th century: *Fortuna Laime* 'goddess of luck' (Brodowski 1730) and *Laima* 'the
pagans' goddess of childbirth, luck and life' (Ruhig 1747).

In Lith. and Latv. folklore, however, the image of L. is somewhat different. L. does not actually feature in it as a goddess of luck. The chroniclers' knowledge of ancient Greek and Roman mythology probably
played a role in this shift. The authors, who had received classical education, knew the Roman goddess of fate and luck Fortuna; because L. was
one of the determiners of fate, they broadened her role to 'lucky fate' as
well. In Balt. folklore, L. mostly appears as a goddess of fate who knows

[101] *Zu den Himmels-Göttern gehören Occopirnus, Layme, Perkunas* [Chapter IV,
§3].
[102] *Leumele ist die Göttin der Geburt, die sie anruffen, wenn eine Kindbetterin
hat oder sol eines Kindes genesen, dabei sie auch sonderliche Ceremonien
haben* [Chapter IX, §23].
[103] *Dann nimmt die Pribuweje, d.h. die Alte eine Kauszel und betet zu der Jun-
gfrau Maria; einige beten noch die Laime an, der sie auch was auf die Erde
giessen* [Chapter IX, §9].
[104] *Wenn der Vater die Taufe bestellt und die Gevattern kommen, geht die
Hebamme ihnen mit der Kauszel entgegen und alle trinken herum. Dann giebt
die Hebemutter ihnen das Kind, indem sie dasselbe auf dem linken Arm, in
der linken Hand die gefüllte Kauszel trägt und die Panna Maria (oder die
Laime) um Hilfe anruft, dass das Kind die Taufe erhalten und seinen Namen
verdienen möge.*

(and in later conceptions also determines) how long a person will live and what will happen to them in their life (→ fate). In Latv. folklore, she usually bears the epithet *mana mūža licējiņa* 'the determiner of my age'. She discusses human fates with → Dievas/Dievs and sometimes they disagree about determining the length of some people's lives. In Lithuania, this song has been preserved:

Tai Dievo duota,	It was given by God,
Laimužės lemta,	Determined by Laima,
Kad per laukelį	That the young man grew up
Bernužis auga.	Far beyond the fields.

(Juškevičius 1883, Nr. 1085)

Probably because of the cooperation with Dievs, in Latv. folklore she also started to appear among the sky inhabitants and in some dainas, she even attends their weddings (→sky inhabitants, wedding). Her other roles are however compliant with the historical records – L. is indeed the goddess of women in childbirth, invoked in Latvia e.g. in this way:

Nāc, Laimiņa, kad es lūdzu,	Come, dear Laima, when I plead to you,
Ir basāmi kājiņām;	Even barefooted;
Ausi kājas, kavēsies,/	You will be putting on shoes
Grūt' manami mūžiņam.	While I will be having a hard time.

(LD 1099)

Baltic women traditionally gave birth in a sauna, which is therefore perceived as the place where L. manifests and where her powers are greatest. Her attributes are a knife, keys and a woven belt – objects symbolically or even directly associated with childbirth. This is because childbirth was subject to many acts of analogical magic: the woman in childbirth e.g. let her hair loose, loosened her belt and untied all knots on her clothing to "be free of all restrictions", so that "nothing was in the child's way into the world". This is also why in some dainas, L. runs to help the woman with her hair loose. In other songs, she has a blanket which she spreads on the sauna floor for the woman in childbirth to lie on.

Beside this specific function, L. was also the goddess of women in general, helping them spin and weave as well as overseeing them and making sure that they were decent and hardworking. This can be inferred e.g. from this popular Latv. daina:

Kura meita godu gaida,	Which girl is honest,
Tai Laimiņa kroni pin,	For her Laima weaves a wreath,
Tai Laimiņa kroni pin	For her Laima weaves a wreath,
Tīra zelta, sudrabiņa;	All of gold, silver;
Kura goda negaidīja,	Which girl is not honest,
Tai no ērkšķu pazarēm,	For her from thorny twigs
Tai no ērkšķu pazarēm	For her from thorny twigs
Un no dadžu lapiņām.	And thistle leaves. (LD 6621,9)

Various folk beliefs related to L. have also been preserved: e.g. that the threshold is a place where the world of human household meets the world of supernatural beings and gods, and so it is not advisable to sweep the sweepings over the threshold, because they would 'fill up mother L.'s eyes'. When a person walks on a path, they should not urinate or spit on their right side, because it is at their right side where L. always walks and protects them.

There are no records of L.'s appearance – probably because the Balts never had a specific idea of it. The folklore materials only describe the aforementioned objects: a key, a knife, a belt, and a blanket; and the fact that she runs to the women in childbed with her hair loose. In addition to that, Latvian folklore also mentions that L. appears in the form of a hen. Hens and sometimes also sheep were sacrificed to L. until mid-19th century. Latv. folk ornaments symbolise L. with a spruce twig or a cross similar to → Perkūnas' cross.

Outside of the Eastern Baltic area, Toporov finds traces of the theonym in Prussian personal male name *Layme* and points out that the trio of gods Okkopirnus (→ *Ukapirnas* / Ockopirnus), L. and → Perkunas could be all Prussian gods. The theonym *Łaume* from the so called Yatviag manuscript found in the 1970s at the Narew River in Belarus is probably also relevant in this context. The manuscript contains cca 200 lexemes and Łaume follows right after the name of the god of thunder *Pjarkuʃ.* Both theonyms are only introduced by the Polish word *pogańske.* In another place in the manuscript, there is the word *łauma,* translated by Pol. *szczęście,* i.e. "luck". The difference in vowels – *au* instead of the expected *ai* – can be explained by a crossover with the name of another Baltic goddess named *Lauma.*

Interpretation of the theonyms is straightforward, cf. Lith. *láimė* "luck, fate", Latv. *laȋma & laȋme* id., Pruss. *laimiskan* "rich", *etnīstis-laims* "abundant in grace"; all the forms are probably derived from a verb the root of which is preserved in Lith. *léisti,* dial. *láisti* "to allow; to set free; to create",

Latv. *laîst* "to let (e.g. free, loose, stg happen)". The original Old Balt. form could then be reconstructed as **laidm(ij)ā*. Alternately, the name L. might be related to the name of the Roman goddess *Līma*, *Leima* in a more archaic epigraphic variant; cf. also Roman god of quick glances *Līmus*.

Bibl.: Biezais 2006, 91–130; Fraenkel I, 333, 351; Gimbutienė 2002, 24–32; LPG 481, 513, 531, 544, 599–600, 611; MEnc II, 207; PŠ 40–54; MV 519–20; Radke 1965, 185; Smoczyński 2018, 657; Toporov, *Prusskij jazyk* V, 26–30.

Laimes māte – Latv. "Mother of Destiny / Good Fortune". Judging by the name it would seem that she belongs to the category of Latv. Mothers (see → Mātes). P. Šmits and V. Toporov, though, are of the opinion that this theonym really is an epithet of the goddess of destiny → Laima.

Bibl.: BRMT 164, 245; PŠ 12, 40; TDz 3396.

*Lauma – Balt. 'goddess of childbirth' (?). In *Idolatria veterum Prusso-rum*, i.e. the 4th part of the book *Preussische Schaubühne* 1684 by Matthaeus Praetorius, "Laumes" is listed as one of the water deities.[105] Cf. also the Prussian place name *Laumygarbis* (1339), i.e. 'L's mountain'. Grammatically, it is probably gen.sg. or nom.pl. of the theonym **Laumė*. As the final -ė suggests, this theonym is of feminine gender, i.e. it denotes a goddess.

Seeing as *Antrimpus*, the theonym that precedes L. in the abovementioned list, is Pruss., the possibility that **Laumė* is a Pruss. theonym as well cannot be discarded. An indirect proof of this theonym's existence in Pruss. could perhaps be the toponym *Laumygarbis*, recorded in 1339 in Pruss. region of Natangia and interpreted as "Lauma's hill", cf. Lith. toponym of the same meaning *Laumėkalnis* and Latv. *Laũmes-kalns*. L.'s name can also be found in some of the first Lith. dictionaries that were published in the 18th century: *Lucina Lauma* "goddess of childbirth" (Brodowski 1730) and "*Laume* – the heathens' goddess of earth; spectre that comes on Thursday nights if the girls have been spinning on a Thursday, and brings misfortune to the house by re-spinning the thread"[106] (Ruhig 1747).

As for Latvian tradition, the name of this goddess was first recorded by J. Lange in his Latvian dictionary (1777)[107] and G. F. Stender in his

---

[105] *Wasser-Götter Antrimpus, Laumes.*
[106] *Laume eine Erdgöttin der Heyden, ein Gespennst, welches, wenn man am Donnerstag spinnt, in der Nacht nachspinnen soll und drauf Unglück machen.*
[107] *Vollständiges deutsch-lettisches und lettisch-deutsches Lexikon*, Mitau 1777.

book on Latvian grammar (1783).[108] Lange's brief article goes as follows:
"Laume – the goddess of earth. […] She had power over the earth."[109]
Stender's article says : "The goddess that has power over the earth; she
was worshipped on the evenings preceding Fridays (Fridays are called
Pìektvakars, i.e. 'the fifth evening'); no girl was allowed to spin on those
evenings. She had special power over rain and hail. Today, *laume* is understood to be 'witch'."[110] In both Baltic languages spoken today, the theonym L. has equivalents – common nouns: Lith. *laumė̃, laũmė* "specific
kind of fairy that does harm to people from time to time", Latv. *laũma*
"flying witch, soothsayeress". Last but not least, let us not forget to mention some interesting idiomatic and frequently also metaphoric phrases
containing L.'s name: Lith. *Laũmės júosta* "Lauma's belt" = "rainbow"
and → Laumės papas, recorded by Ruhig in 1747; also the phrase denoting "mistletoe" in Lith. *Laũmės šlúota* = Latv. *Laumas sluota*, literally
"Lauma's broom". The word has found its way into other languages, too:
cf. Pol. *ławma* "forest fairy", Beloruss. *laŭma* "witch".

As for etymology of this theonym and word, there are several interpretations. However, it is only the etymological interpretation based on
the IE root *$(H_l)leud^h$- "to grow; to be fruitful" that explains the functional characteristics of this goddess of childbirth and probably also soil
fecundity. What is more, the same root can be identified as the source of
names of deities with similar functions in several other IE traditions: cf.
Venetic *Loudera*, Lat. *Līber* 'god of vegetation', Gr. Hom. Εἰλείθυια, Cre-
tan Ἐλεύθυια 'goddess of childbirth', Mycenian *e-re-u-ti-ja*, and others.
The Proto-Balt. form can therefore be reconstructed as *Laudm(ij)ā*.

L. was traditionally associated with both the earth and the sky; also,
with thunder god → Perkūnas. She was active on Thursdays (Thursday is
considered to be the thunder god's day) and small stones called *Laumės
papas* were sometimes referred to as *Perkūno kulka* "Perkūnas's bullet".
Lith. mythologist N. Laurinkienė uses these facts to deduce that L. was
originally the wife of Perkūnas and lived with him in the sky. One day,
though, she made a terrible mistake (of being unfaithful to him, perhaps?)

---

[108] *Lettische Grammatik*, Mitau 1783.
[109] *Lauma eine Erdgöttin .. Diese herrschete über der Erde.*
[110] *Göttin der Erde, die über der Erde herrschte, welcher der Abend vor dem
       Freytage, der Peektswakkars hiess, geheiligt war, an welchem kein Mäd-
       gen spinnen durfte. Besonders soll sie Macht über Regen und Hagel gehabt
       haben. Heutzutage ist lauma soviel als eine Hexe.*

and Perkūnas threw her off the sky down on the earth. That is how little stones called belemnites or *Laumės papai* (see also → kaukaspenis), found lying on the ground up to this day, came to be.

In Lith. folklore, L. is portrayed as a beautiful woman with long blond hair and large breasts who does not have a home. People sometimes catch a glimpse of her bathing. In some tales, a human boy falls in love with her, marries her and they have children, but Perkūnas is jealous of them and kills one of the children. In other tales, the boy leaves her, she loses her home, wanders aimlessly and secretly changes people's children for her own ones, for people to take care of them and for Perkūnas not to be able to find them and kill them. In some tales, she is described as an ugly woman with large teeth, impossibly long arms, iron nails, and her legs are the ones of a hen. Some tales tell a story of her being abducted by → Velnias and marrying him. Both her ugliness and her relationship with Velnias might somehow be related to her becoming more corporeal after Perkūnas made her live on the Earth. Baltic folklore portrays sky inhabitants as beautiful, dignified, dressed in gold and silver (see e.g. → Saules meitas), but she could not be that anymore, living on the earth. She became the subject of demonization and merged with the witch figures of Baltic fairy-tales (→ ragana). This would explain the fact that witches are sometimes referred to as *laumė ragana* in Lithuanian fairy-tales.

To conclude, let us tell this brief tale known in Lithuania:

Kazys Drobnė from the village of Raitininkai in Čepeliškė district once overheard L. talking to her children. It was in the evening, the sun had already set. He heard her say: "Unrest, Unrest! Give Attack a swing!" "Unrest isn't here, the thunder's killed him!" one of the children replied.[111]

Bibl.: Fraenkel I, 345–346; Laurinkienė 1996, 172–183; LPG 532, 612, 617, 629; ME III, 261; MV 539; Smoczyński 2018, 675; Toporov, *Prusskij jazyk* V, 156–170.

Laumės papas see → kaukaspenis

---

[111] *Kazys Drobnė Raitininkų kaime, Čepeliškės raiste girdėjo laumės pasikalbėjimą su savo vaikais. Taip jau saulei nusileidus, vakare, girdi jis laumę šnekant: 'Nerimai, Nerimai! Pasupk Priepuolį!' 'Nėra Nerimo, dundulis užmušė!', atsako kažkoks jos vaikas.*

*Lazdona – Lith. 'goddess of hazelnuts and hazel trees'. The first scholar to list this deity was J. Łasicki in *De Diis* 1584: "They also have a god of hazel trees Lasdona and Babilos, the god of bees."[112] Save for a few exceptions, all scholars agree that this deity was most likely a goddess, not a god – seeing as the theonym ends with -*a*, which is usual in female names. According to German mythologist W. Mannhardt, it is more likely that her name was *Lazdonė*; this theory is based on the Lithuanian word *tėvonė*, the feminine form of *tėvonis* "heir".

Little is known about this goddess. According to Lith. mythologist Rimantas Balsys, it is likely that her cult really existed, as "hazelnuts have long been an important secondary source of nutrients" and in Lithuania, "the hazel tree has a special status among trees – it is said that the Devil [*velnias*, → *Velinas] is afraid of it but still uses it as a hiding place […] the reason probably being that it is shorter than other trees and therefore Perkūnas never hits it".[113]

Vytautas Mažiulis, in his *Etymological Dictionary of Prussian*, derives the theonym L. from Lith. *lazdà* "[hazel] rod, cane", adding that earlier, in all Baltic languages, this word probably meant "plant that grows wide and trails on the ground". Later, in Lithuanian, the meaning of the word was gradually narrowed down to one part of the plant, and by adding suffixes -*ona* and -*ynas* derivations were created that refer to one specific tree/ bush that "grows wide", i.e. a hazel tree, and its goddess.

Pēteris Šmits supports the theory of both Baltic words denoting a hazel tree (Lith. *lazdýnas*, Latv. *la(g)zda*, Pruss. *laxde*) having been derived from a word that means "rod, cane" because Latv. folk songs advise on making a walking cane out of a hazel tree branch, for

Visi koki ļaunu vēl / lazdiņš ļauna nevēlēja

"All trees can be mean / but the hazel tree does not wish anyone harm." (LD 34351)

Bibl.: Brückner 1922, 179; Fraenkel I, 348; LPG 378; Mažiulis III, 54–56; ME II, 399; MV 541–43; PŠ 213; RB 353 > Vėlius 1987, 73; Smoczyński 2018, 677–78.

[112] *Lasdona avellanarum, Babilos apum dii sunt.*
[113] The god of thunder and eternal enemy of devils in folklore and Velinas in mythology

*Lietuonis (recorded as **Lituwanis**) – Lith. 'god of rain'. Polish chronicler M. Stryjkowski mentioned that a god called *Lituwanis* was responsible for sending rain down on the earth and that Lithuanians would sacrifice white, black and speckled hens to him. The theonym is derived from Lith. *lietùs* "rain", which, in turn, is derived from the verb *líeti* "to pour". A similar derivational suffix can be identified in Lith. *ligónis* "sickly person, patient", which is derived from the noun *ligà* "illness, ailment".

Bibl.: LPG 330, 339; Smoczyński 2018, 700–01.

*Ligyčius, *Lygėjus (Ligiczus, Lygieigus) – Lith. 'god that gives and keeps peace'. Samogitian (Žemaitian, i.e., western Lithuanian) god, recorded in J. Łasicki's *De Diis* 1584: "*Ligiczus,* that is a god who creates and guards harmony among people."[114]

This is the only preserved original piece of information we have on this god, although he was later mentioned by M. Praetorius in *Deliciae Prussicae oder Preussische Schaubühne* 1684 as *Lygieigus* (which is usually transcribed in modern Lithuanian as *Lygėjus*). There are two possible reasons for this: a) it is the same deity whose name differs depending on place and time (Łasicki wrote about Samogitian deities of the 16th century, while Praetorius recorded mostly Prussian 17th century deities); b) Praetorius borrowed the information about this god from Łasicki but adapted his name so that it fit in the Lith. language as he knew it. This is not entirely impossible because, according to Pranas Skardžius and Rimantas Balsys, he did something similar to the name of god Prigirstytis. Praetorius himself writes indignantly at the end of the paragraph that mentions L.: "It is obvious, though, that Łasicki did not know the Lithuanian or Samogitian language because he recorded a number of names in incorrect form. He also seems to me to have been too gullible, as he believed without hesitation what was told to him without making the effort to find out whether it is true or not. That is why some of the gods have such unseemly names that one cannot believe that Samogitians who respected their gods so much would endow them with such odd names."

The meaning of the theonym *L. is transparent enough – most mythologists consider it a derivation from the Lith. verb *lýginti* "to make peace, to settle, to smooth over", Pruss. *līgint(on)* "to judge, to try".

[114] *Ligiczus is Deus esse putatur, qui concordiae inter homines et auctor est et conservator.*

Łasicki believed L. to be a god; however, most mythologists do not discard the possibility that L. was a famous human judge.

There is also a third possibility – i.e. *L. could have been a sobriquet of one of the supreme gods (for more information, see → Derfintos).

Bibl.: BRMŠ II, 581, 594; Fraenkel I, 370; LPG 356, 368; RB 355–356, 385 > Jaskiewicz 1952, 88.

Līkcepure, Līkcepurs, Līccepuris & Nagcepure – Latv. 'chief devil, chief jods', literally "Crooked Cap" & "Cap of Fingernails and Hooves". These names cannot be found in any of Latv. folk tales, but their bearers appear often. The chief of all devils features prominently in Latv. folklore, but under the names *vecais velns* "old devil", *velnu tēvs* "father of devils", *Lūcifer*s or *Lucipers*. The name *Līccepuris* can already be found in G. F. Stender's writing, who says "*Līccepuris* or devil walks around and often manifests," and P. Šmits says "the names *Licepurs* or *Liceporis* are not unfamiliar to Latvian mouths." This suggests that Latv. peasants transformed the foreign word *Lucipers* into the compound of *līks* "crooked, bent" and *cepure* "cap", more comprehensible to them, even though no tales featuring the "chief devil" under this name have survived. This folk etymology was supported by the fact that in Latv. folk tales, devils wear caps made, or with their visors made, of cow, sheep and pig hooves and also human fingernails (Latv. *nags* means "hoof", "fingernail" as well as "visor"). This motif went so far that some tales consider visored caps a devil's invention. Latvians probably adopted the basis for this motif, that is, the cap of hooves and fingernails, from Estonians; it can e.g. be found in the Est. national epos *Kalevipoeg*. In Latvian folklore, *Lūcifer*s is not very different from the usual European representations of Lucifer. L. was made famous by the epic poem *Lāčplēsis*, where the poet A. Pumpurs gave him the role of 'chief jods' (→ jods; jodses in the epic are crueller and more dangerous than devils – see → Velinas) and helper of the enemy army. It is L. who summons a dragon in The Devil's Pit and threatens Kangars with feeding him to the dragon if he does not betray → Lāčplēsis to the Teutonic Knights. See also → world, → underworld.

Bibl.: APL 164–167; KL 192, 206, 210–211; L 91–92; LPT II, 13, III, 238; ME II, 486; PL 281–282; Pumpurs 1987, 23–25.

Magyla – Lith. 'assistant to the goddess of death Gìltinė'. According to Praetorius, she does the hard work for → Gìltinė: "This goddess [Gìltinė] keeps Magyla as her assistant to throttle people or make them suffer until they die, and also to execute punishments."[115]

Prussian lexicographers from the first half of the 18th century comment on the function of M. in similar ways: Brodowski (1730) mentions her as *Furia Magyla*, Ruhig (1747) as *die Zorngöttin der Heyden*, "the heathen goddess of fury". The most likely etymology of this theonym is Lith. *magýla* "burial mound" which is an adaptation of Pol. *mogiła* id.

Bibl.: Fraenkel I, 395; LPG 544, 612.

Mājas kùngs, also **Mājas gars** – Latv. "Lord of the House" or "House spirit", were the most common names for the spirit who resided at a place in a homestead, most often behind the stove, in the barn, in the sauna, under a large stone, under a pile of stones or in a tree.

The house spirit's task was to protect the household, as well as securing ample amounts of food and protecting the inhabitants of "his" house from illnesses. There are also local variants such as → Ašgalvis, → Bēlis, → Cēlis, → Cepļa dievs, → Ciemnieks and → Vecainis.

Reports about M.k. are included in collections of folk beliefs and church protocols from the 17th to 19th centuries, because he was among the Balt. deities whose cults survived the longest. The Balts worshipped him until the 19th century, despite many diligent efforts by church officials to wipe out his cult, because it was inherently connected to family traditions and rituals (celebrations, offerings) and did not require gatherings in public places. Some of the records about the cult of the house spirit are included under the specific local entries. Another report comes from the priest A. W. Hupel in the year 1789. According to this source, Latvians in the Valka Municipality (Valka is a town in Northern Latvia, at the border with today's Estonia) still knew M. k. during Hupel's life, i.e. at the end of the 18th century. Here and there, the farmers would pile up stones at their houses, call the pile M.k. and begin to regard it as a sacred place under the protection of the house deity. On St. Michael's Day, they sacrificed a rooster at the pile and poured out a little beer, which was both

---

[115] *Diese Göttin [Giltine] Dienerin wird gehalten Magyla, gleichsam die Jemand erstickt oder quelet, gleichsam die Executorin* ("Idolatria veterum Prussorum", volume IV of his book *Deliciae Prussicae*).

an expression of their gratitude for the spirit's protection so far as well as a plea for continuing protection in the following year. If the place was damaged, they feared a catastrophe would befall the homestead. However, this belief was not known everywhere.[116]

The offerings mentioned by Hupel were probably particular sacrifices conducted at special occasions like holidays and family celebrations. However, Latv. folklore bears witness to the fact that offerings were made to the spirit regularly, before every meal. The protector of the farm had a right to be the first to taste every meal, and therefore every time before his protectees began eating, they broke away a little piece of bread or meat for him, poured out a little porridge or drink. This offering was always conducted at the place where the M.k. resided. When a new member joined the household, for example a young bride, they had to put a gift, for example new gloves, under the threshold or place it on the fireplace, to gain the house spirit's good will. M.k. insisted on his right to offerings so thoroughly that if he did not receive them, he was capable of causing an illness in a household member, or even leaving the house and setting fire to it (similarly to Lith → áitvaras). For Baltic house spirits, a certain petulance and vindictiveness is therefore characteristic, similarly to Scandinavian house spirits.

Latvian M.k. allegedly preferred men over women, and so it was only men who conducted the sacrifices on holidays. He usually manifested as a person dressed in white, a frog, a bug or a → grass snake. In many households, the belief was that he resided above the fireplace, in the hook on which the cooking pot was hung. He was named after this hook – *kāsītis*, Latv. "little hook". The food offerings to him were skewered on the hook. This *kāsītis* was also the protector of farm animals and keeper of the fire. If the fire died in a household, the landlord or landlady went to ask their neighbours for it, but they had to greet their *kāsītis* politely, ask for the fire politely and then also thank for it.

Namiņš kūp, namiņš kūp,	There is smoke coming from the house
Kas namiņu kūpināja?	Where does the smoke come from?
Kāsīts tup namiņā,	Kāsītis is squatting in the house,
Guni tur rociņā.	He holds the fire in his hand.

---

[116] This text is not included in any of the collections of historical sources this book uses. It is based on the Latvian translation by P. Šmits, to be found at the.

Kur guntiņu tad dabūtu,	Where would we get fire
Kad kāsīts nesargātu?	If kāsītis did not give it?
Labrīt, kāsīt, labrīt, kāsīt!	Good morning, kāsītis, good morning!

(LTD XI, 55334)

There are many theories about the origins of the cult of M.k. For example, it is his connection with the fireplace that led the historian A. Johansons and the Finnish folklorist Lauri Honko to see his origins in the cult of fire, which would have later transformed into the cult of the fireplace. The Latv. *Mitoloģijas enciklopēdija* sees a connection to the cult of earth, probably namely Mother of Earth (→ Zemes māte), because a rooster sacrificed on a stone is an offering typical for earth and fertility deities. The German mythologist J. Grimm was of the opinion that the cult of House Spirit had arisen from the cults of forest and vegetation deities. Latv. *mãja* means "house, building" and it might be an adaptation of Est. *maja* "house", cf. also Finn. *maja* "house". Latv. *kùngs* "sir, master" and OLith. *kùnigas* "master, chief" (recorded first in 1653), in modern Lith. "priest", are borrowings from Middle High German dial. *kunig* "king". Latv. *gars* means "steam; spirit"; cf. related words such as Pruss. *garrewingi* "burning, boiling, steaming", OCS *gorěti* and others.

Bibl.: Fraenkel II, 320; Kursīte 1996, 320–322; LTT 19322–19347; ME I 603–604; II, 314, 577–78; MEnc II, 207–208; PŠ 55–57; PŠ > Hup IV, 408; Smoczyński 2018, 632–33; Vykypěl 2011, 245–251.

Màldinâtãjs – Latv. 'ghost that makes people lose their sense of direction'. It is one of the names of the ghosts of → Vadātājs category that makes people get lost in forests. As to the etymology of this name, cf. Latv. *màldinât* "to confuse, to mislead; to cause sby to lose sense of direction, to lead in a different direction".

Bibl.: ME I, 556–557.

*Markẵ-po[t]is or ***Markẵ-po[co]lis** – Pruss. 'god of wealth & nobility' and / or 'earth god'.

The richest survey of forms occurs in the document *Der vnglaubigen / Sudauen ihrer bockheiligung mit sambt andern Ceremonien, so sie tzu brauchen gepflegth*, known from several manuscripts from the 16th cent.:

Markopole "die Erdleuthe" = "subterranei", and alternatively "die Edelleuthe";

Merkopele "die erdtleutchen";

Marckoppole, Marckopole, Markepole, Markkopole, Merkopete "Edelleute" (Mannhardt 1936, 246).

The latinized form *Marcoppolum* "deum magnatum et nobilium" was used by Johannes Maeletius [Jan Malecki] in his book *De Sacrificiis Et Idolatria Vetervm Borvssorvm, Liuonum, aliarumque uicinarum gentium* (1551), followed by J. Łasicki in his book *De Diis Samagitarum Caeterorumque Sarmatarum et falsorum Christianorum* (1615), see Mannhardt 1936, 295, 362.

The form *Markopotis* was used by M. Praetorius in his *Idolatria veterum Prussorum*, Chap. IX, §22, representing the fourth book of his *Deliciae Prussicae* finished in 1703 (Mannhardt 1936, 544). The same author (Chap. IV, §3) classifies *Markopete* as 'one of the three fortune-gods' (Mannhardt 1936, 532). After Praetorius Grienberger (1896, 84) also quoted the form *Marcopullei*. Concerning the vacillation *t ~ l*, he reminded of the place-name *Wetau = Welau* (the former and older after Praetorius; one of these letters must be a scribal error). Accepting the *t*-variant based on Praetorius' record *Markopotis* and the variant *Markopete* (besides *Merkopete* quoted above), the second component of this transparent compound is etymologizable from Baltic **patis* > Old Lithuanian *patìs*, later *pàts* "husband", *patì* "wife", Latvian *pats* "housekeeper", *pati / pate / paša* "(house)wife", Prussian (*Ench.* 5.14) *pattiniskun* "marriage", (*Ench.* 45.18; 61.6) acc. *waispattin* "lady", *butas waispattin* "housewife" = Old Lithuanian *viešpatni* (Fraenkel 1962–65, 551–52). Corresponding compounds occur in Lithuanian:

Dimstapatis ~ Dimstipatis "deus domesticus" (Mannhardt 1936, 432–35);

Laukpatis "Herr des Feldes" (Mannhardt 1936, 373);

Raugupatis "der Gott, der die Gehr hilft, wenn das Bier volgiert, den Teig wohl säuert" (Mannhardt 1936, 545);

Wejopattis "Herr des Windes", cf. also *Wejpons* with the second component borrowed from Slavic, and *Wejdiews* "Windgott" (Mannhardt 1936, 542);

Zemepattis ~ Zemepatys "Herr der Erden" (sic, see Mannhardt 1936, 544). This is not the only solution. Accepting the *l*-records, Grienberger (1896, 84) assumed metathesis of the 2nd and 3rd syllables, reconstructing **Mār-pecolis* where the latter component should correspond to the divine name *Pecols* "Pluto", cf. also *Pocols* "Furiae" (Georg von Polenz & Paul Speratus, "Sambiensis Constitutiones Synodales", 1530), *Pocclum* "deum inferni et tenebrarum" & *Poccollum* "deum aëriorum spirituum"

(Joannes Maeletius, *De Sacrifiis Et Idolatria Vetervm Borvssorvm Liuo-num, aliarumque uicinarum gentium*, 1563), etc. This idea can be devel-oped by suggesting haplology **Marco-pocol°* > *Marcopol°*. The vacil-lation *l ~ t* is explainable alternatively too, if *Pocols* is substituted by his infernal colleague, *Patollus ~ Potollos* etc. "god of the dead" (see Mannhardt 1936, 312).

In the final *-e* occuring in most of the quoted forms Grienberger (1896, 84) saw the Latin plural ending *-ae*. But this ending could be identified as the original Prussian vocative (Baltic **-ei* > Lithuanian *-iẽ*) or dative (Baltic **-ei* > Lithuanian *-ie*, Prussian *-ei*; see Stang 1966, 211, 207). The vacillation *-ei ~ -e* in the final position is well attested, e.g. *istwei ~ istwe* "to eat" (*Ench.* 65.31 vs. 65.32) or *assei ~ asse* "thou art" (*Ench.* 45.2, 51.18, 53.1, 81.3 vs. 7.4, 65.33).

It remains to explain the first member of the compound. There are two alternatives: a) **marka-* (cf. EV 654 *paustocaican* "wild horse" < **pausta-* & **kaika-*, see Mažiulis III, 237, or the place-name *Ray-stopelk* < **raista-* & *pelkī with the components corresponding to Lith-uanian *raĩstas* "swamp" & Prussian *pelky* "morass", see Gerullis 1922, 138; Mažiulis IV, 8), b) **markā-* (cf. EV 665 *paustocatto* "wild cat" < *paustā & *katā, see Mažiulis III, 238), depending on the gender of the first member. The semantic definitions "Erdleute" / "subterranei", "Edel-leute" / "deus magnatum et nobilium" and "Glücksgott", look rather enigmatic. The existing attempts to etymologize the stem **markă-* do not solve this semantic dispersion. Let us confront the published compara-nda: (1) Lithuanian *markà*, "pit for retting flax or hemp", Latvian *mãrks*, *mãrka* "flax-retting" (so G.F. Stender in the chapter *Lettische Mythologie* of his *Lettische Grammatik*, Mitau 1783; see Mannhardt 1936, 618–20); (2) Polish *mrok* "dusk, twilight" (G. Ostermeyer, *Kritischer Beytrag zur altpreussischen Religionsgeschichte*, Marienwerder 1775); (3) Lithua-nian *isz marios kopa* "to rise from a sea" (Praetorius; see Grienberger 1896, 84); (4) Lithuanian *Mergu pàts* "lord of virgins" (Brückner 1922, 170). Finally, Grienberger (1896, 84) reconstructed the starting point *mār-pecolis with metathesis of the 2nd and 3rd syllables, interpreting it as "der grosse *Pecolis*" (see above). Let us add that **mār-* is postulated only on the basis of other IE languages, cf. Welsh *mawr*, Old Icelandic *már* (Pokorny 1959, 704).

It seems the most exact cognate is to be found in the Italic deity *Mer-curius* who has a wide spectrum of functions: (1) 'patron of merchants'; (2) 'he who brings a gain'; (3) 'bearer of felicity'; (4) 'conductor of souls

of the dead into the infernal regions', etc., cf. the epithets and character-
izations as (1) *mercator* (*CIL* XIII 6294), *negotiator* (*CIL* XIII 7360),
nundinator (*CIL* XIII 7569); (2) *lucrorum potens et conservator* (*CIL*
V 6594), *Mercurius lucrum promittit* (*CIL* XIII 2031); (3) *felix* (*CIL* IV
812, XII 5687 10); (4) *Iuppiter iutumuit, quaque est non usa modeste,* |
eripuit linguam Mercuriumque vocat. | *'Duc hanc ad manes locus ille
silentibus aptus* | *nympha, sed infernae nympha paludis erit'* (Ovid,
Fasti II 607–10). In Rome a temple was dedicated to Mercurius in 495
BC (Livius II.21). The same god *Mircurios, Mirqurios* was honored in
Praeneste. The discovery of the so-called *'titoi mercui efiles'*-inscrip-
tion at Mercurius' temple in Falerii indicates the parallel form **Mercuvius*. Since antiquity (e.g. St. Augustin, *De civitate Dei*, IV, 11; Servius,
Aeneis IV, 638), the divine-name *Mercurius* with its variants has been
explained on the basis of *merx, -cis* "ware" (Plaut.), *mercātus* "purchase;
market", *mercātor* "merchant, trader", *mercēs, -ēdis* "earnings, wage,
rent", and further Oscan abl. sg. *amiricatud* "handelsmässig", acc. sg.
amirikum "commercium", together with the divine name *Mirikui* (dat.
sg.) confirming the Faliscan form without *-r-*, all probably borrowed
from Latium (Untermann 2000, 85–86, 479). A primary verb could be
sought in Hittite *mark-* "to divide, separate; distribute, apportion; cut up,
butcher" (Güterbock & Hoffner 1989, 187f; cf. Tischler 1990, 137–38).
On the other hand, with respect to the chthonic function of the Prussian and Latino-Faliscan deities, there is a tempting cognate in Hittite
ᵈ*Markuwaya-* 'deity in depth of the earth' (Tischler 1990, 139), especially with respect to the variant **Mercuvius*. Only to the world of death
and destruction is limited semantics of hypothetical Indo-Iranian counterparts: Old Indic *Márka-* "a demon presiding over various sicknesses
of childhood; name of the Purohita of the Asuras", *marká-* "seizure", i.e.
"eclipse (of sun); annihilation, death" = Avestan (Late) *mahrka-* "death,
destruction", (Old) *marəkaē-čā* "and in ruin", from *mark-* "to destruct,
ruin, kill", Sogdian *mrync* "to destruct", *mrc* "death", Middle Persian
marg id. (Mayrhofer II, 323–24).

Balsys (2006, 81–85) brings a survey of other etymologies. Among
them should be mentioned the idea of Šmits (PŠ 111) about adaptation
or interference of the name of the traveller Marco Polo (1254–1323). His
description of the richness of the Far East was introduced into Balticum
with delay, but it became very popular. But this idea does not explain the
relation of this deity with death.

Bibl.: Blažek 2001, 351–54; Fraenkel 1962–1965, 551–552; Grienberger 1896, 84; Güterbock & Hoffner 1989, 187f; Kregždys 2016; LPG 246, 295, 312, 362, 373, 432–435, 532, 542, 544, 545, 618–620; Mayrhofer, EWAI II, 323–324; Pokorny 1959, 704; Smoczyński 2018, 755; Tischler 1990, 137–139; Untermann 2000, 85–86, 479.

Mātes – Latv. "Mothers", maternal goddesses or supernatural beings. "As far as I know, no author has yet tried to explain why there are so many more mothers than fathers among our gods," wrote Latv. mythologist Pēteris Šmits in 1926. What he had in mind were supernatural beings from Latv. folklore that oversee various landscape features, natural phenomena etc. (see also → world), and their names contain the word *Māte* "Mother". For example, Ūdens māte "Mother of Water", *Zemes māte* "Mother of Earth", *Vēja māte* "Mother of Wind", and many others. M. are specific to Latvians among the Balt. nations. No similar cult of Mothers can be found with the Prussians, nor with the Lithuanians. P. Šmits undertook the task of explaining the numerous appearances of M. in Latvian mythology himself. He theorises that they used to be the goddesses of the original matriarchal, pre-Indo-European inhabitants of Latvia who lived in the area at the beginning of the Common Era and were later assimilated into the Baltic and Fenno-Ugric tribes. The fact that old Gauls and Germanic tribes had a similar cult (inherited from pre-Indo-European nations with matrilineal descent systems) also speaks in favour of Šmits' theory. The supposed pre-Indo-European inhabitants of Northern Latvia left a deep mark on both Latvian language and culture. This consequently played a role in the division of the Eastern Baltic language into Latvian and Lithuanian, and Latvians likely also acquired the cult of mother goddesses from these tribes. However, in competition with the Latvians' Indo-European gods (→ Dievs, → Pērkons and others) these goddesses have eventually lost their standing and become mere spirits.

This theory is opposed by Latvian mythologist Vilma Greble, who disputes the notion that Latvians adopted the cult of M. from a pre-Indo-European nation in the Common Era. She proposes that its roots lie in "matriarchy as a stage in the development of humanity as a whole". Contemporary Latvian mythologist Janīna Kursīte more or less agrees with Greble's notion: according to Kursīte, there was a time in the history of Europe when nearly all nations worshipped mother goddesses. She also derives the origin of these M. from a Great Mother, the chief matriarchal goddess who ruled over both life and death. The other M. would have perhaps represented individual characteristics of this one chief Mother; or, the Mother eventually "dissolved" into individual M. and each of them began to represent a single aspect of the one original Mother and took over one area of her responsibilities.

Most information concerning M. available now is preserved in Latvian dainas. As a certain part of dainas is generally accepted to be the oldest part of Latvian folklore,[117] the images of M. presented in these dainas are also considered the oldest and most reliable ones. The oldest concepts are those of M. of Wind, M. of Forest, M. of Fields, M. of Souls, M. of Manure, M. of Sea, M. of Fire, M. of Earth, M. of Water, M. of Milk and several others. There are, however, also dainas about M. which, according to Šmits, are later creations of folk singers who composed new dainas, inspired by the original ones. Among the newer M. are evidently the Mothers of Tobacco, of Rīga, and of Money (since Rīga was founded in 1201 and money is a fairly recent phenomenon, to say nothing of tobacco); the Mothers of Flowers, Waves, Leaves, Bushes, Deers, Sand and several others are probably relatively new as well. It is immediately clear that M. were originally responsible for natural phenomena of importance to agriculture, fishing and gathering, i.e. the sources of living for ancient and early medieval cultures. Above all, the M.s' spheres of influence concerned unpredictable elements that could provide people's living (sea, forests) or destroy it (fire, wind). In later times, M. were also in charge of those natural phenomena that were not necessary for people's living (flowers, leaves, bushes, animals such as deer etc.).

In the 1930s, Latv. theologian, religionist and minister of education Ludvigs Ādamovičs proposed a theory that combines P. Šmits' and J. Kursīte's theories. Ādamovičs argues that M. evolved by differentiation from a single mother goddess, 'M. of Earth'. At first, several basic M. emerged: Mother of Forest, Water etc. Those then divided further into more specific Mothers: 'Mother of Forest' evolved further into 'Mother of Deer', 'Mother of Leaves', 'Mother of Bushes,' and 'Mother of Berries'; 'Mother of Water', analogically evolved into 'Mother of River,' 'Mother of Waves' and so forth.

According to contemporary folklorist and mythologist Aldis Pūtelis, M. evolved as a personification and deification of the phenomena they

---

[117] More in PŠ 125 and Kursīte 1996, p. 139.

were then responsible for: thus, 'Mother of Wind' is personified wind, 'Mother of Fire' is personified fire, etc.

However, setting aside the question of the origin of the cult, scholars agree that due to the insufficient number of historical sources, it is impossible to determine with any certainty when the Northern Baltic tribes did adopt it.

What did Latvian M. look like and in what manner were they worshipped? There is very little record of sacrifices made in their honour. It is, however, certain that M. were not only characters in narrative myths like most of the sky inhabitants were. Latvians did indeed keep their cult, that is, worshipped them, invoked them and brought offerings to them. For example, there are records of a white hen with chicks sacrificed to Mother of Fire (more under the respective entries). A popular sacrificial phrase used to address M. was *Še, ... māte, tava tiesa; neņem pate (ar) savu roku!* "Here, Mother of…, is your share; do not take it with your own hand!"

M. can be divided into 3 categories depending on their appearance. (i) Some are anthropomorphised, and in that case their figures are surprisingly exaggerated, asymmetrical or even disfigured: they could have cow horns, a large bottom lip, thick fingers, or unnaturally long legs. *Ceru māte* "Mother of Bushes" appears as a woman taller than the tops of trees. (ii) Some M. manifest to humans as animals: e.g. *Gausu māte* "Mother of Plenty" appears as a toad or as a mouse. J. Kursīte believes that both these types of appearances prove the M.'s archaic origins. (iii) The third category of newer M. encompasses M. that are completely identified with the element or phenomenon they oversee: for example, *Uguns māte* "Mother of Fire" manifests simply as a small flame.

According to Kursīte, a total of 115 M. can be found in the old chronicles, dictionaries, collections of dainas, folk beliefs and incantations. The number is very uncertain, though, as there is a distinct possibility that not all of these M. were really mother goddesses overseeing certain natural phenomena; it is not even certain whether all of them were indeed goddesses or spirits at all. As Vladimir Toporov and Elza Kokare noted, the Latv. word *māte* was historically used not only to denote mothers and goddesses, but also middle-aged or elderly women, usually those that were respected in the community. Hence, the address *Vasariņa, Ziedu māte* = "Dear Summer, thou Mother of Blooms" (LD 28253) could merely be a poetic way of addressing and personifying summer as a respected woman that is associated with flowers or gives flowers to people, not an actual reference to a goddess of flowers.[118] In the song

Man uzauga pūcenīte	A rowan tree grew
Zirgu staļļa galiņā;	Behind my stable;
Ik rītiņus skauģa māte	Every morning, the mother of envy
Garām gāja šņaukādama	Went by, snorting through her nose.

(LD 29835)

it is also difficult to determine whether the words "mother of envy" refer to an envious woman, or if this envious woman is likened to the supernatural being / goddess "Mother of Envy", or if the supernatural being / goddess herself is referred to here. A similar problem arises with the interpretation of songs about *Bišu māte* "Mother of Bees", which may simply refer to the queen bee. Unfortunately, it is not possible to dedicate an individual entry to each of the 115 M. in this Lexicon. Moreover, some of these 115 M. are only mentioned in a single song, or they are only referred to by a single chronicler, without giving further details. The following list only contains the 57 most frequently mentioned M., listed alphabetically according to their Latv. name. All three categories of M. are represented: i.e. there are 1) M. of elements, 2) ancient M. (such as Mother of Manure, *Rīšu māte*, Mothers of Plenty, Mother of Veļi (souls), Mother of Path/Journey) and 3) more recent M. (Mothers of Deer, Livestock Enclosures, Forest Berries, Leaves).

The names marked with an arrow have their own separate entries:
→ *Bangu māte* "Mother of Waves", *Bišu māte* "Mother of Bees", *Briežu māte* "Mother of Deer", → *Ceļa māte* "Mother of Path/Journey", *Ceru māte* "Mother of Shrubs/Bushes", *Dārzu māte* "Mother of Livestock Enclosures", *Debess māte* "Mother of Sky/Heavenly Mother", *Gaisa māte* "Mother of Air", → *Gaujas māte* "Mother of Gauja [river in Northern Latvia]", → *Gausa/Gausu māte* "Mother of Plenty", *Gov(j)u māte* "Mother of Cows", *Igauņu māte* "Mother of Estonians", → *Jūŗas māte* "Mother of Sea", *Kapa/Kapu māte* "Mother of Grave/Graves", *Kaŗa māte* "Mother of War", *Krūmu māte* "Mother of Bushes", *Laimes māte* "Mother of Luck", *Lapu māte* "Mother of Leaves", *Lauka/Lauku māte* "Mother of Field/Fields", *Lazdu māte* "Mother of Hazels", *Lopu māte* "Mother of Livestock", *Ļekatu māte* "Mother of Jumps" (most probably just another name for Gausu māte), *Mēra māte* "Mother of

[118] See BMRT 165 and Kokare 1999.

Measure/Measuring Cup", *Mēŗa māte* "Mother of Plague", → *Mēslu māte/
bāba* "Mother/Hag of manure", → *Meža māte* "Mother of Forest", *Miega māte*
"Mother of Sleep", *Miežu māte* "Mother of Barley", *Miglas māte* "Mother of
Fog", *Mūža māte* "Mother of Age/Life", *Nakt(e)s māte* "Mother of Night",
→ *Naudas māte* "Mother of Money", *Nāves māte* "Mother of Death", *Ogu
māte* "Mother of Forest Berries", *Piegulas māte* "Mother of Horse Pasture"
(invoked when the herdsman went to the pasture for a longer period of time,
e.g. overnight), → *Piena māte* "Mother of Milk", → *Puķu māte* "Mother
of Flowers", *Rauga māte* "Mother of Sourdough", *Rīgas māte* "Mother of
Rīga", → *Rīšu/Rīšķu māte* (the meaning of her name is not clear), → *Rūšu
māte* "Mother of Graves / Burial Mounds", *Sātā māte* "Sated Mother", *Sēņu
māte* "Mother of Mushrooms", *Skauģa māte* "Mother of Envy", → *Smilšu
māte* "Mother of Sand", *Tabakas māte* "Mother of Tobacco", *Tirgus māte*
"Mother of Market", → *Ūdens māte* "Mother of Water", *Uguns māte* "Mother
of Fire", → *Upes māte* "Mother of River", *Vidzemes māmuliņa* "Mommy
of [North-Latv. region] Vidzeme", → *Vēja māte* "Mother of Wind", → *Veļu
māte* "Mother of veļi [= the souls (of the dead)]", → *Zemes māte* "Mother
of Earth", → *Ziedu māte* "Mother of Blooms", *Ziemeļa māte* "Mother of
North Wind", → *Zirgu māte* "Mother of Horses".

Aside from the aforementioned, there are two further categories of M.
to be found in Latv. folklore: 1) M. of various body parts and illnesses,
e.g. *Sirds māte* "Mother of Heart", *Krampju māte* "Mother of Cramps",
or *Guļas māte* "Mother of Lying Down", which is a metaphorical name
for illness. 2) The other group consists of M. of other gods: *Velna māte*
"Mother of Velns", *Jāņa māte* "Mother of Jānis", *Laimas māte* "Mother
of Laima" and *Jumja māte* "Mother of Jumis". These are mothers (or, as
V. Toporov proposes, wives or female variants) of the respective mythical
beings; see also the relevant entries (→ Jānis, → Jumis etc.).

The motif of mother goddesses was so old and important in the Eastern Baltic area that it can be found in the very first description of the
region. It was compiled by Roman historian Publius Cornelius Tacitus,
using merchants and soldiers' stories, in §45 of his book *Germania* in the
1st century CE: "Turning, therefore, to the right-hand shore of the Sue-
bian sea, we find it washing the country of the Aestii, who have the same
customs and fashions as the Suebi, but a language more like the British.
They worship the Mother of the Gods…"[119]

---

[119] *Ergo iam dextro Suebici maris litore **Aestiorum** gentes adluuntur, quibus ritus
habitusque, lingua Britannicae propior. Matrem deum venerantur* [http://data.

The idea of M. spread from the Balts into the neighbouring Fenno-Ugric traditions as well, as suggested by the Est. *Maa-ema* "Mother of Earth", *Tule-ema* "Mother of Fire", *Vete-ema* "Mother of Water", *Tuule-ema* "Mother of Wind", *Marum-ema* "Mother of Storm"; Liv. *Nurme-imä* "Mother of Field", *Kala-imä* "Mother of Fish", *Mier-imä* "Mother of Sea"; Mordv. *Moda-ava* "Mother of Earth", *Veď-ava* "Mother of Water", *Kov-ava* "Mother of Moon", *Varma-ava* "Mother of Winds", *Viŕ-ava* "Mother of Forest", *Nar-ava* "Mother of Flood Plains", *Jurt-ava* "Mother of House", *Veľ-ava* "Mother of Community/Municipality", etc. The large number of mother goddesses in Mordv. tradition suggests that the ancestors of the Mordvins were the Balts' eastern neighbours, as is also evidenced in the Balt. origins of the names of rivers in the upper reaches of the Volga.

Bibl.: Ajxenvaľd, Petruxin, Xelimskij 1982, 167, 175; BMRT 165; Kokare 1999, 178–188; Kursīte 1996, 317, 325, 328, 337; Kursīte 1999, 50–91; PŠ 129–131.

Medeina – Lith. 'goddess of forest'. The first book to mention her name is J. Łasicki's *De Diis* 1584: "Medeina and Ragaina are forest deities."[120] Later, we find similar information about her in Daukša's 1595 Samogitian (Žemaitian) translation of the appendix to a catechism: "Especially those who worship the fire, the goddess of Earth, snakes, grass-snakes [note: the Lith. word for "grass-snake" was sometimes also used to denote poisonous snakes such as adders], Pęrkûnas, the trees, the groves, Mędeinas, Kaukas's and other devils; and then also those who perform magic, incantate, brew potions, pour tin and wax, tell the future from foam and testicles and those who believe in all this; all those people abandon God and enter Devil's service and behave as if they were equal to the Lord"[121].

perseus.org/citations/urn:cts:latinLit:phi1351.phi002.perseus-lat1:45]. Visited on June 2, 2021. Translated by Alfred J. Church & William J. Brodribb (1942). The word Aestii most likely refers to a population speaking a Baltic language, not to the ancestors of Estonians, even though it gave the name to the latter's country.

[120] *Modeina et Ragaina sylvestres sunt dii.*

[121] (in the original orthography): *Szitie îpaczei, kurie gárbiną vgnį, źęmîną, giwatés źálczius, Pęrkûną, mędźiús, ałmíś, Mędeinés, kaukús ir kitús biéssus: ir anié, kurie źinauia búrę, nůdiią, ałwu yr waßkú łâia, ant' pútos ir ant pâuto węźdi: ir kurie tã tiki: ßitie wissi Diewo atsiźada, ir pristôia węlnóp ir vź Wießpaty sau ápturi.*

The theonym is derived from Lith. *mẽdis*, *mẽdžias* "tree", East Lith. also "forest", *medìnis* "wooden, of forest", *mediena* "wood" (~ Latv. *mežs* "forest", Pruss. *median* "forest").

Bibl.: Fraenkel I, 423–425; LPG 356, 402; MV 589–90; Smoczyński 2018, 771–73.

*Medeinas (recorded as **Mějdějnъ**) – Lith. ʻgod of forests and wild-life'(?). The only record of this theonym is provided by *Galician-Volhynian Chronicle* in the description of the year 1252: "His baptism was a mere artifice and he continued to offer sacrifices to his gods in secret: to *Nonadej*, *Teljavel*, *Diverikis*, to the hare god (and) *Mejdejn*. Whenever he rode into a field and saw a hare running into it, he felt he was not allowed to step into a forest, let alone break a branch there. He sacrificed to his gods, cremated his dead and did not care if anyone sees that he continues living as a pagan." [122] This theonym is derived from Lith. *mẽdis*, *mẽdžias* "tree", in Eastern Lith. dialects also "forest", *medìnis* "wooden", *mediena* "wood material" (~ Latv. *mežs* "forest", Pruss. *median* "forest").

Bibl.: Fraenkel I, 423–425; LPG 51, 55; MV 589–90; Smoczyński 2018, 771–73.

Medžiojma – Latv. ‚goddess of hunting'. She is mentioned in the ten-volumed *Dzieje starożytne narodu litewskiego* ʻAncient stories of the Lithuanian people' by Teodor → Narbutt. The author deals with M. in the 1st volume called *Mitologia litewska*. He described her as "… Laima, which lives in forests, hunts animals and terrifies them and sometimes she pastures herds of elks, roes and other game". Narbutt's followers, e.g. Romanticist A. L. Jucevičius described her as the Lithuanian goddess of hunting, imagined as a giantess with a masculine face, dressed in a bear's skin and with a bow on her shoulder. In the West Lithuanian region Žemaitia (= Samogitia) in the district Raseiniai there supposedly stood her sanctuary. Rather suspicious is that Łasicki never mentioned her, although he recorded a lot of other Žemaitian deities. Together with the fact that this goddess does not appear in folklore, it seems, M. represents

---

[122] *Kreščenie že ego lьstivo byst: žrjaše bogomъ svoimъ vtaině, pervomu Nъnadějevi, i Teljaveli i Diverikъzu, zaejačemu bogu₍,₎ Mějdějnu: egda vyěxaše na pole i vyběgnjaše zajacь na pole, v lěsъ roščenija ne voxožaše vnu i ne smějaše ni rozgy ulomiti, i bogomъ svoimъ žrjaše, i mertvyxъ telesa sožigaše, i pogaньstvo svoe javě tvorjaše.*

probably again a product of Narbutt's imagination, perhaps inspired by
the goddess → Medeina.

Bibl.: Narbutas 1998, 123; RB 358.

*Medžiorys, pl. ***Medžioriai** (recorded as **Medzorei**) – Lithuanian ‚tree-
priests'. A kind of the Prussian and West Lithuanian (Žemaitian) priests,
described by M. Praetorius (see → priests). The term was formed from
Lith. *mēdis*, *mēdžias* "tree". From Praetorius' description it is possible
to judge that in the middle of the 17th cent. the function of tree-priests
already did not exist or had a different name: "To such [→ vaidilas, which
care for forest] it is possible to add the *Medzorei*, whose task was to consecrate specific trees […] they undoubtedly cared for such the woods and
thickets, which exist still today, especially in Žemaitia."

Bibl.: BRMŠ III, 167, 276; Fraenkel I, 423; LPG 554; Prae 4, Chap. 14, §XXII;
Smoczyński 2018, 771–73.

Meletette – Lith. 'deity of plants used by dyers and of colours, especially
blue colour'. Praetorius says: "Meletette – deity responsible for all plants
used by dyers… in fact, a goddess of blue colour."[123] There is an obvious
relation to Lith. *mélas* "blue", *mélys* "blue colour", *mélė* "dyer's woad,
also known as glastum, Lat. *Isatis tinctoria*". Mannhardt was of the opinion that this theonym is a compound with the second component being
Lith. *tetà* "aunt"; however, this theory appears to be too forceful.

Bibl.: Fraenkel I, 430–431; LPG 513, 545; Smoczyński 2018, 778.

Mēness, Mēnestiņš, Mēnestinis, Mēnesīts, Mēnestiņa, Mēnesnīca – Latv.
"Moon", and its diminutives. A celestial body that features both as an
anthropomorphic representation, and not personified in Latv. mythology
(→ sky). The word M. and its derivatives have their origin in the Proto-In-
do-European *mēnōt "Moon", gen. *mēneses, and they are also related to
the names for this celestial body in many contemporary Indo-European
languages. The forms *Mēnestiņa*, *Mēnesnīca* etc. (the list above is not
exhaustive) are feminine; according to H. Biezais they were formed for
reasons of rhythm, by adding the fem. ending -a: the metre of Latv. dainas

---

[123] *Meletette der Farben Gott über die Färbenkräuter, … doch eigentlich die
Göttin der blauen Farben (Idolatria veterum Prussorum*, i.e. volume IV. of
his book *Deliciae Prussicae).*

uses predominantly trochaic or dactylic-trochaic feet, therefore it usually works best with two- or four-syllabic words. M. appears most often in dainas; an impressive number of dainas speaking of M. has survived, around 900.

Similarly to the Morning Star, M. in dainas is also treated both as the celestial body itself and as its anthropomorphic representation. Aside from dainas, M. also appears in a certain kind of myths, discussed further at the end of this entry. Some dainas use poetic language to tell very simple facts about M.: that he shines at night and the Sun during the day, or that he shines in winter and the Sun in summer. Observations of the Moon are used for calendar purposes, and its constant changes of shape are a parable for fickle men (LD 33843). Dainas also speak of M. as a great helper of humans – he shines for orphans whom their stepparents force to work all day and night, orphaned girls without brothers who would split lighter wood for them, and other people who need to work at night. This part of his responsibilities was still pronounced well into the 19th century, because Latv. serfs often had to work all day on their lords' fields, and only had time for sewing their own clothes, maintaining their homes etc. in the evenings and at night. Latvians therefore formed a special relationship to M.

The dainas often call him "old man, old fellow, wise man" etc.; but also "lazy" or "slacker" when he does not shine at night. Sometimes, M. is even called lazy because he does not shine during the day:

Ai, Mēness, veco brāl,	Hey, Moon, you old fellow,
Kam tu dienu netecēji?	Why did you not shine at day?
Kam tu savu augumiņu	Why did you only wander
Nakti vien maldināji?	Over the sky at night? (LD 33846)

In some dainas, therefore, the difference between Moon and its anthropomorphic representation disappears. However, some dainas that feature M. only as a non-personified celestial body can also be found. There are only several such dainas, but they represent a very important record of old Latv. cosmology (the beliefs concerning the order of the universe). These dainas follow this type:

Bērziņš auga trim lapām,	There grows a birch tree with three leaves,
Saules taka maliņā.	The Sun's path is on its side.
Tai vienāi diena ausa,	In one leaf the day breaks,
Tai otrāi Mēnestiņš,	In the other Moon rises,
Tai trešāi lapiņāi	And in the third leaf

Lec Saulīte vizēdama.   The glowing Sun rises. (LD 33749)

This daina describes the Tree of the → world and the division of the universe into three parts. In this cosmological belief, M. is an important part of the universe.

Dainas that treat M. as an anthropomorphic representation often focus on his clothes, which are rich and sparkly:

Mēnestiņis nakti brauca,	Moon drove through the night,
Es Mēneša ormanīts;	I was his driver;
Man iedeva Mēnestiņis	Moon gave to me
Savu zvaigžņu mētelīti.	His starry cloak. (LD 33852)

M.'s cloak could be not only starry, but also golden (LD 33854, 2), silk, silver, waxed (LD 33834), or in some cases a fur coat. He wears a golden ring on his hand (LD 33852, 1), sturdy boots on his feet (LD 33740) and he often carries a sword (LD 33853, 34043, 14).

The dainas do not speak very clearly as to the relations between M. and the other inhabitants of Latvian skies. There is no hierarchy or familial relations like those between e.g. Greek gods. Most often, M. appears together with the Sun (→ *Saulijā*), in many cases as the Sun's bridegroom (the role of M. in → sky wedding is further discussed in that entry, see also → sky inhabitants, sauna; for M.'s relationships with stars, see → Auseklis). Several songs mention his son or sons (LD 22049, 33803), but they give no further details. Moreover, H. Biezais believes that in the name *Mēness dēls* "Son of Moon", the word *Mēness* is merely a *genitivus appellativus*. According to this theory, the phrase would mean simply "Son Moon" and emphasise that Moon is young, even unmarried, and therefore has no family.

It is apparent that a personified, deified Moon only features in literary myths, i.e. only as a character in stories. Unlike with Auseklis, however, it is still possible that the Baltic tribes worshipped the Moon, because there are also several surviving dainas that hail the Moon and the Sun. There are, however, no records of sacrifices to the Moon. See also → world.

Bibl.: ME II, 616; SLDDG̦ 35, 57.

Mėnuo – Lith. "Moon". In Lith. mythology, one of the key characters in the stories of the wedding of sky inhabitants (see → sky inhabitants, wedding), also generally of the Lith. mythological → sky.

The Lith. folklore has preserved fewer songs with pre-Christian mythological elements than Latv. folklore. One of these rare witnesses of the pagan past is a daina recorded at the beginning of the 19th century by the folklorist Liudvikas Rėza (Rhesa) not far from the town of Tilžė (Germ. Tilsit, today's Sovetsk in the Kaliningrad Oblast). The text below has been transcribed into modern Lithuanian orthography (copied from Ivanov & Toporov 1974, 19):

Mėnuo Saulùžę vėdė	Moon was marrying Sun
pìrmą pavasarėlį.	In the early days of Spring.
Saulùžė ankstì kėlės,	Before Sun got up with the dawn,
Mėnùžis atsiskýrė.	Moon walked away from her.
Mėnuo víens vaikštinėjo,	Moon walked the sky alone,
Aušrìnę pamylėjo.	He loved the Morning Star.
Perkúns dideí supýkęs	Perkūnas was enraged,
jį kárdu pérdalyjo.	He cut him in half with his sword.
Ko Saulùžės atsiskýrei,	Why did you walk away from Sun,
Aušrìnę pamylėjei,	Loved the Morning Star?
Víens naktý vaikštinėjei?	Why did you wander alone in the night?

The motif of the newlywed husband-Moon's unfaithfulness can be found here alongside a cosmogonical motif, i.e. an attempt at explaining why the Moon appears to be cut in half in some parts of the month. See also → Mēness and → world.

Bibl.: Fraenkel I, 438; Parolek 1996, 18; Smoczyński 2018, 782–83.

Mēra māte – Latv. "Mother of Measure / Measuring Bowl". One of about a hundred Latv. Mothers. Latv. *mẽrs* "measure, measuring bowl (to determine the amount of grain)", together Lith. *mierà* id. is an adaptation of the Slavic word *měra*. See also → Mātes.

Bibl.: ME II, 620.

Mēŗa māte – Latv. "Mother of Plague".One of about a hundred Latv. Mothers. The first component of her name is the gen.sg. form of Latv. *mēris* "plague", cf. *mir̃t* "to die". See also → Mātes.

Bibl.: ME II, 619.

Mēslu māte/bāba – Latv. goddess "Mother / Hag of Manure".

One of approx. a hundred Latv. Mothers (→ Mātes). Similarly to other Mothers, she was not anthropomorphic or there are no preserved records of her appearance. Unlike many other Mothers, though, she is not only mentioned in folklore, but also in historical sources – her name can be found in the works of two predecessors to Latv. national revival, J. Lange and G.F. Stender, called *Vecais Stenders* by Latvians, "Stender Senior". He explains her name in the dictionary appended to his work *Lettische Grammatik* (1783) in this way: "*Mehslu bahba* goddess of sweepings, for whom the housekeepers would always leave three small piles of sweepings in the garden." Contemporary Latvian mythologist Janīna Kursīte points out that in folklore material, the words "dumping ground" (*skaidiena*) and "dung-yard" (*mēslaine*) are sometimes used interchangeably and that the word *mēsli* "manure" originally meant "everything that is swept away". It is possible that originally Latvians did not differentiate between a dumping ground and a dung-yard and M. m. was the goddess of both sweepings and manure.

Latvian mythologist P. Šmits considers her one of the older universally known Mothers, but unfortunately both Stender and Latvian folklore only bring information about the sacrifices offered to her by Latvians. Her other characteristics, functions or even the information who invoked her can only be guessed at. J. Kursīte believes that she was the goddess of fertility of fields and animals or possibly even humans – that is understandable since manure assists the fertility of fields. J. Kursīte sees another parallel in the fact that while some folk songs and traditions (including Czech tradition) say that children are brought by storks or crows, Latvians find their children as little beetles on a manure heap:

Es redzēju vaguliņu	I saw a little beetle
Mēslienā rāpojot;	Crawling in manure;
Saņēmām, satinām	We took it, we wrapped it
Dārgajos lakatos.	In richest cloths. (LD 1161)

The motif of this song suggests that M. m. could indeed be a goddess of fertility.

It is possible that even the aforementioned three piles of sweepings in the garden or yard were not a sacrifice, but that Latvians were in this way providing this goddess with a dwelling. If the Mother of Horses could live under the floor in a stable, it is quite possible that the Mother of Manure dwelled in the sweepings in the yard. According to Kursīte, women and girls sacrificed to her, aside from the sweepings, also wool and colourful yarns. For example, when they were shearing sheep, they did not start the shearing until they laid a tuft of wool from a sheep's forehead on the ground, saying: *Še, Mēslu māte, tava daļa; neņem pate savu roku!* "Here, Mother of Manure, is your share; do not take it yourself with your hand!" This kind of sacrifice is also recorded in this daina:

Mēslu bāba priecājās	The Hag of Manure rejoices,
Meitiņām piedzemot:	When girls are born:
Kur adīja, kur rakstīja,	Where they knit, where they weave,
Tur palika dzīpariņi.	There will be colourful yarns left.

(LD 1171)

Bibl.: BRMŠ IV, 198 > Stend 1783, §218; Kursīte 1996, 328 > Etnogrāfiskas ziņas par latviešiem 1892, 122.

Meža māte – Latv. goddess "Mother of Forest". One of cca. a hundred Latv. mother goddesses (→ Mātes); according to P. Šmits and L. Ādamovičs she is one of the primary, older Mothers, together with e.g. Mother of Field, Water or Wind. Unlike the latter two, however, she does not have such an ambiguous personality, doubtless because a forest can neither harm nor help humans as much as wind or water can. M. m. is very popular in texts from the 18th and 19th centuries: the writers describe her as wearing impressive clothes, a cloak of leaves and needles and a hat of flower buds. In newer dainas, she is often presented as a loving and caring mother: she knows where every forest animal lives and calls all birds by their name:

Meža māte putnus sauc,	Mother of Forest calls the birds,
vai ir visi vakarā:	If there are all of them on the eve:
Krauklis Juris, sīlis Ancis ...	Juris the raven, Ancis the jay…

(LD 30623)

She also helps lumbermen and herdsmen and, according to Paul Einhorn, a chronicler from the 17th century, also hunters.

Krūmu māte, Mežu māte,	Mother of Bushes, Mother of Forest,
Gani manas avetiņas;	Look after my grazing sheep;

Kad es iešu tautiņās,   When I will marry,
Ik pie krūma ziedu metu.   I will throw flowers to the bushes.

(LD 34048)

Neither the chronicles nor the folk songs mention M.m.'s appearance. J. Kursīte believes she could have manifested as a nightingale. Kursīte derives this theory from the old folk belief that herdsmen, when they first sit down in the forest to graze horses during the night, must tear off a small piece of their clothing and throw it into the fire, saying:

Še, lakstīgala, tava tiesa;   Here you have, nightingale, your share;
neņem pate ar savu roku!   do not take it yourself by your hand!

Then, it is said, there is no danger of their clothes catching fire while they are half asleep. This incantation might admittedly also concern *Pieguļas māte* "Mother of Night Pasture" or *Uguns māte* "Mother of Fire". The appearance of a forest bird, however, suggests that it is M.m. this incantation was directed at.

See also → world. Latv. *mežs* means "forest, grove, brush", in some exceptional cases also "tree"; it is equivalent to Lit. *mēdžias* "forest, tree", Pruss. *median* "forest".

Bibl.: Einh 485; Fraenkel I, 423–425; ME II, 611; MV 589–90.

Mežauckus – name of a strongman in Latv. tales. He is a son of a woman and a → bear. The name is derived from Latv. *mežs* "forest" to emphasize the fact that M. grew up in a forest. Once he grew up, M. disdained the part of his personality that was related to natural world and animals, i.e. to his father, the bear. He found a way out of the forest for himself and his mother, and he joined people. According to G. Ozoliņš, this story symbolizes the victory of man over natural world. The strongman of Latv. folk tales is better known as Lāčausis or → Lāčplēsis, though.

Bibl.: LPT IX; Ozoliņš 282–286.

Miega māte – Latv. "Mother of Sleep". One of about a hundred Latv. Mothers. Latv. *mìegs* means "sleep" (~ Lith. *miẽgas*, Pruss. *maiggun*). See also → **Mātes**.

Bibl.: ME II, 651; MV 572–73; Smoczyński 2018, 794–95.

Miežu māte – Latv. "Mother of Barley". One of about a hundred Latv. Mothers. Latv. *miezis* means "barley" (~ Lith. *miežỹs*, Pruss. *moasis*). See also → **Mātes**.

Bibl.: Adams & Mallory, EIEC 51–52; ME II, 657; MV 608–09; Smoczyński 2018, 798–99.

Miglas māte – Latv. "Mother of Mist / Fog". One of about a hundred Latv. Mothers. Latv. *migla* means "fog, mist" (~ Lith. *miglà*, OCS *mьgla*). See also → **Mātes**.

Bibl.: ME II, 624; Pokorny 1959, 712; Smoczyński 2018, 799.

Milda – popular Lithuanian and Latvian "goddess of love", but she is merely romantic literary creation of T. → Narbutt, together with → Kaunis.

Bibl.: PŠ 117–118.

*Motergabija (recorded as **Matergabia**) – Lithuanian deity. The only available information on this theonym is these two sentences in J. Łasicki's *Di Diis* 1584: "To *Motergabia, a cake made by a woman is sacrificed […] It is baked in the furnace […]"[124] The first component of the name is a latinized form of Lith. *mótė*, gen. *móteres* "woman, wife", in dialects also "mother". See also *Gabija.

Bibl.: Fraenkel I, 126–127, 465; LPG 352, 357–358, 372–373, 389; Smoczyński 2018, 822–23.

Mūža māte – Latv. "Mother of Age / Life".One of about a hundred Latv. Mothers. Latv. *mûžs* means "age; length of life".See also → **Mātes**.

Bibl.: ME II, 680.

Nakt(e)s māte – Latv. "Mother of Night".One of about a hundred Latv. Mothers. Latv. *nakts* means "night" (~ Lith. *naktìs*, Pruss. *naktin*). See also → **Mātes**.

Bibl.: ME II, 690–691; Smoczyński 2018, 838–39.

nãra – Latv. "water fairy". First used by poet Auseklis (published in 1888): *es ęsmu ūdens meita – nãra* "I am a daughter of water – *nãra*".

---

[124] *Matergabiae deae offertur a foemina ea placenta, ... In furno coquitur ...*

This name is derived from the verb *nìrt* "to dive" (~ Lith. *nérti*; Ukrainian *nerty*).

Bibl.: Smoczyński 2018, 855.

Narbutt, Teodor (1784–1864) – Polish historian, engineer, writer and last but not least, the author of ten-volume history of Lithuania *Dzieje starożytne narodu litewskiego* (1835–1841). For this book, he used, without critically evaluating them, not entirely reliable resources on mythology, such as the work of chronicler Simon Grunau or of the collector of mythologic texts A. L. Jucevičius. Narbutt's history of Lithuania was influenced by the dominant literary style of that time – romantism – and the eloquent and enthusiastic Narbutt adapted and altered a number of fictitious mythical beings. He even created several new gods and wrote new stories about the existing ones. These stories became very popular in the Baltics and now they are a part of general knowledge. In this Lexicon, these are entries on gods probably created by Narbutt: → Jūratė, → Kastytis, → Kaunis, → Medžiojma, → Milda and → Nijolė. Several other gods were created by the author of the epic Lāčplēsis, Andrejs → Pumpurs. Also, the Prussian high-priest → Krivė is now considered to be one of the, let's say, "altered" characters. However, some Balt. deities appear in fiction without having been idealized or altered, such as → *Perkūnas in the novel by Kazys Boruta *Baltaragio malūnas* ("Baltaragis' Windmill").

Natrimpe – Pruss. deity. This theonym can be found in the complaint by the bishop of Warmia, *Collatio episcopi Warmiensis*. He wrote this complaint in 1419, in support of the Order of German Knights against the kings of Poland. The text of the complaint, which is addressed to the Pope, contains this paragraph: "For they [The Order of German Knights] had a great faith in God, they are trying with immeasurable and difficult effort to gain the country of Prussia, from which, since the very beginning, there was an effort (which has now succeeded) to drive out the tribes that serve demons like slaves, worship *Patollus, Natrimpe* and other shameful figments of imagination…"[125] That is all we learn about N. in this complaint – simply the fact that he is listed alongside the god

[125] *Nam quantam fidem ad deum habuerit (Ordo fratrum Teutonicorum), probat primo multiplex et difficilis labor acquisicionis terre pruwsie, de qua ab inicio expellende erant et expulsi (sic) sunt gentes seruientes demonibus, colentes patollum Natrimpe et alia ignominiosa fantasmata, …*

of underworld → Patulas. For etymological analysis see → *Trimpas and entries on other deities whose names end with -trimpas.

Bibl.: LPG 153–154.

Naudas māte – Latv. "Mother of Money". One of more than a hundred Latvian Mothers (see → Mātes). Latvvian mythologist Pēteris Šmits puts her among other relatively recent popular creations – Mothers that were created, based on older Mothers like Mother of Wind and Mother of Sea. These original Mothers (with the exception of Mother of Souls, see → Veļu māte) controlled the elements of nature that the lives and health of Latvians quite obviously depended on (wind and fire are useful but also very dangerous; forests, fields, and the sea were necessary for people to make a living off). With time, money became necessary as well; that is why a supernatural being or a deity that could be addressed in regard to money came to be.

N. m. can only be found in several *dainas*. Here are some examples of how the singers would address her:

Ei, naudiņa, Naudas māte,	Hey, money, Mother of Money,
Es ar tevi vadāšos:	Let us make a wager:
Tev bij man zirgu pirkt,	You will buy me a horse,
Man atvest līgaviņu.	I will bring myself a bride. (LD 11031)
Ai, naudiņa, Naudas māte,	Hey, money, Mother of Money,
Nekrīt ceļa maliņā,	Do not fall at the edge of a road,
Krīt vadziņas galiņā,	Fall down at the end of a furrow
Lai saņem arājiņš.[126]	For a plougher to pick you up. (LD 27904)

As can be seen in these *dainas*, N. m., unlike older Mothers, does not have specific traits and is not clearly separable from the money she provided. According to folklorist and mythologist Aldis Pūtelis, N. m. is essentially a personification of money. "Money" might not necessarily have meant "metal coins", as fur, salt and amber were also valid currencies for a long period of time in what is today's Latvia.

Latv. *nauda* /naûda/ means "money" as well as "use, profit, property". Cf. Lith. *naudà* "gain, property, profit, benefit". There are interesting par-

---

[126] This *daina* was probably meant to express the wish for "one of us" to get the money, as *arājiņš* ("plougher") was often used to mean "village boy" in general and fields were the domain of peasants, i.e. the authors of *dainas*; roads, on the other hand, were also used by German, Jewish and Russian merchants.

allels in Germanic languages: Old Norse *nautr* "valuable piece of property", *naut* "piece of cattle", Old English *notu* "profit", Goth. *niutan* "to reach, to gain; to enjoy; to use", *nuta* "hunter".

Bibl.: Fraenkel I, 487; PŠ 130; Kursīte 1999, 123; Pūtelis – personal consultation.

Nāves māte – Latv. "Mother of Death". One of the many Latvian Mothers. Latv. *nâve* means "death". For more information see → Mātes.

Bibl.: ME II, 703.

Nelabais – Latv. "devil". Alternative name for the devil (usually called *Velns*, see → *Velinas) that only appeared after the introduction of Christianity; literally, it means "the not-good one". The name is dervied from Latv. *labs* "good", *nelabs* "bad, horrible" (~ Lith. *lãbas*, Pruss. *labs* "good" : Lith. *nelãbas* "evil"). For more information see → *Velinas, → underworld.

Bibl.: ME II, 397, 719; MV 512–13; Smoczyński 2018, 651.

Nijolė – Lith. goddess, which was abducted by Poklius (→ Pikulas), who made her a queen of → underworld. Again an artificial romantic construction of → Narbutt.

Bibl.: RB 225.

Nīkšķis – Latv. deity. It is an alternative name for the god *Vẽļns* (→ *Velinas). Literally "ruination-maker, evil enemy; whining, groaning". The name is formed from the Latvian verb *nīkšêt* "to weep, cry, blare", which itself is derived from the noun *nīka* "destruction, doom".

Bibl.: ME II, 747.

northern lights – an astronomical phenomenon known in Latvia as well, although it does not appear there as often as it does in e.g. northern Finland (→ world; → sky). It is noteworthy that Latvian has five names for this rather rare natural phenomenon: *jodi, baigi, kāvi, murgi, pāvi*. Latvians used to believe that it is the manifestation of evil spirits or the souls of fallen soldiers. A similar idea could be found with the Finns, Scandinavian nations and even Inuits. Lutheran priest G. F. Stender (Latv. *Vecais Stenders*, Stender senior) provided a concise and apt description of the belief in his book *Lettische Grammatik* (1783): "*Jods* – a devil of fields and forests, a spectre. The plural *Jodi* has a different meaning – those are aerial spirits and souls of the dead. Even today, some Latvians say about the northern lights: *Jodi kaujas* 'aerial spirits are fighting'; and because this phenomenon was terrible to look at, they also said: *baigi, kas kaujas,* 'terrible spirits that fight'. Others explain it thus: *karu ļaužu dvēseles kaujas* 'the souls of fallen soldiers fight'".

This folk belief was widespread throughout Latvia. Because it was exotic, even scholars who recorded the customs of Latv. peasants took a liking to it. For example, one of them wrote in the magazine *Latvijas avīze* in 1830: "I myself have heard one fool say upon seeing the northern lights, with a deep sigh: 'Oh God, what will become of us now?'" That is because Latvians considered n. l. to be a bad omen: of war, epidemics, or famine.

And what are the meanings of the individual names for n. l.? The word *jodi*, as already mentioned by Stender, is pl. of *Jods*, which designates an evil spirit (→ Jods). The word *baîgi* is probably derived from the adj. *baîgs* "terrible" or the identically sounding subst. that means "spectre", "phantom", "feverish hallucination". The name *kàvi* is derived from the verb *kaût* "to beat" and most likely means "those who have killed". The word *pāvi* is either a lettonised pl. of the German *der Pfau* "peacock" that Latvians may have heard and associated the peacock's colourful tail with the colours of the n. l.; or it is a taboo substitution for *kāvi*, so that one would not summon the bad omen by uttering the real name. And the word *murgi* originally designated various apparitions, among others also bad dreams, nightmares – this is the only meaning of the word that has been preserved in Latv. to this day. According to etymologist K. Karulis, the word is related to the IE root **mer-* "to shimmer, to glisten".

N. l. therefore, despite their beauty, played no happy role in the minds of Latv. peasants. Nowadays, n. l. are already stripped of the mythological context and the word *ziemeļblāzma* "northern light" is used for the phenomenon. However, the older name still appeared in the title of the 1989 novel *Kāvu blāzmā* by Visvaldis Lāms.

Bibl.: BRMŠ 195, 203 > Stend 1783; Karulis I, 357; Kursīte 1996, 344–346; LPG 627; LTT 14182–14207; ME I, 250; ME II, 179, 205, 669.

Nukirptoja see fate.

*Numa-deivas (recorded as *Nъnadějъ*) – Lith. 'god of the household'; for more information see → Numejas – Lith. 'household deity'. The only record of this theonym is provided by *Galician-Volhynian Chronicle* in the description of the year 1252: "His baptism was a mere artifice and he continued to offer sacrifices to his gods in secret: to *Nonadej, Teljavel, Diver-*

ikis, to the hare god (and) *Mejdejn*. Whenever he rode into a field and saw a hare running into it, he felt he was not allowed to step into a forest, let alone break a branch there. He sacrificed to his gods, cremated his dead and did not care if anyone sees that he continues living as a pagan." [127]

Numejas – Lith. ‚home deity'. In his *De Diis* (op. cit.) J. Łasicki informs us that "they called home [gods] Numeias".[128] Mannhardt adds that the word *numejas* [*numijas*] was used in the meaning "belonging to homestead" in the district of Telšiai. Its phonetic form indicates Žemaitic dialectisms *numas* "home", *numaĩ* "house", loc.sg. *nùmij* "at home", versus the standard Lithuanian forms as *nãmas*, pl. *namaĩ* "house, home", Latvian *nams* "summer kitchen, entry hall in bath, hut". Maybe the theonym *Nъnadĕevi* (dat.; the expected nom. is reconstructible as **Nъnadĕjь*), known from the Hypatian redaction of so-called Volhynian Chronicle to AD 1252, belongs here too, if it reflects the compound **Numa-dievas*, i.e. "house-god", proposed by Mierzyński. The Old Lithuanian theonym corresponds formally to the name of the Avestan deity *Nmāniia-*. It was probably consecrated to houses, since it means "belonging to the house" (= Old Persian *māniya-* "domestic staff"). It is formed from the noun *nmāna-* "home, house (for people and gods)". The unambiguously positive character of this deity is indicated in the verse [*Gāh* V, 5]: *ya xᵛāθrauuaiti Nmāniiāiti* "beatific is that {woman}, which is together with Nmāniia".

Promising parallels may be seen in the names of two Old Italic cultural heroes. The first one was *Numitor*, grandfather of Romulus and Remus, the second one *Numa Pompilius*, the legendary second king of Rome. Their connection with "house" is indirect, through the cult of the goddess Vesta, the guard of the family hearth. *Numa* was described by Ovid in his *Fasti* VI, 263–64: *Hic locus exiguus, qui sustinet atria Vestae,/tunc erat intonsi regia magna Numae.* "This little spot, which now supports the Hall of Vesta, was then the great palace of unshorn Numa." (translated by

---

[127] *Kreščenie že ego lьstivo byst: žrjaše bogomъ svoimъ vtaině, pervomu Nъnadějevi, i Teljaveli i Diverikъzu, zaejačemu bogu₍ᵣ₎ Mějdějnu: egda vyěx-aše na pole i vybĕgnjaše zajacь na pole, v lěsъ roščenija ne voxožaše vnu i ne smějaše ni rozgy ulomiti, i bogomъ svoimъ žrjaše, i mertvyxъ telesa sožigaše, i poganьstvo svoe javě tvorjaše.*

[128] *Numeias vocant domesticos.*

James G. Frazer). And according to Dionysius of Halicarnassus [II, 65], the cult of Vesta was introduced in Rome by Numitor.[129]

Bibl.: Blažek 2001, 355–57; Fraenkel I, 482–483; LPG 52, 357, 377; Smoczyński 2018, 840–41.

Ockopirmus see *****Ukapirmas**

Ogu māte – Latv. goddess "Mother of forest fruits". One of numerous goddesses-mothers. Latv. *oga* /uôga/ means "strawberry". Related are Lith. *úoga*, Church Slavonic *agoda*. For more information see → Mātes.

Bibl.: ME IV, 413–144; Smoczyński 2018, 1563–64.

*****Pakulas** (recorded as **Pocols, Pacols, Pikoliuni**) – Prussian ‚flying evil ghost'. First this theonym was recorded by G. von Polenz and P. Speratus in

---

[129] Origin of the proper names in *num°* has been sought in Etruscan anthroponymy, but the same root also appeared in the space outside of the area, where the Etruscans lived (e.g. the city of *Numāna* in Picenum by present Ancona; Rutulian warrior *Numānus Remūlus*, a bridegroom of the younger daughter of Turnus, king of the Rutuls, which were rivals of Aeneas – see Vergil, *Aeneis* IX, 592n). In this perspective is understandable the interpretation *Numa* = "belonging to house (= to a broader community or to a ruling clan?)". In this case it is possible to see in *Numa* the protoform *$dṃmā$ formed from IE *dem- / *dom- "house" or "family clan". The city of *Numāna* (*$dṃmānā$) would mean the collective "houses", formed from an analogical form, which is preserved in Avestan *nmāna*- "house" (*$dmāno$-). An alternative etymology based on the main characteristics of Numa as "legislator" (cf. Greek νόμος "custom, regulation, law") was proposed already by ancient authors (e.g. Servius, *Aeneis* VI, 808). Let us add still Greek νομός "pasture, dwelling, district", νωμέω "I share", νωμήτωρ "manipulator, distributor", Lat. *numerus* "number, quantity, list, share, place" (*$nomes$-o-), Avest. *nəmah*- "loan", Lith. *núoma* "rent, lease", Latv. *nuõma* id. (*$nōm$-), all from the verb *nem- "to share, take", cf. Greek νέμω "I distribute, possess, receive legally"; νεμέτωρ "judge", Goth. *niman* "to take, accept, get, receive", *ga-niman* "to learn", *arbinumja* "heir", Latv. *ņemu* : *ņemt* "to take". Some linguists also include here the Baltic words for "house" (Fraenkel I, 482–483; Frisk II, 302–304; Hamp 1980, 44; Illič-Svityč 1963, 54–55; LIV 453; Pokorny 1959, 763; Trautmann 1923, 193). Otherwise Smoczyński 2018, 879: Lith. *núoma* < *nuo-ima.

1530. They added the Roman equivalent: *Pocols – Furiae*.[130] The Roman *Furiae* has been interpreted as "goddess of revenge", but it also designated "evil ghost". *P. are frequently characterized as "flying ghost or devils".[131] Already in the middle of the 16th cent. J. Maeletius/Malecki[132] ascribed to Prussians the belief in "atmospheric ghosts". And at the end of the 17th cent. the deity *Pacols* was introduced without any other characteristics by Ch. Hartknoch.[133] The theonym probably originated thanks to contamination of two theonyms → *Patulas (recorded as *Patollus, Patollo*) ,god → underworld' and → *Pikulas (recorded as *Pecols, Pikols, Pykullis*) ,god of underworld and darkness'. It can therefore be explained as a construct of chroniclers. Perhaps the name was created by a clerical error by replacing the original *t* with *c*, and it is probably not a name inherited from the Baltic or even Indo-European pantheon. Further see → world.

Bibl.: Ivanov & Toporov, MNM II, 296–297; Kregždys 2018a & 2019a; LPG 233, 245–246, 295.

Parckuns see *Perkūnas

pareģis, pareģuonis – Latv. "seer". The designation is formed from the verb *paredzêt* "to sight, observe, foresee, anticipate" : *redzêt* "to see" (~ Lith. *regéti* "to see"; MHG *regen* "to bestir oneself"). Further see → priests; → soothsayer.

Bibl.: Fraenkel II, 712; LIV 498; ME III, 89, 502; Smoczyński 2018, 1075–76.

Pargrubrius see *Grubrius

---

[130] Georg von Polenz & Paul Speratus: *Episcoporum Prussie Pomesaniensis atque Sambiensis Constitutiones Synodales*, 1530.

[131] *Pockols – die fliegende geister oder Teufell*, podle *Sudauerbüchlein – Der vnglaubigen Sudauen ihrer bockheiligung mit sambt andern Ceremonien, so sie tzu brauchen gepflegeth*; the text is preserved in several manuscripts from the 16th cent. *Pikoliuni – die fliegende Geister oder Teuffel*, according to *Chronicon des Landes Preussen Collogirt durch Joannem Bretkium Pfahrern zu Labiau*, 1588.

[132] *Quos ipsi Deos esse credunt, uidelicet Pocollum – aëreorum spirituum*, according to *De Sacrificiis Et Idolatria Vetervm Borvssorvm, Liuonum, aliarumque uicinarum gentium*, 1551.

[133] *Selectae dissertationes historicae de variis rebus Prussicis*, 1679.

Parstuken see **barzdukai**

*__Patulas__ (recorded as **Patollus, Patollo**) – Pruss. ‚god of → underworld'
(→ world). His name was first mentioned by the Bishop of Warmia in his
complaint to the Pope (1419) *Collatio episcopi Warmiensis*. The complaint was meant to support the Order of German Knights against Polish
kings. We can read in the text: "With regard to its great confidence in
God, [Order of German Knights] tries to reach the Prussian territory with
a big and difficult effort. From the beginning the tribes serving demons,
worshipping Patollus, Natrimpus and other ignominious fantasmata were
driven out."[134] The ideas of the Prussians about the god of underworld
*P. were introduced by the chronicler Simon Grunau[135] into his descrip-
tion of the banner of the legendary king Widewuto: "The banner was
a white baize 5 cubits long and 3 cubits wide. There were depicted three
human-like figures. Their clothes were blue and their upper torsos were
portrayed as follows: one was [depicted] as a man of a young form without a beard, crowned with a wreath of spikes, with a cheerful face, the
god of grain, called *Potrimppo*. The second [was depicted *Perkūnas*] like
an angry man of middle age, whose face was like fire, crowned by flames,
His beard was curly and black. That is why they are [portrayed] with
their characteristics, the jolly one smiling to that angry one, and the latter
becomes swollen in wrath. On the third portrayal there was an old man
with long green beard. His face was quite deathly, decorated by white
linen resembling a turban. He looks up at both of the aforementioned
gods from below. He is called *Patollo*. Besides them there was [depicted]
a shield with two standing horses and among them there was placed a figure with a human torso but a face like a bear with an open muzzle. On
the shield and banner there were also letters in a script unknown to us, in
such a form and manner as is possible to see below {in the book a picture

---

[134] *Nam quantam fidem ad deum habuerit* (*Ordo fratrum Teutonicorum*), *probat
primo multiplex et difficilis labor acquisicionis terre pruwsie, de qua ab inicio
expellende erant et expulsi* (sic) *sunt gentes seruientes demonibus, colentes
patollum Natrimpe et alia ignominiosa fantasmata, …*

[135] Dominican Simon Grunau, living in the village Tolkemit near Frauenburg
(today Fombork) in the northeast of Poland today, worked on his chronicle
*Cronica und beschreibung allerlüstlichenn, nützlichsten und waren historien
des namkundigenn landes zu Prewseen* in the years 1517–1521 and 1529. It
was printed under the title *Preussische Chronik* in Leipzig only in 1876–1889.

follows}."[136] Further Simon Grunau mentions a huge, evergreen, oak, where are depicted three upper gods: Perkuno, Potrumppo {*sic*} and Patollo. "The third picture belongs to Patollo and is located on the third side. It consists of [three] skulls: of human, horse and cow, and in the time of their feasts they were exhibited on the top [of the tree] to be worshipped."[137] After it in connection with Prussia Grunau wrote about an archaic solar cult, which was replaced by a cult of the triad Patollo, → Potrimpo, → Perkuno, with the underworld-god on the first position: "In the beginning inhabitants of the lands of Prussia still knew something about worship of gods or goddesses, with exception of the Sun. But when the *Cimbri* came they brought three idols of their gods – one was called Patollo, the second Potrimpo and the third Perkuno."[138] The important role of the underworld-god was confirmed by the following words of Simon Grunau: "Patollo – the highest idol of Bruteno, somehow named by the inhabitants of Brudenia {sic}, now called the Prussians. This [god] was

---

[136] *Das bannir war ein weisz tuch 5 elen langk, 3 elen brett und hett in sich gewurcht 3 bilde der gestalt wie mennir, blo waren ire cleider und woren brustbilder in solcher formen: das eine war wie ein man junger gestalt ane bardt, gekronett mit saugelen und frolich sich irbot und der gott vom getreide und hies Potrimppo. Das ander war wie ein zorniger man und mittelmessigk alten, sein angesicht wie feuer und gekronet mit flammen, sein bart craus und schwarcz, und sogin sich beide an noch iren geschiglichkeiten, der eine frolich wie er des andern zornigen lachete und der ander auffgeblosen in zorn. Das dritte bilde war ein alter mann mit einem langen groen bardt und seine farbe gantz totlich, war gekronet mit einem weissen tuche wie ein morbant unde sag von unden auff die andern an unde his Patollo mit namen. Sust aber wu es ein schilt war, woren stetis 2 weise pferde, die in hilden zwischen in, auff dem schilde war ein brust bilde wie ein mensch und ein angesichtt wie ein beer mit offenem munde. So woren im schilde und im bannir buchstaben und schriffte unsz unbekant noch solcher form und weise, wie hie undene ist gemerckt und gesehen ...*

[137] *Das dritte bilde Patolli hilt inne die dritten seitte, und sein cleinott war ein todten Kopff vonn eim menschin, pferde und ku, und diesen zu zeiten in iren festen in eim toppe unslitt brandten zur erungk.*

[138] *Von anbegin die einwoner des landes zu Preussen wusten noch von gotte noch von gotthin zu sagin, sundir die sonne sie geerht haben. Do aber die Cimbri qwomen, die brochten mit ihn 3 bilde ihrer abgotte, den einen Patollo sie nanten, das ander Potrimpo, das dritte Perkuno.*

a horrifying deity of night …"[139] From the name of the deity it is possible to separate the prefix *pa-* "under-" and the base **tul(a)-* "earth, ground", which appears in various apophonic grades also in Pruss. *talus* "floor", Lith. *pã-talas* "bed", Latv. *pa-tali* "small pillows", Old Russian *tьlo* "bottom", Old Norse *þel* "soil, ground, base, bottom", Lat. *tellūs* "earth, ground", cf. the Roman deities *Tellus, Tellurus, Tellumo*, further *meditullium* "inland" etc. Uncertain is any connection with Sanskrit *pātāla-* "underworld", which has been derived from the noun *pāta-* "fall", but is alternatively derivable from the same base as *talātala-* "hell", plus the prefix *pā-*.

Bibl.: Fraenkel I, 549, 552; II, 1093; Ivanov & Toporov, MNM II, 293–294; LPG 154, 192, 195–197; MV 675–76; Pokorny 1959, 1061; Puhvel 1974, 79–81; Radke 1965, 298.

pauṛi – Latv. ‚invisible ghosts [of death]‘; details see → vėlės.
Bibl.: ME III, 129.

*Pelengabija – Lith. ‚goddess of fireplace‘. In the end of the 16th cent. J. Łasicki in his *De Diis* (op. cit.) recorded: "They believe, Pelengabija is a goddess, which cares for permanently shining fireplaces."[140] The first component consists of Lith. *pėlenas* "open fireplace" (~ Latv. *pęlns* "fireplace", Prus. *pelanne* "ashes"). The second component see → **Gabija.
Bibl.: Fraenkel I, 126–127, 566; LPG 352, 357–358, 372–373, 389; MV 684–85; Smoczyński 2018, 938.

Perdoytus see **Bardaits**

Pergrubrius see ***Grubrius**

*Perkūnas – Balt. ‚Thunder God‘ and one of the triad of main gods of the Baltic pantheon. The theonym is well-attested in all documented Baltic languages:

Lithuanian *perkū́nas*, also *perkuonas* (Daukantas) "thunder, thunderbolt", personified as "Thunder God"; *perkūnija* 'storm with thunder and

---

[139] *Patollo der obirster abgott der Bruteni also ettwan genant die einwoner Brudenie itzundt Preussen genant. Dieser war ein irschrocklicher got des nachtes …*

[140] *Polengabia diva est, cui foci lucentis administratio creditur.*

lightning' is a collective to *perkū̃nas*, in like manner as *kelmijà* "place with many tree stumps" to *kélmas* "tree stump"; Latvian *pḕrkûns* "thunder", with ablaut variants *pḕrkuôns, pḕrkauns, pḕrkàunis* id., also with the meaning "Thunder God"; Prussian *percunis*, glossed "Donner", i.e. "thunder", as the item Nr. 50 in Elbing Vocabulary (with the "false" *i*-stem, originating from the form **perkūns < *perkūnas*);

"Narewian" *Pjarkuſ*, together with Łauma, are identified as "pogańske [bogi]" (Zinkevičius 1984, 17). The Baltic name of ‚Thunder God' also spread into some Fenno-Ugric languages: Fin. *perkele*, dial. *perkeles, perkule* "devil", Karelian *perkeleh* id., Votic *pẹrku* "hell", Est. (arch.) *pergel, pärkel, perkläne* "devil", *põrgu* "hell", OEst. *Perckun Nohl / perkuni-nōl'/* "lightning" (Göseken 1660, apud Thomsen), literally "Perkun's arrow"; Mordv. Erzya: Erzya *puŕg'ińe, p'iŕg'ińe, p'iŕg'ide* "thunderstorm".[141]

The name of the Baltic god of thunder was first recorded in the appendix to the Russian-Church Slavonic translation of *Chronographia* of Ioannis Malalas of Antioch (AD 491–578) from 1261. In this appendix there is the information about the cultural hero Sovij who introduced among Baltic nations (Lithuanians, Yatvingians, Prussians, also Livs and Yäms) a worship of several pagan deities: *prelestъ Sovij vъvede vně i prinositi žrъtvu skvernymъ bogam Andaevi i Perkunovi rekše gromu i Žvoruně rekše sucě i Teljaveli isgkuznecju skovavše jemu slъnce jako světiti po zemli i vъverъgšju jemu na nebo slъnce* "Sovij introduced the superstition of bringing sacrifices to terrible gods *Andai* and *Perkunъ*, called 'thunder', and to Žvoruna, called 'bitch', and to *Teljavelъ* – the smith who forged out the Sun to shine upon the Earth and who placed the Sun upon the heavens." Still in the end of the 13th century the name of Perkūnas appeared in the form *Perkune* in the so-called Livonian rhymed chronicle (*Livländische Reimchronik*) by an anonymous author, describing the history of the Teutonic Knights in the territory of modern Latvia and Estonia in 1143–1291 (see LPG 71, verses 1434–1437):

> *zû Swurben vûren si ubir sê.*
> *das ist genant daz Ôsterhap,*
> *als ez **Perkune** ir afgot gap,*
> *daz nimmer sô hart gevrôs.*

---

[141] Thomsen 1890, 207; SKES 523–524.

The chronicle was written in Middle High German probably by a member of the Order who knew the internal structure and documentation, maybe a herald of the Order.

The role, played by P. in Lithuanian folklore, may be illustrated by one of the most beautiful dainas with a remarkable mythological content. In the beginning of the 19th cent. it was recorded by folklorist Rėza (Rhesa) near the city of Tilžė (Germ. Tilsit, today Sovetsk in the Kaliningrad Enclave). The text is quoted according to Schleicher (1857, 3):

Ménuo Saulùžę védė	Moon married Sun.
pìrmą pavasarėlį	It was in the first spring days.
Saulùžė ankstì kélės,	Earlier than Sun got up in the dawn,
Mėnùžis atsiskýrė	Moon moved away.
Ménuo víens vaikštinėjo,	Moon alone walked on the sky,
Aušrìnę pamylėjo	made love with Morning Star.
Perkúns didei supýkęs	Therefore Perkūnas got angry
jį kárdu pérdalyjo	by his sword he chopped it in two halves.
Ko Saulùžės atsiskýrei,	Why did you move away Sun,
Aušrìnę pamylėjei	(why) did you make love with Morning Star,
Víens naktý vaikštinėjei?	(why) did you alone wandered in nights?

Lithuanian tradition also knows the situation, when Dievas (→ *Deivas) was preceded by P., cf. *kad Dievo nebūtų, tai jis* (= *Perkūnas*) *būtų Dievu, bet kadangi Dievas esąs, nes jis niekados nemìrštąs, tai ir Perkūnas negalįs būti Dievu, nors pirmiaus jis valdęs svietą ir neretai nužengdavęs ant žemės...* "If *Dievas* was not, he (= *Perkūnas*) would be *Dievas*, but with regard to the fact that *Dievas* is, because he never dies, *Perkūnas* (they say) cannot be *Dievas*, although he ruled over the world earlier and frequently he came down on the earth" (Balys 1937, 151; Toporov 1972, 294).

From an etymological point of view the closest cognate to the Baltic Thunder God **Perkūnas* appears in the Old Norse theonym *Fjǫrgyn* ,mother of Thor', i.e. of ,Thunder God', but also personified "earth" [*Oddrúnargrátr* 10]. Its masculine counterpart *Fjǫrgynn* had to be a father of the goddess Frigg. The feminine is apparently primary and can be projected back to PGmc. **fergunjō*. This form or the neuter **fergunja^n* became bases for other related Germanic appellatives and proper names: Gothic *fairguni* "mountain (ridge)", South Swedish toponym *Færghin(s)gyl* (1349), OEng. *firgen-holt* "mountain forest", Old High German name of the mountain ridge *Fergunna* (*Chronicon Moissiacense*, AD 805), Middle High German *Firgunnea* designating the mountains "Krušné hory" or "Český les". Till the present time no satisfactory etymology of the name *P. has been proposed. Usually the theonym has been explained on the basis of the verb *per- "beat, strike, hit"[142]. We add the second, nominal, member of the hypothetical compound *per-kun-, the root *kun-, which continues in Lat. *cuneus* "wedge, plug" (cf. Germ. *Donnerkeil* "lightning", lit. "thunder-wedge"), further Tocharian A nom.sg. f. *käñ "stone", instr.pl. *kñās-yo* (**kuni̯ā*), and maybe Hittite *kunkunuzzi*- "a kind of stone (diorite?)"[143], which was used as "millstone". Let us mention that the compounds with the first verbal and second nominal components are not so frequent as the compounds with the opposite order, but they exist and are well-attested in the Baltic languages too.[144] The proposed compound *per-kun° can be interpreted as a *nomen agentis* "striking by [thunder] wedge/stone" → "Thunder God" or as a *nomen instrumenti* "strike of [thunder] wedge/ stone" → "lightning/thunder". An exact functional counterpart to Baltic *Perkūnas is the Slavic Thunder God *Perunъ. But the missing -*k*- in the Slavic theonym remains enigmatic. It might be explained as a result of the name of *Perunъ and the word *pьrvьnjь "first, earlier". In the hypothetical, but quite probable, formulation **Perkunъ – pьrvьnjь(jь) bogъ* "Perkunъ – the first of gods", the comparative *pьrvьnjь together with the gen.pl. *bogъ may also express the superlative. There is an exact parallel in the name of the highest god of the Prussian pantheon (→ *Uka-pirmas): *Ockopirmus – der erste Gott Himmels vnd Gestirnes* "the first god of sky and constellations", recorded in the 16th cent.[145]

P. is one of the triad of the highest Baltic gods (see → *Deivas/Dievas). The Lithuanian mythologist G. Beresnevičius means that P. had

---

[142] Lith. *periù, peřti* "to beat; to lash by broom in bath", Latv. *peṛu, pèrt* id.; OCSl. *perǫ, pьrati* "to beat; to wash", *pьrjǫ, pьrěti* "to dispute", *pьrǫ, perti* "to stamp, press", Lat. *premō* "I press", Albanian *pres* "to cut out", Armenian *orotam* "to thunder", Avest. *parət*- "fight, battle", Skt. *pṛ́t*-, *pṛ́tanā* "fight, contention" (Pokorny 1959, 818–19).

[143] Ved. *aśáni*- "strike of lightning, (bolt of) lightning": *áśan*- "stone, rock", *áśman*- "lightning" & "stone, rock"; Lith. *Perkū́no akmuõ* "lightning" = "Perkunas' stone" (Schrader & Nehring I, 396; Gimbutas 1973, 475; LKŽ IX, 834).

[144] Cf. Lith. *kreĩpratis* "steering wheel" < *kreĩpti* "to turn; give direction" & *rãtas* "wheel"; Latv. *val̃bacis* "that who rolls eyes" < *valbât* "to roll" & *acs* "eye".

[145] *Sudauerbüchlein – Der vnglaubigen Sudauen ihrer bockheiligung mit sambt andern Ceremonien, so sie tzu brauchen gepflegeth*; see LPG 245–246.

a position more or less equal to the God of sky, fairness and vegetation, Dievas, and formulates the theory that P. was a son of Dievas. They are in a very good relation, but P. persecutes → *Velinase/Velniase at Dievas' request, while Dievas does not fulfil any wish of Dievas. The Lithuanians and Žemaitians frequently addressed P. as *dievaitis*, where the suffix *-aitis* formed diminutives and designations of descendants. These relations indicate that *Perkūnas* really can be a son of *Deivas*, with such distribution of roles that *Deivas* represents a 'legislative' power, *Perkūnas* an 'executive' power and both share of 'legal' power. With regard to his specialization, P. comes down among people much more frequently than *Deivas*. Thanks to his earthly activities P. belonged amongst the very popular gods in Lithuania and became a main patron of Lithuanian rulers and warriors. During the 13th-14th cent. P. was the most important god of the Lithuanian Grand Duchy. The church built in Vilnius on the occasion of baptism of the Lithuanian king Mindaugas in 1251 and his crowning by the King of Lithuania in 1253, was after his assassination in 1263 superseded by a temple dedicated to Perkūnas, and Mindaugas' followers returned to paganism. Thanks to archaeological research it is possible to imagine, how Perkūnas' temple looked. The building was lacking a roof in order to keep the contact with the sky. The floor consisted of glazed bricks. On the floor there were 6 fireplaces and the stony altar stood by the wall. The altar had on every side six parts, which were meant to symbolize every month, expressed by signs of the zodiac. Another sanctuary of Perkūnas was mentioned by Peter von Dusburg (14th cent.) in → Romowe in the Prussian region Nadruva, which was the seat of a priest → Kriwe. Two centuries later Simon Grunau concluded that the sanctuary consisted of a massive oak, where were carved portraits of the gods → Potrimppo, Perkuno and → Patollo, and a so-called eternal fire, which was maintained by the priest Kriwe with oaken logs. The priest together with important representatives of people sacrificed under the oak a he-goat. The chronicle *Sudauerbüchlein* described in detail the ceremonial sacrifice of the he-goat, devoted to 14 Prussian gods including P. The Lutheran priest M. Praetorius, in *Deliciae Prussicae oder Preussische Schaubühne* (op. cit.) from the end of the 17th cent., wrote about the experience of one of his colleagues from the Prussian village Metirkviečiai on the border with Žemaitia (Samogitia or Žmuď): His parishioners led by a *vaidilutis* came in a big crowd to the oak growing near the village. By the oak there lay a stone and there stood a long pole with the hanging skin of a he-goat, flowers and grain spikes. On the stone stood a vessel with

some kind of drink. Suddenly there came a ceremonially clothed woman
with a jug and poured something from it into the vessel on the stone. →
Vaidilutis had a drink from it and expressed thanks to some god for food
and shelter. After it the young people present took each other's hands and
began to dance around the pole. They stopped their dance at the moment
the vaidilutis began to pray. Then he again drank, touched the pole and
took away from it the he-goat's skin, with which he clothed himself and
distributed grain to the people present. Finally they sat down around him
and he talked about the Old Prussian religion and mentioned the goddess
Žemyna and P. This indicates that a common denominator of the sacrifices devoted to P. were he-goat, oak and fire.

Lithuanian mythologist N. Laurinkienė characterizes P. as "active,
fiery, full of energy – typical Indo-European masculine god". P. is really
very similar to other Indo-European masculine gods of the younger gener-
ation, e.g. Scandinavian Thor, Vedic Parjanya and Indra (see → *Velinas/
Velnias). According to the witness of folklore, P. rode on an iron or fiery
wagon pulled by two he-goats or four white horses. When P. drove these
he-goats or horses with whip, the lightning bolts appeared. If the typical
weapon of *Deivas was the sword, P. was characterized by the axe, like
other thunder gods. P. was frequently connected with the oak. Lithuanians
believed that in the crown of an oak P. fought with Velnias and this mighty
tree was an intermediary between P. and people. For this reason the sacrifices devoted to P. were conducted under the oaks. In Latvia Perkōns
was not so popular as his Lithuanian counterpart. Here he represented
a personified storm and was perceived as a celestial being. P. participated
at → sky wedding according to both the Lithuanian and Latvian dainas.
The Latvians also connected P. with oaks, but instead of he-goats they
sacrificed grain to him, usually with a request for abundance of rain:

Ko dosim Pērkoņam	What do we give to Pērkons
Par vasaras grandumiņu?	for summer thundering?
Lasti rudzu, lasti miežu	One wagon-load[146] of rye, one wagon-load of wheat,

---

[146] *Lasts* or *laste* is a unit of contents and weigh, used especially in Hansa. Into
Latvian it was borrowed from German (Germ. *die Last*). It corresponds c. 2
tuns, or the load of one wagon. It means, the daina promises to *Pērkons* 4 tons
of grain.

Pusbirkava apinīšu.   half-pud[147] of hops. (LD 28818)

Remarkable is P.'s. family, the most numerous one in comparison with other Baltic gods. In Latvian folklore P. has a wife and daughters[148], which "bind sieves and make rain drizzle" (LD 33699, 33708), daughter-in-law, which "only rumbles aloft" (LD33707), and 4, 5, 6 or even 9 sons, which …

Cits spēra, cits rūca,	One hit, one thundered,
Cits zibināja,	one shot lightning,
Cits laida migliņu	another released fog
Avota malā.	on the edge of a spring. (LD 33704,1)

According to the Latvian folklore tradition, all members of P.'s. family are apparently various personified elements of the storm. In the Lithuanian folklore the situation is rather different: P. has also (sometimes) four sons, but also one or three brothers, mother and former wife. From three brothers or four sons everyone has been connected with one cardinal point and is important concerning various predictions. E.g. the first spring storm, if comes from the north, implies a cold year; if it comes from the west and is oriented to the east or north, the early seeding will yield a good harvest of grain, but that year many children will die. V. N. Toporov, N. Vėlius, G. Beresnevičius and N. Laurinkienė mention noticeable connections between P. and the goddess or fairy Laumė and think that she could be P.'s. wife (see → Lauma). It is rather surprising that the Lithuanian folklore does not know any mother of P. But she appeared in the book of J. Łasicki *De Diis* (op. cit.) from the 16th cent.: "*Percuna tete* is the mother of thunder and lightning, which washes Sun in a bath, tired and dusty, and the following day she releases Sun, clean and shining."[149] Although Łasicki explicitly wrote *mater*, in Lithuanian the word *tetà* designates "aunt" and this relation to P. cannot be excluded. In principle, it is

---

[147] The Russian unit of weigh, c. 164 kg.
[148] Mother of Wind in Latvian mythology weaves white sea waves, while Perkunas' wife and daughters make sieves with very small holes and then push water through them in order to create gentle rain. That's a contrast to Perkunas who creates storms and heavy rain.
[149] *Percuna tete mater est fulminis atque tonitrui, quae solem fessum ac pulveruntum, balneo excipit, deinde lotum et nitidum posteradie emittit.*

possible that → Teljavelis was only one of the epithets of P. In this case, P. would also be a sky smith, like other thunder gods.

Bibl.: Balys, J., Perkūnas lietuvių liaudies tikėjimuose. Tautosakos darbai III, Vilnius 1937, 151; Blažek 2011/2014; BRMŠ I, 333–334, 344 > Dusb; BRMŠ I, 555, 576 > Dl; BRMŠ II, 581, 593 > Las; BRMŠ II, 66–67, 104 > Grun; BRMŠ II, 127–133, 144–148 > Sud; BRMŠ III, 130–133, 246–249, 254 > Prae; EH II, 228; Fraenkel 1962–1965, 575; Kokare 1999, 27–31; Kraukle 2008, 31; Kregždys 2012, 250–51, fn. 377; Id. 2019a; Larsson 2002, 219; Laurinkienė 1996; Lehmann 1986, 104–105; LPG 56–60, 87–88, 194, 246–251, 356, 533–540; Mažiulis III, 265; ME III, 208–209; II, 424; MV 699; Parolek 1998, 75; Schleicher 1857, 3; Schrader & Nehring I, 397; Smoczyński 2018, 946–47; Toporov 1972, 294.

Piegulas māte – Latvian goddess "Mother of the horse-pasture". One of numerous mother-goddesses (see → Mātes), whose name is derived from Latv. *piēgula*, "night guarding".

Bibl.: ME III, 253.

Piena māte – Latvian goddess "Mother of milk". One of numerous goddesses-mothers. Her name is derived from Latv. *piẽns* "milk", corresponding to Lith. *pienas*. See → Mātes; → Brēķina.

Bibl.: ME III, 276.

*Pikulas (recorded as **Pecols, Pikols, Pykullis**) – Baltic ‚god of → underworld and darkness'. Prussian *Pekols/*Pikols was characterized by the most trustworthy chroniclers of the 16th cent. as *Pecols – Pluto*,[150] i.e. Greco-Roman ‚god of the underworld'; *Peckols* – "god of hell and darkness";[151] [*credunt..*] *Pocclum* (acc.) – "[they believe in the] god of underworld and darkness ";[152] *Pikols* – ‚god of hell and darkness'.[153] His Lithuanian counterpart called *Pikulis* was described by M. Praeto-

---

[150] Georg von Polenz & Paul Speratus: *Episcoporum Prussie Pomesaniensis atque Sambiensis Constitutiones Synodales*, 1530.

[151] *der helle vnd Finsternus ein Gott* (*Sudauerbüchlein – Der vnglaubigen Sudauen ihrer bockheiligung mit sambt andern Ceremonien, so sie tzu brauchen gepflegeth*; the text is preserved in several manuscripts from the 16th cent.).

[152] *deum inferni et tenebrarum* (J. Maeletius/Malecki: *De Sacrificiis Et Idolatria*, op.cit. 1551).

[153] *der Hellen vnd der Finsternis Gott* (*Chronicon des Landes*, op. cit. 1588).

rius in *Idolatria veterum Prussorum,* in the 4th volume of *Preussische Schaubühne* (op. cit.); firstly in a triad with typically Lithuanian deities: "Besides it there are also the gods of anger and misfortune: *Pykullis, Giltyne, Magyla*"[154]; secondly in a society of gods, amongst which one, **Potrimpas*, is known only from the Prussian tradition: " ... so in Romowe they chiefly worship other [gods], which are called *Pykullis, Perkunas, *Potrimpas*".[155] In his last message Praetorius mentions that *Pykullis* has his own subordinate personnel: "Another kind of godlings are these, which are called kobolds; Old Prussians regard them as servants of *Pykullis*, i.e. devil."[156] Lexicographers of Lithuanian from the 18th cent. are more or less in agreement on the characteristics of P.: Brodowski (1730) *Pikuls – Irae Deus* "god of anger"; Ruhig (1747) *Pikullus – der Zorngott der Heyden* "god of anger of the pagans". The corresponding Latvian theonym was modified by *Volksetymologie*. In his Latvian dictionary J. Lange recorded *Pihkals /Pīkals/* = "*Peekalnis* mountain god of the heathen Latvians".[157] It was caused by the phonetic proximity of Latv. *piekalne* "slope of mountain", *piekalnaîns* "hilly". Similarly in his Latvian grammar G. F. Stender characterizes *Pihkols* as "mountain god", from *pikolns* instead of *peekalns* ,hill'."[158] The Baltic languages also know the corresponding apellative: Prus. *pickūls* "devil", *pyculs* "hell", Lith. *pikùlas* "devil", Latv. *pikuls* "evil ghost, devil". The designation of "devil" and "god of → underworld" has been explained in two ways. The first etymology presupposes an inherited Baltic term of the same origin as Lith. *pìktas* "evil, bad", *pìkčius* "devil", *pỹkti* "to be angry, be evil", *peĩkti* "to defame, slander", Latv. *pikts* "evil", *pîkt* "to become evil, angry". According to the alternative explanation both the term "devil" and theonym represented by Lith. *pikùlas* & *Pykullis* etc. appeared in the Baltic traditions thanks to adaptation of the Slavic term for "hell" or its inhabitants, cf. OCS *pьkъlъ* "hell, lord of hell", besides the more frequent meaning "resin",

[154] *Sonsten sind auch noch Zorn- und Unglückgötter Pykullis, Giltyne, Magyla.*
[155] *... so sie in der Romove vor allen andern angebetet haben, geheissen Pykullis, Perkunas und Padrimpus.*
[156] *Eine andere Art der Götterchen sind diejenigen, die man Kobold nennet, die die alten Preussen vor Diener des Pykulis, i.e. des Teufels gehalten.*
[157] *Peekalnis der heydn. Letten Beggott* (*Vollständiges deutsch-lettisches und lettisch-deutsches Lexikon,* 1777).
[158] *Der Berggott; von pikolns anstatt peekalns ein Anberg* (*Lettische Grammatik,* chapter *Lettische Mythologie,* Mitau 1783).

which also belongs to the palatalized doublet *pъcъlъ*, further OPol. *piekeł*, *pkieł* "hell", ORuss., RCS *pъklъ*, *peklъ*, *pъkъlъ*, *pekolъ* "hell", ORuss. also "resin"[159] etc. The meanings "devil" and "hell" apparently came into Balticum with the Christian religion. The rich variants of the East Slavic forms indicate that a source of the Baltic terms should be sought just here. The phonetic proximity of genuine Baltic words meaning "angry" or "to be angry" caused some semantic shifts.

Bibl.: Fraenkel I, 563, 589; Gerullis 1926, 119–120; Ivanov & Toporov, MNM II, 296–297; Krappe 1932; Kregždys 2019a; LPG 233, 245–246, 295, 532, 544, 612; Mažiulis III, 279–280; ME III, 213, 230, 255; MV 709–10; Smoczyński 2018, 959–60.

*Pilnitis/*Pilwitis – Pruss. ‚god of a rich harvest'. His name cannot be reconstructed unambiguously. The attested records indicate that the form **Pilwitis* is more frequent than **Pilnitis* by a ratio of 5 : 3. The replacements *u/v* for *n,* and vice versa, are among the most usual scribal mistakes and so it is not necessary to speculate about any parallel existence of both alternatives. **P.* has been connected with ‚wealth' and ‚full barns'. In the first feature he corresponds to the Greek god Πλούτων ‚god of wealth', in the latter one of the authors compared him with the Roman goddess of harvest, Ceres. **P's.* primary function can be reconstructed as ‚god of a rich harvest'. The following eight more or less chronologically arranged sources bring together almost all the information known about **P.* at all:

Georg von Polenz & Paul Speratus: *Episcoporum Prussie* (op. cit., 1530): *Piluuytus – Ceres.*

Sudauerbüchlein (op. cit., te text is preserved in several manuscripts from the 16th cent.): *Pilnitis* – "God, who creates wealth and makes full barns."[160]

A close "print A": *Piluitus* – "God, who creates wealth and makes full barns."[161]

---

[159] Vykypěl, ESJS 12, 738–739; Vasmer III, 226; Shevelov 1964, 340, 437; about the third palatalization – see Shevelov 1964, 344–345: **k, *g, *x* after the vowel **ь* (and **ī, *i*) > **c, *z, *ś/*š*; the velar was preserved, if was followed by a consonant or **ъ, *y*. For this reason OCS *pъkъlъ* is regular and the doublet *pъcъlъ* can reflect the adaptation of Lat. *picula*, which is a diminutive of *pix, -cis* "resin".

[160] *Der Gott macht reich vnd füllet die Scheuren.*

[161] *Der Gott macht reich vnd füllet die scheunen.*

J. Maeletius/Malecki: *De Sacrificiis* (op. cit. 1551): *Piluitum* – "Of god of wealth, who is called Pluto in Latin."[162]

J. Łasicki *De Diis* (op. cit.; 1582 or 1584, published 1615): *Pilnitum* –„Of god of wealth."[163]

Chronicon des Landes Preussen (op. cit. 1588): *Piluitus* – "He is supposed to be a god of abundance, who creates wealth."[164]

I. C. I. Behm: *Duae orationes* (op. cit. 1644): *Pilvuvytus* – *Cererem.*

I. B. Ch. Hartknoch: *Selectae dissertationes* (op. cit. 1679): *Polunytis.*

In etymological perspective it is easier to analyze the *n*-variant, which is close to Lith. *pìlnas*, Latv. *pil̃ns* "full", Pruss. *pilnan* "whole". The more frequent variant with **w* resembles the semanticaly more distant Lith. *pilvas* "[thick] belly, stomach", although both forms originate from the same root attested in the verb Lith. *pìlti* "to fill, pour", Latv. *pil̃t* "to drop". Among the external cognates should be added Archaic Pol. *oplwity*, Pol. *obfity* "abundant", and Greek πλοῦτος "wealth, abundance", besides the theonym Πλούτων ,god of wealth'.

Bibl.: Fraenkel I, 591–593; Gerullis 1926, 119–120; Kregždys 2019a; LPG 233, 245–246, 295, 299, 362; Smoczyński 2018, 962–64.

Potrympus – Prussian deity. The theonym P. appeared in the following contexts: *Potrympus & Bardoayts ... Castor & Pollux*; *Potrimpus der Gott der fliessender Wasser*; *Potrympum fluviorum ac fontium*; *Potrimppo* (Grunau Chron.). See → *Trimpas; → *Patulas.

priests, also **soothsayers, enchanters, sorcerers** etc. – people with magical abilities, as well as intermediaries between this world and the world of gods, spirits etc. Unfortunately, records about them are highly unreliable. German and Polish chronicles adjusted the reports about priests so that they would fit their own religious views; usually, they turned Balt. priests into a twisted image of Christian priests. They exaggerated their cruelty and emphasized their connection to the Devil.

Unlike e.g. ancient Greeks and Romans, Balt. tribes had no temple buildings – according to G. Beresnevičius, this was because a roof would block the direct contact with the nature and light. Prussians and Lithuanians most probably had priests who lived near sanctuaries and organised rituals

---

[162] *Deum divitiarum quem latini Plutum uocant.*
[163] *Deum divitiarum. sal sein ein Gott der fulle, vnd der Reich machet.*
[164] *Sal sein ein Gott der fulle, vnd der Reich machet.*

for the gods. As far as Latvians are concerned, E. Kokare believes that "…
old Latvians managed without intermediaries." Undoubtedly, though, Balt.
tribes had various soothsayers (→ soothsayer), who interpreted the gods'
will to people and foresaw the future as well; there were also sorcerers,
enchanters, herb women, → witches (see also → Ragaina) etc. We use the
term p. purely for practical reasons to encompass all these various categories.

Following terms for the individual categories can be found in historical sources and contemporary Baltic languages:

Soothsayer: Lith. (→ *Viduronys), → *Seitonys, → *Sietonys, →
Lekkutones, → žynỹs, → būrė̃jas; Latv. → zĩlniĕks, → zĩmlēmis, →
pareģis, → gàišreģis.

Sorcerer: Lith. → žynỹs, → bùrtvis, bùrtininkas = Latv. bùrvis, burt(i)
nieks.

Enchanter/Charmer: Lith. → užkalbétojas; Latv. → vārdotājs.

The word *žynỹs* is universal; it can denote a soothsayer, a sorcerer as
well as a pagan priest and sage. Another universal word is Lith. → *vaidilà*, "sorcerer, minstrel; a kind of exalted old Pruss. priest"; *vaideliòtas*
"old Lith. and Pruss. priest", beside Pruss. *waidelotte* "Pruss. priest and
sorcerer" (compare *waidleimai* in 1st person pl. conjunctive "so that we
conjure", known from the Third Catechism, *Enchiridion*).

The word *waidelotte* is garbled by its adaptation into German, the language in which Simon Grunau described the Pruss. cultic place Romowe
or Rikoiot. It was a shrine with a giant oak and undying fire. It was kept
by the waidelottes and the high priest called *Krivė Krivaitis* (→Krivė),
revered by all Balt. tribes. Grunau's reports met with a strange fate: they
were very popular and many chroniclers adopted them into their books.
In the second half of the 19th century, German scholars M. Töppen and
W. Mannhardt renounced almost the entire body of Grunau's work as fab-
rications. Nowadays, most mythologists and historians agree that some
of Grunau's data are reliable, but other facts are probably fabricated. For
example, it is quite possible that there existed a Prussian sanctuary with
an oak in the centre where sacrifices by fire would be conducted. Oak
was a holy tree for Balt. tribes and the tradition of sacrifice by fire at trees
was even known in the 18th century Latvia. On the other hand, it is quite
impossible for a single high priest of all Baltic tribes to have existed,
because the tribes in question waged continuous wars with one another.

From the 16th century onwards, many records of Prussian, Lithuanian
and Latvian sorcerers', soothsayers' and witches' activities can be found,
particularly in church documents: proceedings of witch trials and visita-

tions in individual parishes. For the area of today's Latvia, these protocols are practically the only source of information we have. Where Prussia is concerned, we are more fortunate, as soothsayers and sorcerers captured the attention of M. Praetorius in the 17th century. He was a Pruss. priest who compiled records about the religion of the Baltic tribes found in earlier chronicles, and also closely observed any demonstrations of pagan beliefs that he himself encountered in Prussia and Samogitia (Žemaitia). He then carefully categorised everything into paragraphs. By this process, the book *Deliciae Prussicae oder Preussische Schaubühne* (1684) was created. This book provides us with two exhaustive chapters on the topic of sorcerers, soothsayers and incantators. This is also why most of the aforementioned types of soothsayers and sorcerers originate in Prussia.

Most of Praetorius's records about this topic are of activities he had witnessed himself, or been told of by reliable witnesses. Beside these, however, he also dedicates several chapters to the description of the old Prussian sanctuary *Romowe* and the high priest *Krywe* – this information is mostly adopted from Simon Grunau, which gives cause for reasonable doubt about its truthfulness.

For each type of sorcerers, Praetorius lists exactly what function they performed and what they were in charge of. His descriptions are, however, limited to the outer demonstrations of their activities, but do not mention if these sorcerers served certain gods or which gods they were, or if their activities were purely practical. In many places in the book, he says that these sorcerers and soothsayers achieved astonishing feats – they told the future correctly, confounded a young man so that he fell in love with an old woman, they said where a stolen object could be found etc. Sometimes, Praetorius' astonishment and inability to explain these feats come through. Unlike his contemporaries, however, he does not judge these people out of hand, because he tends to consider their connection with the Devil not deliberate. ("… this woman, to the best of my knowledge, leads a very decent life. But that does not prevent her from acting as a *vaidilutė*, because the Devil can take on the appearance of an angel of light."). Praetorius' writings show that the longest lasting pagan belief in Prussia and Lithuania Minor was the belief in the power of certain places, trees and animals, various kinds of magic and also sorcerers, soothsayers and incantators.[165]

---

[165] This is supported by the fact that various herb-women, fortune-tellers, astrologers and "salons of white magic" are still very popular in Lithuania and Latvia – so popular, in fact, that in 2010 a Lutheran priest delivered a homily against

Bibl.: Fraenkel II, 1179–1180; LPG 192; Smoczyński 2018, 1583–84.

*Prigirstytis – Lith. deity ‚listening god or spirit', which is described only by J. Łasicki in his *De Diis* (op. cit.): "Prigirstitis is that one, who hears whispering persons. For this reason two who are whispering should whisper most quietly, otherwise Prigirstitis might hear them."[166] With regard to the fact that Łasicki was the only chronicler who mentions P., the Lithuanian mythologist Rimantas Balsys concluded that in West Lithuania (Žemaitia) P. was already unknown in the 17th cent. The theonym represents a transparent derivative from the Lithuanian verb *prigirsti*, *gir̃sti* "to begin to hear". The reconstruction **Prigirstytis* agrees with the rules of Lithuanian and its standard orthography, since the ending *-titis* does not exist. On the other hand, it is possible that Praetorius created his 'forest god' → Girstis according to **Prigirstytis*. A god with only a single function – to listen to whispering – is a rather exceptional phenomenon and implies the idea that P. represents a tabuistic name for some important and unpredictable god, or it belonged only to a spirit without any more concrete features. This theory was supported by N. Vėlius, who wrote that Łasicki (better to say [his source] Laskowski) called … all deities, mythical beings and worshipped objects uniformly as ‚gods'.

Bibl.: BRMŠ II, 576, 594 > Las 48; LPG 369; RB 355; Smoczyński 2018, 348.

pūķis see **áit(i)varas**, and **velis**

Puķu māte – Latvian goddess "Mother of flowers". Together with Ziedu māte "Mother of blooms", these represent two of the numerous Latvian maternal goddesses. Mythologist Pēteris Šmits classified them among the more recent Mothers, created by folk singers according to the pattern Mother of wind, Mother of fire, Mother of forest and other oldest Mothers. He deduced this from the fact that there was no known cult of flowers in any Indo-European or Fenno-Ugric tradition. Flowers did not play any important role in lives of the Baltic tribes, since contrary to forests or fire,

---

them, similar to those from the 17th century, even though practising Christians do not seek out these fortune-tellers. One of the authors met with a case of a woman from a small Latvian town who went to see a sorcerer to ask him to arrange an early death of her husband.

[166] *Prigirstitis hic est, qui murmurantes exaudire putatur. Iubent igitur vt quis sumisso murmure, hoc vel illud loquatur, ne clamantem Prigirstitis audiat.*

flowers were not beneficial, nor did they do any harm to people (see →
Mātes). In the case of *Ziedu māte* it is possible that she was no supernatural being at all. Latvian mythologist E. Kokare thinks that the following
daina illustrates that it was simply an epithet of summer:

Vasariņa, Ziedu māte,	Oh summer, my Mother of blooms,
Dod tu man visu labu,	give me all the best,
Visupirms noziedēt	at the earliest to be in blossom
Manam miežu līdumam.	my barley field. (LD 28253).

Puķu māte is also one of the younger Mothers. Her name appears in *Lettische Grammatik* (1783) by G. F. Stender (called *Vecais Stenders* "Stender
the Older"), but he did not inform us about her functions or sacrifices.
Bibl.: BRMŠ IV, 198 > Stender 1783, §218; Kokare 1999, 179; PŠ 131.

Pumpurs, Andrejs (1841–1902) – the Latvian author of the epic →
Lāčplēsis about a strongman of the same name. He created several new
personages, such as Koknesis, or perfected the figure of ‚fairy of the cliff
of Staburags‘ (→ Stabradze/Staburadze).

*Puš(k)aitis or ***Putskaitis** – Pruss. ‚god of fertility of earth; guard of
sacred groves, symbolized by elder or lilac‘. His name appears in the
most important sources of Prussian mythology from the 16th and 17th
cent.: *Puschkayts* – "Puškaits, Latin *Sambucus* – subterranean god [occur-
ring] under the holy grove of elder."[167] *Putscaetus* – "… [in] which gods
they themselves believe, namely … of the god Putskaytus, who guards
the sacred groves".[168] *Putscetus* – "… [in] which gods they themselves
believe, namely … Putskaitus, the guard of the sacred groves".[169] *Puschkaitus* – "… is said to be a god over the fruits of the earth, as of all kinds of

---

[167] *Puschkayts – latine Sambucus – der Erden Gott vnter dem heiligen holtz des
Holunders.* Viz *Sudauerbüchlein*, op. cit.; the text was preserved in several
manuscripts from the 16th cent.
[168] *..quos ipsi deos esse credunt, videlicet … deum qui sacros lucos tuetur.* See J.
Maeletius/Malecki: *De Sacrificiis* (op. cit. 1551).
[169] *… quos ipsi deos esse credunt, videlicet … Putscetum sacrorum lucorum
tutorem.* See *De Diis* (op. cit.).

grain".[170] *Pušaitis* [recorded as *Pufszaitis*] – "… among deities of Earth there are Zemepatis, Zemine or also Zemele, Zemelukštis, Pušaitis".[171]

The theonym is written in two basic variants and each of them implies a different etymology. The variant *Puš(k)ait-* is explainable thanks to Latvian *puškuôt*, *puškuôt* "to decorate [by flowers]", cf. *puškis*, *pušks* "bunch of flowers". Similarly is formed the name *Pūṣán* of the Vedic god of fertility, namely from the verb *púṣyati* "is in flower". Related theonyms of the same origin appear in other traditions: the Avestan evil ghost *Apaoša-* (*„unblooming"), the Greek god of herds, fields and forests, Πάν < *pāusōn*. In Lithuanian the derivational suffix *-aitis* forms usually diminutives, e.g.. *jaunikáitis* "boy" : *jaunikis* "young man", and patronyms, e.g. *kálvaitis* "son or descendant of a smith" : *kálvis* "smith" or *gimináitis* "blood-related, member of kin" : *giminẽ* "kin, clan". A corresponding suffix in Prussian forms designations of fruits of various trees: *krichaytos* "cherries", *sliwaytos* "plums", *wisnaytos* "sour cherries". The alternative variant *Putskait-* can be explained with help of Lith. *pùtinas* "viburnum, bush with white flowers and red fruit, *Viburnum*", dial. *pùtelis* id., Latv. *putenes* "rowan, viburnum", which may be derived from a verb of the type Lith. *pùsti*, *puntù*, *putaũ* "to bloat, swell". Unclear is the second part of this theonym, if it is analyzed as a compound. It is tempting to speculate about existence of the Prussian word *kait-* "forest", which would correspond to such Celtic forms as Breton *coet*, Old Welsh *coit* "forest", and further Goth. *haiþi* "field", *haiþiwisks* "wild", Germ. *Heide* "heath" etc. The expected Prussian appellative *kait-* could also be identified in some place-names, e.g. Koitelauken (AD 1308), where the second component represents Pruss. *laucks* "field" (~ Lith. *laũkas*, Latv. *laũks*). See also → world.

Bibl.: Fraenkel II, 677–678, 681; Gerullis 1926, 119–120; Ivanov & Toporov, MNM II, 353–354; LPG 246, 295, 362, 532; Mažiulis 2004, 33; ME III, 438, 440; Otrębski II, 261; Pokorny 1959, 521: IE *kaito-* "forest"; Smoczyński 2018, 1048; Toporov 1974, 3–36; Toporov, *Prusskij jazyk* III, 158; IV, 147–152.

---

[170] *Puschkaitus sal sein ein Gott vber die fruchte der Erden als allerleÿ getreÿdes.* See *Chronicon des Landes* (op. cit. 1588).

[171] … *unter den Erd-Göttern sind Zemepattys Zemyne oder auch Zemele, Zemelukfztis, Pufszaitis.* See Matthaeus Praetorius in the 4th volume *Idolatria veterum Prussorum* of his compendium *Preussische Schaubühne* from the 1680's and published 1703.

Ragaina – Lith. 'goddess of forests'. The only chronicle that mentions her name is J. Łasicki's *De Diis* 1588: "*Medeina* and *Ragaina* are gods of forests."[172] Her name is derived from the Lith. verb *regė́ti* "to see" (~ Latv. *redzêt*). Some mythologists trace its origins to the Lith. word *rãgas* "horn", though (~ Latv. *rags*; hence adj. *ragaina* "with horns"; Pruss. *ragis*, Russ. *rog* "horn"). Lithuanian mythologist M. Gimbutienė sees the term *ragaina* as a merge of both concepts. The name R. bears a striking similarity to Lith. word *rãgana* "witch, sorceress, female prophet" (~ Latv. *ragana*). This caused several mythologists to try and find a link between R. and witches; even more so because the witches of Lith. fairy-tales live in forests. For example, the above-mentioned M. Gimbutienė takes R. to be a lunar goddess[173] of night, winter, death and birth. This concept, inherited from the Indo-European period, gradually declined after the baptism of the Baltics, and the area of R.'s influence was limited to the forests. Her name was then transferred to her female servants living in them.

W. Mannhardt, on the other hand, discards the existence of a forest goddess called R. altogether. His theory states that Łasicki did not understand fully the difference between deities, spirits, spectres and people. From his informant, Łaskowski, he received messages about a soothsayer living in a forest and proceeded to present her as a goddess by mistake.

R. Balsys draws his readers' attention to a different possible connection: Fairy-tale witches often appear in situations that can be interpreted as initiations, i.e. the hero must fight them or set a trap for them to prove his maturity (e.g. Latv. → Velna māte). And seeing as Mircea Eliade claims that this phase of initiation usually featured the tribe's ancestors, totem animals or deities, it is entirely possible that it was R. in this role for the Baltic tribes. Her part as the "strict examiner" later contributed to her degradation to an ugly, evil sorceress.

Bibl.: BRMŠ II, 581, 594 > Las 47; Gimbutienė 2002, 55; DLKŽ 648, 663; LPG 55, 356, 374, 400; ME III, 464, 502; RB 345, 348; Smoczyński 2018, 1075–76.

ragana see witch

*Ratainyčia (recorded as ***Ratainicza***) – Lith. 'goddess of horses'. J. Łasicki in *De Diis* 1584 lists her name along with a brief description

---

[172] *Modeina et Ragaina sylvestres sunt dii.*
[173] Her relation to the moon is explained by the word *rãgas* "horn" in her name also bearing the meaning "moon crescent".

in male gender: "Ratainicza was considered to be the god of horses".[174]
The name of this goddess is derived from Lith. *rãtas* "wheel", pl. *rãtai*
"wagon", analogically Latv. *rats*, pl. *rati*. There are related words in several ancient and mediaeval languages, e.g. Old High German *rad*, Old
Irish *roth*, Lat. *rota* "wheel", Ved. *rátha-*, Avest. *raθa-* "wagon"; the original IE root was probably the one preserved in the Old Irish verb *rethim*
"I am running" and Lith. verb *ritù : rìsti* "to roll".

Bibl.: Fraenkel II, 703; LPG 357; Pokorny 1959, 866; Smoczyński 2018, 1067,
1099.

Rauga māte "Mother of dough" see **Mātes** and **Raugupatis**.

Raugupatis – Pruss. 'god that makes dough rise / god that oversees fer-
mentation processes'.

Matthaeus Praetorius in the 4th chapter of his book *Preussische
Schaubühne* 1684, 1703, called *Idolatria veterum Prussorum*, mentions
a deity by the name R. This theonym can be interpreted as "master of fer-
mentation", cf. Lith. *ráugas* = Latv. *raûgs*, Lith. *rū́gti* "to rise (of dough),
to ferment, to become sour", Latv. *rûgt* id.

Bibl.: Fraenkel II, 705, 746; LPG 545; Smoczyński 2018, 1069, 1112.

Rīgas māte "Mother of Riga" see Mātes

Rīšu/Rīšķu māte & Vīkala – Latvian "Mother of fate" and ‚spirit connected with human fate' or ‚spirit spinning a thread of life' (?). The word
māte in his name should not be understood precisely as „mother" (as
e.g. Jānis' mother), nor "administratrix" (e.g. Mother of forest cares for
forests and Mother of winds takes care of all kinds of wind). According to
E. Kokare, it belonged to the third group of 'Mothers', where *māte* meant
simply a female being and not 'mother' (see also → Mātes). In the case of
R. m. the word *māte* probably only indicated a female spirit. That is why
we write her name with *m-* and not *M-*. This conclusion agrees with the
witness of Latvian folklore. But it is possible that R. m. degraded from
a primarily divine status to a mythical being on a lower level as a consequence of collapse of the old religious system. These spirits have tendency
to remain in the subconscious mind of people in a role of evil ghosts. In
one folk concept R. m. is identified with a spirit called → Vīkala. For this

---

[174] *Ratainicza equorum habetur deus.*

reason the following description is devoted to both together. In collections of Latvian folktales and superstitions there two types of subjects about Vīkala and R. m. In the first one they do not influence anybody and " … the walk in the night, invisible to human eyes, to spin on spinning wheels, which belong to girls. If some girl is able to creep up so quietly that she is not audible and to stop the spinning wheel, it quits its spinning". In other tales it is not possible to stop spinning. This has been interpreted so that the ghost announces a death of somebody from the house. According to J. Kursīte it is unusual, if the death is symbolized by the act of spinning itself and not snapping the thread of life, typical for some other Indo-European traditions. She explains both names with two synonymous Indo-European roots meaning "to turn, bind, bend": R. m. should be derived from the verb continuing in Latv. *ràisît & rist*, Lith. *raišýti & rišti* "to tie, attach; tether, bind", Pruss. *per-rēist* "to bind" < **u̯roi̯k̂-* "to bend, crook, turn, wind", which represents an extension of the root **u̯er-* "to turn, wind", which is also a source of Latv. *vẽrpt* "to spin". Similarly, the name *Vīkala* would be derived from the verb attested in Latv. *vīt* "to wind, plait" = Lith. *výti* "to roll, wind (thread into a ball, or onto a spool); twist fibres (to make twine, rope, tethers, reins, a whip); shape sth by weaving, plaiting, tying, especially: plait garlands, plait hair, build a nest (of a bird), weave a web (of a spider)", all from IE **u̯i̯eH₁-* (LIV 695), hence e.g. Lat. *vīēre* "to wind, plait", OCS *poviti* "to weave" etc. It implies that in the past the Latvians believed that R. m. and Vīkala were really the beings which spun the thread of human life.

Bibl.: Fraenkel II, 690, 1267; ME III, 470; Kursīte 1996, 341; Latviešu tautas ticējumi IV, 2016; MEnc I, 136; Pokorny 1959, 1158–1159; Smoczyński 2018, 1100, 1686–87.

Rugių bóba – Lith. deity "Rye old woman". A spirit or deity of a lower rank, who cared for a good harvest. She was worshipped by people of East Prussia speaking Lithuanian till the end of the 19th cent. Lexicographer F. Kurschat defined R. b. as "goddess – protector of seeding". She was symbolized by a sheaf of grain, tied together in the form of a woman, which villagers transported together with the last load of rye into the village, where they poured water on the sheaf and danced with it. At the same time they also carried the sheaf, which was reaped in the field as the last one and which was called *bámba*, i.e. in Lithuanian "navel". The reaper, who harvested this last sheaf, was called *bambėrėža*, "cutter of the navel". Lithuanian philosopher and mythologist A.J. Greimas saw in this ritual a cutting the umbilical cord and that is why he thought that the cult of R. b. replaced the older cult of 'Earth-Parent'. R. b. was responsible for fertilization of the earth in spring and a successful birth, i.e. a good harvest, in summer. During the celebration of the end of harvest (Lith. *javapjūtės pabaigtuvės*) it was usual to eat a black or white rooster, sometimes a hen. The offering of poultry is typical for rituals connected with deities of fertility of fields and fecundity of domestic animals, described by Stryjkowski. Here the following deities can be mentioned: *Krūminė Pradžių Varpų* (the only deity!) or *Chaurirari*. The poultry was probably sacrificed for its high fruitfulness. It is also a reason, why the egg was a symbol of fecundity and a new life in the spring. R. b. probably appeared also in one enchantment, which was written in a record from the judicial process with Kotryna Gailiuvienė, suspected of witchery, from AD 1560. Striking is the reference about the rooster: *Baba thawa walla, Baba ne thawa walla, wanicku Gaidin, neschith wischtha, milam Diewa*. A. Augstkalns understands this sentence only as fragments, which can be transformed into modern Lithuanian spelling: *Boba – tavo valia, Boba – ne tavo valia... vainiką... gaidys... nešit vištą... mielam Dievui*, i.e. "Old Woman – at thy will, Old Woman – against thy will ... wreath ... rooster ... you carry? a hen ... to beloved God." R. Jasas and R. Balsys mention the notice about the wreath, which could be woven from spikes as a typical symbol of the end of harvest. The enchantment should be a magic formula addressed just to R. b. It seems that there are several possibilities concerning her position: 1) R. b. is an old Prussian goddess of general fertility, earlier called by a different name, whose activities, over time, were restricted to the fertility of fields (in a similar way as Latvian 'Mother of dung' → Mēslu māte). 2) Originally R. b. had not this role, but adopted it after the cult of Earth – Parent' (see above the notice about A. J. Greimas) and later she again lost it. 3) K. Gailiuvienė did not know the functions of individual gods and turned to the first deity which came to mind. Independently of the development from the goddess of fertility to a spirit, or not, after the 16th cent. R. b. was going through the process of degradation, leading to a role as simply a bogey. In the 20th cent. she was mentioned only in the setting when it was necessary to discourage children from trampling the grain fields: "In rye there is crouching R. b. and catches children. She squeezes them on her iron chest until she smotheres them or she forces them to suck axle grease from her breasts. She is an old woman with a cruel gaze. In her right hand she keeps a twig. Sometimes she has iron shoes and puts them on to step on the naughty children."

Bibl.: BRMŠ II, 213–217; Greimas 2005, 484–485; LKŽ XI, 892; RB 134–136 >
Balys; Smoczyński 2018, 1111–12.

Rūšu māte – Latvian goddess "Mother of burial mounds" or "Mother of burial pits"; together with the goddesses **Smilšu māte** "Mother of sand" and **Kapu māte** "Mother of graves" they form a specific triad among c. one hundred of the Latvian Mothers (general information – see → Mātes). The functions of Mother of graves and Mother of sand are clear, together with Mother of earth they cared for graves and corpses of buried people (in contrary of → Veļu māte, who took care of their souls and led them away in the Country of souls). In the case of Mother of sand her name is motivated by the fact that in Latvia the burial hillocks were usually built from sand. R. m. is the most enigmatic Mother from this group. It is only known that she was in some relation to Veļu māte, 'Mother of souls of the dead':

Rūšu māte, Veļu māte,	Rūšu māte, Mother of souls of the dead,
ved bariņu galiņā!	lead people beyond the village!
Drīz gulēt man jāiet	I am going to lie down soon
baltā smilšu kalniņā.	on a sandy white hillock. (LD 27528)

The last distich apparently represents a metaphorical designation of death. The colour white has frequently been used in connection with death and with Mother of souls of the dead. And in East Balticum there was a long tradition of burials on tops of hills. The component *Rūšu* has nothing in common with the souls of the dead and so *Rūšu māte* and *Veļu māte* should be thought of as distinct mythical personages. The most convincing solution was probably formulated by J. Kursīte, who explained her name from Latv. dial. *rūsis*, gen.sg. *rūšu* "heap, mound, furrow". It is possible to conclude that R. m. was probably "Mother of burial hillocks" or "Mother of burial pits".
Bibl.: Kursīte 1996, 329–331.

Sāta māte – Latvian goddess "Mother of satiety" or "Satiated mother"; one of around one hundred of Latvian "Mothers". Latv. *sāts* means "satiating". See → Mātes.
Bibl.: ME III, 809.

Saulės duktė "daughter of Sun" – see Latv. → **Saũles meîtas** "Daughters of Sun"

Saûles meîtas – Latv. deities "Sun's Daughters". They are beings from
Balt. literary myths and inhabitants of the Latvian mythical sky (→ sky, →
world). They also appear in Lith. dainas, under the name *Diẽvo dukrýtės*
"Dievas' daughters", or rather "sky daughters", because the word Dievas
here has retained its original meaning "sky". S. m. were also preserved
in several tales under the name *Sáulės dùkros* "Sun's Daughters". Their
number is not fixed – sometimes only one Sun's Daughter is mentioned;
in those cases, according to H. Biezais, Sun itself is meant (→ sky inhabitants, wedding). Most of the time, however, Sun's Daughters are discussed without further specification of their number.

Opinions on their role in mythology differ. P. Slavėnas and astronomer J. Klētnieks consider them to be personified planets, mythologist
E. Kokare argues they are personified dawn, mythologist W. Mannhardt
claims them to be personified dawn and dusk. The fact is that out of the
folklore material available to us (they are not mentioned in historical
sources), it is not possible to positively determine whether they were
a personification of a natural phenomenon or not.

Let us first consider Sun's Daughters in Latvian dainas. There are 4
characteristics typical of them: 1) genteel appearance – like other sky
inhabitants, they are dressed in silks, gold and silver, and their tools and
personal possessions are also made of precious metals:

Saules meita sudrabota,	Sun's Daughter is all silver,
Pūriņš zelta lapiņām;	Her hope chest laid with golden leaves;
Zīda cimdi, zīda zeķes,	Silken gloves, silken stockings,
Zīda visi prievitiņi.	All her garters silken, too. (LD 33980)

2) women's chores – no matter how exquisitely they are dressed, they are
similar to human daughters in not avoiding any of women's chores:

Kas tur spīd, kas tur zvēro	What is shining, what is glittering
Viņā lauka galiņā?	There at the other end of the field?
Saules meita sienu grāba	Sun's Daughter is raking hay
Ar sudraba grābeklīti.	With a silver rake. (LD 33816)

3) horses – like all sky inhabitants, they have their horses:

Saules meita savus zirgus	Sun's Daughter drenched
Jūriņā peldināja;	Her horses in the sea;

Pate sēd kalniņā, Sitting on a hillock,
Zelta groži rociņā. Holding golden reins in her hand.
(TDz 10192)

4) relationship with *Auseklis* – he is the "right", "true" bridegroom of Sun or her daughters; despite that, in some songs the courtship is not successful:

Trīs rītiņi neredzēja For three days we did not see
Auseklīša uzlecam; Auseklis rising;
Saules meita ieslēguse Sun's Daughter had shut him
Ozoliņa kambarī. In an oaken chamber. (LD 34022)

In other songs, Moon entices S. m. away from Auseklis. But most often, the folk songs sing about the relationship of Sun's Daughters to Dievs' sons (→ Dieva dēli), similar to the relationships of young people on Earth – Sun's Daughters and Dievs' sons are playing together, watch one another in secret, play tricks on one another and also court one another (for more information on the courtship, see → sky inhabitants, wedding):

Dieva dēli, Saules meitas Sun's Daughters, Dievs' sons
Rotaļām spēlējās, Were playing together,
Rotaļām spēlējās Were playing together
Pa rociņu rociņām. Holding their hands. (LD 33758)
Dieva dēli klēti cirta, Dievs' sons were building a barn,
Zelta spāres spārēdami, Roof of golden beams,
Saules meita cauri gāja, Sun's Daughter walked through,
Kā lapiņa drebēdama. Trembling like a leaf. (LD 33754)
Saules meitas danci veda Sun's Daughters were dancing
Zaļas birzis pakrēslī; In the shadow of a green grove;
Dieva dēli lūkojās Dievs' sons were watching them
Caur ozola lapiņām. Through leaves of an oak-tree. (LD 33959)

In Lithuanian tales, the image of Sun's Daughters is very different. They carry the characteristics of characters from folk tales, but at the same time they are also deities, and they communicate with humans. We also learn their names: *Aušrìnė* ("Morning Star"), *Vakarìnė* ("Evening Star"), *Indraja* ("Reed, Cane" / "Henrietta"), *Vaivora* ("Blueberry"), *Žiezdrė* ("Sandbank"), and *Salyja* ("Riverside Meadow"). The tales distinguish those of sun's Daughters who still live with their mother, and those who are already married. One of the latter is *Indraja*, whose husband's name is *Salys* (sometimes also *Sielys*); he is notable for owning a palace that has sunk into the ground. *Indraja* is, in general, the most frequent character in the tales: they present her as a traveller who wanders after the Sun, either to the east or to the west, and finds Sun's palace on the sea. She also watches over humans and teaches them about useful plants.

The name Saules meita penetrated into Estonian tradition as well; in the epic *Kalevipoeg*, there is a maiden called *Salme,* called by the more archaic name *Salve* in some dialects.

Bibl.: Aixenval'd, Petruxin, Xelimskij 1982, 167; Blažek 2004, 189–190; DLKŽ 56, 135, 156, 700, 909; Gimbutienė 2002, 108–111; Kokare 1999, 42–44; ME II, 592, III, 772; SLDDG 255–270, 281–289.

*Saulijā – Baltic ‚goddess of Sun‘. The oldest witness about the solar cult among the Prussians was mediated by Peter von Dusburg in his *Cronica terre Prussie* z roku 1326: "And since they did not come to know God, it came to pass as a consequence of leaving God, that all creatures were worshipped, namely Sun, Moon, stars, thunderstorm, birdlife, quadrupeds, including toad. They also had sacred groves, fields and waters ..."[175] Unfortunately, none of sources register the original Prussian theonym. The first reference about Sun in the Lithuanian mythological tradition appeared in the Church Slavonic / Old Russian supplement to the translation to the book *Chronographia* of Ioannes Malalas (Ἰωάννης Μαλάλας; 491–578) from Antiochia, dated to AD 1262: "Sovij introduced the superstition of bringing sacrifices to terrible gods *Andai* and *Perkunъ*, called 'thunder', and to *Žvoruna*, called 'bitch', and to *Teljavelь* – the smith who forged out the Sun to shine upon the Earth and who placed the Sun upon the heavens."[176] The original Lithuanian designation of the solar deity was recorded only by Jonas Bretkūnas (Germ. Johann Bretke) in his *Postille* written in Lithuanian in 1591: "According to their silly nature

---

[175] *Et quia sic deum non cognoverunt, ideo contigit, quod errando omnem creaturam pro deo coluerunt, scilicet solem, lunam et stellas, tonitrus, volatilia, quadrupedia eciam usque ad bufonem. Habuerunt eciam lucos, campos et aquae sacras..*

[176] *.. prelestь Sovij vъvede vně i prinositi žrъtvu skvernymъ bogam Andaevi i Perkunovi rekše gromu i Žvorunĕ rekše sucĕ i Teljaveli isgkuznecju skovavše jemu* **slъnce** *jako světiti po zemli i vъverъgšju jemu na nebo* **slъnce.**

the pagans thought that there were many gods and that is why they fabricated and worshipped them. One told that the Sun is a god, another that the Moon [is], yet again some saw a god in other things, in like manner as Lithuanians stupidly prayed to Žemepatis and Kaukas."[177] The Latvian counterpart was recorded in its historical spelling by G. F. Stender in his 'Register': "Saule, [goddess of] ,Sun', married Moon according to pagan Latvians. From this bond of marriage the firstborn were the stars. In this place in old Latvian songs one has heard about *Saules meitas*, ,daughters of Sun'. *Dieva dēli*, ,sons of [supreme] god', courted them and the daughters had got small presents."[178] In his 'Latvian Grammar'[179] Stender devoted an independent chapter to Latvian mythology. Here he published the following song, which is written in the present Latvian orthography:

Saule Mēnesi sacirta	Sun cut Moon
ar asajo zobeni	by a sharp sword,
kam paņēma Auseklam	why has he taken from Morning Star
saderētu līgaviņ?	the engaged bride?

The name of the solar goddess is identical with the designation of "sun" in the Baltic languages, where it is feminine: Lith. *sáulė*, Latv. *saũle*, Pruss. *saule*. Feminines are also Old Norse *sól*, Middle Welsh *haul* (also masc.), while Goth. *sauil* and OCS *slъnьce* (*sulniko-*) "sun", are neuters, and Greek Ἥλιος and Ved. *Súrya-* are masculine deities, whose names agree with their Baltic feminine counterparts in the common derivational suffix *-(i)io- / *-(i)iā-*. In the east Baltic folklore the ,daughter of Sun' plays an important role, Lith. *Saulės duktė*, Latv. *Saules meita*. This name was adopted even into the Estonian tradition, where in the epic *Kalevipoeg*

---

[177] *Pagonis sawa durna prigimima sekdami, daug Diewu tare essanczu, tūgi ir daug Diewu patis saw pramane ir garbinoia, kits tare iog **Saule** butu Diewas, kits iog Menu, kits kita daikta Diewu essant tikeia, kaip ir durnai Lietuwa pirmschu metu, meldessi Szemepaczus, Kaukas* [we owe the revision of translation to Vaidas Šeferis].

[178] *Saule, die Sonne, war bey den Heidnischen Letten verheiratet und zwar an den Mond. Aus dieser Ehe wären die ersten Sterne gezeugt worden. Daher hört man in den alten lettischen Liedern Saules meitas, Sonnen Töchter, nach welchen die Deewa dehli Gottessöhne gefreyt und eine kleine Mitgabe bekommen.*

[179] *Lettische Grammatik*, Mitau 1783.

appears the girl *Salme*. In Estonian dialects the more archaic variant *Salve* has been preserved. Further see → world; → sky.

Bibl.: Aixenval'd, Petruxin, Xelimskij 1982, 167; Blažek 2004, 189–190; Fraenkel II, 765; LPG 58–59, 87, 425, 623, 627; MV 822–23, 825; Pokorny 1959, 881; Smoczyński 2018, 1142–43.

*Seitonys (recorded as the Latin pl. **Seitones**) – Lithuanian ‚soothsayer from tied amulets'. One of several types of Prussian and Žemaitian (West Lithuanian) soothsayers (→ soothsayer), which were described by M. Praetorius (see the introduction to the entry → priests). The name is derived from the verb continuing in Lith. *siẽti* "to bind, fasten, tie" = Latv. *sìet* "to tie, make a knot". Praetorius wrote about them: *"Seitones* tied certain things and amulets on the sick man or animal and after removing them they were able to predict his life or death. Such people are still numerous in Nadruva and Skalva [parts of Prussia], but only some of them are competent and many of them are cheaters."

Bibl.: BRMŠ III, 163, 273; Fraenkel II, 783; Prae 4, Chap. 15, §XI.

Sēņu māte – Latvian goddess "Mother of mushrooms". One of more than one hundred goddess-mothers. The first component of her name represents Latvian *sẽne* – "mushroom", which was borrowed from a Balto-Fennic source, cf. Liv., Est. *seeń* "mushroom". See → Mātes.

Bibl.: ME III, 827.

Sergėtoja – one of the Lithuanian Weird sisters. It it the feminine from the noun *sergėtojas* "guard, watch", which is formed from the Lithuanian verb *sérgėti* "to protect, guard, look after (children, a sick person), oversee". See → osud.

Bibl.: Fraenkel II, 776; Smoczyński 2018, 1158.

*Sietonys (recorded the Latin plural **Sietones**) – Lithuanian ‚seer from a sieve'.

One of several types of the Prussian and Žemaitian (West Lithuanian) soothsayers (→ soothsayer), which were described by M. Praetorius (see the introduction to the entry → priests). Their name is motivated by the word for "sieve", known in Lith. *síetas* = Latv. *siêts*. From M. Praetorius we learn only the following information: *"Sietones* were *vaidilas*, which were able to prophesy with the help of circular movements of the sieve. Such people are still numerous in Nadruva and Skalva" [i.e. historical Prussia].

Bibl.: BRMŠ III, 163, 273; Fraenkel II, 783; Prae 4, Chap. 15, §XII; Smoczyński 2018, 1166.

Siliniczus see **Kerpyčius**

Skalsa – Lithuanian ‚goddess of abundance'. M. Praetorius informs us that "… Skalsa is the same as cornucopia; for this reason her feast is celebrated".[180] Lith. *skalsà* means "abundance, copiousness, happiness", cf. *skalsùs* "abundant, nourishing".

Bibl.: Fraenkel II, 794; LPG 545; Smoczyński 2018, 1182, 1190.

Skauģa māte – Latvian goddess "Mother of envy". One of more than one hundred goddess-mothers. Latv. *skàuģis* means "envier" (~ Lith. *skáugė* "envy"). See → Mātes.

Bibl.: ME II, 876; Smoczyński 2018, 1188.

sky – one of the layers of the → world in Baltic mythology and the place where sky inhabitants interact in → sauna and have their → weddings. Some of the most notable Baltic gods, phenomena and celestial bodies are associated with the s.; see → Auseklis "Morning Star", → Debess bungotājs, → Debess māte, → Debesstēvs, → *Deivas, → Dieva dēli, → Mēness/Mėnuo "Moon", → Perkūnas, → northern lights, → Saules Meitas, → *Saulijā "Sun", → *Teljavelis.

sky; blacksmith see →*Teljavelis, →*Perkūnas and → *Velinas

Sky inhabitants, sauna (Lith. *pirtìs*, Latv. *pìrts*; cf. ORuss. *pьrtь*, Russ. dial. *pert'*; Balt. > Finn. *pirtti*) – the sky sauna is the place where the inhabitants of Latvian sky (→ sky), usually the Sun (→ *Saulijā), Sun's daughters (→ Saules meitas), Dievs' sons (→ Dieva dēli), sometimes also the Moon (→ Mēness or → Mėnuo), → Auseklis and the stars, meet for their body hygiene and love games. Latvians are probably the only Euro-

---

[180] *Skalsa ist gleichsam Cornu Copiae, dem zu Ehren sie auch ein Fest gehalten.* (*Idolatria veterum Prussorum*, representing the IVth volume of *Deliciae Prussicae*, op. cit. 1703).

pean nation with a similar motif in their mythology. It can be found in 34
dainas in total. The majority of them tell a simple story – the Dievs' sons
built a (golden) sauna at a (silver) water, the Sun or her daughters waited
for them there and they bathed together:

Sudrabupes maliņā	"On a silver river's bank
Dieva dēli pirti taisa;	Dievs' sons are building a sauna.
Tur Saulīte pērties gāja	There the Sun went to bathe
Ar visām jumpravām;	With all her maidens;
Dieva dēli garu lēja	Dievs' sons poured the steam,
Zābakos stāvēdami.	Sturdy shoes on their feet." (LD 55050)

In other songs, it is not only the river that is silver. In s.s., most objects are
made of silver, gold, gems or silk. Even the sauna itself is sometimes pure
gold, as opposed to the black-smoked saunas on earth. This is the most
typical aspect of the sky inhabitants' life – it marks an ethereal world,
where everything is more genteel than in the world of humans:

Dieva dēli pirti dara	"Dievs' sons are building a sauna
No sīkiem olīšiem;	Of tiny pebbles;
Saules meitas pērties gāja,	Sun's daughters went to bathe
Zelta slotas padusē.	Golden whisks under their arms.
Auseklītis garu lēja	Auseklītis poured the steam
Ar sudraba biķerīti.	With a silver goblet.
Leji, leji, Auseklīti,	Pour slowly, Auseklītis
Izpatapu siltumiņu.	Pour us warmth." (LD 33844.1)

What are the roles of the individual beings in the sauna? Dievs' sons
(or a single son of Dievs) usually build it, then, sometimes, also heat it,
standing there in sturdy shoes, pouring water, and at the same time they
are using the sauna as well: they are sweating and swatting themselves
with golden whisks. The Sun or Sun's daughters have a central role in s.s.
and appear in all songs related to it. They never go to the sauna without
golden whisks and silk chemises folded under their arms (an analogy to
Latvian women who would never enter a sauna without birch whisks and
linen shirts). Sometimes they heat the sauna themselves and then wait
for Dievs' sons. If the Sun appears, she often swats them herself. The
Moon (*Mēness*) and the Morning Star (*Auseklis*) also pour water on the
hot stones (then they are referred to as *gara metēji*, "steam throwers"),

while sweating and swatting themselves. In one song, even → *Pērkons appears in this role, but according to H. Biezais, that is a mistake. Last but not least, stars (zvaigznes)* can appear in s.s. They also have a specific task: to bring into s.s. water in diamond vessels, from a nearby spring, lake or river. The songs about s.s. have most probably sprung up because the sky inhabitants participate in similar activities that Latvian peasants did. Sauna played an important role in their life – sweating in saunas was a widespread method of cleansing and immunity strengthening, children were born in saunas and → Dievs and the goddess → Laima visited saunas – there was no reason why the sky inhabitants should not use a sauna as well. It also widens the sphere of activities Dievs' sons and Sun's daughters participate in together. Finally, other, romance-type dainas should be mentioned. To the motif of s.s., they add the motif of an orphan:

Man māmiņa šautru svieda,	"My mommy threw a chunk of wood at me,
Es iebēgu lejiņā;	I ran into a valley;
Es atradu lejiņā	I found in the valley
Zelta pirti kuroties.	A golden sauna heated up.
Dieva dēli kūrējiņi,	Dievs' sons were heating,
Saules meitas pērējiņas,	Sun's daughters were swatting themselves,
Auseklītis garu lēja	Auseklītis poured the steam
Ar sudraba biķerīti.	With a golden goblet.
Es tev lūdzu, Auseklīti,	I beg you, Auseklītis,
Lej gariņu pamazām,	Pour the water slowly,
Lai tā man neizkusa	So that the heat does not melt
Zelta slota peroties,	My golden whisk,
Lai pārnesu māmiņai	So that I can bring my mommy
Jel ar' vienu žagariņu,	At least one twig from it,
Jel ar' vienu žagariņu	At least one twig from it
Par šautriņa sviedumiņu.	For the chunk of wood thrown."
	(LD 33844)

This daina couples the earthly with the ethereal: a human mingles with the beings in s.s. – an orphan driven there by their wish to escape from their malevolent stepmother. The sky inhabitants, again, play the role of helpers and defenders of the weak. See also → world.

Bibl.: SLDDĢ 322–28; Smoczyński 2018, 971.

Sky inhabitants, wedding (Lith. *dañgiškos vestùvės*, Latv. *debesu bûtņu kãzas*). The sky wedding is a motif of both Lithuanian and Latvian myths, telling the story of Sun's or the Sun's daughter's wedding. This topic is typical for Baltic mythology; however, Baltic mythologists have so far paid it less attention than other themes, such as → Perkūnas, → Velinas, → Laima, trees, → *velijā, creation of the world (→ world) etc.

The theme of sky wedding in Baltic mythology breaks further down into individual motifs: looking for the bride, courting, the wedding itself, disagreements about potential bridegrooms. Fragments of similar stories can be found in other Indo-European traditions as well. The most detailed one is in Greek mythology, where the beautiful Helen plays the main role, together with her twin brothers Castor and Polydeukes (known for their fast horses), the so-called Διόσκουροι, "Zeus' sons", and Helen's countless suitors.[181] In the Vedic tradition, the central role falls on Sūryā́, the daughter of the Sun god (Sū́rya); her father recommended she marry the Moon god Sóma, while she preferred the Aśvins, the famous twin riders.[182] The motifs in this entry and the → Dieva dēli (Dievs' sons) entry obviously differ from their Greek and Vedic counterparts, but they are generally considered to have common origins.[183] However, some of the stories could have sprung to life on their own in the Baltic area, as a metaphorical explanation of what people could observe happening in the sky. For example, the following Lithuanian song can be interpreted as a story about Sun's wedding, but also as a poetic description about the end of night and sunrise. This ambiguity is further supported by the fact

---

[181] The reasons of Menelaus´ victory in competition of numerous suitors wooing Helen are rather unromantic – Menelaus prevailed, because he gave the greatest gifts [Hesiod, *Catalogues of Women* 68.98–100], how already Odysseus anticipated and sent no gifts [ibid., 21–27]. In the fragment 197, also ascribed to Hesiod, the decision in favor of the wealthiest suitor was realized by Dioscurides, i.e. brothers of Helen (cf. West 2007, 232).

[182] R̥gveda I, 116.17 (compare translator Griffith's commentary 1889[1987], 165, 167); I, 119.2 about the epithet Ūrjānī "power". According to the 19th century mythologist Albert Pike, Sun's Daughter is the star Sirius near the Gemini constellation, i.e. the two stars Castor and Pollux. Interesting parallels and differences between this story and the Baltic sky wedding suggest themselves (see the reprint of his fundamental work, published 1992).

[183] Compare recently Jackson 2006; Janda 2006.

that the Lith. words *tekėjo* and *ištekėjo* mean both "was getting married" and "was rising".

Bitel, dobilėliau,	Little bee, little clover,
Dobiliau,	Clover,[184]
Kas tai ištekėja,	Who was rising/who was getting married here,
Dobiliau?	Clover?
Saulala tekėja,	The Sun was rising/was getting married,
Dobiliau.	Clover.
Žvaigždeles lydėja,	The stars were accompanying her,
Dobiliau.	Clover.
Atsigrįžk, Saulala,	Turn around, Sun,
Dobiliau,	Clover,
Beg visas žvaigždeles,	Are all the stars here,
Dobiliau?	Clover?
Visos, kaip ne visos,	All of them, how could not all of them be here?
Dobiliau.	Clover.
Da vienos nėra,	Only one of them is missing,
Dobiliau.	Clover.
Da vienos nėra,	Only one of them is missing,
Dobiliau,	Clover,
Žvaigždeles rytines,	The morning star,
Dobiliau.	Clover.
Kur buvai, žvaigždela,	Where have you been, little star,
Dobiliau?	Clover?
Kur tu uliavojai,	Where have you been wandering,
Dobiliau?	Clover?
Buvau, ašan buvau,	I have been, I have been away,
Dobiliau,	Clover,
Rinkau Saulai vietelį,	Choosing a place for Sun,

---

[184] The words *dobilėliau* and *dobiliau* can be translated as addresses "little clover" and "clover". In this song, they work as an acoustic constant or chorus, a very frequent phenomenon in Lithuanian folk songs. The clover is probably also mentioned because the song speaks about early morning, i.e. the time when clover was cut – before the dew sets, otherwise it would not dry properly. The word for clover was also used as a polite address for a close person.

Dobiliau.	Clover.
Bega giedras rytelis,	Is the morning clear,
Dobiliau?	Clover?
Beg ne ūkanotas,	Is it not misty,
Dobiliau?	Clover?
Giedras, kaip negiedras,	Clear, how could it not be clear,
Dobiliau,	Clover,
Bet neūkanotas,	Not misty,
Dobiliau.	Clover.

(Dundulienė 2008, 118)

The genre typical for the theme of s. w. are folk songs. The majority of them are Latv. dainas that include detailed descriptions of the individual stages of the wedding; they form the largest source of information for this entry. In Lithuanian, only brief folk beliefs are known, together with only several songs, which however tell fuller stories than the Latv. ones (see also → Mėnuo):

Mėnuo Saulùžę vėdė	Moon was marrying Sun
pìrmą pavasarėlį.	In the early days of Spring.
Saulùžė ankstì kėlės,	Before Sun got up with the dawn,
Mėnùžis atsiskýrė.	Moon walked away from her.
Mėnuo víens vaikštinėjo,	Moon walked the sky alone,
Aušrìnę pamylėjo.	He loved the Morning Star.
Perkū̃ns dideí supýkęs	Perkūnas was enraged,
jį kárdu pérdalyjo.	He cut him in half with his sword.
Ko Saulùžės atsiskýrei,	Why did you walk away from Sun,
Aušrìnę pamylėjei,	Loved the Morning Star?
Víens naktý vaikštinėjei?	Why did you wander alone in the night?

Or this song:

Aušrinė svotbą kėlė,	Morning Star was celebrating her wedding,
Perkūns pro vartus jojo,	Perkūnas rode in through the gate,
Ąžuolą žalią parmušė.	He dashed a green oak in half.
Ąžuolo kraujs varvėdams,	The oak's blood was dripping
Apšlakstė mano drabužius,	Staining my dress,
Apšlakstė vainikėlį.	Staining my wreath.
Saulės dukrytė verkiant	Crying, the Sun's Daughter
Surinko tris metelius,	Was picking for three years
Pavytusius lapelius.	The wilted leaves.

O kur, mamyte mano,	Where shall I, my dear mother,
Drabužius išmazgosiu	Wash my dress,
Kur kraują išmazgosiu?	Wash the blood off it?
Dukryte, mano jaunoji,	My daughter, my bride,
Eik pas tą ežeraitį,	Go to the lake,
Kur tek devynios upatės.	Where nine rivers flow. (Biržiška 1925, 74)

These examples alone make it clear that the main character in the s. w. is Sun. In both surviving Baltic languages the word for "sun" is a feminine, making Sun most often the bride. Sometimes, Sun is replaced by her daughter or several daughters. Latvian mythologist Haralds Biezais points out that the phrase → Saules meita "Sun's Daughter" can mean Sun herself in the sense of "Sun maiden", i.e. "Sun the bride". In this case, the word *Saules* could be a *genitivus appellativus,* a denominative genitive. This form is also commonly used in modern Latvian: *profesora kungs,* "Mr. professor", a polite address of a professor, translates literally as "professor's mister". It is plausible that *Saules meita* can sometimes designate Sun as a daughter, a young, unmarried girl. For example in this daina:

Saules meita rozes sēja	The Sun's Daughter sowed roses
Sudrabiņa dārziņā;	In a silver garden;
Ik rītiņu Dieva dēli	Every morning, Dievs' sons
Jāja Saules lūkoties.	Rode to look at Sun. (LD 33977)

The identity of Dievs's sons is similarly ambiguous. We never learn who exactly they are. Some mythologists believe them to be one of the constellations; the astronomer J. Klētnieks argues that they are the planets Mars, Jupiter and Saturn; and many mythologists claim that they are the Baltic equivalent of the Indian twin riders Aśvins and the Greek Dioscuri, or, often, the morning and the evening star. The Latvian morning star is → Auseklis, and therefore e.g. H. Biezais is convinced that Auseklis is one of Dievs's sons whom Sun befriended and was to marry.

The identities and the roles of other sky inhabitants are clearer in the songs and it is not necessary to create hypotheses about them. Each of the beings, however, has several roles that differ between individual songs. It is more illustrative to follow the s. w. chronologically:

1) The first step usually consists of looking for a bride and testing her qualities. This activity is called *lūkoties* in Latvia. The most important factor in the final decision was the potential bride's diligence, described

by the words *gòds*, *gòdiņš* in the songs. Nowadays, this word means "honour":

Celies agri, Saules meita,	Get up early, Suns's daughter,
Mazgā baltu liepas galdu,	Scrub a linden table white,
Rītu nāks Dieva dēli	In the morning, Dievs' sons are coming
Tev godiņu lūkoties.	To look at your honour. (LD 34032)

Dievs's sons are also looking for brides during their games with Sun's daughters.

2) When the bride is chosen, a matchmaker or more matchmakers go to her. They take with them food that is then used to prepare a feast in the bride's house. This activity is most often called *derēt* or *līgt* "to negotiate, to arrange, to make a contract" in Latvian, hence also Latv. *līgava* "bride". In real life, the matchmaker in Latvia and Lithuania was usually one of the bridegroom's older relatives or a neighbour; but in the dainas, it is usually Sun herself who arranges her daughter's wedding. This break with tradition, H. Biezais argues, emphasises the central role Sun plays among the sky inhabitants. Sometimes, the thunder god Pērkons takes over the matchmaking. The agreement was settled by shaking hands:

Dieva dēls, Saules meita	Dievs' son and the Sun's daughter
Pār jūriņu rokas deva.	Shook their hands across the sea.
Kā tie zelta gredzeniņi	Their golden rings
Nesabira jūriņā.	Spilled into the sea. (LD 33757,1)

Beside Dievs' sons and Auseklis, the arranged bridegroom can also be → Dievs himself, Auseklis' son, Moon, Pērkons, Pērkons' son or the personified Wind.

3) The wedding itself follows. In the Baltic region, it often lasted up to 6–7 days. For three days, there were celebrations in the bride's house, and then the bride with her dowry was escorted festively into the bridegroom's house, where the celebrations continued for another three days. The dowry was very important. It was the first duty of the bride's family – very often, they collected it over many years and it was very elaborate and carefully selected:

Saulīt' gauži noraudāja	Sun was weeping sadly
Kalniņā stāvēdama.	Standing on a hill.
Kā tai bija neraudāt,	How could she not weep,
Žēl meitiņas, žēl pūriņa:	Sorry for her daughter, sorry for the dowry:
Pūriņš zelta kaldināts,	The chest was all golden,
Sudrabiņa dāvaniņas.	All the gifts made of silver. (LD 33782,3)

The gifts are mentioned, because on her way to the bridegroom's (i.e. her new) home, a Latvian bride was supposed to give gifts to all the attendants at the wedding, particularly to her new family. There were unspoken rules for the kind of gifts: the father-in-law was usually gifted colourful mittens, the mother-in-law received a large woollen shawl, the bridegroom's brothers and other male relatives usually got socks or garters[185], and female relatives were given smaller shawls, mittens, towels or fabric "tiaras" or "wreaths". In the previous daina, all these gifts are silver, because in Latvian tradition all objects used by the sky inhabitants are made of rich fabrics, precious metals or gemstones. The transportation of the chest with the dowry falls on Sun herself in the dainas:

Kam tie tādi kumeliņi	Why are horses standing here
Sudrabiņa podziņām?	With silver buttons?
Dieva dēlu kumeliņi,	The horses of Dievs' sons,
Saules meita vedamā.	Come here for Sun's daughter.
Pate Saule pūru veda,	Sun herself carries the dowry,
Visus mežus veltīdama:	Giving gifts to all the trees:
Ozolam raibi cimdi,	Colourful mittens for the oak,
Liepai velšu villainīte,	A woollen shawl for the linden,
Smalkajam kārkliņam	For the tiny poplar
Apzeltīti prievitiņi.	Gilded garters. (LD 33804)

However, in terrestrial weddings, the escort of the dowry was the duty of the bridegroom's closest relatives. This is one of the aspects in Latvian weddings that still mirror the customs of the pre-Christian era. The bridegroom, his relatives and friends used to abduct the bride, while her relatives were trying to catch them and were coming up with various ways

---

[185] Here, "garter" means a long strip of fabric (usually woven), tied around the leg at the top of a sock, a stocking or a footwrap, by which means the footwear is secured to the leg.

to hinder them. In the end, when they caught up with the abductors, the bridegroom had to pay for the bride. This old custom has survived in several aspects of the wedding tradition. The bride's dowry was carried (i.e. as if "abducted") by the bridegroom's relatives; sometimes, they also had to overcome various obstacles or to win in games prepared by the bride's relatives. Other such aspects are the designations of several wedding attendants: e.g. the bridegroom's companions were called *vedē-jtēvs* and *vedējmāte* in Latvian, derived from *vest* "to carry, to transport"; they were also responsible for the escort of the dowry. The bride's party was called *panāksnieki*, literally "chasers". Later on, the terms lost their unambiguous meanings and the words *vedējtēvs* and *panāksnieks* began to designate someone akin to a best man or an usher, a man who organises the wedding. In Latvian myths, this best man is Auseklis or more often Pērkons; sometimes, he gives gifts to the attendants.

In the last daina, there are, surprisingly, trees present, which does not fit with the usual picture of the s. w. The wedding is elsewhere attended exclusively by the inhabitants of the Baltic sky; only sometimes the goddess → Laima mixes with them as well. H. Biezais believes that in this particular daina, two notions blended: a) the giving of gifts at the s. w., b) the appearance of the landscape at sunset: when sun is setting behind trees, their tops turn to a golden hue, which could give rise to the idea that Sun is giving them colourful or golden gifts.

4) The wedding banquet is rarely mentioned in Latvian dainas and the food hardly ever. The most usual type of dainas is a simple announcement of the fact that Sun wedded off her daughter:

Saulīt' meitu pārdevuse	Sun wedded off her daughter
Pār deviņi novadiņi;	Beyond nine counties;
Meitu veda pār jūriņu,	She led her daughter beyond the sea,
Pati rauda jūrmalē.	Now she is weeping alone on the shore.

(LD 33940)

The phrase "beyond nine counties" is more or less equivalent to the English "far, far away"; it designates an unknown or very far off place. In other dainas, the s. w. takes place "in the midst of the air", which is synonymous with the sky.

Mythologists have paid great attention to the time the s. w. takes place and their hypotheses are very conflicting. Lithuanian mythologist Pranė Dundulienė believes that s. w. took place in the first spring after the creation of the world – see the second song in this entry and the phrase *pirmą pavasarėlį* (literally "in the first spring"). The Latvian "nature school" in the first half of the 20th century argued that in the original views, s. w. was taking place every month, and only later Latvians ascribed it to the summer solstice. This view is supported by this daina:

Jāņu diena svēta diena	John's Day is holy,
Aiz visām dieniņām.	The holiest of all.
Jāņu dienu Dieva dēls	At St John's Day Dievs' son
Saules meitu sveicināja.	Greeted Sun's daughter. (LD 32919)

The word "to greet" is sometimes used in the meaning "to court" in Latvian folklore.

According to H. Biezais, it is impossible to determine whether the old Balts believed the s. w. to have taken place at a specific time, and the question is irrelevant. It seems that in Lithuania, the prevailing notion was that the marriage of Sun and Moon was harmonious until they fell out because of Morning Star. For example, in Eastern Lithuania, near the town of Molėtai, it was told that, at night, Moon takes care of Sun as she is tired after a whole day's work. There are indications in Lithuanian tradition which suggest that, originally, stars were perceived as the children of Sun and Moon, although this notion is completely absent from Latvian tradition:

Vakarinė žvaigždelė	The Evening Star
Visą dangų išvaikščiojo,	Walked all over the sky
Visą dangų išvaikščiojo	Walked all over the sky
Ir pas Mėnulį sustojo.	And stopped by Moon.
Oi Mėnuli, oi tėveli,	Oh, Moon, oh, my father,
Aš šią naktį – tai dėl tavęs,	Tonight, I am because of you,
Aš šią naktį – tai dėl tavęs,	Tonight, I am because of you,
O jau rytoj – dėl Saulelės	And tomorrow – because of Sun
Debesėliais apsileidus,	Covered with clouds,
Skaudum lietum apsiliejus!	Flooded by doleful rain!
	(Dundulienė 1989, 130)

5) The theme of s. w. also partly involves the topic of disagreements and fallouts between the sky inhabitants. There are four motifs to the disagreements and all of them involve Sun. In the first one, already cited, Sun is angry with Moon because of his love affair: in Latvia, he lured away Morn-

ing Star's promised bride (probably Sun's Daughter); in Lithuania, on the other hand, he was unfaithful to Sun with Morning Star. These differences most probably stem from the fact that the Latv. word for Morning Star is masculine, while the Lith. word is feminine. It is notable that in the Latv. myth, Sun herself punishes the culprit; while in the Lith. version, Perkūnas takes on this task, perhaps because Perkūnas had gradually attained the role of the disperser of justice. H. Biezais ascribes the story to the projection of human stories on the sky inhabitants. Another opinion, popular in the Baltic countries, says that the myth explains the origin of lunar phases. Why is there only half Moon every once in a while? Well, because Sun cut him in half with a sword in anger. In Lithuania, we not only find this motif in the preceding daina, but also in folk beliefs recorded in Dzūkija, i.e. in Southern Lithuania. When Sun rises and Moon is still to be seen on the sky, they say that Sun has caught Moon with Morning Star.

In the second motif, Sun is angry with Moon, because he did not shine during the day. He does not argue back, only replies matter-of-factly:

Saule bāra Mēnestiņu,	Sun scolded Moon,
Kam dieniņu netecēja.	Why did he not run during the day.
Mēnestiņis atsacīja:	Moon replied:
Tev dieniņa, man naksniņa.	Yours the day, mine the night.
	(LD 33909,3)

Thus, the daina poetically explains the alternation of the day and the night.

The third motif is very frequent: it is a fallout between Sun and the Latvian Dievs, concerning the behaviour of their children. Dievs' sons upturned the Sun's Daughters' sled, or they took the wreaths from their heads or rings from their fingers. Sometimes it is, conversely, the Sun's Daughter who breaks the Dievs' son's sword:

Trīs dieniņas, trīs naksniņas	For three days and three nights
Saul' ar Dievu ienaidā:	Sun and Dievs are angry with each other
Saules meita pārlauzuse	Sun's Daughter broke in half
Dieva dēla zobeniņu.	Dievs' son's sword. (LD 34019)

In one daina the disagreement goes so far that Dievs throws a stone at Sun; this motif is one of the literary myths where the sky inhabitants act like humans; it is a consequence of the games that Sun's Daughters play with Dievs' sons.

As for the fourth motif, it is not quite clear whether it is truly a fallout or just an unfortunate accident:

Pērkons rūca, zibinēja,	Pērkons was roaring, hurling thunderbolts,
Sasper zelta ozoliņu;	He clove a golden oak;
Trīs gadiņi Saule raud,	For three years, Sun was crying,
Zelta zarus lasīdama.	Gathering golden branches.

(LD 34047,10)

H. Biezais sees in this daina a parallel with the wedding custom in which the best man embraced the bride's waist with his left arm and with a sword held in his right he cut a sign, meant to protect the house from evil spirits, into the door-frame and the threshold of the bride's new home. Then he embraced the bridegroom's waist and repeated the ritual. Because Pērkons usually plays the role of best man in s. w., there is no reason why he should not do the same – but in his own way, as thunder is wont to do – he hits a tree. On the other hand, W. Mannhardt interprets the daina as a projection of a natural phenomenon into a myth: the rays of the setting sun are vaguely resemblant of a tree and the colour of sunset is similar to the colour of blood – it could, therefore, be the blood of a tree, as referred to e.g. in the second Lith. daina about s. w listed here.

Bibl.: DLKŽ 115, 848, 934; Dundulienė 2008, 117–127; Gimbutienė 2002, 108–113; Laurinkienė 1996, 129–134; ME I, 360, 690; II, 206, 483, 519; Pike 1992, 531; SLDDG 297–321.

Smilšu māte – Latvian goddess "Mother of sand". One of more than one hundred Latvian "Mothers". Latv. *smìl(k)ts* means "sand". See details in → Rūšu māte and → Mātes.

Bibl.: ME III, 963–964.

soothsayer (Lith. *būrė̃jas*, Latv. *gàišreģis*) – a person of important social standing, believed to be able to foresee and interpret things to come correctly. Due to the relatively late arrival of Christianity, Balt. nations differentiated between various types of soothsayers, usually based on the manner in which they foretold the future. For more information on the individual groups of soothsayers, see → priests; → būrėjas; → bùrtvis; → gàišreģis; → Lekkutones; → pareģis; → *Seitonys; → *Sietonys; → *Vandelučiai; → *Viduronys; → zīlniẽks; → zīmlēmis; → žynỹs.

Sovij – Lithuanian mythological being and a cultural hero. The name *Sovij* (**Sovius*?) appears in the supplement to the Church Slavonic / Old Russian translation of the book *Chronographia*, in the Greek original written by Ioannes Malalas (491–578), from AD 1262: "There was one man [named] Sovius, he hunted a boar. He took away him 9 spleens and gave them to his descendants, to roast them."[186] In another passage we can read: "Oh, great devil's blindness, which seduced the Lithuanian tribe and Jatvingians and Prussians and Jäms [= Estonians] and Livonians and further with many other languages, to call Sovij's [tribes] and to believe in Sovij's role as a guide of their souls in underworld. That [Sovij], who lived in the time of Abimelek. Till the present time they burn their dead on funeral pyres as the Hellens [burnt] Achilleus and Aiant according to their custom. Sovij introduced the superstition of bringing sacrifices to terrible gods *Andai* and *Perkunъ*, called 'thunder', and to Žvoruna, called 'bitch', and to *Teljavelь* – the smith who forged out the Sun to shine upon the Earth and who placed the Sun upon the heavens.."[187] The name S. is not of Baltic origin. The attempt to connect it with the possessive pronoun of the type Lith. *sãvas* "suus" makes no sense. More promising is an adaptation of some such Byzantine name like Εὐσέβιος or Σάβας. Recently a new and quite original solution was proposed by the Prague Baltist Ilja Lemeškin. It is based on a hypothesis that the order of the first two words in the formula *Sovij bě člověkъ* was originally **bě Sovij*; thus, in reality, it should be a single word, Old Russian *běsovij* "devil's". If this is the case, the sentence can be translated as: "the Devil's man hunted a boar." See also → underworld.

Bibl.: Lemeškin 2009, 36–37, 184, 328; LPG 56–68.

---

[186] *Sovij bě člověkъ. Ulovivšju emu divij veprь. Izemše iz nego 9 slezenicь i izdastь ei ispeči roženymъ dětem nego.*

[187] *O velikaja prelestь diavolьskaja jaže vъvede vъ litovskyj rod i jatvezě i v prusy i vъ etь i vъ livь i inym mnogo jazyki iže soviceju naričjutsja. Mnjašče i dъšamъ svoimъ sušča provodnika vъ adъ Sovьja. Byvšu emu vъ lěta Avimelexa iže i ině mrtva telesa svoja sъžigajutь na kradaxъ jakož Axileos i Eantъ i inii po rjadu Ellini. Siju prelestь Sovij vъvede vně i prinositi žrъtvu skvernymъ bogam Andaevi i Perkunovi rekše gromu i Žvoruně rekše sucě i Teljaveli isgkuznecju skovavše jemu slъnce jako světiti po zemli i vъverъgšju jemu na nebo slъnce.*

Spalvaînis – Latvian ‚fairytale strongman‘, or at least one of his names, although the best-known is the strongman → Lāčplēsis appearing in the epic of the same name. The name S. is derived from Latv. *spaĺva* "feather, animal's hair; colour of animal's hair" (~ Lith. *spalvà* "colour"), means either "feathered" or "hairy, furry". This hero is known only from several tales. In one of them his father is a → bear, which abducted a girl from a nearby village into his cave. Another motif is common to many European folktales. In this tale the hero together with two other strongmen set out in the world. He saves three princesses, but his companions betray him and inform the king that only they two saved the princesses. Remarkable are the names of these companions: *Kokupļāvējs* "He who scythes trees" and *Kalnugāzējs* "He who overturns mountains". These names inspired Andrejs Pumpurs to create the literary personage Koknesise.

Bibl.: LPT II; ME III, 983.

Stabradze, Staburadze – Latv. "nymph of the Staburags cliff". Her name is derived from the 18 m high cliff Staburags, which used to tower above the Daugava, the largest Latv. river, near the town of Koknese in central Latvia, and was a popular destination until 1965, when the Soviet government had it levelled during the construction of the water power station Pļaviņas. The name of the cliff itself is a composite of *stabs* 'column' and *rags* 'horn, cliff'. S. is a character from Latv. folk songs and tales, made famous by the national epic *Lāčplēsis*. In this work, she is a beautiful nymph who mourns her dead lover and lives on the bottom of the Daugava River in a crystal palace under the Staburags cliff. She saves the drowned and takes care of orphaned girl. One of these girls is Laimdota, who the hero → Lāčplēsis meets in S.'s palace.

The author of the epic, Andrejs Pumpurs, based the character of S. freely on folk tales and 11 dainas published by professor of the Tartu university F. Krūze in his book *Urgeschichte des Estnischen Volkstammes un der kaiserlich Russischen Ostseeprovinzen Liv-, Esth- und Kurland* (1846). In his commentary, Krūze says that he received the dainas from a certain 103–year-old village woman, via Stender, a priest. Scholar Jāzeps Rudzītis believes it was J. H. Stender, the grandson of G. F. Stender (the Stender Senior often mentioned in this book). On the basis of these dainas and tales, F. Mālberģis wrote his epic *Staburags un Liesma* (Staburags and Flame), which was a major influence on Pumpurs' image of the nymph Staburadze.

The expression "based freely on folk tales" was used deliberately in the previous paragraph, because none of the songs or tales mention a beautiful nymph S. who lives in a crystal palace and cares for orphaned girls. The stories about the Staburags cliff are rather typical local tales that sprang to life because of the cliff's appearance. Period photographs show a fairly slim, tall rock formation that vaguely resembles a human figure. Near the surface of the water, there were many indentations and holes and a large cave in the cliff. Thin streams of water flowed through the holes and the imagination of folk authors supplied the idea that the cliff was spinning and weaving:

Stabas-raga māmuliņ	Staburags' Mommy
Zīdu diegu šķeterēj';	Spun a silk thread;
Zīdu diegu šķeterēj',	Spun a silk thread,
Nēzdaudziņu rakstīja.	A patterned handkerchief. (KL 273–279)

Another of the 11 dainas conveys the idea that Staburags has girls in its care:

Es tev lūdzu, Stabu-rags,	I plead from you, Staburags,
Dod man vienu nēzdaudziņ',	Give me one handkerchief,
Dod man vienu nēzdaudziņu,	Give me one handkerchief,
Nēzdaudziņu audējiņ'.	A weaver of handkerchiefs.

The weaver in this song is probably a girl from one of the villages in the vicinity of the cliff. In other songs and tales, "daughters and sons of Staburags" also denote the people from the surroundings who revere the cliff as a landmark and associate their identity with it.

Other, more specific stories have survived as well, in which a maiden lives in the cliff and by weaving helps both young girls, who then get enough cloth for their dowry, and married women, who are tasked so heavily by the nobility that they do not have time at home to weave cloth for their families' clothes.

The fact that the cliff resembled a human figure gave rise to many tales about its origins. Let us mention two of them: "A very long time ago now, a certain young man took his boat on the Daugava to catch fish. All of a sudden, terrible waves arose, the boat overturned and the bridegroom drowned. The poor bride spent days and nights weeping on the riverbank, until she turned into a cliff." And another: "There is a grey-haired old man living in the Staburags cliff, who gives out his wealth to those who ask him at midnight. In the evenings, a maiden sits in front of the rock and washes herself and her long hair in the clear water." These dainas and

tales then formed the basis for the image of the nymph S., as described by
the poet A. Pumpurs in the epic *Lāčplēsis*.

Bibl.: APL 150–152, 168–171; KL 273–279; L 75–77, 93–96, 109, 149, 151;
Pumpurs 1987.

Sumpurṇi [the exact transcription with intonation is *sùmpur̃ṇi*] – Latvian
'dogheads'. These mythical beings from Latvian legends and tales looked
like humans with dogs' heads. However, some s. could also have bird's
heads or only one eye, one ear or one leg, walking by holding hands with
another similar person with their eye, ear or leg on the other side of their
body. As the name suggests, though, people with dogs' heads were the
majority among s.: *suns* is Latv. "dog" and *pur̃ns* "snout, muzzle". Similar
is Lith. *šumbur̃nis* and *šun(i)aburnis*. It would appear that s. are similar to
werewolves and some legends confuse them – e.g. a sorcerer could change
humans into werewolves or dogheads by girding them with a magic belt.
But as the origins of these beings are traced, they appear separate – two
distinct kinds of beings with the following differences: 1) Baltic werewolves
were often not dangerous to humans. Sometimes they were even humans
who tried the change into a wolf out of curiosity, took a walk in a forest
and then changed back to humans. On the other hand, s. were cruel, they
always hunted humans, ate their flesh and drank their blood. Sometimes they
also kept humans captive, feeding them up. 2) A werewolf was a human,
who could change appearance and character from human to wolf and back,
unless someone burned their wolf skin, touched their clothes etc., but a s.
was a doghead from birth. 3) Werewolves appeared alone or in groups,
but s. were a whole nation with their own country (usually deep in the
forest), they kept together and always charged in packs. Besides, s. had
a hierarchy: a kind of kings or chiefs, who could be recognised by their
long tail. S. were also said to wear clothes made of leaves and sleep "like
pigs" – on a pile, with their heads at other dogheads' feet. When a human
wandered into their country and they started hunting them, they could save
themselves by putting on their sandals or rawhide shoes[188] backwards and
pouring ashes into them, which would confuse their scent track. Climbing
a tree was also recommended, because s. cannot raise their heads. The
dogheads appear in the Latvian epos *Lāčplēsis*, which is partly based on
Latvian legends. The hero → Lāčplēsis sails to an unknown island, but he

---

[188] Baltic shoes were basically a piece of rawhide tied to the foot. Similar shoes
are worn with folk costumes in other parts of the world as well.

cannot stay there, because he and his companions are attacked by s. The island is a variant of the "land of the dogheads." According to the Latvian *Mitoloģijas enciklopēdija*, the belief in s. could be based on an attack of an ethnic whose members' faces resembled the faces of dogs. P. Šmits also argues that s. are an amalgamation of mythical beings and memories of an ancient tribe. S. differ from → Vadātājs, who can be very unpleasant but one can be rid of him easily, or pūķis (see → áit(i)varas and → vilce) who can burn down a person's house and take their soul to hell, but will only do so if the person makes a deal with him or treats him with disrespect. S., on the other hand, are unambiguously evil and not even innocents are safe from them. In all the Latvian mythical beings, s. are the most dangerous and cruel.

Bibl.: APL 214–216; LTT 28985–28993; ME III, 419, 121–123; MEnc II 220–221; PLP 60; PŠ 103.

Sun see *Saulijā; → **Saules meitas**; → **sky wedding**.

*****Sutvaras** (recorded as **Sotwaros**) – Lith. 'god of cattle'. The Polish chronicler Stryjkowski recorded several Lith. theonyms that aren't analoguous to any of the theonyms mentioned by other authors. Among those is *Sotwaros*, 'the god of cattle'. Stryjkowski says that Lithuanians sacrifice capons to him in front of fires. According to Mannhardt, this theonym is actually a distorted word *sùtvaras* "creator, demiurg; creation", which is a derivate of the prefixed verb *sutvérti* "to create". However, it could just as well be an adaptation of the Polish word *stwór* "creature, being", or a similar one.

Bibl.: LPG 330, 339.

Szullinnijs see → *Šulininis

*****Šilinyčius** (recorded as **Siliniczus**) – Lith. 'deity of lichen and moss'. Lichen and moss was used in building, to fill the gaps between logs. For more information see → *Kerpyčius & *Šilinyčius.

*****Šulininis** (recorded as **Szullinnys**) – Pruss. god or spirit 'guardian of wells'. This supernatural being was worshipped in Prussia, where it was recorded by M. Praetorius in *Deliciae Prussicae* 1684: "They assign to almost all things a god, or rather, a demon, under whose rule this or that grows, dies and generally happens. That is why they call for their help from time to time. ... *Szullinnys* stands [as a ruler] over wells."[189] His name is obviously Lithuanian, which was the language of most peasants in Prussia in Praetorius' times. It is quite clearly derived from Lith. *šulinỹs* "well" : *šùlė* "barrell".

Bibl.: BRMŠ III, 148, 260; Fraenkel II, 1032; LPG 521, 545; Prae 4, kap. 9, §XXIV; Smoczyński 2018, 1424.

Tabakas māte "Mother of Tobacco", see → **Mātes**

Tarškulis – one of the sobriquets os Lith. thunder god → Perkūnas. It is derived from the Lith. verb *tarškėti*, which means "to make noise, to rattle" (and other, similar, meanings).

Bibl.: BMRT 111; Fraenkel I, 1063; Smoczyński 2018, 1452.

Tavvals – Lithuanian deity. Chronicler J. Łasicki (known better under the Latin version of his name, Lasicius) described numerous Lithuanian gods in his book *De Diis* 1584. Among other gods, he mentions T. and characterizes him this way: "God – a supporter of art (or crafts and skills)."[190] T. might be a distortion of the theonym → *Teljavelis. This god has been described as a sky blacksmith – a craftsman indeed. According to other interpretations, T. is a distortion of the Lithuanian word *tėvėlis* "daddy", i.e. the diminutive form of *tėvas* "father". Nevertheless, it is also possible that the name T. is a cross between the theonym *Teljavelis and the word *tėvėlis* "daddy".

Bibl.: Kregždys 2011b; LPG 54, 67, 68, 356; Smoczyński 2018, 1476.

*Teljavelis – Lithuanian ,celestial smith'. The first reference about this deity appears in Galician-Volhynian annals of AD 1252: "His baptism was only a trick and he secretly worshipped his gods, first Nonaděj, Teljavel, Diverikis, the hare god [and?] Mějdějn. When he took a ride on a field and on this field ran into a hare, he must not walk into a forest, nor break off a twig. He worshipped his gods, allowed the burning of

[189] *Sie schreiben noch fast einem jeglichem Dinge einen Gott, oder einen Dae-mon vielmehr, zu, unter dessen Regierung dieses oder jenes fortgeht, wächst oder zu nicht kömpt, deswegen sie sie auch bisweilen als Helfer anrufen. ... Szullinnys der den Brunnen vorsteht.*
[190] *Deus auctor facultatum.*

bodies of the dead and apparently clung to paganism."[191] More detailed is the supplement to the Old Russian / Church Slavonic translation of the world's history called *Chronographia* by Ioannes Malalas from Antiochia (491–578), referring to AD 1261. We are informed about Sovij and his introduction of several pagan deities among the Baltic tribes, namely Lithuanians, Jatvingians, Prussians, and also Livonians and Jäms [= Estonians]: "... Sovij introduced the superstition of bringing sacrifices to terrible gods *Andai* and *Perkunъ*, called 'thunder', and to *Žvoruna*, called 'bitch', and to *Teljavelь* – the smith who forged out the Sun to shine upon the Earth and who placed the Sun upon the heavens."[192] The quoted fragments imply that in the 13th cent. in the Lithuanian pantheon *T. occured in the neighbourhood of the Thunder-God, independently of his name → Perkunas or Diviriks.[193] *T. is a smith, who forged the Sun and placed it on the sky (→ sky). From numerous etymologies of his name only two reflect his role as a smith. According to the Baltic etymology the theonym represents a corruption of the Lithuanian diminutive *kalvēlis* from the word *kálvis* "smith" (Wolter). The change of vowels in the first and second syllables can be accepted as a common scribal mistake in transcription of an unknown proper name. The substitution of *t-* for *k-* looks less probable, but it was also possible. Polish Baltist Smoczyński mentions that scribes writing in German mutually exchanged *k* and *t* in positions before front vowels. Still more probable is this explanation in the case of a scribe, whose mother tongue is East Slavic, where the softness correlation plays a much stronger role than in German. A more attractive solution was proposed by Toporov (1970, 537–43). He judged that the names of *Teljavelis* & *Tavvals* represent adaptations of the Old Norse name *Þjálfi*, a helper of the Thunder-God *Þórr*. Etymologically connected with *Þjálfi* is the name of the cultural hero *Þjelvar*, who after *Gutasaga* established the Island of Gotland as a dry landmass, when he went round the

---

[191] *Kreščenie že ego lьstivo byst: žrjaše bogomъ svoimъ vtaině, pervomu Nъnadějevi, i Teljaveli i Diverikъzu, zaejačemu bogu*(,) *Mějdějnu: egda vyěxaše na pole i vyběgnjaše zajacь na pole, v lěsъ roščenija ne voxožaše vnu i ne smějaše ni rozgy ulomiti, i bogomъ svoimъ žrjaše, i mertvyxъ telesa sožigaše, i poganьstvo svoe javě tvorjaše.*

[192] *.. prelestь Sovij vъvede vně i prinositi žrъtvu skvernymъ bogam Andaevi i Perkunovi rekše gromu i Žvoruně rekše sucě i Teljaveli isgkuznecju skovavše jemu slъnce jako světiti po zemli i vъverъgšju jemu na nebo slъnce.*

[193] His name can be explained from Lith. *Dievo rykštė* "Dievs' whip", i.e. "lightning", one of main attributs of Thunder-God.

island with a fire. The name *Þjálfi* is derivable from **Þelban-*, while *Þielvar* represents the compound **Þelba-harja-*. The further etymology is not unambiguous. The following comparanda were proposed: (i) Icelandic *þjálf* "work" by Much; (ii) Old Norse *þiálfi, þálmi* "cuffs, loop".

Bibl.: Blažek 2009, 72–73; Brückner 1886, 1–3; de Vries 1957, 129–30; LPG 51, 58–60; Smoczyński 2000, 147–149; Toporov 1970, 537–543; Wolter 1886a, 640–641.

Tikkla/Tīkla see **Dēkla**

Tirgus māte – Latv. "Mother of Market". One of the hundred Latv. Mothers. Latv. *tìrgus* means "market". Cf. Lith. *tur̃gus* < ORuss. *tъrgъ* "market". For more information see → Mātes.

Bibl.: ALEW 1136; ME IV, 194–195; Smoczyński 2018, 1541.

Trenktinis – Lith. sobriquet of thunder god → Perkūnas. It is derived from Lith. verb *treñkti* "to hit, to strike", and therefore means "the one that has the power to strike by lightning and thunder".

Bibl.: BMRT 111; Fraenkel II, 1118.

*Trimpas/*Trimpā/*Trimpus – Baltic deity of unclear function, but represented in all three Baltic traditions. Lith. *Trimpas* or *Trimpa* survives in the malediction *eik sau po Trimpų* "Go to hell!", which was recorded by the Lithuanian writer, ethnographer and historian Simon Daukantas (1793–1864). Latv. dial. *Trinpus* preserved in enchantments of the type *Laj Trinpus nuo taviem laùkiem, lùopiem, pļavām, dārziem un ganīklām nuogriežās* "Let Trinpus turn away from your fields, animals, meadows, gardens, and pastures." (Trejland 1881; translated by Tereza Kabeláčová); Prussian toponym *Trympauwe*, till the 20th cent. known as Trömpau. In the function of theonym it appears in the Prussian tradition in as many as three or four variants with different prefixes: a) *Antrimpus sal sein Gott des Meers vnd der See*; *Antrimpum, deum maris*; *Wasser-Götter Antrimpus*; *Antrympus Neptunus*; b) *Autrympus*; *Autrimpus der Gott des Mehres vnd der grossen Sehe*; c) *Natrimpe*; d) *Potrympus & Bardoayts ... Castor & Pollux*; *Potrimpus der Gott der fliessender Wasser*; *Potrympum fluviorum ac fontium*; *Potrimppo* (Grunau, *Chron.*). It cannot be decided whether or not the prefix *an-* is a result of a scribal mistake instead of the prefix *au-*. And the rare occurence of the prefix *na-* allows us to speculate about replacement of *na-* for *an-*, which should be finally *au-*. The four variants are thus reduced to only two prefixes *au-* and *pa-*. The Prussian prefix *au-*

corresponds to Slavic *u*-, e.g. Pruss. *aumūsnan* "washing", *aulāut* "to die", while the Prussian prefix *po*- (Balt. **pa*-) corresponds to Slavic *po*-, e.g. Pruss. *podāst* "submits (to somebody)" vs. Czech *poddá se* id. The theonym has been derived from a verb of the type Lith. *trem̃pti* "to stamp", *patrem̃pti* "to make a path by treading (on snow)". V. N. Toporov drew attention to a remarkable parallelism in the Roman hymn *Carmen Saliare* devoted to Juppiter: *Quomne tonas, Leucesie, prai tet tremonti* "When thou thunderest, O god of Light [= Jupiter], men tremble before thee."[194]

Bibl.: Fraenkel II, 1116–1117; Kregždys 2019a; Mažiulis III, 302, 334; MV 751–52; Smoczyński 2018, 1510; Toporov, *Prusskij jazyk* I, 176.

tukšumi – Latv. "emptiness". This word is derived from Latv. *tukšs* "empty". It's the name for Northern parts of the world in Latv. folklore and mythology (→ Ziemeļmeita). See also → world.

Bibl.: ME IV, 256–258.

Ūdensdepis, sometime only **Depis** – Latvian ,water ghost in the shape of a toad'. In 1920´s Latvian mythologist Pēteris Šmits recorded this popular superstition: "Till the present time in Lower Kurzeme [West Latvia] people often speak about Depis or Ūdensdepis, which supposedly lives in water and at noon he pulls down into the water the people, which remained on the shore." Janīna Kursīte adds that the Latvian word *depis* means "toad", *ūdens* "water". The compound indicates a water-being in shape of a toad.

Bibl.: Kursīte 1996, 332; LTT I, 356; ME I, 455.

Ūdens gars – Latvian "Water spirit". Similar to → Ūdensdepis, another water spirit was described in Šmits' collection of superstitions as follows: He looks like an old man. He lives in rivers, lakes and marshes and feeds on fish. By daylight he does not appear and leaves water only at night. During quiet nights he sails in an empty boat without oars. At midnight wizards walk to him for water and with the help of it they treat sick persons." Latv. *ūdens /ûdens/* means "water" and *gars* "steam; spirit" (~ Lith. *gãras* id.).

Bibl.: Kursīte 1996, 331–332; LTT IV, 1883; ME I, 603; IV, 404–405;.

---

[194] Marcus Terentius Varro: *De Lingua Latina*, 7.27. Translated by Roland G. Kent.

Ūdens māte "Mother of water" and **Jūŗas** (in the new, simplified, spelling **Jūras**) māte "Mother of the sea". One of the most important mothers among more than one hundred Latvian Mothers (see → Mātes; → world). According to L. Adamovičs (1937) she is even the oldest one of them and from her other, more specialized Mothers had to develop. Although Ū. m. has broader functions than the more specific Mother of sea, she is mentioned only in two historical sources (*Lettische Grammatik* by G. F. Stenders from 1783 and *Vollständiges deutsch-lettisches und lettisch-deutsches Lexikon* by Jakob Lange published 1772–1777), several dainas and one popular superstition, while Mother of the sea appears much more frequently not only in dainas, but also in enchantments and also in three historical sources. G. F. Stenders and J. Lange also mentioned her in their dictionaries. Further she was described by the superintendant of Couronian dukes, Paul Einhorn, AD 1649 (hence much earlier) in the book *Historia lettica*: "... they had special gods and goddesses, as Mother or Goddess of the sea, which were invoked by fishers [...]. And moreover, I heard, the fishers lamented, that Mother or Goddess of the sea was angry with them and caused their unsuccessful fishing." Characteristics of these three deities were closely connected with the elements ruled by them – waters. That Ū. m. could cause damage, is apparent from the following daina:

Dod, māmiņa, kam dodama,	Give me to whom you want, mamma,
Nedod mani zvejniekam:	do not give me to a fisher:
Zvejnieciņa dvēselīte	whole fisher's soul
Ūdens mātes rociņā.	Mother of water keeps in hands.

(LD 9549)

but also the following popular superstition: "When somebody bathes after sunset, Mother of water pulls him down into the depths."[195] But the Mothers of the water element could also be useful to people, e.g. to give them a big catch and even to transform their health or life. The Latvians believed in the existence of so-called "healthy water" or "water of health" (*veselības ūdens*), which can be asked for on a certain day from a source flowing to the east. In this ambivalent character of Mother of water and Mother of sea they resemble the Mother of wind. The folk singers are not

---

[195] *Kad pēc saulītes norietēšanas iet peldēt, tad Ūdens māte ierauj dziļumā* (LTT IV, 1883).

only interested in whether these three goddesses can benefit or do damage, as in the case of most other mothers, but they also describe their attributes. For the Mother of wind it was a ray of a reed and a weft of foam, for Mother of water & sea it was money (i.e. probably amber):

Es redzēju Ūdens māti	I saw the Mother of water,
smiltīs naudu skandinot.	how she clinks with money in the sand.

(LD 30731)

Es redzēju jūriņā	What saw I in the sea?
Uz akmeņa uguntiņu;	Fire on a stone;
Tur žāvēja Jūras māte	there the Mother of sea dried
Savu zeltu, sudrabiņu.	her gold, silver. (LD 30914)

In contary to Mother of wind and Mother of water, only Mother of sea had daughters, although it is not clear, if they were really her daughters, since their name *Jūras meitas* means "Daughters of sea" and not "Daughters of Mother of sea". It is certain that she had maidservants:

Jūras māte, Jūras māte,	Mother sea, Mother sea,
Valdi savas kalponītes:	tame your maidservants:
Sasegušas baltas sagšas,	they got dressed in white shawls,
Nelaiž mani maliņā.	they do not want to let me go ashore.

(LD 30772)

Let us add that Latvian *ūdens* /ûdens/ "water" corresponds to Žemaitian (= West Lithuanian) *unduõ*, besides Standard Lith. *vanduõ*, Pruss. *unds* (*Enchiridion*), *wundan* (Elbing Vocabulary). Latv. *jūra, jūŗa, jūre*, OLatv. *jūris* "sea" corresponds to Lith. *jūra*, pl. *jū́ros, jū́rės, jū́rios, jū́riai* id., and Pruss. *iūrin* (*Enchiridion*), *iuriay instead of *luriay* (Elbing Vocabulary) id.
Bibl.: Einh 584; Fraenkel I, 198 & II, 1163, 1194–1195; LTT IV, 1883; ME II, 122; IV, 404–405.

Uguns māte – Latvian goddess "Mother of fire". One of around one hundred Latvian "Mothers". The first component represents Latv. *uguns* "fire" and is related to Lith. *ugnis* and Common Slavic *ogъnь id. See → Mātes.
Bibl.: ME IV, 294–295.

*Ukapirmas (recorded as **Ockopirmus** and in other variants) – Pruss. "first god of the sky and the stars", or perhaps "first god of the sky and the earth". The most specific information on this deity is provided in the 16th century *Sudauerbüchlein*. This book states that *Ockopirmus* was "the first god of the sky and of the stars"[196] (similar information is later provided by Łasicki and in the "A print", this time calling *Ockopirmus* "the first god of the sky and of the earth"). The etymology confirms the accuracy of this description: the name literally means "the very first one", cf. Pruss. *ucka*- "the most… " (*ucka kusaisin* "the weakest one", *ucka isarwiskai* "in the most faithful way") and *pirms* "the first one". The theonym was also recorded by several other authors; more or less correctly, but pairing the god misleadingly with various Ancient Roman counterparts (*interpretatio Romana*): *Occopirmus = Saturnus* (von Polenz & Speratus 1530; Behm 1644), *Occopirmum – deum nautarum, qualis olim apud Romanos fuit Portunnus* (Malecki 1551). The theonym is also included in several lists of Pruss. gods. In these lists, the name is written incorrectly, though, probably due to inattentive reading of the previous source or due to the scribe's mistake. The most frequent mistake is confusing *m* with *n*: *Okopirnus* (Bretkunas 1588), *Occopirnus* (Hartknoch 1679), and further *n* with *u*: *Occopiruum* (Łasicki 1615). Mislenta even goes as far as to record the variant *Occopurnus*, that is, not only mistaking *m* for *n*, but also changing *i* into *u*. Toporov is of the opinion that the name **Uka-pirmas* "the very first one" denotes "a deity in itself", analogically to Lith. *Dievas* and Latv. *Dievs* that simply mean "god / God". Taking this theory into account, we can reconstruct the original Proto-Baltic formation **Ukapirmas Deivas* "the very first god", of which the first part was preserved in the Western Baltic mythology and the second part in the Eastern Baltic mythology. The first part in shortened form could penetrate into the Balto-Fennic pantheon as the name of the supreme god: Finn. *Ukko* and Est. *Uko* (Kalevipoeg), if this theonym indeed is an adaptation of a Baltic word. Let us mention some details about both the gods, *Ukko* and *Uko*:

Ukko 'highest god of the Finnish pantheon, lord of thunder and air'. His functions are described in Kalevala:

> [9.33–34] *Tuo Ukko, ylinen luoja, itse ilmojen jumala…*
> "That Ukko, the highest creator, god of the heavens himself…"

---

[196] *Der erste Gott Himmels vnd Gestirnes.*

[9.403–04] *Oi Ukko, ylinen luoja, taivahallinen jumala!*
"O Ukko, the highest creator, the god up in the sky!"
[48.356–57] *Oi Ukko, ylijumala, Ukko, pilvien pitäjä*
"O Ukko, high god, cloud-keeper…"

Similar formulations appear in the 'Spell to prevent rain', recorded in 1881 [Honko et al., 1993, 213; translated by K. Bosley]:

Oi Ukko ylijumala	"O Ukko, high god
tahi taatto taivahinen	heavenly father
taivahallinen jumala	god up in the sky
Ukko pilvien pitäjä	Ukko, cloud-keeper
hattaroijen hallitsia!	vapour-governor"

Similar attributes characterize his Estonian colleague *Uko* who is analogically the highest god of the Estonian pantheon (Ajxenvaľd, Petruxin & Xelimskij 1982, 167). The theonyms *Ukko & Uko* have usually been interpreted as "old man", regarding Finnish *ukko* id., cf. also one of his characteristics from Kalevala [12.279–80]:

Oi Ukko, ylijumala, taatto vanha taivahinen
"O Ukko, high god, old father up in the sky"

But the epithet "high" or "highest" and the celestial functions allow us to identify here an adaptation of Baltic **uka-* > Prussian *ucka-* 'prefix expressing the superlative'.
      For more information, see also → **Deivas*; → sky; → world).
Bibl.: Blažek 2004, 193–194; Kregždys 2019c: otherwise; LPG 245; MV 923; Toporov 1972, 294.

underworld – lower sphere of the → world in Baltic mythology and a home of some important gods, the dead, but also devils and hell beings, whose demonization was often caused by Christianity. See namely → Barzdukai; → Bauba; → Drebkulis; → Jods; → Jupis; → **Kaukas*; → Līkcepure; → Nelabais; → Nijolė; → **Pakulas*; → **Patulai*; → **Pikulas*; → [+]Sovius; → **Trimpas*; → velija; → velinas; → Velna māte.

Upes māte – Latv. "Mother of River". One of the hundred Latv. Mothers. There are not many folklore texts mentioning her. Let us have a look at one of the few *dainas* with U. m. as a protagonist:

Upes māte, Jūras māte,	Mother of River, Mother of Sea,
Sargi manus bāleliņus!	Guard my brothers!
Vēju māte, cilā viegli	Mother of Wind, keep lifting lightly
Baltajos zēģelīšus!	Their white sails! (LD 30890)

Etymological analysis of this name is simple: Latv. *upe* means "river, stream", analogically, also Lith. *ùpė*.

Bibl.: ME IV, 300.

Upinis *Deivas – Lith. "river god". His name is mentioned in the *Chronicle*[197] by Matys Stryjkowski as *Upinis Dewos*. He notes that the god rules over rivers. White sucking piglets are sacrificed to him so that rivers have pure, clear water. Lith. *ùpinis* is an adj. form meaning "of river", derived from the word *ùpė* "river".

Bibl.: LPG 331.

urguči – Latv. "spirits; ghosts or souls of the dead". As to the etymology of this name: cf. Latv. *urgučas* "tragedy, catastrophe". For more information see entry → velijā.

Bibl.: ME IV, 304–305.

Ūsiņš, also **Ūsenis, Ūsinis** – Latv. 'god of bees and patron of horses'. The first information about this deity comes from the Jesuit monk Joannis Stribingius, who included it in the report about 1606 missions in the Latv. part of Livonia: "To the god of horses whom they call *Deviņ Ūšiņe* every one of them individually sacrifices two solids, two loaves of bread and a piece of fat by throwing them into the fire."[198] It is also in Latv. dainas where Ū. is mentioned in connection with horses:

---

[197] *"Która przedtem nigdy światła nie widziała", Kronika polska, litewska, żmudzka i wszystkicj Rusi kijowskiej, moskowiewskiej, siewierskiej, wołyńskiej, podgórskiej etc. w Królewcu u Jerżego Osterbergera* (1582).

[198] *Deo Equorum, quem vocant Dewing Vschinge, offerunt singuli 2 solidos et duos panes et frustum pinguedinis, quem in ignem conijciunt.*

Ūsiņš jāja pieguļā   Ūsiņš was riding to the night pasture
Ar deviņi kumeliņi.   With nine horses.
Es tev lūdzu, Ūsiņ brāl,   I plead with you, brother Ūsiņš,
Dod man pāri ceļa zirgu.   Give me a pair of riding horses.

                                                              (LD 30082)

The author of *Lettische Grammatik* (1783), *Lettisches Lexikon* (1789) and one of the first compilers of Latv. folklore material G. F. Stender (1714–1796; often referred to as "Stender Senior"), recorded: *Uhsinsch, swehts uhsiņsch der Bienen Gott, von uhsas, der Bienen gelbe Wachshosen.* "*Ūsinš, svēts ūsiņš* – god of bees; from *ūzas* 'trousers, the yellow wax trousers of bees". It is obvious that Stender's etymology is misguided. Latv. *ūzas* "trousers" is a relatively recent adaptation of the Swedish word *huso* "long trousers" and differs from the theonym by the consonant *z*. Formally, the closest relative to the theonym is the Latv. word *ūsa* "beard", adj. *ūsainis, ūsaîns* "bearded"; but together with Lith. *ūsaī* and Est. *ūz*, these words are mere adaptations of Russ. *usy* "beard". There is also no connection whatsoever between "beard" and "god of bees and horses". It is therefore necessary to find a different interpretation.

The Rgvedic character called *Auśijá-* comes to mind as a suitable candidate.[199] He appears in the hymns dedicated to the divine twins-riders Aśvins; the texts imply that *Auśijá-* is their protégé. Two verses of Rgveda mention his relation to honey and bees,[200] which led the translator of Vedas R. Griffith to believe that he actually is the honey-bee. This double functional parallelism makes this interpretation more plausible than the

---

[199] Etymologically, this is a patronym derived from Ved. *uśíj-* 'epithet of sacrificers and god Agni' (~ Avest. *usij-* 'sacrificer who refuses to accept Zoroastrianism'). It is probably derived from a verb related to Ved. *vaś-/uś-* "to wish, to desire" or *vāś-* "to roar, to moo", cf. Ossetic *wasun* "to sing" (EWAI I, 234–235; II, 527–528, 547–548).

[200] *yắbʰih sudānū auśijắya vaṇíje dīrgʰáśravase mádʰu kóśo ákṣarat/ kakṣívantaṃ stotắraṃ yắbʰir ắvataṃ tắbʰir ū ṣú ūtíbʰir aśvinā gatam* [RV I, 112.11] ("Those through which, o you of good drops, a cask streamed honey for for Dīrghaśravas Auśija the merchant, with which you helped Kakṣīvant the praiser – with those forms of help come here, Ó Asvins."); *utá syắ vām mádʰuman mákṣikārapan máde sómasyauśijó huvanyati* [RV I, 119.9] ("And the little fly whispered honeyed {speech} to you, {and now} in the exhilaration of soma, {Kakṣīvant}, the son of Uśij, cries out {to you}.") Translated by Stephanie W.Jamison and Joel P.Brereton (2013).

one of Elizarenkova and Toporov, who see the theonym as derived from
the root *aus-, which denotes the Morning Star in the Baltic tradition (see
Lith. → Aušrinė, Latv. → Auseklis).

Bibl.: Blažek 2012; Elizarenkova 1999, 134, 148, 608, 616; Elizarenkova &
Toporov 1964, 66–84; EWAI I, 234–235; Griffith 1889[1987], 173; Ivanov &
Toporov, MNM II, 551; Jonval 1929, 139; LPG 442, 625; ME IV, 409–411.

užkalbétojas – Lith. "incantator". The verb *užkalbéti* "to heal by chanting
incantations" consists of the prefix *už-* and the verb *kalbéti* "to speak" :
kalbà "speech, language". More information on u. can be found in the
entry → priests.

Bibl.: Fraenkel I, 207; II, 1173–1174; Smoczyński 2018, 473–74.

Vadātājs – Latv. 'spectre that lures people away from their path at night'.
It is a mythical being of the lowest rank, a spectre that confuses people's
way. Allegedly, it is the soul of a person who died a premature or violent
death and now has to wander among the living and disorient them, until
a certain number of people lose their way because of it, so it can rest in
peace. V. appears in the form of an old woman or a friendly traveller and he
confuses people by enchanting their sight so that they see something else
than what is really around them – e.g. instead of a house, they see a forest.

V.'s tradition is already Christianised, perhaps partly because the
records about him come from as late as the end of the 19th century. The
most efficient aid against the influence of V. is said to be crossing oneself
and saying the Lord's Prayer. The advice to put the right shoe on the left
foot and vice versa, so that the world is "turned the other way round" and
one sees it clearly again, is probably older. The motif of swapped sandals
also appears in the Hittite myth about the god Telepinu.

The name of this Latvian spectre that causes the loss of orientation is
derived from the verb *vadât* "to lead (to and fro)".

Bibl.: ME IV, 429.

vaidilà – Lith. 'magician, troubadour; type of high-ranking priest with
Old Prussians'. Variants: female equivalent *vaidilė* "priestess of pagan
Lithuanians" or *vaideliòtas* "priest of pagan Lithuanians and Prussians";
Prussian parallel *waidelotte*[201] "Prussian priest or wizard" (**waidlōtojis*;

---

[201] Based on this Prussian word, the Latvian word *vaidelis* "pagan priest" was
later created (ME IV, 434).

cf. verb *waidleimai* in 1ˢᵗ person plural conjunctive "for us to do magic", from so called "Third Catechism", *Enchiridion*) is distorted by being germanized, as German is the language of Simon Grunau's chronicle, in which he described the Prussian sacred place of worship Romove, or Rikoiot. It was an open-sky sanctuary consisting of a mighty oak tree, an eternal fire, *waidelottes* who tended to it and the high priest called *Kriwe* who was, according to Grunau, respected by all Baltic tribes. The title *waidelotte* is probably derived from a word related to Lithuanian *váidas* "vision, figment of imagination", cf. Pruss. 3ʳᵈ person singular *waidinna* "to show".

Bibl.: Fraenkel II, 1179–1180; MV 926–27; Smoczyński 2018, 1584.

*Valgina (recorded as **Walgina**) – Lithuanian ‚god(dess) of domestic animals bred for consumption'. A Žemaitian, i.e. West Lithuanian, deity, recorded by J. Łasicki in *De Diis* (op. cit.): *Ratainicza equorum habetur deus, ut Walgina aliorum pecorum.* "Ratainicza is deemed to be the God of horses, while Walgina is a deity of other cattle". The theonym **Valgina* can be of either the masculine or feminine gender, since Łasicki did not explicitly determine the gender. In Lithuanian the nom.sg. in -*a* usually indicates feminines, but may also belong to masculines (e.g. *viršilà* "sergeant" vs. *viršus* "top of something, summit"). In etymological perspective the name was apparently derived from the verb attested in Lith. *válgyti* "to eat", Pruss. *walge* ‚esseth' (Grunau), while Latv. *vaļģît* "to eat a lot quickly" was adopted from Lithuanian. H. Usener thought that the theonym designated the god of feeding of domestic animals, while according to R. Balsys **V.* had to be responsible for nourishment of countrymen, which was based on the meat of cattle.

Bibl.: BRMŠ II, 582, 594; Fraenkel II, 1189–1190; LM I 426; RB 160–161; Smoczyński 2018, 1596–97.

*Vandelučiai (written **Wanduolutti**) – Lithuanian ‚water-seers'.
One of the kinds of Prussian and Žemaitian (West Lithuanian) soothsayers (→ soothsayer), as described by M. Praetorius (see the introduction to the entry → priests). Their name was derived from Lith. *vanduõ* "water". According to Praetorius it was a general term for all *vaidila*s, which were specialized in divinations from water, its waves, foam etc. Their alternative name should be *Udones*. In his book, Praetorius described their special category, recorded by him as *Nerutti* (in modern spelling it would be **Neručiai* from older **Nerutiai*), transparently derived from Lith. *nérti* "to dive" = Latv. *nìrt*). Praetorius characterized them as beings

which "dive under the water and are able to say exactly, if there are or are not fish and if it is possible to hope for a good catch, but also in good or bad weather. It was said that they enchanted fish so that it was not possible to catch them. Once this happened to a warden in Passenheim, who after his prohibition of farmers fishing in the Lake of Leliškės, could not catch any fish there. For this reason he invited one such *Nerutte* [**Nerutė*], i.e. *vaidilė*, who dived into the lake, but could not [or did not want to] oppose magic spells, lest the warden would die together with fish in the lake. Similar witchcraft was described by Hennenberger and Simon Grunau".

Bibl.: BRMŠ III, 164, 273; LPG 552; Prae 4, Chap. 15, §XIV; Smoczyński 2018, 1602–03.

vārdotājs – Latv. "incantator". The word is derived from the verb *vàrduôt* "to enchant", cf. Lith. *var̃dyti* "to name; to hex, to incant, to enchant", all derived from an East Baltic word for "name": Lith. *var̃das*, Latv. *vàrds* id., also "word, speech, invocation". See also → priests.

Bibl.: Blažek 2019, 62; Fraenkel II, 1198; ME IV, 500–502; Smoczyński 2018, 1605–06.

Vęcainis – one of regional Latvian names for a house spirit of the → Mājas kungs category. Literally "old man, old one", cf. Latv. *vęcs* "old".

Bibl.: ME IV, 514, 517; MEnc II, 207.

*Vecais tēvs (written down as Wazzajs Tehws) – Latvian "Old Father"; one of the epithets of → Pērkons. G. F. Stender, the precursor of Latvian national revival (also known in Latvia as *Vecais Stenders* "Stender senior"), in his book *Lettische Grammatik* (1783) and its chapter *Lettische Mythologie* mentions the Latvian term *Wazzajs Tehws* (in the contemporary orthography), which he explains thus (Latvian words are presented in modern orthography): "Old Father, or simply *vecais* – old man; that is how Latvians most often referred to the god who resided in the sky and rode on the clouds to see what people were doing. To this day, Latvians say when there is a storm: *vecais baras* 'the old man is arguing' or *vecais kājās* 'the old man has gotten up'." This implies a reference to Pērkons and V. t. was therefore one of his cognomens. The name consists of Latv. *vęcais* "old" (~ Lith. *vę̃čas*) & *tę̃vs* "father" (~ Lith. *tévas*). The same cognomen for the god of thunder can also be found in Estonian: *Vana-Esä* "Old Father".

Bibl.: ALEW 1228, 1096, 1099; Laurinkienė 1996, 142; LPG 627; ME IV, 177, 514, 517; MV 906, 914; Smoczyński 2018, 1645–46, 1476.

Vēja māte – Latvian "Mother of Wind". Best documented of the Latvian Mothers (see also → Mātes; → world). She is mentioned in 70 dainas and also in folk beliefs, collected by P. Šmits (*Latviešu tautas ticējumi,* vol. 1 and 4. Rīga 1941), and in several tales. Similarly to other Mothers, she is not a chthonic deity and is closely connected to the element she rules – her characteristics also derive from the characteristics of wind. She is, therefore, unpredictable. She can be kind and motherly, to help with winnowing of grain (she can be called to help by whistling), to rock babies and forest animals, and thus help with the genesis of life:

Zīlīte, žubīte, kur tavi bērniņi?	Little tit, little finch, where are your children?
Kas viņus šūpo, kas viņus auklē?	Who rocks them, who takes care of them?
Vējmāte šūpo,	Mother of Wind rocks them,
Vējmāte auklē.	Mother of Wind takes care of them.
	(LD 2094)

But she can also rage, whizz and tear down – that means taking away property and life:

Ai, lielā Vēja māte,	Oh, you great Mother of Wind,
met jel mieru vakarā,	Calm down in the evening,
daža laba dvēselīte	Many a living soul
uz ūdens līgojās	Is rocking on the sea. (LD 30693)

However, even with this activity she occasionally helps humans, by sweeping away evil forces:

Nu var iet tumšu nakti,	Now we can go into the dark night,
Nu nav velnu šai zemē:	There are no devils left on earth:
Vēja māte apēduse	Mother of Wind has already
Velna māti launagā.	Snacked on the Mother of Devil.
	(LD 34057)

If Mother of Wind was too enraged, she could be calmed down with an invocation that started with the words *Ai, lūdzama, Vēja māte* or *Ai, lielā Vēja māte* etc., and that conveyed the wish for her to go to sleep into a dry tree's crown or into dry grass. Dry, i.e. passive plants, in opposition to green, i.e. active plants, were in Latv. invocations and enchantments often used to neutralise an activity or a being dangerous to humans.

Mother of Wind is similarly unpredictable – once caring, once dangerous – in literature, e.g. in *The Tale of Sprīdītis*, the 1905 play by Anna Brigadere (also shot as a film in coproduction with Czechoslovakia in the 1980s). Here, V. m. gives Sprīdītis a formidable task: to watch over her four sons. During this task, Sprīdītis nearly freezes to death; however, even though he does not manage to keep watch over Mother of Wind's sons in the end, she gives him a magic flute. Wind had a similarly double-faced character in ancient Greek mythology as well.

Beside these two faces, V. m. is also tasked with three activities: 1) accompanying → Pērkons and after the storm, throwing gold into the sea (which probably symbolises golden sunlight after a storm):

Pērkons brauca pa jūriņu	Pērkons rode across the sea
Ar sidraba ratiņiem;	In a silver carriage;
Vēja māte pakaļ skrēja,	Behind him, Mother of Wind
Zeltu meta jūriņā.	Is throwing gold into the sea. (Tdz 10505)

2) Sweeping the courtyard and path in → Dievs' and Moon's (→ Mēness) house. According to contemporary Latv. mythologist J. Kursīte, this was her original and most important function, also because sweeping was, in Latvia, one of the symbols of renewal and constituted part of cleansing rituals on significant holidays and in important, transitional moments of human life, such as weddings or the birth of a child.

Apsagrieza Vēja māte	Mother of Wind turned
I veinādi, i otrādi,	To one side, to the other side,
Dieva namu slaucīdama,	When she was sweeping Dievs' house,
Mēnestiņa istabiņu.	Moon's room. (LD 34049)

3) V. m. was also (like many other Latvian goddesses) tasked with spinning and weaving and with helping women with these activities. In the Latvian conception of the → world, these activities were connected to the creation of Earth. This is corroborated by the fact that V. m. wove on a loom with a reed[202] made of real reed / cane, with weft spun of foam –

---

[202] A large comb-like part of the loom, used to batten the weft to the already woven cloth.

dainas suggest that Latvians believed that life was created when water
began to whirl around a stone in the midst of a sea and foam began to
appear:

Skataties jūriņāi,	Look at the sea,
Kādi balti audekliņi:	What white cloths:
Niedru šķieti, putu audi,	Reed of cane, weft of foam,
Vēja māte audējiņa.	The weaver is Mother of Wind.

(LD 31003)

As to the etymology of V. m.'s name, the form *vēja /vẽja/* is gen. sg. of
Latv. *vējš /vẽjš/* "wind" = Lith. *vėjas.*
Bibl.: Forssman 2001, 113–114; Kursīte 1996, 12, 336, 338; ME IV, 552–254.

*Vėjdeivas – Lithuanian "god of wind". In the form *Wejdiews*
"Windgott" the theonym was recorded by M. Praetorius in his *Preussische Schaubühne* (op. cit.). It is a transparent compound consisting of
Lithuanian *vėjas* "wind" & *diẽvas* "god". It is tempting to see a parallel in
the Roman god of the underworld, known as *Vēdiiovis* (Gellius) / *Vēdīus*
(Martianus Capella) / *Vējovis* (Varro). The same origin can be proposed
for the Indo-Iranian god of wind: Ved. *Vāyú-*, Avest. *Vaiiu-*; primarily
"wind; air".
Bibl.: Ivanov & Toporov, MNM I, 227; KEWA III, 190–191; Radke 1965, 306–
310; Smoczyński 2018, 1626.

*Vėjonys (recorded as ***Wejones***) – Lithuanian 'wizards ruling wind'.
   One of the specialized Prussian and Žemaitian (West Lithuanian)
wizards (see also the introduction to the lemma → priests), described
by M. Praetorius: "*Wejones* observed winds and storms and were able to
change or to orient them according to their will. Some people from Nadruva [a part of historical Prussia] master this art and during wildfire it is
possible watch with astonishment, how easily the direction of wind can
be changed. I myself was a witness of it in Nybudžiai in October 1648.
Some of these 'direction-makers' are also able to enchant fire. When they
address by name the fire-angel, they can command him not to do damage." The name of the Lithuanian ‚wind-direction-makers' is also formed
from Lith. *vėjas* "wind" = Latv. *vẽjš.*

Bibl.: BRMŠ III, 163, 273; Fraenkel II, 1216; LPG 552; Prae 4, Chap. 15, §XIII; Smoczyński 2018, 1626.

*Vėjopatis (recorded as **Wejopat(t)is**) – Lithuanian deity "lord of wind". The name V. was first recorded by Praetorius in *Preussische Schaubühne* (op. cit.). He wrote that V. was depicted as a man with two faces (cf. Roman *Jānus*), with open mouth, wings on his shoulders, with spread out arms, in one arm a keg, in the second arm a fish, on the head a rooster. The name consists of Lith. *vėjas* "wind" (= Latv. *vėjš*) & OLith. *patìs* *„lord", later *pàts* "husband; alone" = Latv. *pats*. Praetorius also quotes the synonym *Wejpons*, where the second component represents an adaptation of Pol. *pan*, which has the same function as OLith. *patìs*), while the first component agrees with the first member of *Wejdiews*. The same origin as the first component in names of both the Lithuanian gods of wind, *Wejdiews* & *Wejopat(t)is*, can be proposed for the Indo-Iranian god of wind: Ved. *Vāyú-*, Avest. *Vaiiu-*; primarily "wind; air".

Bibl.: Fraenkel II, 1216; I, 551; Ivanov & Toporov, MNM I, 227; KEWA III, 190–191; LPG 542; Smoczyński 2018, 1626.

*velijā, pl. ***velijās** – East Baltic designation for ‚souls of the dead'. The East Baltic terminology describing the other world (→ underworld) is remarkably rich in both the number of forms and number of their derivatives. As a good illustration may serve Lith. *velė̃*, *vėlė̃* "soul of the dead", pl. *vilės*, *vėlės* "figures of the dead similar to ghosts", with many derivatives like *vėlìnės* and *veliaĩ* "feast of the dead, All Souls' Day", *vėlinas* "devil", with several shortened variants *vélnias*, *velnas*, *veln(t)s*, *véls* id., *velinuvà* "evil ghost", *velniavà* & *velniuvà*, archaic also *velinuvà* "hell"; similarly Latv. *velis*, pl. *veḷi* "ghosts of the dead; time of ghosts", *velēnieši* "ghosts of the dead", *veḷns* "devil". Already in 1793 Josef Dobrovský[203] connected the Baltic designations of "devil" with the corresponding Old Czech pagan god called *Veles*. For the first time it appeared in the beginning of the 15th cent. in the text *Tkadleček* („small weaver") in company with the devil and dragon: *Ký jest črt, aneb ký veles, aneb ký zmek tě proti mně zbudil?* "What is the devil, or what veles, or what dragon did incite thou against me?". Further it appears in the sermon of one priest from the Czech city Litoměřice (AD 1471): *O nechme již těch hříchuov u velesa!* "Oh, let us leave already these sins by veles!". Without the final -*s* the

---

[203] In the letter dated to May 5, 1793. See Jakobson 1969, 585.

name was first recorded in one song already in 1426: *Vele, vele, stoji dubec prostřed dvora* "Vele, vele, there is standing an oak in the middle of a court" (Jakobson). In the East Slavic tradition, there were even two deities of similar name: *Velesъ* corresponds exactly to Old Czech *Veles*, while *Volosъ*, always with the epithet "god of cattle"[204], was limited only to the East Slavic area. Nevertheless, the relation to cattle can be traced also in the case of Latvian *velis*, as documented in the following daina, chosen by Jakobson (1969, 585):

Kas tur skani gavilēja	Who ever does sing loudly
Kapu kalnu galiņā?	up there on graveyard?
Mūs māsiņa gavilēja	Our sister sang there,
Veļu govis ganīdama.	{by her} soul she pastured cows.

In spite of the proximity of the Baltic and Slavic languages, there were preserved, surprisingly, only a few common mythological terms. The derivatives from the root **vel-* represent just such a case. With regard to the semantics of the Baltic forms, the origin has been sought in the Indo-European root **u̯el(H)-*. Its primary meaning "to die" is reconstructed on the basis of Tocharian A *wäl-/wal-* "to die", Hieroglyphic Luvian *arha wala-/wara-* id., and Cuneiform Luvian *walant-/ulant-* "the dead". Other cognates shifted their meanings to "die in a fight" → "to fight": Hitt. *walḫ-* "to fight"; Pruss. *ūlint[wei]* "to fight"; Czech *válka* "war", Ukrainian *valjava* "battle field covered with corpses"; ONor. *valr* "the dead on the battle field"; OEng. *wal-dād* "murder", etc. Among the Slavic traditions Ivanov found a corresponding form in the name of the fairy *Vela* in Macedonian folklore. Other terms with similar semantics appear in Latv. *iļǵi*; *ļeļi*; *pauri*; *urguči*; *vecīši* ,souls of the dead'.

Bibl.: ALEW 1212f; Fraenkel II, 1218; Ivanov 1986, 53; Ivanov & Toporov 1973, 15–27; Jakobson 1969, 580–599; LIV 679; ME IV, 529–532; Melchert 1993, 250–251; MV 923; Niederle 1924, 112–115; Pokorny 1959, 1144; Smoczyński 2018, 1627.

*velinas / *Velinas / *velnias / Vę̃lns – East Baltic ,devil' and a member of the triad of the highest Baltic gods besides → **Deivas* and → Perkūnas/ Pērkons. Lit. *vēlinas* "devil", with shortened variants *vélnias, velnas, veln(t)s, véls* id., *velinuvà* "evil ghost", *velniavà & velniuvà*, archaic also

---

[204] *skotii bogъ, skotьja bogъ, bogъ skotьja.*

velinuvà "hell"; Latv. *vẽlns* "devil". The apparent Baltic loanword in Mordvinian *Velen-pas* designated ‚god – protector of community'. The semantic shift can be explained so that the worship of the dead was transformed into the cult of a domestic godling. For more about the etymology see East Baltic → **velijā* ‚souls of the dead'. *V. is common to both the Lithuanian and Latvian mythology and also his depiction is similar in both traditions. On the other hand, he differs from *Deivas and Perkūnas/Pērkons in several features: 1) V. has no family; 2) V. appears practically exclusively in folktales and superstitions, but only rarely in dainas; 3) V. is not a celestial god, but was connected with the lowest layer of the → world (→ underworld); 4) There is no information about V.'s cult. After the introduction of Christianity V. was quickly identified with Satan and every mention of him was punished by manorial lords. Originally he had apparently nothing in common with the Biblical Satan, nor the European devil. As already noted, he belonged to the triad of the highest Baltic gods and according to the Lithuanian mythologist G. Beresnevičius he was a brother of the supreme god *Deivas and uncle of *Perkūnas. In most folktales, recorded only in the 18th-20th centuries, i.e. in the time of full Christianity of Lithuania and Latvia, V. stands against *Deivas and *Perkūnas. *Deivas and Perkūnas had to keep order and fairness in the world, while V. was connected with chaos. V. has been described as unpredictable: sometimes clever, at other times extremely silly or awkward. He had various strange whims and behaved as a typical trickster. In this perspective he is similar to the Scandinavian god Loki, including his usual antagonist Thor – thunder-god. In etiological myths, which could have been mediated by Slavs from Iranian tradition, V. together with Dievas created a world. Although the main creator was Dievas, V. was more hardworking and inventive. In the world created by them they both appear as bailiffs, but in unequal positions. E.g. V. possesses big herds of cattle and uses a scythe, while Dievas mows his corn with a chisel. Myths do not inform us how V. gained his herds and tools. They concentrate on depicting how Dievas outwitted V. and attained his property and better harvest. In these stories V. is already more silly, trustful and sometimes he behaves as a trickster: he tries to create animals like Dievas, but instead of birds he creates toads and instead of people he creates → wolves. According to M. Gimbutienė V. was the oldest among the three main Baltic gods: Dievas had a shape of a young man, Perkūnas looked like a mature man and V. like an old, gray-haired man. In some folktales V. has several heads (→ Jods). V. is also able to transform into any man of whichever appearance, but also into animals or things, usually of a black colour: black dog / tomcat

/ horse or black pillar. It is possible to recognize three shapes and characters of him, which originated at various times and in different cultural contexts. Although these faces shade into each other, let us describe them separately. V. frequently appears as a hobbling man, is humpbacked and one-eyed. As N. Vėlius mentions, in Baltic mythology these features are typical for "such beings as personify chaotic, violent forces of the earth and underworld". It is V.'s oldest shape, when V. concentrates in his personage the features corresponding to several gods of other Indo-European traditions. M. Gimbutienė mentions that V.'s one eye can be compared with a similar feature of the Scandinavian god Odin [Óðinn], who sacrificed one of his eyes to drink from the well of wisdom *Mímir*, flowing out of the roots of the world-tree Yggdrasill. Cf. *Poetic Edda – Völuspá* 28[205]:

Ein sat hon úti,	Alone she sat outside,
þá er inn aldni kom	when in old there came
yggjungr ása	Yggjungr, Aesir,
ok í augu leit.	and in her eye gazed:
Hvers fregnið mik?	'What wouldst thou ask me?
hví freistið mín?	Why temptest thou me?
allt veit ek, Óðinn!	I know all, Óдinn!
hvar þú auga falt:	Where your eye fell:
í inum mæra	in the mighty
Mímis brunni;	well of Mími'
drekkr mjöð Mímir	Mead drinks Mímir
morgin hverjan	every morning
af veði Valföðrs.	from Valfathers pawn.
Vituð ér enn eða hvat?	Understand ye yet, or what?

In some Lithuanian folktales V. also smears his eye with water from a well, to become all-knowing. But if any man repeats the same procedure, V. pierces such an eye. In Latvian folktales it is the devil, who gives a party with witches, where all participants smear their eyes with a magic salve. They are followed by a man, who sneaked into the party and immediately he sees all in a real light: instead of sausages they eat roasted snakes and instead of meat there are consumed children's hands. The following day in an inn the man recognizes that one visitor is the devil, but he pierces him

[205] <http://originemundi.xsrv.jp/norse/2017/02/voluspa-28/>. Cf. also Kure 2006.

in the eyes. For this reason M. Gimbutienė identifies in V. an "all-knowing god" and stresses his similarity to Odin. The second image of V. connects him with cattle: on his head there grow cow's horns, he has a he-goat's beard and legs and a cow's tail. With regard to V.'s possession of big herds of cattle according to the creation myth, it is possible to deduce that the East Baltic V. corresponds to the East Slavic god of cattle, *Volosъ*. Frequently V. appears in folktales explaining the origins of some landscape features, usually a cave or a big stone: "According to one legend, in the deep past V. carried a big sack with stones along the Lėvuo River. There were a lot of small stones and one big stone. This big stone finally wore a hole and the stone fell down on a meadow by the village Smilgiai. After this the other stones followed and tumbled out onto a field. From that time on the shore of the Lėvuo River lie a lot of stones and this place is called Akmenutė [lit. "Little stony"]. And till the present time on a horse pasture near Smilgiai lies a big stone, lost by V." According to some other Lithuanian and Latvian folktales V. wanted to use the stones as a dam closing a river. Sometimes it is the first morning rooster who prevents him doing it, at another time the thunder-god Perkūnas/Pērkons. In these stories N. Laurinkienė sees a connection of V. with the Vedic demon Vṛtra, who dammed up rivers with stones. And the thunder-god, Indra, punished him and released the rivers. The last face of V. is Baltic. According to the Lithuanian and Latvian traditions there are two typical characteristics of V. = devil: he lives in marshes and it is possible to outwit him. The marshes are "gates" into the lowest parts of the world and is connected with V.'s link with → underworld. Certain mental constraints of V. represents restraints on the world of chaos (→ Velna māte). In Latvian mythology V. also has opponents among animals – he fears a wolf and a bear, which persecute him. But V. has also been a trickster, is strong and laughs at other gods as well as people. He entices them into marshes or teaches them to distill hard liquor. According to one Lithuanian folktale V. skins a man. In one subject of the Lithuanian folktales the devil (= V.) is introduced as an owner of an underground forge, a strong and skillful smith, who offers to a hero a blacksmith's duel. On the basis of this story A. J. Greimas judges that V. was originally the smith, to whom Kalvelis (→ Teljavelis) stole a secret of processing iron, and thanks to it he forged the Sun. More frequently in the Lithuanian and Latvian folklore the motif of permanent combat between V. and the thunder-god Perkūnas / Pērkon is documented. Laurinkienė identifies here the archaic Indo-European motif of the fight of the thunder-god with the representative of chaos, but with some spe-

cific Baltic details. In some Lithuanian folktales V. is hiding in an oak
or spruce or hazel tree (→ Lazdona). Sometimes he directly fights with
Perkūnas, namely in the oak or on the hill – i.e. on the places, which are
characteristic for Perkūnas. In the first plan, it is possible to speculate that
Perkūnas pursues V. for his abduction of Perkūnas' wife, → Laumė, as it
is narrated in some Lithuanian folktales. It resembles the story in which
the trickster Loki abducted Idun, the wife of Bragi (Snorri's *Prose Edda*:
Skáldskaparmál 1). N. Laurinkienė proposes two other hypotheses about
reasons for this fight. According to the first one Perkūnas persecutes V. for
his theft of some important object. This motif is known from Scandinavian mythology, when the giant Thrymr stole from the thunder-god Thor
his main tool, weapon and iconic attribute – the hammer called Mjöll-
nir. In Lithuania similar motifs are known in stories in which V. steals
from Perkūnas a pipe, knife, axe or stone for building a house. The second hypothesis explains the conflict between V. and the thunder-god as
an old Indo-European heritage, having analogy in the Vedic mythology.
N. Laurinkienė sees a parallel motif in the fight between the thunder-god
Indra and some Asuras, especially Varuṇa, Vṛtra and Vala. Varuṇa was first
connected with the Ocean[206]. He had also a relation to horses and cattle[207].
Together with Mitra, Varuṇa belonged among the Asuras. They both cared
for the world order and fairness, and ruled the sky and earth[208]. When Indra
overcame Vṛtra, they became Devas[209]. Although M. Gimbutienė judges
that V. represents a Baltic counterpart of Varuṇa and they have some common features (waters; cattle), V. had other common features with Vṛtra
(building the stony dam across a river), and outside of India the closest
parallels connect him with the East Slavic cattle-god *Volosъ* and the Scan-
dianavian gods Odin and Loki, besides the giant Thrymr. It is possible that
in the Baltic traditions characteristics of several mythic personages inherited from the Indo-European layer merged into one. Not excluded is also
the influence of Christianity, which could have caused the merging of all

[206] Cf. RV 1.161.14: *divā́ yānti marúto bʰū́myāgnír ayáṃ vā́to antárikṣeṇa yāti /
adbʰír yāti **váruṇaḥ samudraír** yuṣmā́m̐ icʰántaḥ **śavaso** napātaḥ.*

[207] Cf. RV 5.85.2: *váneṣu vy **àntárikṣaṃ** tatāna vā́jam **árvatsu** páya **usríyāsu** /
hṛtsú krátuṃ váruṇo apsv **àgníṃ** diví sū́ryam adadʰāt sómam **ádrau.***

[208] Cf. RV 5.63.3: *samrā́jā ugrā́ vṛṣabʰā́ diváḥ pátī pṛtʰivyā́ **mitrā́váruṇā** vícarṣaṇī
/ citrébʰir abʰráir **úpa** tiṣṭʰatʰo rávaṃ dyā́ṃ varṣayatʰo **ásurasya** māyáyā.*

[209] Cf. RV 7.60.12: *iyáṃ **deva** puróhitir yuvábʰyāṃ yajñéṣu **mitrāvaruṇāv** akāri /
víśvāni durgā́ pipṛtaṃ tiró no yūyám pāta svastíbʰiḥ sádā naḥ.*

masculine deities with at least slightly negative connotation into one. With regard to the negative expectations the name V. was replaced by various tabu-names, e.g. Lith. *nelabasis*; → baubas; → būkas; Latv. → Līkcepure; → nelabais; → Jupis; → Nīkšķis; → Jods etc.

Bibl.: Ajxenval'd, Petruxin, Xelimskij 1982, 175; ALEW 1214; Beresnevičius 2004, 153–158; Fraenkel 1218–1219; Gimbutienė 2002, 124–128; Greimas 2005, 153–155; Ivanov & Toporov 1973, 15–27; Jakobson 1969, 585; Kokare 1999, 192–197; Laurinkienė 1996, 141–166; MEnc 222–223; PŠ 157; Pūtelis, p.c. 2011; Smoczyński 2018, 1629–30.

Veliuonà (with Łasicki, recorded as **"Vielona"**) – Old Lith. 'goddess of ancestors' souls'. The first scholar to describe her was J. Łasicki in *De Diis* 1584: "*Vielona* – the deity of souls that receives sacrifices so that the dead are satisfied."[210] The theonym is derived from Lith. *veliónis* "the deceased", *veliónė* "the deceased (f.)". For further etymological analysis, see East Baltic → *velijā, i.e. 'souls of the dead'.

Bibl.: Fraenkel II, 1218–1219; LPG 357; Smoczyński 2018, 1628.

Velna māte "Mother of Velns (devil)" and **Joda māte** "Mother of jods (demon)" – two Latv. mythical beings of lower rank (→ underworld), whose functions are mostly overlapping. Their names are somewhat misleading, because they are rarely associated with → Velns and → Jods in Latv. folklore. The other part of their names places them into the category of Mothers (see →Mātes). Aldis Pūtelis' theory that the name "Mother" suggests the mythical being in question is a personification or essence of a given thing would also speak for categorising these beings as Mothers: Mother of Wind could be the essence of wind and Mother of Velns would be a sort of "supra-Velns". (That would also explain why Velns is usually not said to be her son.)

However, readers who have already familiarised themselves with the entries Mother of Wind, Mother of Forest etc. can easily see that these are a different kind of beings. Mother of Forest is the keeper of the forest, but Mother of Demon being "the keeper of a demon" does not really make sense. She falls under a different category of Mothers: not Mothers of elements, but rather Mothers of other mythical beings. The Mothers in this category are particular in that they, most probably, were not objects of any

---

[210] *Vielona Deus animarum, cui tum oblatio offertur, cum mortui pascuntur.*

cult. Read: we encounter them in myths rather than in invocations, sacrificial formulas etc. It is logical: Latv. peasants needed to placate Mother
of Fire with offerings so that she would not put their houses on fire, fishermen wanted to placate Mother of Sea so that she would not trip their
boats. But V. m. or J. m. were not of any practical use for them.

Their role was different: they symbolised the danger and at the same
time a certain kind of narrow-mindedness of the world of chaos. In folk
beliefs, V. m. steals people's children and changes them for her own. In folk
songs, both these Mothers are usually part of other myths about
a magical bean, told by a young singer. The basis of these myths is similar to the English tale about Jack and the beanstalk, but then evolves into
a typically Balt. story: the hero is given a white (or "Turkish") bean; he
sows it in his garden and it grows into the sky. The hero climbs up the
beanstalk and in the sky he meets the mythical inhabitants of the Latv.
sky or watches the sky wedding (→ sky inhabitants, wedding). In some
variants, he wins over V. m. or J. m with their help. Interestingly, this is
another common point with the English tale in which Jack kills a giant:
according to Janīna Kursīte, V. m. carries some characteristics of a giantess (e.g. she eats lizards and frogs). J. Kursīte says that these variants are
initiation songs. Nowadays it would be extremely difficult to reconstruct
the proceedings of initiation rituals in Balt. tribes and the role V. m. and
J. m. played in them. But it is fairly safe to say that every Latv. young
man probably had to prove his adulthood by defeating and killing one of
these Mothers – in song, in a pretend fight or by defeating a substitute
enemy:

Es nokalu zobentiņu	I forged myself a sword
Deviņiemi asmiņiem,	With nine blades,
Es sacirtu Joda māti	I cut Mother of Demon
Deviņiem gabaliem.	Into nine parts.
Apskrien mani brūni svārki	My brown cloak is soaking
Joda mātes asinīm.	With the blood of Mother of Demon.
[…]	[…] (LD 34043)

V. m., however, also loses a fight with Mother of Wind:

Nu var iet tumšu nakti,	Now we can go into the dark night,
Nu nav velnu šai zemē:	There are no devils left on earth:
Vēja māte apēduse	Mother of Wind has already

Velna māti launagā.	Snacked on the Mother of Devil.

(LD 34057)

What did these mythical beings look like? A typical characteristic is sparkling hair or fingernails:

Es redzēju Velna māti	I saw Mother of Devil
Ābelē koklējam:	Play a kokle[211] in an apple tree:
Pieci pirksti, pieci nagi	Five fingers, five fingernails,
Piecas uguns dzirkstelītes.	Five fiery sparkles. (TDz III, 8260)

Beside fire, both Mothers are often associated with air and wind: "Ķēves-dēls had not ridden a long way when he heard a hollow howl, as if a windstorm were rising. He looked back and lo: he saw the Mother of devil following him and hissing." (Kursīte)

J. m. is also closely connected with water:

[...]	[...]
Es uzkāpu debesīs	I climbed into the sky
Pa pupiņas zariņiem.	On the beanstalk's twigs.
Es atradu Dieva dēlus	There, I found Dievs' sons
Kumeliņu seglojot.	Saddling a horse.
Es tev lūdzu, Dieva dēls,	I beg of you, Dievs' son,
Seglo cieti kumeliņu,	Saddle the horse firmly,
Seglo cieti kumeliņu,	Saddle the horse firmly,
Kaldin' asu zobeniņu,	Forge a sword for me,
Lai es jāju pār jūriņu	So that I can, beyond the sea,
Jūdu māti sakapāt. –	Cut the Mother of demons. –
Sakapāju Jūdu māti	I cut the Mother of demons
Deviņos gabalos,	Into nine pieces.
Man noskrēja brūni svārki	My brown coat got soaked
Jūdu mātes asinīm.	With Mother of demons' blood.
Es tev lūdzu, Dieva dēls,	I beg of you, Dievs' son,
Kur es viņus izmazgāšu?	Where am I to wash it?
Tai upē izmazgāsi,	Wash it in the river,
Kur deviņas straumes tek.	Where nine currents flow. (LD 34043, 11)

---

[211] Latvian traditional string instrument.

In these songs, J .m. is always killed beyond the sea. J. Kursīte and etymologist K. Karulis point out the possible connection with the name of
an Indian water monster (crocodile?) called *Yādas-* in Classical Sanskrit.
In the older Vedic Sanskrit, the word *yádas-* meant, among other things,
"liquid substance".

Bibl.: Karulis I, 357; KEWA III, 17; Kursīte 1999, 67–69; Latviešu tautas pasakas
par velniem 153; LTT 32388–32400.

Veļu māte – Latvian goddess "Mother of *veļi*". One of a hundred of Latvian Mothers (→ *Mātes); together with Mother of Wind, Mother of Sea,
Mother of Earth, Mother of Manure and others is V. m. one of the oldest
and most widely mentioned mother-goddesses. Surprisingly, there are no
records of her name coming from any of the early-modern chroniclers.
That might be because she did not oversee any apparent parts of practical
life. Veļi* is a Latvian word for souls, usually souls of the departed (see
→ velijā). V. m. was the ruler of *veļi*. According to older interpretations
she could originally have been (like similar goddesses of other nations)
the soul of an important and powerful woman, perhaps a queen, who had
passed away. In the 1920s, Latvian mythologist Pēteris Šmits disputed
this interpretation, arguing that it seems to him "very naive to believe that
the véls would live in a republic for thousands of years and the moment
a woman of high social standing died, they would become a monarchy."
The interpretation was later abandoned completely. More likely, V. m. is
a real goddess, though of a "lesser order" than e.g. → Laima. She manifests either as a cow or in the form of a woman with cow's legs (many
goddesses, not only IE ones, took on the form of a cow), or as a woman
dressed in white (among the Balts, white colour symbolised the non-ma-
terial = the other world):

Balta sēd Veļu māte	White sits the Mother of *veļi*
Baltābola kalniņāi.	On the hill under a white apple tree.
Pilna roka baltu puķu	Her hand is full of white flowers,
Klēpei balta villainīte.	Her lap is covered with a white woollen wrap. (TDz 49478)

Folk songs often describe her as rich. In Latv. folklore, the word applies
to beings who have access to an unlimited amount of certain things. In
this case, rather than things it speaks of the souls of the departed, the
number of which constantly keeps growing. The role of V. m. was, first,

to cunningly lure people to herself in order to gain more véls for her realm:

Veļu māte pievīluse	Mother of *veļi* has lured
Manu vecu māmuliņu:	my old mother to come to her:
Ielikuse medus bļodu	she laid a bowl of honey
Pašā dobes dibinā.	on the very bottom of a pit. (LD 27536, 4)

V. m. also spoke to recently deceased people and gave them advice on crossing an expanse of water or a bog in order to reach the realm of *veļi*. J. Kursīte believes this to be an initiation ritual:

Velāniešu māmuliņa,	My dear mother of véls,
Kā pār purvu pārbridīšu?	Haw am I to cross the bog?
Cel, meitiņa, lindraciņus,	Raise your skirt, my daughter,
Bried basām kājiņām.	Wade through barefooted. (LD 34264)

Beside cunning, one of the most distinct characteristics of V. m. was maliciousness. She would rejoice when someone died and she gained a new soul for her realm:

Veļu māte priecājās	Mother of *veļi* was dancing
Kapa virsū dancodama:	With joy on the grave:
Redzēj' manu māmuliņu	She saw my dear mother
Skaistu, baltu novedam.	Being carried away, white and beautiful.
	(LD 27539)

When V. m. fell asleep, a human's fire of life was extinguished and the person died. This belief transpires in this daina:

Kur, Anniņa, tu tecēji	Where are you running, Annie,
Ar uguns vācelīti?	With fire in your basket?
Aizmigusi Veļu māte,	Mother of *veļi* fell asleep,
Izdzisusi uguntiņ.	Her fire has died out. (LD 27523)

Elza Kokare argues that this song springs from the old tradition of maintaining a fire in a house, which gradually came to symbolise the succession and togetherness of generations; but also the belief that the afterlife not only follows immediately after the life before death, but is also very similar to it. Just as a living person needs fire and warmth in this world, so do Mother of *veļi* and her subjects. V. m. was the subject of a cult – in songs, people turn to her politely and respectfully, likely because she was feared. J. Kursīte notes that politeness and respect were common in dainas and invocations to dangerous beings, while – paradoxically – Latvians did not express such respect when they addressed *veļi*, who could not do any damage to them and were the souls of their revered ancestors; sometimes, after the funeral banquet, the souls of the departed were even chased out. As for sacrifices, forest berries were reserved for the Mother of *veļi*. In Latvian mythology, forest berries are an old symbol of death, as well as fertility:

Kur, māsiņa, tu tecēsi	Where will you run, sister,
Ar to krūkļu vācelīti?	With the buckthorn basket?
Es tecēšu odziņās,	I will run to pick forest berries,
Veļu māte ogas prasa.	Mother of *veļi* is asking for them.

(TDz 49487)

Lastly, an interesting fact is that dainas only describe V. m.'s activities in this world and almost never describe her rule over her realm. It therefore remains unknown how she took care of the *veļi* and whether she was a cruel, or a kind ruler.

Bibl.: Kokare 1999, 186–189; Kursīte 1996, 319, 330–331; Kursīte 1999, 63–66; PŠ 12, 14, 30.

Verpiančioji – one of Lithuanian "weavers of fate" (→ fate). Her name is derived from the verb *verpiù : ver̃pti* "to spin".

Bibl.: Fraenkel II, 1227; Smoczyński 2018, 1637–38.

*Viduronys (recorded as **Widdurones**) – Lithuanian ‚seers from entrails'.

One of the kinds of the Prussian and Žemaitian (West Lithuanian) seers (→ soothsayer), which are described by M. Praetorius (see also introduction to the lemma → priests). Their designation is formed from Lith. *vidurỹs* "middle of something; inside; belly", pl. *viduriaĩ* "entrails, internal organs"; OLith. sg. "neighbourhood, person's environment", derived from *vidùs* "inside, middle" = Latv. *vidus* "middle, centre; middle part of trunk, belly or waist". Prophecy from entrails was probably usual in the Indo-European society. As the textbook example the Roman *haruspices* can serve. Praetorius wrote about them as follows: "*Widdurones* are seers or explainers of signs, who are able to predict {the future} from entrails of animals sacrificed to gods. Even in the present time some people from Nadruva, studying a pig's spleen or liver, are able to foretell the next winter, harvest, which seeding should grow up better – early or late."

Bibl.: BRMŠ III, 162, 272; Fraenkel II, 1238–1239; LPG 551; Prae 4, Chapter 15, §VIII; Smoczyński 2018, 1649–50.

Vidzemes māmuliņa – Latvian "Mamma of the Vidzeme region [North Latvia]". One of many Baltic goddesses-mothers. See → Mātes.

Vīkala – Latvian ‚goddess of hard-working girls. She comes to them in the night to weave instead of them'. The Latvian word *vīkala* originally designated a part of women's dress. It was probably formed from such verbs as *vīkst* "to prepare, make ready", *vèikt* "to make, act" etc. See also Latv. → Rīšu/Rīšķu māte.

Bibl.: ME IV, 636; 524.

vilce – Latvian alternative designation of *pūķis* (see → *áit(i)varas*) prevalent at the borders with today's Estonia. It is a female being who brings her master money and foodstuffs. Her name is probably derived from the verb *vìlkt* "to drag, to pull, to tow", most often used by Latvians to denote the activities of vilce and pūķis. V. most frequently manifested in the shape of a fiery snake. Two kinds of v. are recognised: *naudas*, money v., who carried money and had a blue hue, and *maizes* or *labības* – bread or grain v., who carried grain and was light-coloured.

Bibl.: Kursīte 1996, 325; ME IV, 585.

vilktakis, vilkolakis (Lith.), **vilkats, vilkacis** (Latv.) see **werewolf**

werewolf (Lith. *vil̃ktakis, vilkãtas, vilkólakis, vilkalokas, vil̃ktrasa*; Latv. *vilkacis, vilkats, vilkateks; kadars*) – 'mythical being, a human with the ability to turn into a wolf, or a human turned into a → wolf against their will'.

Tales about w. were popular and widespread with all Baltic nations. The belief in humans who can turn into an animal can be found all around the world and the belief in w. was once spread all across Europe. Many theories have been formulated as to the origin of these beliefs. One of them ascribes it to a mental illness (lycanthropy) that causes the afflicted to believe they are wolves; another sees the inspiration for the concept of w. in criminals who hid from justice in the wilderness and lived there on their own. According to Latvian *Mitoloģijas enciklopēdija,* the belief in human ability to become wolf was, if not triggered, certainly strengthened by the desire of poor peasants for the ability to hunt for as much meat as they wished. Lithuanian mythologist N. Vėlius and Russian linguist and mythologist V. N. Toporov trace the belief back in time to the era of totemic belief that the wolf is an old ancestor and protector of the nation. This could have given rise to rituals in which attendants dressed as wolves to please the protector of their tribe, and also the shamanic custom to communicate with wolves in trance. This theory seems to be supported by Herodotus' record from the 5th century BC, about a nation of Neuroi, who, according to his account, lived in the area of today's Belarus: "These men it would seem are wizards; for it is said of them by the Scythians and by the Hellenes who are settled in the Scythian land that once in every year each of the Neuroi becomes a wolf for a few days and then returns again to his original form. For my part I do not believe them when they say this, but they say it nevertheless, and swear it moreover." (Herodotus IV, 105; transl. G. C. Macaulay[212]) Some historians believe he is talking about Slavs, while Latvian mythologist P. Šmits is convinced that the text concerns Balts, because part of Belarus was once inhabited by Baltic tribes. Baltic tales about w. are also, in comparison to similar tales of other nations, highly archaic. Very few of them succumbed to the influence of Christianisation and only few of them feature w. explicitly described as a not baptised person. Neither do Baltic tales reflect the late mediaeval and early modern fear of wolves and w. and the conviction that they are servants of the devil.[213] Interestingly, the nobility and clergymen were convinced that only a person's soul incarnates into a wolf, while Lithuanian and Latvian serfs believed that human body turns into that of a wolf.

---

[212] London and New York: MacMillan 1890 <http://www.sacred-texts.com/cla/hh/>. Visited on June 2, 2021.

[213] Paradoxically, this fear was kindled by the inquisition that claimed to be Christian, but in the Bible all animals are God's creation and nowhere in it are w. mentioned. American writer Barry Lopez ascribes the witch and w. hunts to the fear of the wild, carnal aspect of human nature which the mediaeval culture suppressed. Because the Baltics at the time was still at the outskirts of European cultural events, the fear of w. was not massively widespread among the ruling classes and affected the peasants only minimally.

Where wolves and w. are concerned, Baltic mythology is closest to Nordic mythology. Wolves are the most important animals in it and stories about w. are marked by exceptional imagination – there are many interesting motifs in them. The importance of wolf and w. in Latvian mythology is corroborated by historical sources. At the beginning of the modern period, the Baltic area was considered to be a "land of werewolves" by the rest of Europe, similarly to how later Balkan came to be associated with vampires. This popularity of w. and the fact that Latvian w. (*vilkači*) are far less dangerous than w. in the West, is probably rooted in Livonian[214] folklore, where w. is a popular figure and not at all always cruel or dangerous. It was also supported by the aforementioned historical records: "Often and many times they turned into wolves and ran as werewolves – that is what they were called...," Salomon Henning says about Latvians in 1589. But this conviction was for the most part based on the popularity of the following account in Swedish cleric Olaf Magnus' book *Historia de Gentis Septentrionalibus* from 1555: "The inhabitants of Livonia, Prussia and Lithuania suffer great losses on their cattle from wolves all year long, because in the woods, once the animals venture only a small distance away from the herd, wolves dismember them and devour; and in spite they do not consider these losses as great as those inflicted on them by humans turned into wolves. On Christmas Day when dusk falls, large numbers of wolves, into whom humans from various parts have turned, meet up in an appointed place, and attack both animals and humans with such unbelievable ferocity that they cause the inhabitants of these countries much greater losses than wolves. [...] They break into beer cellars, drink several barrels of beer and also simple, home-made beer[215], and then stack the empty barrels on top of one another in the centre of the cellar; in this manner they differ from wolves. [...] Between Lithuania, Samogitia and Curonia there is a wall, a ruin of a castle, where thousands of them meet at a certain time of the year, and they try their prowess in jumping: those who cannot jump over the wall, as happens to the fatter among them, those are whipped by their leaders. Finally, it is said that also great lords and even most respected members of the nobility can be

---

[214] An ethnicity speaking a Balto-Finnic language. Originally, Livonians lived along the whole Baltic coast in today's Latvia. Only two speakers of the Livonian language survived into the 21st century, and after 2010, it is most probably a dead language.

[215] In Latvian translation *miestiņš* "home-made beer".

found among them. […] Whoever wants to can be turned into a wolf and all his life meet with his fellows at certain times and bring destruction, yes, even death to humans and animals, he will receive from a person who is a master of these enchantments this art of transformation so completely opposed to nature, and this happens in this manner, that he will give him a cup of beer to drink […] and pronounces certain words." A similar way of transforming was also described by Paul Einhorn, superintendent of the Dukes of Courland, in 1627.

In Baltic folklore, there were three different ways of transformation into a wolf: 1) it could be a curse inflicted by a sorcerer, witch or simply an envious person, and in that case the afflicted person could not turn back into a human on their own; 2) it could be a curse under which the person had to turn into a wolf and back on a regular basis (sometimes only for a night, sometimes for a period of up to 3 years; in contrast to Western European tales, this did not happen at full moon but at new moon); 3) it could be a person who turned into a wolf on their own volition, out of curiosity of because they wanted to wonder about the forest without supervision, eat meat, or avenge themselves on somebody by killing their cattle or even killing the person.

And how can w. be recognised among humans? Both Lithuanian and Latvian folk beliefs consistently say that w. can be recognised by a wolf's tail – w. have it even in their human form. The easiest way to find out is to pour cold water over them in sauna: the tail will show. According to Lith. sources, the tail is short and the human-w. sometimes also has remarkable empty spaces between his teeth. Latvian sources mention wolf's eyes or ears. Lithuanian and Latvian sources however disagree considerably on the manner of discerning whether a wolf is actually a transformed human: Latvian sources say such a wolf has the hind part of his body taller than the front. Another way of uncovering him can be applied when you meet him with his catch in his muzzle: either you greet him and the prey will turn into a snake, frog or manure at once, or if you address him: "Dear godfather, give me too!" If the w. is really a man, he will leave half his catch to you. According to Lithuanian sources, such a wolf has a white spot under its neck (if he had a white kerchief around his neck before the transformation), a necklace around its neck, or human teeth.

The first cause of the transformation into a wolf that we listed, enchantment, is less frequent in the tales and folk beliefs. In such a case a person became a wolf against their will when a sorcerer girdled them with a magic belt (the Balts adopted this motif from Russians). The sorcerer could also give a person a magic drink in which a tiny wolf floated, and say: "What I am, so shall you be!" Or the sorcerer cursed a person during their wedding – in Lithuania, these stories often do not end well: somebody shoots a wolf dead and finds out it had a fresh wedding bouquet under its fur. This plot probably sprang up as a result of the old belief that after the birth, at transitional times of the year (solstices, holidays) and during a wedding, a human is most vulnerable and evil spirits, on the contrary, most powerful.

According to Lithuanian sources you could turn back into a human only if a) the magic belt tore; b) someone addressed you by your name; c) you met your sorcerer again. According to Latv. tradition, an honest person had to give you a slice of bread or to wound you.

The second cause of transformation was explicit intention to turn into a wolf, which was used by both sorcerers and ordinary people who had heard about this possibility and wanted to try it. In Lithuania, one could become wolf by somersaulting over one or two tree stumps or between two stumps where in addition a knife was thrust into the ground.

Other ways of transformation were somersaulting over several twigs thrust into the ground, or jumping over several wooden combs or simply taking off one's clothes. Aside from that, Latvian folklore also refers to the possibility of howling and three times going round a tree with its crown reaching to the ground. Similarly, you could also crawl under a tree bent so low that its crown has stuck root, or through a black shirt or a horse-collar. All these acts are complicated and unusual, probably in order to ensure that nobody would become w. by accident. The only exception is taking off one's clothes, but this act emphasises the voluntary secession from human society and disregard for its norms, similarly to the very frequent motif of Latvian tales about W.: stories in which a person becomes w. by crawling naked under the roots of a tree that rise above the ground. Latvians most probably adopted this motif from Livonians, but Latvian folklore sometimes adds that the tree has to be bent and its crown has to reach almost to the ground. Some sources say that one had to pronounce "I want to become a wolf!" during this act, or that the transformation had to happen at a certain time (at night, at full moon etc.).

It might seem that the last manner of transformation is not very risky. However, for a tree to have roots high above ground it has to be exposed to strong gusts of wind or a strong water stream and to stand in an open plain or at the edge of a forest, where it is clearly seen, or at a lake shore, where paths often lead. Even though the transformation took place at night, one still risked being seen (the most well-known Latvian "W. pine-tree", Latv. *Vilkaču priede*, stands on the banks of the Salaca River near the town of Mazsalaca, next to a path through the natural park Skaņaiskalns).

The transformation back to human was simple: you dressed, did a somersault or went round the tree in the opposite direction, or crawl through the root, shirt or horse-collar back. Latv. stories about w., however, often point out that if somebody touched your clothes in the meantime, you had to stay a wolf forever.

Balt. tales also tell the stories of people who were not able to turn themselves back to human. Almost all of them stress the sorrow of people forced to be someone else and eat what they would not eat normally. They compensate by hunting only animals humans eat as well. In some tales, such a man-wolf eventually starts to live with wolves, but never really fits in: he goes to watch people in his old home through the window, and when among wolves, he has to sleep upwind so that they would not smell him and find out he is actually a man; sometimes, he has to hide from them and occasionally they even find him and dismember him. According to N. Vėlius, these tales existed to point out the feelings of people unjustly segregated from human society.

To conclude, let us focus on the origin of the words designating w.: Lithuanian and Latvian terms are usually similar, but the similarity is misleading, because the words *vilkólakis* and *vilkalokas* are lithuanised loan-words from Polish (Pol. *wilkołak* "werewolf" means literally "wolf skin"; *-łak* is shortened old Slavic word **dlaka* or **dolka*, meaning "pelt, skin"; the Czech equivalent *vlkodlak* retains the *-dl-* segment), while the other variants, like Lith. *vil̃ktakis, vilktãkas vilkatakỹs* and Latv. *vìlkataks, vilkatęks* represent a composite of the words "wolf" & "run": Lith. *vil̃kas* (Latv. *vìlks*) "wolf" and *tekéti* (Latv. *tecēt*) "to pour, to run". W. is therefore someone who runs like a wolf. Lith. *vil̃kakis* and Latv. *vilkacis* "wolf" are sometimes believed to be a composite "wolf eye", compare Lith. *akìs* and Latv. *acis* "eye", but they could also be the aforementioned composite of "wolf" and "run", with the *t* dropped for ease of pronunciation. Latvian *kadars* means "werewolf".

Bibl.: BRMŠ I, 118, 124; BRMŠ II, 325, 337, 689, 690 > SalHenn; BRMŠ III, 582, 594 > EinhAbg; EH I, 573; DLKŽ 848, 944–945; Fraenkel II, 1252–1253; Lopez 2004, 228–242; LPG 315, 414, 419, 444, 462, 466, 489, 630; LPT XIII; LTT 32913–32949; Machek 1971, 695; ME IV, 587–588; OlMag; Smoczyński 2018, 1665; Vėlius 1977, 268–279; <https://spoki.lv/aktuali/Latviesu-dievp ibas-paganu/135645>. Visited on June 2, 2021.

Widewuto – character from Prussian mythology; 'one of the two legend-
ary brothers that created a new form of rule for Prussians; this form of rule
relied heavily on the religious reform represented by his brother Bruteno'.
The legend was recorded in the 16th century by Dominican monk Simon
Grunau, who was born in Tolkemit, not far from Frauenburg (today's
Fombork) in north-eastern Poland, in *Cronica und beschreibung... zu
Prewssen*. This chronicle was first printed and published as *Preussische
Chronik* in Leipzig as late as 1876–1889. For more information see →
Bruteno and → *Patulas.

witch – (Lith. *rãgana,* Latv. *ragana*) and wizard, sorcerer – (Lith. *bùrtininkas*, Latv. *bùrvis*). Like in other mythological systems, in Baltic mythology these are people who have supernatural powers and use them mostly
to harm animals and people. There are more records of female witches
than those of male wizards. As the word for a witch is derived from the
root that can be distinguished in Lith. *regéti* "to see", it is possible that
the main activity of these people was not originally causing pain. More
probably, they were soothsayers that saw things other people could not
see: they foretold future and searched for lost things. Perhaps they knew
how to heal and help people by magic as well. It is likely that they ful-
filled several functions of soothsayers and sorcerers that are described in
the entry → priests.
    Some mythologists are convinced that the words *ragana* and Lith.
laũmè rãgana (with similar meaning) were originally names of goddesses
that gradually transferred to their servants – priestesses (see → Laumè
and → Ragaina). Whether that is true or not, one thing we can be certain of: that the concept of witchcraft was later degraded and demonised
by the Christian church, very much in the same way as e.g. *Rugių boba*
was reduced to a dangerous spectre or → Velinas (Velns) took the role
of biblical Satan and European devil. In the case of witches and wizards,
however, not only mythological concepts suffered but also living people.
Those believed to have special powers were spiteful villagers who liked
to scare their neighbours, or mentally ill people, harmless healers, herb-
women, or women who heard about an incantation and tried it out of
curiosity. As we say in the entry → werewolf, witch– and werewolf–hunts
did not reach such a massive level in the Baltics as they did in Western
and Central Europe, nevertheless, numerous witch trial protocols are preserved. They are very useful to us, as we can see what the village wom-
en's magic looked like and what was the common image of a witch in the

Baltics. Most witch trial protocols there come from the 16th and 17th century. To the modern reader, it is clear that in most cases, the accused was not guilty of anything; the prosecutor simply suffered several losses in an unusually short period of time and therefore thought that black magic was at large. Like other European nations, Lithuanians and Latvians believed witches to be able to influence weather: to call a thunderstorm, to cause a lightning to strike or hail to fall on a neighbour's field. → analogical magic was a frequent case, too. For example, in a protocol written in Lithuanian Upytė in 1614 we read about a squire's wife who felt great pain after giving birth, and therefore invited a village herb-woman and asked her to relieve her pain. The herb-woman took two rag dolls, said an incantation over them, threw them under the squire's wife's bed and told her the pain would now be over. The dolls were obviously supposed to symbolise the patient. She, however, felt much worse and died eventually. Her husband later accused the herb-woman of murder by magic.

After Baltic folklore material, it is possible to reconstruct a detailed image of the Baltic witch. This image is quite homogeneous – i.e. there are not many differences between Lithuanian and Latvian witches – and it is even quite similar to the image of a Slavic witch: usually, the witches are old, ugly-looking women who use magic ointment to be able to fly on a broomstick to a hill where they have congress with devils. However, the Baltic witches have some specifically Baltic traits as well: they are not associated with black cats nor bats and they do not only fly on broomsticks, but also on shovels or dry logs. Some mythologists claim these to be fallic symbols; according to Marija Gimbutienė witches generally dealt and were associated with dry wood as with the symbol of death. One of their duties was to remind people of the unavoidability of death and the course of life. Baltic witches knew how to cut the Moon in half by flying over it and how to take on the form of various animals, e.g. a tailless magpie, a fly, a toad or a snake. Amphibians and snakes in general are associated with female figures in Baltic mythology because soil and water are female elements. In some tales, however, the above mentioned animals are mere messengers or servants to witches.

In reading the Baltic folklore material, it seems that the favourite activity of witches was believed to be jinxing, removing by magic or simple stealing of milk from cows. This was done in various ways: the witches either sneaked to the cows without being seen by the cowherds, and then they were able to jinx the milk; or, they took on the form of a toad or a grass-snake and drank directly from the udders. There are many reports of witches being envious of neighbours' good milk and therefore jinxing their cows.

How did people protect themselves from the witches' magic? Let us look at one Latv. "instruction for use of analogical magic" to reveal who has been jinxing one's cows: "If cows do not give milk or if the milk is bluish, creamless and sort of stretches, it means the cows are jinxed. To find out who is behind this, take a broom and sweep the dust from all four corners to the middle of the room. Then, take a woman's blouse, wipe one of your cows clean with it from the head down to the legs, then pour the dust into the blouse, tighten all openings with a string, put the blouse in the threshold and start to beat it with something. You shouldn't beat the waist of the blouse, though, because then you would kill the witch instantly. A witch will come running and pleading for mercy. If it happens that no witch or wizard comes, you will hear later from your neighbours about someone who was rolling on the ground, screaming with pain, at the time when you were beating the blouse."

The times when witches were most powerful were the so-called transition times: the noon, the sunset, the midnight, holidays and solstices. During these times, people would take most precautions against witches' activities: they would stick nettles, brier branches or thistles in the corners of rooms or stables, in the thresholds and ceilings, for the witches to prick themselves on them. Sometimes, they used the pentacle against them (also called the pentagram), which is a five-pointed star drawn with a single line. The pentacle was usually considered to be the best precaution against succubi and incubi (→ lietuvēns), but it was also used against witches and wizards.

Bibl.: BRMŠ II, 213–217 > NarkGail; BRMŠ III, 379–450; DLKŽ 97, 648; Gimbutienė 2002, 55–61; LTT 25285–25343; ME I, 355; RB 345–348; Straubergs 1939; Vėlius 1977, 218–255.

wolf – beast of prey that played an important role in the Baltic culture and mythology and is, together with the → bear, probably the most important animal in them.

Unlike the negative perception of wolves in Western Europe, which gained ground particularly in the Middle Ages (here, wolves were considered to be loving parents, but also cruel, sly animals), in Baltic tales w. was a more positive figure. According to some authors, this could mirror the perception of w. with ethnicities originally living only on hunting, gathering and fishing (then people would have no reason to hate w. if they did not keep farm animals, these authors argue). But more probably, even with the Baltic nations, this treatment was a magical manipulation with the figure of w. as a cruel enemy who in the Middle Ages caused losses to herdsmen and in years of hunger endangered even gatherers of berries. The totemic relation of Baltic ethnicities to w. as a founder and protector of the nation (more → werewolf) can be explained as a kind of magical protection against w. by establishing a kinship.

But beside the positive aspects, even in Baltic mythology w. has many negative ones, which survived mainly in Latvian folk beliefs, tales and legends. Latvians had probably the largest number of taboo names for w.: "Forest God", "Forest Robber", "Forest Man" (→ Meža tēvs), "Dievs' Dog", "Master", "Little Brother", "Dear Godfather" etc.

In Lithuanian and Latvian folk beliefs, w. has supernatural abilities – he has the wit of 9 men and the ability to take away a person's voice. When a w. crossed a Lithuanian's or a Latvian's path or they dreamed about w., they believed it to be a good omen. When a girl dreamed about w., it meant that soon matchmakers would come to arrange a wedding. A dream about a w. also plays an important role in the legend about the foundation of the city of Vilnius (see Appendices). In Lithuanian folk beliefs, w. meat and teeth even heal illnesses.

W. played an interesting role in etiological myths about creation of the world, animals and humans. The Baltic designation of w. with the name "Dievs' Dog" has a special relation to this myth: → Velns watched → Dievs create the man and breathe life into his nostrils. He wanted to model a man from clay himself, but he only kept making wolves. When he tried to breathe life into them, he could not manage, no matter how hard he blew. He went to Dievs to ask for advice. Dievs told him that the wolves would come to life if he cried: "Get up, wolves, devour Velns!" And so Velns started shouting: "Get up, wolves, devour Dievs!", but the wolves did not move. In the end, he hid behind a bush and whispered: "Get up, wolves, devour Velns!" The wolves got up right away and dashed after him. And so they chase him to this day. In some myths the task of chasing Velns also falls on the bear.

W. could be called "Diev(a)s' Dog" because he chased Velns "in Diev(a)s' service", but N. Vėlius believes this designation only came to be under the influence of Christianity.

Otherwise, the Balt. languages preserve the word for w. inherited from the IE proto-language: Lith. vil̃kas, Latv. vìlks, Pruss. wilkis. Closest to the Baltic words are Slavic forms, like Old Church Slav. vlьkъ, Pol. wilk; from other language groups then Albanian ulʼk, ujk, Ved. vŕ̥ka-,

Avest. *vəhrka-*, Tokharian B *walkwe*; everything is derived from the IE stem **u̯lku̯o-*. Related forms have been preserved in other IE language branches as well, with greater or smaller deviations; the greater changes probably came about because of taboo: Goth. *wulfs*, Old Norse *ulfr* id., beside the more archaic feminine form *ylgr (*u̯lku̯í-*), Lat. *lupus*, Gr. λύκος, etc.

Bibl.: EIEC 646–648; Fraenkel II, 1251–1252 ; ME IV, 588–589; 65, 71, 108, 136–138, 148–149, 155–159, 161–162, 164, 166–167, 169, 173, 180–181, 186, 223, 226; MV 946–47; Smoczyński 2018, 1664; Vėlius 1977, 276–277.

world – According to archaeological discoveries, various mentions in folklore and chronicles, it is possible to judge that the Baltic tribes interpreted the world in a perspective of binary opposites, as other communities at a comparable social level, e.g. west – east, day – night, fire – water, old – young, low – high. The opposites were not absolute and no one member of the pair was preferred in relation to the second one, perhaps with exception of the east, connected with sunrise, Morning Star (→ *Auštra, → Auseklis), which was understood as a little more positive than the west, connected with the sea and the Empire of the dead (→ *velijā), located in → underworld. It is interesting that with the exception of the myths about the → sky wedding, the opposition between woman vs. man does not appear in Baltic mythology. The Balts imagined the earth as flat, and in the middle there was supposed to be a huge world-tree, similar to the Scandinavian world-tree, called *Yggdrasill*. In Lithuania such a tree was oak or maple, in Latvia oak or birch, and sometimes only a wooden column. This central tree was divided into three parts. The first part is represented by roots, which were connected with underground, water, amphibians and reptiles, but also with the specific Lithuanian musical instrument called *kañklės*, Latv. *kuõkle(s)*.[216] The second part is the stem, growing above the earth and so relating to all that is on and above the earth: people, domestic and wild animals, bees, plants. The third part is formed by twigs reaching as far as the sky. They were connected with birds, air and celestial bodies. The following lemmas also belong to various natural phenomena: → *Bangputīs; → Bangu māte; → *Beržulis; → *Deivas; → Drebkullis; → *Ežerinis; → Gaujas māte; → *Grubrius; → *Ievulis; → Mātes; → Mēness; → Meža māte; → Mėnuo; → northern

---

[216] PBalt. protoform **kantlijā* is confirmed by the Baltic loan in Fin. *kantele* "harp" (Fraenkel I, 215).

lights; → *Patulas; → *Perkūnas; → *Puš(k)aitis; → Ragaina; → Saûles meîtas; → *Saulijā; → sky sauna; → sky wedding; → Ūdens māte; → *Ukapirmas; → Vēja māte; → Zemes māte; → Ziemeļmeita; → *Zwaig-stikas; → *Žemepatis.

Bibl.: Laurinkienė 1996, 99; MEnc II, 220; Vėlius 1983.

Zemes māte – Latvian goddess "Mother of Earth". She is one of about a hundred Latvian Mothers (→ Mātes, → world). The first part of her name is gen. sg. of *zeme* "earth" (~ Lith. *žẽmė*, Prus. *semmē*). In Latvian folklore, she appears in similar contexts as → Veļu māte, or as a person-ified but further unspecified Earth. In many cases, it is not clear if the source concerns Mother of Earth or Earth as such:

Māte, māte, mīļa māte,	Mother, mother, my dear mother,
Ne tā mana mūža māte,	Is not my eternal mother,
Zemīt, mana mūža māte,	Earth is my eternal mother,
Glabā manu augumiņu.	She cradles me.[217] (LD 27730)

Mother of Earth is most often mentioned as a deity that "has the key to the grave" (LD 27519), waits for the dying humans, welcomes them and, together with the Mother of Veļi, rules over their souls in the Land of Veļi. However, unlike the Mother of Veļi, she usually deals with a person's body upon death:

Lai ir grūti, kam ir grūti,	Life be hard for whom it will,
Grūt' veciem ļautiņiem:	It is the hardest for old people:
Zemes māte kaulus prasa,	Mother of Earth longs for their bones,
Veļu māte dvēselīti.	Mother of Veļi for their souls. (Tdz 49320)

Z. m. also differs from the Mother of Veļi in not being cruel – she does not lure the dying person to herself and does not dance with joy upon their death. She only, like a good mother, embraces them and sometimes also cradles them in her arms:

Šūpo mani, māmuliņa,	Cradle me, my mommy,
Neba mani daudz šūposi;	You will not cradle me for much longer;

---

[217] Literally "she keeps my body".

Šūpos mani Zemes māte   Mother of Earth will cradle me
Apakš zaļa velēniņa.   Under a green turf. (LD 27406)

Some sources suggest that the importance and field of activity of Z. m. were originally much larger. For example, the Lutheran priest A. W. Hupel writes about the goddess *Erdgöttin* ("the Goddess of Earth") in the 4th volume of his extensive report *Topographische Nachrichten von Lief- und Ehstland*; it is highly likely that he is writing about Z. m.: "They have a custom of fencing a tree or empty space, especially in the place of an old house that burnt down, or a pile of rocks, and there they bring in sacrifice to the Goddess of Earth the first milk, butter, wool and money. On the 23rd of April they cut a black rooster's throat in sacrifice to her; there is usually a special rock set aside for this purpose on the above-mentioned site. They hold such a place, which is to them something of a house-guarding god, in extraordinary respect: to climb over the fence and pick a strawberry or a raspberry etc. is in their eyes a crime that inevitably results in misfortune or sudden death. This peasant belief is very old and probably common to all Latvians, Livonians and Estonians." Z. m. also appears in this daina:

Sabarōju kumeliņu,   I fed my horse,
Na ar auzom sabarōju;   But not with oats;
Zemes mōte sabarōja   Mother of Earth fed him
Ar ōrysku ōbuleni.   With a nice apple. (Tdz 54451)

W. Mannhardt proposed that Z. m.'s responsibilities originally also included plants and animals. The above daina had not yet been recorded in his time, but in retrospect, it supports his theory.

    Based on this and several similar dainas, J. Kursīte argues that Mother of Earth was originally not only associated with death and the realm of souls, but with the circle of life itself and also fertility. P. Šmits believes she was indeed one of the main Latvian deities: most Indo-European mythological systems contain the duality of Heavenly Father – Earth Mother, and therefore Šmits concludes that Latvians had a similar couple in Dievs – Debesstēvs and Z. m.

Bibl.: Hup IV, 1789; Kursīte 1996, 329; LPG 622; ME IV, 708; PŠ 26, 92; Toporov 2000b, 239–371.

234 Zemessieva – Ziemeḷmeita

Zemessieva – Latvian "Earth / Underground wife", a specific bogey, which replaces human children with its own children. The human parents can get their child back, if Z.'s child is treated awfully by alternative parents. In this case Z. runs up and says to the mother: "I care for your child so well and you care for my child so badly, that it is permanently weeping! Take it back!" In some folktales appear indications that Z. was supposed to belong to a specific underground people, characterized by big heads and small bodies. According to Janīna Kursīte Z. is a more recent variant of Mother of earth (→ Zemes māte). In other subjects Z. has been compared to → Laume. The first member of the compound is gen.sg. of the word *zeme* "earth", the second component is the word *siêva* "wife" (related are OHG *hīwa* "wife" : *hīwo* "husband").

Bibl.: Kursīte 1999, 67; LTT 16339–16341; ME III, 861; IV, 708; Smoczyński 2018, 1727.

Ziedu māte – Latvian goddess "Mother of blossoms". She belongs among c. a hundred goddess-mothers. Her name was derived from Latv. *ziêds* = Lith. *žiedas* "flower". See → Puķu māte "Mother of flowers".

Bibl.: Fraenkel II, 1305; ME IV, 739; Smoczyński 2018, 1735.

Ziemeḷa māte – Latvian goddess "Mother of North wind". She also belongs among c. a hundred Latvian goddess-mothers. Lot. *ziemelis*, gen. *ziemeḷa* "north wind" is formed from the word *zìema* "winter", cf. Lith. *žiemà*, Pruss. *semo*, Common Slavic **zima*. See → Mātes.

Bibl.: ME IV, 742; Smoczyński 2018, 1736–37.

Ziemeḷmeita – Latv. "Daughter of the North/North Wind.

A being known from Latv. folk and imaginative literature, one of the most popular characters of Latv. mythology. However, her function is not certain; her name itself is ambiguous: it is not clear whether it is a contraction of *Ziemeḷu meita* "Daughter of the North" or *Ziemeḷa meita* "Daughter of the North Wind". (Czech Baltic scholar and translator Radegast Parolek also interpreted her as "Queen of the North" in one of his translations and as "Daughter of Winter" in another.)

J. Kursīte believes that Latvians originally adopted this figure from the mythology of nations living further to the North. In the Finnish epic *Kalevala*, there is a character called *Pohjolan tytär* "Daughter of Pohjola"; Pohjola is the Northern kingdom in the epic. If Kursīte's theory is correct, Z. should be translated as "Daughter of the North".

Except for Ūsiņš, there is no other being in Latv. folklore that offers so many possible interpretations. 1) In dainas, Z. is found in wedding songs in the role of the daughter of farmer Ziemelis:

Kur jūs jājat, bandenieki,	Where are you going, hinds,
Riņķotiemi kažokiem?	In your embroidered fur coats?
Ziemeļami viena meita,	*Ziemelis* has one daughter,
Tās mēs jājam lūkoties.	We are going to court her.
Vai jūs jājat, vai nejājat,	You can court her all you want,
Jūs jau viņas nedabūsat;	You will never get her;
Tai pašai līdzi auga	From childhood, there grew up with her
Gobas zemes arājiņš.	A ploughman who ploughs good soil.
	(LD 14425, 4)

2) Sometimes, she is a personification of North and Winter (cold, snow); 3) elsewhere, she is an empress of the North, which is called *tukšumi* in Latv. "North, Northwest" and, similarly to the West, is usually associated with the realm of *veļi* – the souls of the dead (→ world). In these cases, Daughter of the North appears as a beautiful woman who lures sailors and fishermen – so that they die in cold seas and the realm of *veļi* receives new souls; 4) sometimes, she also commands the northern lights, and just like them, she is beautiful but unattainable.

The image of the Daughter of Pohjola in The Kalevala is similarly ambiguous: she is the beautiful daughter of a wicked witch, who is however not at all supernatural herself; and yet she is seen sitting on an arch of light and weaving a golden cloth in the 8th song. Nonetheless, all these figures have something in common: they are beautiful female creatures who attract men, but the men never get them.

This is the most popular folk song about Daughter of the North in today's Latvia:

Tēvis, tēvis, tais' man laivu,	Build, build me a boat, my father,
Aud, māmiņa, zēģelītes,	Mother, weave sails for me,
Lai es braucu jūriņā	So that I can sail on the seas
Ziemeļ'meitas lūkoties!	To meet the Daughter of the North!
	(LD 30875)

In the 19th century, Daughter of the North assumed a fifth aspect. The revivalist authors' imagination was mostly captured by her beauty, and so she is a thoroughly positive figure in their works. For example, in the epic *Lāčplēsis*, she figures as a benevolent ruler of the northern seas and the northern lights who saves the hero → Lāčplēsis and his friends from her father, the Northern Wind, and shows them their way. The most sophisticated portrayal of Z. can be found in Kārlis Skalbe's neoromantic tale *Kā es braucu Ziemeļmeitas lūkoties* ("How I Went to See the Daughter of the North"). In this story, she has similar characteristics and plays a similar role she did in *Lāčplēsis*, but in addition, she also symbolises the dreams of the young writer: she is gentle, beautiful, she is well-travelled, she has high moral standards and a will to change the world; with these characteristics, she helps the hero to rise above his environment and flee from the narrow-minded Land of the Fat Pig.

Bibl.: APL 207–214; KL 317–321; Kursīte p.c. 2011; L 121, 133, 134–140, 146; Pumpurs 1987, 55–59; Skalbe 1983, 23–31.

zīlnieks – Latv. "fortune-teller". One of numerous types of Baltic sorcerers and fortune-tellers (see → priests, → fortune-teller). This particular one specialized in telling the future by the direction in which certain birds flew at certain moments. His name is derived from the verb *zīlêt* "to tell the future", which in itself is a derivate of *zīle* "titmouse; bird used for fortune-telling". This Latvian noun is related to Lith. *žýlė* "titmouse". The primary meaning must have been "blue titmouse", cf. Latv. *zils* "blue", Lith. *žìlas* "gray", besides the semantic parallels in Russ. *sinica* "blue titmouse" : *sinij* "gray", Czech *sýkorka modřinka* "blue titmouse" etc.

Bibl.: Fraenkel II, 1308–1309; ME IV, 732–733; Smoczyński 2018, 1739.

zīmlēmis – Latv "interpreter of ominous and good signs". One of numerous types of Baltic sorcerers and fortune-tellers (see → priests, → fortune-teller). No details are known as to which signs z.s used to tell the future from. Their name itself is derived from the Latv. verb *zīmlemt* "to tell future from signs", which is derived from Latv. *zìmêt,* cf. Lith. *žyméti* "to denote, to mark; to draw" : Latv. *zìme* and Lith. *žymẽ* "sign" < Balt. **źinm-*, cf. Lith. *žinóti* "to know".

Bibl.: Fraenkel II, 1309; ME IV, 735.

Zirgu māte – Latv. "Mother of Horses". One of approximately one hundred Latv. Mothers (for more information see → Mātes). Judging by her name she was believed to take care of horses. There is not much folklore material on her and therefore nothing is known as to sacrifices Latvians may have offered her or the form she took on. What is worthy of attention, though, is the fact that she is one of the very few Mothers who is mentioned as having a place to live:

Jauni puiši nezināja,	Young boys did not know
kur guļ zirgu māmulīte:	Where dear Mother of Horses lies:
vidū staļļa apakš grīdas,	Inside the stable, under the floor
zaļa zīda nēzdogā.	Wrapped in a green silk scarf. (LD 32499)

This *daina* supports the theory that some Mothers had a specific place of the household dedicated to them (→ Mēslu māte, → Piena māte, Govju māršava). Latvian word *zir̃gs* means "horse"; with parallels in Lith. *žirgas* "horse used for ploughing" and Pruss. *sirgis* "stallion".

Bibl.: ME IV, 726–727; MV 851–52; Smoczyński 2018, 1747.

*Zwaigstikas – Prussian ‚god of celestial lights'. In lists of the Prussian gods his name stands six times in the second position and one time in the fourth position. It was usually recorded as *Suaixtix* (von Polenz & Speratus 1530; Mislenta; Hartknoch 1679), with minor variants like *Suaixtis* (Behm 1644), *Suaistix* ("Sudauerbüchlein"), but also more differently *Swaikticks* (Bretkunas 1588) or *Schwaytestix* ("print A"). Three times he is connected with light, in two cases with Sun (von Polenz & Speratus 1530; Behm 1644). M. Praetorius in his *Deliciae Prussicae* (op. cit.) offered the following comments: "Furthermore no other objects [lit. 'creatures'] are as divinely worshipped less than Sun, Moon, and Stars. They are, I suppose, included under the name *Szweiksduks*. The word itself can mean "ruler of stars" [Praetorius apparently replaced the final -*tix* by -*duks*, probably under the influence of Lat. *dux* "leader, prince"]".[218] Praetorius' conclusion may also be supported in etymological perspective. The Prussian noun in acc.sg. *swāigstan* means "shine, light", the verb *erschwāigstinai* "illuminates, lights up". The closest cognate has been sought in the Balto-Slavic designations of "star": Lith. *žvaigždė̃* & *žvaigzdė̃*, dial. *žvaizdė̃* "star", Latv. *zvài(g)zne* id.; further East & South Slavic **zvězda* id., besides the depalatalized variant in West Slavic **gvězda*. The difference in derivational suffixes led

---

[218] *Ausser diesen sind nicht minder göttlich geehrt worden andere Creaturen als: Sonn, Mond und Sterne. Diese sind, halte ich, unter dem Namen der Szweiksduks angebetet worden. Denn selbiges Wort bedeuten kann ein Sternregierer.*

Fraenkel to an alternative etymology of Pruss. *swāigstan* "shine, light", *erschwāigstinai* "illuminates, lights up", and the theonym *Suaixtix*, namely to the Balto-Slavic root **śveit-* > Lith. *šviẽsti* "to shine, be clearly visible (from a distance), appear, shine, glow; illuminate", OCS *světъ* "light; world (= place, where is light)". In principle, both solutions are acceptable. See also → world.

Bibl.: Fraenkel II, 1043–1044, 1324; LPG 546; MV 893–94; Smoczyński 2018, 1861–62.

*Želus (recorded as **Zelus**) – Lith. ‚divinity responsible for growth of grass'.

Recorded by Praetorius in the fourth book of his *Deliciae Prussicae* (finished in 1703) titled *De idolatria veterum Prussorum*, Chap. IX, §24: They worship one god … [called] *Zelus*, to stimulate growing grass, according to *zelu* ‚I become green'[219]. The correct Lithuanian parallels are *želiù*, *žélti* "to grow up, sprout, become overgrown", *žel̃vas* "greenish, yellowish", *želvỹs* & *žel̃vis* "young tree", *žolė̃* "grass", etc. (Fraenkel 1962–65, 1297, 1322), from IE **ǵʰelH₃-* "green, yellow" (Pokorny 1959, 429–31). In the Old Italic theonymy there is an excellent correspondence in the Latin divine- & grove-name *Helernus*, cf.

> *Adiacet antiquus Tiberino lucus Helerni*
> *pontifices illuc nunc quoque sacra ferunt.*
> Near to the Tiber lies an ancient grove of Helernus;
> the pontiffs still bring sacrifices thither.
> (Ovid, *Fasti* VI, 105–06; translated by James G. Frazer)

Dumézil (1973, 308) proposed an earlier syncopy from **heles-ino-s*, like *ornus* "ash" < **osinos*. It is natural to seek a starting point in *(h)olus*, pl. *(h)olera* "vegetable, soup greens", earlier *helus, helusa* (on the testimony of Paulus Diaconus who recorded the witness: *helus et helusa antiqui dicebant quod nunc holus et holera*, see Dumézil 1973, 307). Outside of Latin there is a promising cognate in Thracian **zelu-* (*u*-stem!) reconstructed on the basis of the compound name Ζηλυ-δηζη (Georgiev 1975, 34), where the latter component should have been related to Greek θεός

---

[219] *So beehren sie einen Gott…Zelus, dass die Grass wohl wachsen, a **zelu** i.e. ich grüne* (see LPG 545).

"god", Armenian *di-k‘* "gods", Oscan *fíísnam* acc. 'templum' etc. < **dʰ₂s-* : **dʰēs-* (Pokorny 1959, 259; Georgiev 1975, 19).

Bibl.: Blažek 2001, 354–55; Detschew 1957, 182; Dumézil 1973, 308; Fraenkel II, 1297, 1322; Georgiev 1975, 34, 19; LPG 545; Pokorny 1959, 429–431; Smoczyński 2018, 1724–25.

*Žemepatis – Lithuanian deity 'Lord of the Earth'. This theonym can be found in the very first printed Lithuanian text, namely the translation of the Lutheran cathechism by Martynas Mavydas (Lat. Martinus Mosvidius, Königsberg 1547) in the rhymed preface: *Kaukus, Szemepatis ir laukasargus pameskiet,/visas welnuwas deiwes apleiskiet* "Throw away all the Kaukas's, Žemepatis's and Laukosargas's,/ leave all the devilish spirits and gods." J. Łasicki in *De Diis* 1584 mentions that *permultos Zemopacios, id est, terrestres ii venerantur*, "they worship numerous Žemepatis's, that is, earthly ones". It is an obvious compound of Lith. *žēmė* "earth" & OLith. *patìs* "lord". See also → world.

Bibl.: Fraenkel II, 1299; I, 551; LPG 280, 356; Smoczyński 2018, 925.

*Žemina – Lithuanian ‚goddess of earth‘. In his *De Diis* (op. cit.) J. Łasicki recorded: "There are still the goddess of earth *Žemina* and goddess of bees Austheia. They believe they both have influence on offspring."[220] It also appears in Daukša's Žemaitic translation of Ledesma's catechism, printed in 1595. In the passage, where the question of who first broke God's law was solved, there were several mythological names: "Especially these {people}, which worship fire, Žemina, snakes, grass snakes [used also for vipers and other poisonous snakes], Pęrkûnas, forests, groves, Mędeina, Kaukus and other devils. Finally these {people} do magic, enchant, prepare potions, cast tin and wax, predict from foam and testicles. And such people who believe in it; these all renounce God, join the devil and behave as equal to our Lord."[221] The name Ž. was transparently formed from Lith. *žēmė* "earth" (~ Latv. *zeme*, Pruss. *semmē* & *same*).

---

[220] *Sunt etiam deae Zemina terrestris, Austheia apum, utraeque incrementa facere creduntur...*

[221] (in historical orthography): *Szitie įpaczei, kurie gárbiną vgnį, žęmî̃ną, giwatés źálczius, Pęrkûną, mędźiús, ałmiś, Mędeinés, kaukús ir kitús biéssus: ir anié, kurie źinauia búrę, nŭdiią, ałwu yr waßkú lâia, ant'pútos ir ant pâuto wężdi: ir kurie tã tiki: ßitie wissi Diewo atsiżada, ir pristôia węlnóp ir vź Wießpaty sau ápturi.*

240   Žemina – Žvėronys

Bibl.: Fraenkel II, 1299; Ivanov & Toporov, MNM I, 439–440; LPG 357, 402; MV 812–13; Smoczyński 2018, 1727–28.

žuvų piemuõ, žuvų karãlius – Lith. spirits "Fish-herder" and "King of Fish". Two kinds of Lithuanian water spirits, known from folk tales. "Fish-herder" was an old man with long hair, who usually sat in reeds and watched over fish "grazing" in shallow waters. He was seldom seen – in the tales, the hero usually only hears his voice as he calls his "herd" or asks fishermen to give back a fish they have caught and which is his. "King of Fish", on the other hand, appeared in the shape of a large fish with a crown on its head. When a fisherman saw such a fish, he knew there were many fish in the waters and the catch would be large. But if he caught the fish with the crown, he had to let it go immediately, otherwise all fish would disappear from the water. Similar spirits are known to Estonians as well.

Lith. *žuvis* means "fish" (Latv. *zivs/zuvs*, Pruss. *suckis*) and *piemuõ* "shepherd, herder" (~ Gr. ποιμήν), plus *karãlius* "king" (< Belarussian *korol'*).

Bibl.: DLKŽ 312, 579, 983; Fraenkel I, 219, 585; II, 1323; MV 890–91; RB 290–291; Smoczyński 2018, 1760–61.

*Žvėronys, pl. ***Žvėroniai** (recorded as **Szweronei**) – Lithuanian ‚priests taking care for sacred forest animals'. One of kinds of Prussian and Žemaitian (West Lithuanian) priests, described by M. Praetorius (see introduction to the lemma → priests). Praetorius mentions only about their worshipping sacred forest animals, especially elks, owls etc. and care for them. Elsewhere Praetorius writes: "Besides grass snakes they considered as sacred also horned owls and elks […]" [on horned owls see → Ievulis]. "Here it is necessary to retell, what is written in the chronicle of Order. There it is written that every man in the mentioned Prussian lands had his own godling, worshipped as his personal god. Some of them worshipped Sun, others Moon, still others stars. Similarly some people took as sacred domestic animals, grass snakes, frogs or thunder. Others took as sacred forests, still others in turn waters. But it is necessary to differentiate the worship of gods from the worship of consecrated things. As gods they worshipped Pikulas, Perkūnas […]. But grass snakes and owls themselves were not sacred and it was necessary to consecrate them. And not only a whole region, but every individual person could choose, what match with gods and what to take for sacred, e.g. one took for sacred

Sun, another Moon, a third stars, that one elk, this one white horse, that one black horses. In this case he partially sacrificed them to gods, partially gave food, partially he only did not slaughter them and spared them in honour of gods [...]. Why this or that animal was taken for sacred, is easily understandable: if they did some work and occasionally this animal appeared and the work finished successfully, then they took this animal for sacred. [...] *Žveronei* belong among Vaidulots, which have worship and take care for the sacred animals in forests, especially elks and owls."[222] Unfortunately, Praetorius did not add anything else, e.g. if Prussians did see in these animals only "messengers of good news", if they thought that they were sent by gods or if they ascribed them any special skills, allowing him to help people. In the 17th cent. the function of Ž. probably ceased to exist or step by step lost its importance. The name of worshipers and protectors of the wild animals is formed from Lith. *žvėrìs* "(wild) animal, game, beast". Related are Upper Latv. *zvêris* "beast", Pruss. acc. pl. *swīrins* "animals", and further OCS *zvěrъ* "wild animals, beasts", Lat. *ferus* "wild" and Greek Hom. θήρ, Aeolic φήρ "wild animal, predator".

Bibl.: BRMŠ III, 167, 255–256; 276; Fraenkel II, 1327; MV 900; Pokorny 1959, 493; LPG 554; Prae 4, Chap. 11, §I–IV, Chap. 14, §XXI; Smoczyński 2018, 1763.

*Žvėruna (recorded as **Žvoruna**) – Lithuanian deity, which appears in the supplement to the Church Slavonic / Old Russian translation of the book *Chronographia*, in the Greek original written by Ioannes Malalas (AD 491–578) to AD 1262. We are informed here about the personage called Sovij, who introduced worshipping several pagan deities among nations in Eastern Balticum, namely to Lithuanians, Yatvingians, Prussians, and also Livonians and Jäms, i.e. probably Estonians): "Sovij introduced the superstition of bringing sacrifices to terrible gods *Andai* and *Perkunъ*, called 'thunder', and to Žvoruna, called 'bitch', and to *Teljavelъ* – the smith who forged out the Sun to shine upon the Earth and who placed the Sun upon the heavens."[223] The closest appellative is Lith. *žvėrìnė* "Evening Star", i.e. ,Planet Venus'. Cf. further *dìdžlóji žvėrìnė* ,Planet Jupiter or Saturn', lit. "Big Evening Star", and *mažóji žvėrìnė* ,Planet Mars', lit.

---

[222] *Item Szweronei sind Weidulotten gewesen, die die geheiligte Tiere in Waldern, insonderheit Elendte, Eulen etc. – beehret und in Acht genommen haben.*

[223] *.. prelestъ Sovij vъvede vně i prinositi žrъtvu skvernymъ bogam Andaevi i Perkunovi rekše gromu i Žvoruně rekše sucě i Teljaveli isgkuznecju skovavše jemu slъnce jako světiti po zemli i vъverъgšju jemu na nebo slъnce.*

"Small Evening Star" (LKŽ). The attribute ‚bitch' is explainable as the Constellation of Dog (*Canis major*; part of it is also the brightest star Sirius), in the Russian tradition *suka*, i.e. ‚bitch'. Lith. *žvėrìnė* is derived from Lith. *žvėrìs* "(wild) animal, game, beast". Related are Upper Latv. *zvệris* "beast", Pruss. acc.pl. *swīrins* "animals", and further OCS *zvěrь* "wild animals, beasts", Lat. *ferus* "wild" and Greek Hom. θήρ, Aeolic φήρ "wild animal, predator".

Bibl.: Fraenkel II, 1327; LPG 56–60, 64–65; MV 900; Pokorny 1959, 493; Smoczyński 2018, 1763.

žynỹs / žynė – Lith. "wizard/witch, prophet/prophetess, soothsayer" and *žynỹstė* "wizardry". Both terms are derived from the verb *žinóti* "to know"; cf. synonym *žiñčius* (**žintius*); Latv. *zìnis* "soothsayer", *zĩṇauka* "prophetess", *zìṇât* "to soothsay" are adaptations from Lith., as *ž-* suggests; normally, phonological change would produce *z-* in the initial position. For the activities of soothsayers see → wizard, → witch, → priests, → soothsayer, and there see references to other articles.

Bibl.: Fraenkel II, 1310; ME IV, 813; Smoczyński 2018, 1742.

Appendices

Lists of Prussians deities

(I) Georg von Polenz, (Lutheran Bishop of the Sambian diocese; 1478–1550) and Paul Speratus (court preacher in Königsberg; 1489–1551): *Episcoporum Prussie Pomesaniensis atque Sambiensis Constitutiones Synodales* 1530 – see LPG 233.

...*sunt autem pro lingua barbara barbarissimi hi:*	*qui Dei, si eorum numina secundum illorum opinionem pensites, erunt:*
1. *Occopirmus,*	*Saturnus,*
2. *Suaixtix,*	*Sol,*
3. *Ausschauts,*	*Aesculapius,*
4. *Autrympus,*	*Neptunus,*
5. *Potrympus,*	*Castor et*
6. *Bardoayts,*	*Pollux,*
7. *Piluuytus,*	*Ceres,*
8. *Parcuns,*	*Juppiter,*
9. *Pecols, atque*	*Pluto,*

The same lists of gods inspired the authors of three other sources. In the left column are theonyms recorded by I.A. Coelestin Mislenta in *Dissertatio prooemialis* (first half of the 17th cent.), in the right column are almost identical variants recorded by I.B.Chr. Hartknoch in *Selectae dissertationes historicae de variis rebus Prussicis* z roku 1679.

Occopurnus	*Occopirnus*
Suaixtix	*Suaixtix*
Auxschautis	*Auxschautis*
Autrympus	*Autrympus*
Potrympus	*Potrympus*
Bardoayts	*Bardoayts*

Polunytis	Polunytis
Parcuns	Parcuns
Pecols atque	Pecollos atque

The third source was written by I.C.I. Behm under the title *Duae orationes historicae de duplici divinae gratiae fundamento*, published in Regiomonti (Königsberg) AD 1644. The left column with the Prussian theonyms was introduced by the words *Nomina nominum, quibus sacrum cultum praestabant, ipso son barbara et horrida fuerunt*, the right column with the Roman equivalents was introduced by the following words *Haec barbara barbarorum Borussoum nomina notabant*:

Occopirmus	Saturnum
Suaixtis	Solem
Auschauts	Aesculapium
Autrympus	Neptunum
Potrimpus	Castorem *et*
Bardoijts	Pollucem
Pilvuvytus	Cererem
Parcuns	Jovem
Pecols	Plutonem
Pocols	infernales **Fur**

(II) *Sudauerbüchlein – Der vnglaubigen Sudauen ihrer bockheiligung mit sambt andern Ceremonien, so sie tzu brauchen gepflegeth*. The text is preserved in several manuscripts from the 16th cent. (see LPG 245–246). After the slash (/) there follows the record of the theonym with its interpretation according to the close „print A" (see LPG 299):

Ockopirmus – *der erste Gott Himmels vnd Gestirnes* / **Ockopirnus** – *den Gott himels vnd der erde*
Swaystix – *der Gott des Lichtes* / **Schwaytestix** – *der gott des lichtes*
Auschauts – *des Gott der Gebrechen Kranken und Sunden* / **Auschlauis** [**⁺Auschkauts**] – *der Gott der gebrechen Kranken und gesunden*
Autrimpus – *der Gott des Mehres vnd der grossen Sehe* / **Antrimpus** – *der Got des mehrs vn̄ der See*
Potrimpus – *der Gott der fliessende Wasser* / **Protrympus** [**⁺Potrympus**] – *der Gott der fliessenden Wasser*

Bardoayts – *der Schiffe Gott* / **Gardoayts** – *der Schiff Gott*
Pergrubrius – *der lest wachsen laub vnd gras* / **Pergrubius** [⁺**Per-grubrius**] – *der lest wachsen laub vnnd Gras*
Pilnitis – *der Gott macht reich vnd füllet die Scheuren* / **Piluitus** – *der Gott macht reich vnd füllet die scheunen*
Parkuns – *der Gott des Donners, Plitzen vnd Regens* / **Parcknus** – *der Gott des Donners Blicksens vnnd Regens*
Peckols – *der helle vnd Finsternus ein Gott* / **Pocklus** – *der Gott der Hellen vnd Finsternus*
Pockols – *die fliegende geister oder Teufell* / **Pockollus** – *die fliegenden Geister oder Teuffel*
Puschkayts – *der Erden Gott vnter dem heiligen holtz des Holunders* / **Puschkayts** – *latine Sambucus, der Gott vnter dem Holtze Holunder*
Barstucke – *die kleinen Mennichen* / **Barstucke** – *die kleinen Menlin, die wir die Erdmenlin oder Wichtole nennen*
Markopole – *die Erdtleuthe* / **Markkoppolle** – *die Edelleute*

(III) Johannes Maeletius [Jan Malecki]: *De Sacrificiis Et Idolatria Vet-ervm Borvssorvm, Liuonum, aliarumque uicinarum gentium* (1551) – see LPG 295.

...quos ipsi Deos esse
 credunt, uidelicet: deum nautarum, qualis olim apud Romanos fuit
Occopirmum, Portunnus*;*

Potrympum,	*deum fluuiorum ac fontium;*
Piluitum,	*deum divitiarum quem latini* **Plutum** *uocant;*
Pergrubrium,	*deum ueris;*
Pargnum,	*deum tonitruum ac tempestatum;*
Pocclum,	*deum inferni et tenebrarum;*
Poccollum,	*deum aëreorum spirituum;*
Putscaetum,	*deum qui sacros lucos tuetur;*
Auscautum,	*deum incolumitatis et aegritudinis;*
Marcoppolum,	*deum magnatum et nobilium;*
Barstuccas,	*quos Germani Erdmenlen, hoc est, subter-raneos uocant...*

(IV) J. Łasicki: *De Diis* (op. cit.; 1615) – see LPG 362. The list of the theonyms, as well as the comments are almost identical with the version of Johannes Maeletius:

...quos ipsi deos essecredunt, uidelicet: deum coeli et terrae,

Occopiruum	*maris,*
Antrimpum	*nautarum,*
Gardoeten	*deum fluviorum ac fontium,*
Potrympum	*divitiarum,*
Pilnitum	*ueris,*
Pergrubrium	*tonitruum ac tempestatum,*
Parguum	*inferni et tenebrarum,*
Pocclum	*aëreorum spirituum,*
Pocollum	*sacrorum lucorum tutorem,*
Putscetum	*incolumitatis et aegritudinis,*
Auscūtum	*magnatum et nobilium,*
Marcoppolum	*quos Germani Erdmenlin, hoc est, subterraneos*
Barstuccas,	*vocant...*

(V) *Chronicon des Landes Preussen Collogirt durch* Joannem Bretkium *Pfahrern zu Labiau* (1588) – see Gerullis 1926, 119–120.
The author introduced his list of 14 Prussian gods as follows: *In sonderheÿt aber list man das die Sudawen vierzehen Götter geehret vnd angebetten haben.*
Als

Okopirnus	*sol sein ein Got des himels vnd gestirns.*
Pergrubrius	*sol ein Gott der Erdengewechs, der laub vnd gras lies wachsen.*
Perkuns	*sal sein ein Gott des donners, plitzens vnd Regens.*
Swaikticks	*sal sein ein Gott des Lichts.*
Piluitus	*sal sein ein Gott der fulle, vnd der Reich machet.*
Auschauts	*Ein Gott der verbrechens* (sic!), *der die menschen wegen ihrer sunden straffet.*
Puschkaitus	*sal sein ein Gott vber die fruchte der Erden als allerleÿ getreÿdes.*

Barstucke	*solten sein kleÿne menlein des Pußkaiten*
	diener die wir
	Wicholt nennen.
Marcopole	*die Erdleute vnd des Pußkeitten diener.*
Antrimpus	*sal sein ein Gott des Meeres vnd der See.*
Potrimpus	*der Gott der fliessender wasser.*
Bardoaits	*Ein Gott vber die Schiffe.*
Pikols	*der Hellen vnd der Finsternis Gott.*
Pikoliuni	*die fliegende Geister oder Teuffel.*

(VI)
Vilnius – Mythical History

Matys Stryjkowski: *Kronika polska, litewska, żmudzka i wszystkicj Rusi kijowskiej,
moskowiewskiej, siewierskiej, wołyńskiej, podgórskiej etc. w Królewcu u Jerżego
Osterbergera* (1582) <https://wolnelektury.pl/media/book/pdf/stryjkowski-kro-
nika-polska-litewska-zmudzka-i-wszystkiej-rusi.pdf>. Visited on June 2, 2021.

*Swinterog Utenussowic wielki xiądz Litewski, w zeszłych leciech staru-
szek, mając pokój od Krzyżaków Pruskich, którzy w ten czas mieli co czy-
nie z Prussy pogany, spokojnie w Litwie panował, a potym syna Germonta
xiążę Zmodźkie za żywota swego, na xięstwo wielkie Litewskie panom
i bojarom zalecił i naznaczył, aby go sobie za pana wczas wybrali. A gdy
z trafunku, z Germuntem przerzeczonym synem swoim wielki xiądz Litewski Swintorog jachał w łowy, podobało mu się miejsce w puszczy bardzo
ozdobne miedzy górami, gdzie rzeka Wilna wpada w Wilją, i prosił syna
swego Germunta przykazując mu, aby na tym miejscu i między tymi rze-
kami po śmierci ciało jego według obyczaju pogrzebu pogańskiego spalił,
i aby już potym nie gdzie indzie, jedno na tymże miejscu jednym, ciała
inszych xiążąt Litewskich, także panów i bojar zacniejszych palono,
i pogrzeby odprawowano: bo przedtym palili trupy martwe na tym miejscu gdzie kto umarł. Potym też Swintorog Utenussowic rychło dokonał
żywota swego w Nowogrodku, zostawiwszy syna Germonta na państwo
Litewskie, a wykonał wieku swego lat 98, a na xięstwie Litewskim tylko
2 lecie. Giermont jeszcze za żywota ojcowskiego, będąc na wielkie xięstwo Litewskie, Ruskie i Żmodźkie, spólnym wszech stanów zezwolenim
wybrany, po śmierci zaś ojcowskiej, roku 1272, w Kiernowie był na stolicę w czapce xiążęcej podnoszony, według obyczaju zdawna zwykłego,*

i od przodków podanego. Potym czyniąc dosić roskazaniu, i wolej ojcow-
skiej, uczynił i założył wielkie zhlisce między górami, na tym miejscu
gdzie Wilna rzeka do Wiliej wpada; lassy wszystki okoliczne kazał wysiec,
a uprzątnąwszy plac szeroki, poświęcił ono miejsce, z worozbitami swo-
imi, obyczajem pogańskim, nabiwszy bydła rozmaitego bogom swoim
na ofiarę; tamże naprzód ciało ojca swego Swintoroga Utenussowica,
według zwyczaju spalił, ubrawszy go w zbroję i w szaty jego co nadroższe,
i szablę, sajdak, włócznią, chartów z wyżłami po parze, jastrzęba, sokoła
i konia żywotnego, na którym sam jezdzywał, i sługę albo kochanka jego,
nawierniejszego i namilszego, żywego z nim pospołu spalili, złożywszy
wielki stos drew dębowych i sosnowych; rysie zaś i niedźwiedzie pazno-
gcie, panowie i bojarowie około stojąc w ogień miotali, dlatego, iż wie-
rzyli o dniu sądnym, na który umarli wszyscy znowu do żywota przywró-
ceni mieli stanąć, a iż bóg jeden jakiś (którego nie znali, tylko o nim tak
wierzyli) wszechmocny i nad wszystkie insze bogi najwiętszy, miał wszyst-
kich ludzi dobre i złe sprawy sądzić, siedząc na górze wysokiej i przykrej,
na którą górę trudno wierzyli wieść bez paznogci rysich albo niedźwie-
dzich. ... A w Trokach się nowa stolica xiążąt Litewskich poczęła; ale nie
długo trwała, bo Gedimin rychło potym zajachawszy w łowy, zwykłym
obyczajem, czynił ostępy nad brzegami rzeki Wiliej, które wony czasy
lasami i puszczami wielikimi, gęstymi a gwałtownymi zawiesisto zarosłe,
łożyskami tylko przechowaniem rozmaitemu zwierzowi tak wielkiemu
jako i małemu były. Tak tedy Gedimin bawiąc się łowami, a z ostępu
na ostęp przejeżdżając, przyjechał ze wszystkim orsakiem dworu i myśli-
stwa swego na zgliska poświęcone przodków swoich, gdzie rzeka Wilna
do Wiliej wpada, od Trok Starych cztery mile, które zgliska, to jest plac
palenia ciał xiążęcych i panów przedniejszych Litewskich, fundował był
na tym miejscu Swintorog, a po nim Germont syn jego, jakośmy o tem
wyższej napisali, gdzie też kapłani Litewscy obyczajem pogańskim bogom
swoim ofiary za dusze zmarłych xiążąt, (bo o śmiertelności dusz, o dniu
sądnym, i o zmartwychwstaniu wielce trzymali) czynili, i ogień wieczny
ustawicznie we dnie i w nocy bez przestanku (jako też ono był w Rzymie
obyczaj ceremoniej Vesti boginiej) na tym miejscu za pilnością kapłanów
k temu ustawionych gorzał, który ogień Litwa i Żmodź, Prussowie,
i Łotwa za osobliwego Boga mieli i chwalili. Tam tedy Gedimin około
przerzeczonych żglisk w puszczy między górami, które dziś Łysymi zowią,
polując, imo inszego zwierzu mnóstwa sam postrzelił tura wielkiego
s kusze, i zabił go na tej górze gdzie dziś wyszny zamek Wileński, która,
górę od tego tura i dziś Turzą górą zowią, a skórę i rogi jego złotem opra-

wione, miasto zacnych klejnotów długo w skarbie chowano, aż do czasów Witołdowych a Witold iż pospolicie s tych rogów na wielkich biesiadach, i częstowaniu posłów postronnych pijał, tedy jeden darował za wielki upominek cesarzowi Rzymskiemu Sigmuntowi, królowi Węgierskiemu, na onym sławnym zjazdzie królów i xiążąt w Lucku, roku 1429, jako o tym będzie niżej. A teras rzecz przedsię wziętą kończę. ... Gedimin spracowawszy się łowami, tudzież iż wieczór był zaszedł, a noc ciemna nadchodziła, do Trok też omieszkał, pocieszywszy się znacznie z zabitego ręką własną tura, nocował w kotarhach ze wszystkim dworem swoim na zgliskach mianowanych na łące Swintorozie od Swintaroha xiążęcia nazwanej, gdzie dziś puszkarnia, stajnie i niższy zamek. A gdy po pracy jak to bywa twardym snem był zmorzony, śniło mu się iż na tej górze i na tym miejscu, gdzie tura ubił, i gdzie dziś Wilno z zamkami stoi, widział wilka wielkiego, i mocnego, a prawie jakoby żelazną blachą warownie przeciw wszelkim postrzałom uzbrojonego, w tym wilku zaś słyszał sto wilków ogromnie wyjących, których głos po wszystkich stronach roznosił. Ocuciwszy się tedy Gedimin, wpadł mu ten sen w myśl. I gryzł się długo sam z sobą, chcąc zgadnąć coby się przez to znaczyło. ... Tym sposobem Gedimin nazajutrz wstawszy, ten sen wszystkim panom i dworzanom swoim opowiedział, radząc się i pytając, coby się im ten sen zdał, a coby znaczyło. Bo Litwa w on czas jako pogani leda czemu wierzyli, o sami burtami, albo wróżkami, jako Rzymianie Aruspicis, extis, avium volatu, etc. tak wojnę jak domowe sprawy zawżdy odprawowali. Lecz ten sen i wykład jego nie dał się żadnemu tak zgoła gryść, aż musiało przyść na Krywe Krywejta biskupa Litewskiego pogańskiego, któremu było imię Lizdejko. A ten, jako Latopiszcze świadczą, za Witenesa ojca Gediminowego był nalezion w orlim gniazdzie w jednej puszczy przy gościńcu, a niktórzy powiadają, iż w kolebce ochędożnej na drzewie zawieszonego sam Witenes nalazł, i chować go dal ućciwie jako syna .... Bo się też tak właśnie i z naszym Lizdejkiem w on czas działo, który będąc na dworze xiążęcym wychowany, w naukach gwiazdarskich, według biegów pogańskich, w wiezdźbierstwach, snów wykładach, (jako niegdy Joseph i Mojżesz w wszelkiej mądrości Egipskiej) był wyćwiczony, aż potym był za Gedimina, nawyszym biskupem albo przełożonym nabożeństw pogańskich, którego z urzędu Kriwe Kriwejto zwano, o którym urzędzie apud Cromerum, Miechovius Długossum, Erasmum Stellam, Dusburchium, najdziesz jasno świadectwa; Ten tedy Lizdejko, biskup nawyższy, nie inaczej jako Joseph Faraonowi ... on sen o wilku na Turzej górze stojącym i o stu wilków inszych w nim wyjących, tym kształtem porządnie i praw-

dziwie wyłożył: „Iż wilk ten któregoś widział, jakoby z żelaza ukowanego, Wielki Kniazie Gediminie! znaczy to: iż na tym miejscu zglisk, przodkom twoim poświęconych, będzie zamek mocny i miasto tego państwa główne, a sto wilków w tvm wilku ogromnie wyjących, których się głos no wszystkie slrony rozchodzi, to znaczą: iż ten zamek i to misto, zacnością i dzielnością obywatelu w swoich, tudzież; wielkimi sprawami potomków twoich Wielkich Xiędzów Litewskich, którzy tu będą mieli stolec swój, rozgłoszy się i rozszerzy z wielką sławą po wszystkich stronach świata, i cudzym narodom w rychle z tej stolice z wielką sławą panować będą. Tak mądry i prawdziwy a ku rzeczy wykład snu Lizdejkowego, Gedimin pochwaliwszy i ofiary bogom swoim na zgliskach odprawiwszy wnet nie długo odkładając, obesłał wołości okoliczne, rzemieśników też rozmaitych, cieślów, murorzów, kowalów, kopaczów i materiej k temu wszelkiej dostatki sposobiwszy, począł murować naprzód wyszny zamek na Turzej górze, na której sam z kusze tura wielkiego był postrzelił. Wymierzył potym plac na nizny zamek na Swintoroze, które miejsce w on czas krzywą doliną nazywano, przy uściu Wilny rzeki, gdzie do Wiliej wpada, tamże zamek nizny z drzewa z wyniosłymi wieżycami, i z blankami Gedimin wielką pretkością, ale z więtszą pilnością, zbudował kosztownie, a dokonawszy obu zamku, mianował ich Wilnem od Wilny rzeki, Także i miasto prętko się przy zamkach nad Wilna i Wilją osadziło, bo Gedimin z Trok stolicę swoje tegoż roku do Wilna przeniósł i tam ją na potomne czassy ugruntował; za czym wielkio zebranie ludzi, jak" orłowie do ścierwu prętko się w wielkie miasto i rozwlokłe possady zgromadziło.

"Svintorog Utenusovic, the great Duke of Lithuania, grew old while ruling happily over Lithuania, for his land was not bothered by the Teutonic Knights, who at that time were busy dealing with the Prussian pagans. He then recommended to the Lithuanian nobility and boyars that his son Germont, who during Svintorog's reign was the duke of Žemaitija (Samogitia), should be the head of the Grand Duchy of Lithuanian and Svintorog suggested that they elect Germont in due time. Once, when the great Duke of Lithuania went out hunting with his son Germont, a very beautiful place struck his fancy in the forested hills where the Vilnia River empties into the Neris (Viliya). He asked his son to cremate him after his death at this place according to the pagan rite. He also determined that the bodies of other Lithuanian dukes as well as other noblemen and boyars should be cremated and buried only here, because earlier the custom was to cremate the dead in the place where they died.

Soon afterwards Svintorog Utenusovič died at the age of 98 in Navahrudak. Of his 98 years he only spent two in the Grand Duchy of Lithuania, leaving the task of ruling over Lithuania to his son Germont. After his father's death in 1272, Germont, who was elected the head of the Grand Duchy of Lithuania, Žemaitija and Russia in a common election of all estates of the realm, was elevated to the throne wearing the princely cap according to the old ancestral custom in Kernov.

Then, to honour his father's wish and will, he founded a large cremation site on the place where the Vilnia River enters the Neris (Viliya). He had all the surrounding forests cleared and he dedicated the resulting open space to a cremation site with the assistance of his seers. According to the pagan custom, they slaughtered various kinds of cattle as a sacrifice to the gods. And on this place, he cremated the body of his father Svintorog Utenusovič according to the old rite – Svintorog was laid out in his armour and his most precious clothes, with his sword, quiver and lance, accompanied by greyhounds and other fine dogs (always in pairs), a hawk, a falcon and a strong horse which he himself had used to ride. His most loyal and favourite servant was burned alive together with him on the funeral pyre made of oak and pine logs. The noblemen and boyars standing around the pyre threw the claws of lynxes and bears into the fire, because they believed that on Judgement Day all the dead would come back to life and that some almighty god (whom they did not know, only thinking about him in this way) superior to all the other gods would fairly judge all people good and bad atop a high and steep mountain. It would be difficult to climb this steep mountain, they believed, without the claws of lynxes and bears…

A new seat of the Lithuanian dukes was established in Trakai, but it did not last long, because Gediminas went hunting, as was the custom, through the hunting grounds over the banks of the river Neris (Viliya), which were covered at that time with large and dense forests serving only as a refuge for various game large and small. As Gediminas enjoyed the hunt and rode from one area to another, he came, accompanied by his entourage, to the cremation site devoted to his ancestors, which was located four miles away from Old Trakai.

This cremation site, where the bodies of deceased dukes and the most prominent noblemen of Lithuania were burned, was founded here by Svintorog and then his son Germont as we already mentioned above. On this cremation site, the Lithuanian pagan priests made sacrifices to their gods for the souls of the dead dukes according to the old rite, because they cared immensely about the journey of the soul in the afterlife, the day of judgement, and the future resurrection. An eternal flame burned continuously day and night there under the watchful eyes of the priest-hood appointed for this task (similarly to the temple of the goddess Vesta in Ancient Rome). This fire was considered a special deity itself and was worshipped accordingly in Lithuania, Žemaitija (Samogitia), Prussia and Latvia. In the surroundings of this cremation site in the hills which are now called the Bald Mountains, Geminidas went hunting. Besides other game, he also shot dead with his crossbow a huge auroch on the hill where the Upper Castle in Vilnius is located today. This mountain is therefore called the Aurochs' Hill today. The auroch's leather and horns were set in gold and kept as a treasure until the time of Vytautas the Great, who drank from these horns during large receptions and when he hosted foreign mes-sengers. He then gave one of these horns to the Holy Roman Emperor Sigismund, the King of Hungary, during one famous convention of kings and dukes in 1429 in Lutsk about which we are going to talk later. And that is the end of this matter.

Gediminas, tired from hunting, returned late to Trakai only after evening came and night was falling. He was overjoyed at the auroch that he had killed with his own hands and he spent the night with his whole court in the tents on the above-mentioned cremation site at the meadow named after the duke Svintorog, where the armoury, stables and Lower Castle are located today. Having been exhausted by the hunt, he fell deeply asleep and dreamed that on the hill, where he killed the auroch and where today Vilnius with its castles is situated, he saw there a large and strong wolf which seemed to be armoured with metal plates as protection against any bowshot. He heard the wolf howl, which sounded as if a hun-dred wolves intensely howled together and this howling resounded from all directions. After he awoke from his sleep, this dream was burned into Gediminas's memory. He thought to himself about this dream for a long time and he wanted to know what it meant. When Geminidas got up the next day in this state of mind, he told all his noblemen and courtiers about this dream and sought their counsel.

In Lithuania at that time, the people (still pagans) believed in all sorts of things, and they sought advice on military and domestic matters from priests and soothsayers, in the same way that the Ancient Romans had consulted their soothsayers who foretold the future from the entrails of animals or the flight of birds. However, no one could explain this dream, besides the Krive Krivaitis, the office of the Lithuanian pagan high priest whose name was Lizdejko. As the Annals from the time of Vitenes father of Gediminas testify, Lizdejko had been found in the forest during a princ´s visit and some sources claim that it was Vitenes himself who found Lizdejko in a cradle hanging from a tree and him brought up as his own son...

Thus went the story of Lizdejko, who was brought up at the duke's court and educated in astronomy, divination and dream interpretation (as once Joseph and Moses were schooled in the lore of the Egyptians), so that he could become the High Priest during the reign of Gediminas. He served as a representative of Lithuanian pagan belief and held an office called the Krive Krivaitis, about which Cromer, Miechovius, Długosz, Erasmus Stella, and Dusburg found clear testimony.

So this Lizdejko, the High Priest, not so differently from Joseph with the Pharaoh, explained to Gediminas the latter's dream about the Aurochs' Hill and the hundred wolves howling:

'The fact that you, the Grand Duke, saw a wolf which seemed to be hammered out of iron means the following: at that place where the burial site devoted to your ancestors is located, one day a huge castle and the capital of this state will stand. The howling of the hundred wolves from the throat of that one wolf which resounded in all the directions means that the fame of that castle and city will spread all over the world. Its inhabitants will be well known for their generosity and diligence. Your descendants, the great dukes of Lithuania, who will have their seat there, will perform great deeds to bring Lithuania fame, and they will rule over foreign nations from this seat with splendour.'

Geminidas praised Lizdejko for his wise, truthful and factual dream interpretation and did not hesitate to bring sacrifices to his gods on the burial site for long. He asked the surrounding villages to send him craftsmen, carpenters, masons, smiths and diggers and plenty of building material and he started with the construction of the Upper Castle on the hill where he himself had shot the auroch with his crossbow. He then demarcated an area for the Lower Castle at Svintorog, which was then called the Crooked Valley. This was near the mouth of the Vilnia River which empties into the Neris (Vilija). At this place, Geminidas had the Lower Castle built at great speed and with even greater diligence. This castle was costly, built from wood with high towers and battlements. Having finished the construction of both castles, he named them Vilno after the Vilnia River. The population of the city around the castles overlooking the Vilnia River and Neris (Vilija) grew quickly, because Gediminas moved his seat from Trakai into Vilno in the same year and confirmed it in the years to come. Therefore, people gathered in multitudes, just as eagles swoop on their prey, and the area turned into a big city."

Translated from Old Polish into English by
Zuzana Handlová (née Malášková) & Václav Blažek

Bibliography

Adamovičs, Ludvigs. 1937. *Senlatviešu reliģija vēlajā dzelzs laikmetā*. Rīga: Kr. Barona biedrības apgāds.

Ajxenval'd, A. Ju. & Petruxin, V. Ja. & Xelimskij, E. A. 1982. K rekonstrukcii mifologičeskix predstavlenij finno-ugorskix narodov. *BSI* [1981], 162–192.

Akeliewicz (Akielewicz, Akelaitis), Mikalojus. 1863. Uwagi. In: *Pisma rozmaite*. T. III, ed. Lelewel, Joachim. Poznań: Żupański.

ALEW = *Altlitauisches etymologisches Wörterbuch*. Unter Leitung von Wolfgang Hock und der Mitarbeit von Elvyra-Julija Bukevičiūtė und Christiane Schiller bearbeitet von Rainer Fecht, Anna Helene Feulner, Eugen Hill und Dagmar S. Wodtko. Bd. I: A-M, Bd. II: N-Ž, Bd. III: *Verzeichnisse und Indices*. Hamburg: Baar, 2015.

APL = Pumpurs, Andrejs. 1988. *Lāčplēsis, latvju tautas varonis*. Rīga: Zinātne.

Balsys, Rimantas. 2006. *Lietuvių ir prūsų dievai, deivės, dvasios: nuo apeigos iki prietaro*. Klaipėda: Klaipėdos universiteto leidykla.

Balsys, Rimantas. 2015. (Review of) Běťáková, M. E. & Blažek, V.: *Encyklopedie baltské mytologie* (Praha: Libri 2012). *Slověne* 2015, N. 2, 247–254. <https://www.researchgate.net/publication/298177261_Encyclopedia_of_Baltic_Mythology_in_Czech_or_As_Some_Sleep_Others_Must_Keep_Vigil> Visited on June 2, 2021.

Baltų religijos ir mitologijos šaltiniai I, II, III, IV, ed. Norbertas Vėlius. Vilnius: Mokslo ir enciklopedijų leidykla, 1996, 2001, 2003, 2005.

Balys, J. 1937. Perkūnas lietuvių liaudies tikėjimuose. *Tautosakos darbai* III, Vilnius.

Bartholomae, Christian. 1904[1961]. *Altiranisches Wörterbuch*. Berlin: de Gruyter.

Beekes, Robert S. P. 1995. *Comparative Indo-European Linguistics. An Introduction*. Amsterdam / Philadelphia: Benjamins.

Bender, Johannes. 1868. *De veterum Prutenorum diis. Dissertatio historico-critica*. Braunsberg: Huye.

Beresnevičius, Gintaras. 2004. *Lietuvių religija ir mitologija: sisteminė studija*. Vilnius: Tyto alba.

Berkholz, Christian August. 1869–1870. Etwas Kirchliches aus Riga, von 1604–1618. In: *Rigasches Kirchenblatt*, Jg. 6, N. 48.

Bertuleit, Hans. 1924. Das Religionswesen der alten Preussen mit litauisch-lettischen Parallelen. In: *Sitzungsbericht Altertumsgesselschaft Prussia*. Heft 25. Königsberg.

Běťáková, Marta Eva & Blažek, Václav. 2012. *Encyklopedie baltské mytologie.* Praha: Libri.

Bezzenberger, Adalbert. 1877. *Beiträge zur Geschichte der litauischen Sprache auf Grund litauischer Texte des XVI. und des XVII. Jahrhunderts.* Göttingen: R. Peppmüller.

Bezzenberger, Adalbert. 1877. Mythologisches in altlitauischen Texten. *Beiträge zur Kunde der indogermanischen Sprachen* 1, 41–46.

Bezzenberger, Adalbert. 1882. *Litauische Forschungen. Beiträge zur Kenntnis der Sprache und des Volkstums der Litauer.* Göttingen: Peppmüller.

Bezzenberger, Adalbert apud Veckenstedt, Edmund. 1883. *Die Mythen, Sagen und Legenden der Zamaiten (Litauer).* Heidelberg: Winter.

Bielenstein, August Johann Gottfried. 1863. *Lettische Grammatik.* Mitau (Jelgava): Lucas.

Bielenstein, August Johann Gottfried. 1868. Einige Bemerkungen zu Dr. Mannhardts ‚Beiträge zur Mythologie der lettischen Völker'. In: *Magazin der Lettisch-Literarischen Gesselschaft* XIV. Mitau (Jelgava).

Bielenstein, August Johann Gottfried. 1892. *Die Grenzen des lettischen Volksstammes und der lettischen Sprache.* Sankt-Petersburg: Eggers.

Biezais, Haralds. 1961. The Latvian Forest Spirit. In: *The Supernatural Owners of Nature.* Stockholm – Göteborg and Uppsala: Almqvist and Wiksell, 15–19.

Biezais, Haralds. 1975. *Baltische Religion.* Stuttgart – Berlin – Köln – Mainz: Kohlhammer.

Biezais, Haralds. 1998. *Seno latviešu debesu dievu ǵimene.* Rīga: Minerva.

Biržiška, M. 1925. *Dainų istorijos vadovėlis,* III. Kaunas: "Vyties" bendrovė.

Blažek, Václav. 2000. Baltic *[ ]lākija-* m. / *[ ]lākijā* f. "bear". *Linguistica Baltica* 8, 49–56.

Blažek, Václav. 2001. On the Baltic Theonyms: Baltic-Italic Correspondences in Divine-Names. *Journal of Indo-European Studies* 29, 351–365.

Blažek, Václav. 2003a. Baltic horizon in Eastern Bohemian hydronymy? In: *Vakarų baltų kalbos ir kulturos reliktai IV.* Klaipeda: Tiltai 14, 14–20.

Blažek, Václav. 2003b. Slavic **ezero* vs. **ozero.* In: *Studia etymologica Brunensia* 2 *(Etymological Symposion,* Brno, Sept 2002), eds. I. Janyšková & H. Karlíková. Praha: Nakladatelství Lidové noviny, 243–257.

Blažek, Václav. 2004a. Balto-Fennic mythological names of Baltic origin. *Baltistica* 39/2, 189–194.

Blažek, Václav. 2004b. Baltský horizont ve východočeské hydronymii? In: *Spisovnost a nespisovnost. Zdroje, proměny a perspektivy. Sborník příspěvků z mezinárodní konference konané ve Šlapanicích* (únor 2004), ed. E. Minářová & K. Ondrášková. Brno: Pedagogická fakulta Masarykovy univerzity, 291–303.

Blažek, Václav. 2006. Baltijskie gorizonty v vostočnočešskoj gidronimii? *Balto-slavjanskie issledovanija* 17, 76–92.

Blažek, Václav. 2010. *The Indo-European „Smith".* Washington D.C.: Institute for the Study of Man *(Journal of Indo-European Studies,* Monograph Series 58).

Blažek, Václav. 2011 / 2014. *Perkūnas* versus *Perunъ*. In: *Baltai ir Slavai: Dvasinių kultūrų sankirtos / The Balts and the Slavs: Intersections of Spiritual Cultures* (International Conference dedicated to the memory of academician Vladimir Toporov; Vilnius, Sept 2011). Vilnius: Valstybės žinios, 55–58 / In: *Baltai ir slavai: dvasinių kultūrųsankirtos / Balty i slavjane: peresečenija duxovnyx kuľtur*, ed. Tatjana Civjan, Marija Zavjalova & Artūras Judžentis. Vilnius: Versmė 2014, 101–114.

Blažek, Václav. 2012. Latvian *Ūsiņš* 'bee-god and patron of horses'. *Baltistica* 47/1, 53–60.

Blažek, Václav. 2016. *Iamos* – the Greek counterpart of the Indo-Iranian Twin-God **Yama-*? *Journal of Indo-European Studies* 44/3–4, 1–30.

Blažek, Václav. 2017. K pojmenování 'medvěda' ve slovanštině. *Slavia* 86/1, 2017, 53–60.

Blažek, Václav. 2019. How many words did the Indo-Europeans use? *WEKWOS* 4, 58–82.

Blažek, Václav & Běťáková, Marta Eva. 2014. Prussian **Grubrius* 'god of spring and vegetation' in perspective of the Italic pantheon. *Baltistica* 49/2, 345–356.

Blažek, Václav & Hofírková, Lucie & Kovář, Michal. 2011. Rané prameny o národech uralské jazykové rodiny. *Linguistica Brunensia* 59/1–2, 189–224.

BMRT = Toporov, Vladimir N. 2000. *Balty mitologijos ir ritualo tyrimai*. Trans. Erdvilas Jakulis. Ed. Nikolaj Mixailov. Vilnius: Aidai.

BRMŠ = *Baltų religijos ir mitologijos šaltiniai* I, II, III, IV. Ed. Norbertas Vėlius. Vilnius: Mokslo ir enciklopedijų leidykla, 1996, 2001, 2003, 2005.

Brigadere, Anna. 1998. *Sprīdītis*. Rīga: Zvaigzne ABC.

Brückner, Aleksander. 1886. Beiträge zur litauischen Mythologie. *Archiv für slavische Philologie* 9, 1–12.

Brückner, Aleksander. 1897. Besprechung von Grienberger *Die Baltica des Libellus Lasicki* [1896]. *Kwartalnik historyczny* 11, p. 99.

Brückner, Aleksander. 1922. Osteuropäische Götternamen. Ein Beitrag zur vergleichenden Mythologie. *Zeitschrift für vergleichende Sprachforschung auf dem Gebiete der indogermanischen Sprachen* 50, 161–197.

Brugmann, Karl. 1906. *Grundris der vergleichenden Grammatik der indogermanischen Sprachen*, II.1. Strassburg: Trübner.

BSI = *Balto-slavjanskie issledovanija*.

Butzke, Petra. 2009. *Symbolika užovek v litevském folkloru. Žalčių simbolika lietuvių tautosakoje*. Praha: Ph.D. Thesis defended at Charles University.

Ciszewski, Stanisław. 1903. *Ognisko. Studium Etnologiczne*. Kraków: Akademia Umiejętności .

Coleman, Robert. 1992. Italic [numerals]. In: J. Gvozdanović (ed.), *Indo-European Numerals*. Berlin – New York: Mouton de Gruyter, 389–445.

de Vries, Jan. 1957. *Altgermanische Religionsgeschichte*, Bd. II. Berlin: Walter de Gruyter.

258 Lexicon of Baltic Mythology

Dějiny pobaltských zemí, ed. by Vladimír Macura, Luboš & Pavel Štoll. Praha: Nakladatelství Lidové noviny 1996.

Detschew, Dimiter. 1957. *Die thrakischen Sprachreste*. Wien: Rohrer.

Dini, Pietro U. & Mikhailov, Nikolai. 1995. *Mitologia Baltica. Studi sulla mitologia dei popoli baltici. Antologia*. Pisa: ECIG.

DLKŽ = *Dabartinės lietuvių kalbos žodynas*. Vilnius: Valstybinė politinės ir mokslinės literatūros leidykla, 1954.

Dumézil, Georges. 1973. (H)Elernus. *Journal of Indo-European Studies* 1, 304–307.

Dundulienė, Pranė. 1989. *Pagonybė Lietuvoje: Moteriškosios dievybės*. Vilnius: Mokslo ir enciklopedijų leidybos institutas.

Dundulienė, Pranė. 2008. *Lietuvių liaudies kosmologija*. Vilnius: Mokslo ir enciklopedijų leidybos institutas.

EH = Endzelin, J. & Hausenberg, E. 1934–1938 & 1956. *Ergänzungen und Berichtigungen zu K. Mühlenbachs Lettisch-Deutschem Wörterbuch*, I & II. Riga: Herausgegeben vom lettischen Kultursfonds & Chicago: Herausgegeben von der Gruppe der Lettischen Baltologen in Chicago.

EIEC = *Encyclopedia of Indo-European Culture*, ed. by J. P. Mallory & D.Q. Adams. London – Chicago: Fitzroy Dearborn Publishers, 1997.

Elizarenkova, Tat'jana Ja. 1999. *Rigveda (Mandaly I–IV)*. Moskva: Nauka.

Elizarenkova, Tat'jana Ja. & Toporov, Vladimir N. 1964. O drevneindijskoj Ušas (Uṣas) i ee baltijskom sootvetstvii (Ūsiņš). In: *Indija v drevnosti*. Moskva: Nauka, 66–84.

Encyclopedia of Indo-European Culture, ed. by J. P. Mallory & D. Q. Adams. London – Chicago: Fitzroy Dearborn Publishers, 1997.

Endzelin, J. & Hausenberg, E. 1934–1938 & 1956. *Ergänzungen und Berichtigungen zu K. Mühlenbachs Lettisch-Deutschem Wörterbuch*, I & II. Riga: Herausgegeben vom lettischen Kultursfonds & Chicago: Herausgegeben von der Gruppe der Lettischen Baltologen in Chicago.

ESIJ = *Ėtimologičeskij slovaŕ iranskix jazykov*, Tom 2, ed. V. S. Rastorgueva & D. I. Ėdel'man. Moskva: Vostočnaja literatura 2003.

ESJS = *Etymologický slovník jazyka staroslověnského*, 1–15, ed. Eva Havlová et alii. Praha: Academia (1–14) / Tribun EU (15).

ESSJ = *Ėtimologičeskij slovaŕ slavjanskix jazykov*, 1n, ed. O. N. Trubačev et alii. Moskva: Nauka 1974f.

Etymologický slovník jazyka staroslověnského, 1–15, ed. Eva Havlová et alii. Praha: Academia (1–14) / Tribun EU (15).

EV = Elbing Vocabulary – see Mažiulis 1981.

EWAI = Mayrhofer, Mannfred. 1986f. *Etymologisches Wörterbuch des Altindoarischen*, I–III. Heidelberg: Winter.

F = Fraenkel, Ernst. 1962–1965. *Litauisches etymologisches Wörterbuch*, I-II. Göttingen: Vandhoeck & Ruprecht / Heidelberg: Winter.

Ėtimologičeskij slovaŕ slavjanskix jazykov, 1n, ed. O. N. Trubačev et alii. Moskva: Nauka 1974n.

Feist, Sigmund. 1939. *Vergleichendes Wörterbuch der gotischen Sprache₃*. Leiden: Brill.

Forssman, Berthold. 2001. *Lettische Grammatik*. Dettelbach: Röll.

Fraenkel, Ernst. 1962–1965. *Litauisches etymologisches Wörterbuch*, I–II. Göttingen: Vandhoeck & Ruprecht / Heidelberg: Winter.

Frisk, Hjalmar. 1973₂–1991₃. *Griechisches etymologisches Wörterbuch*, I–II. Heidelberg: Winter.

Gamkrelidze, Tamaz V. & Ivanov, Vjačeslav V. 1984. *Indoevropejskij jazyk i indoevropejcy*. Tbilisi: Izdatel'stvo Tbilisskogo univerziteta.

Georgiev, Vladimir I. 1975. Die thrakischen Götternamen. Ein Beitrag zur Religion der alten Thraker. *Balkansko ezikoznanie* 18/1, 5–56.

Gerullis, Georg. 1922. *Die altpreussischen Ortsnamen*. Berlin – Leipzig: Walter de Gruyter.

Gerullis, Georg. 1926. Bretke als Geschichtsschreiber. *Archiv für slavische Philologie* 40, 119–120.

Gimbutas, Marija. 1963. *The Balts*. London: Thames & Hudson.

Gimbutas, Marija. 1973. Perkūnas/Perun: The Thunder God of the Balts and the Slavs. *Journal of Indo-European Studies* 1, 466–478.

Gimbutienė, Marija. 2002. *Baltų mitologija. Senovės lietuvių deivės ir dievai.*Vilnius: Lietuvos rašytojų sąjungos leidykla.

(Anonym) *Gottesidee und Cultus bei den alten Preussen. Ein Beitrag zur vergleichenden Sprachvorschung*. Berlin: Peiser 1870.
< http://archive.org/stream/gottesideeundcu00unkngoog#page/n12/mode/2up > Visited on June 2, 2021.

Graves, Robert. 1972–1974 *The Greek Myths*. Harmondsworth: Penguin Books.

Greimas, Algirdas Julius. 2005. *Lietuvių mitologijos studijos*. Vilnius: Baltos lankos.

Grienberger, Theodor. 1896. Die Baltica des Libellus Łasicki. Untersuchungen zur litauischen Mythologie. *Archiv für slavische Philologie* 18, 1–86.

Griffith, Ralph T. H. 1889[1987]. *Hymns of the Ṛgveda*, I–II. New Delhi: Munshiram Manoharlal.

Grimm, Jacob Ludwig Karl. 1865. Namen des Donners. In: Grimm, Jacob L. K.: *Kleinere Schriften*. Bd. II, *Abhandlungen zur mythologie und Sittenkunde*. Berlin: F. Dümmler, 402–438.

Güterbock, Hans G. & Hoffner, Harry A. 1989. *The Hittite Dictionary* (L–N). Chicago: The Oriental Institute of the University of Chicago.

Haličsko-volyňský letopis, translated by Jitka Komendová from Old Russian original *Galicko-Volynskaja letopis'*. Praha: Argo, 2010.

Hamp, Eric P. 1980. *nãmas, namiẽ*. *Baltistica* 16/1, 44.

Heger, Ladislav (translator). 1962. *Edda*. Praha: Státní nakladatelství krásné literatury a umění.

Herodotus, *The Histories*, with an English translation by A. D. Godley. Cambridge: Harvard University Press 1920.

260   Lexicon of Baltic Mythology

Holthausen, F. 1916. Etymologien. *Zeitschrift für vergleichende Sprachforschung* 47, 307–312.

Hofírková, Lucie & Blažek, Václav. 2011. Baltic loanwords in Saami. *Acta Linguistica Lithuanica* 64–65, 51–64.

Illič-Svityč, Vladislav M. 1963. *Imennaja akcentuacija v baltijskom i slavjanskom*. Moskva: Izdatel'stvo Akademii nauk SSSR.

IT = Ivanov, V. V. & Toporov, V. N. 1974. Baltijskaja mifologija v svete sravnitel'no-istoričeskix rekonstrukcij indoevropejskix drevnostej. *Zeitschrift für Slawistik* 19, 144–157.

Ivanov, Vjačeslav V. 1986. O mifopoétičeskix osnovax latyšskix dajn. *BSI* [1984], 3–28.

Ivanov, Vjačeslav V. & Toporov, Vladimir N. 1973. A comparative study of the group of Baltic mythological terms from the root **vel-*. *Baltistica* 9/1, 15–27.

Ivanov, Vjačeslav V. & Toporov, Vladimir N. 1974a. Baltijskaja mifologija v svete sravnitelno-istoričeskich rekonstrukcij indoevropejskich drevnostej. *Zeitschrift für Slawistik* 19, 144–157.

Ivanov, Vjačeslav V. & Toporov, Vladimir N. 1974b. *Issledovanija v oblasti slavjanskix drevnostej*. Moskva: Nauka.

Ivanov, Vjačeslav V. & Toporov, Vladimir N. 1983. K probleme ltš. *Jumis* i baltijskogo bliznečnogo kul'ta. *BSI* [1982], 140–175.

Ivanov, Vjačeslav V. & Toporov, Vladimir N. 1987. Baltijskaja mifologija. In: *Mify narodov mira*, I. Moskva: Sovetskaja Énciklopedija, 153–159.

Jackson, Peter. 2006. *The Transformations of Helen. Indo-European Myth and the Roots of the Trojan Cycle*. Dettelbach: Röll (Münchener Studien zur Sprachwissenschaft, Beiheft 23, Neue Folge).

Jacobson, Heinrich Friedrich. 1837. *Geschichte der Quellen des katholischen Kirchenrechtes der Provinzen Preussen und Posen*. Königsberg: Bornträger.

Jakobson, Roman. 1969. The Slavic god Veles" nd his Indo-European cognates. In: *Studi linguistici in onore di Vittore Pisani*, Vol. II. Brescia: Paideia, 579–599.

Jamison, Stephanie W. & Joel P. Brereton (translators). 2013. *The Rigveda: The Earliest Religious Poetry of India*. Oxford: University Press.

Janda, Michael. 2005. *Eleusion. Entstehung und Entwicklung der griechischen Religion*. Innsbruck: IBS 119.

Jaskiewicz, W. C. 1952. A study in Lithuanian Mythology: Jan Łasicki's Samogitian Gods. *Studi Baltici* I (IX), 65–106.

Jonval, Michel. 1929. *Les chansons mythologiques lettonnes*. Paris: Picart.

Jouet, Philippe. 1989. *Religion et mythologie des Baltes. Une tradition indo-européenne*. Milano – Paris: Archè „les belles lettres".

Juškevičius, Antanas. 1883. *Liėtùviškos svotbìnės dájnos*. Kazań: *Učenye zapiski Imperatorskago Kazańskago universiteta*.

Kalevala. Karelofinský epos, translated by Josef Holeček. Praha: Státní nakladatelství krásné literatury, hudby a umění 1953 (1st edition 1894).

Karulis, Konstantīns. 1992. *Latviešu etimoloģijas vārdnīca*, I–II. Rīga: Avots.

Kawiński, Paweł & Szczepański, Seweryn. 2016. *Szkice o religii Prusów*. Olsztyn: Towarzystwo Naukowe Pruthenia.

KEWA = Mayrhofer, Mannfred. 1976. *Kurzgefasstes etymologisches Wörterbuch des Altindischen*, Band III. Heidelberg: Winter.

KL = Rudzītis, Jānis. 1988. Komentāri. In: Pumpurs, Andrejs. *Lāčplēsis, latvju tautas varonis*. Rīga: Zinātne.

Krappe, Alexander Haggerty. 1932. Pikuls. Ein Beitrag zur baltischen Mythologie. *Indogermanische Forschungen* 50, 63–69.

Kregždys, Rolandas. 2008a. Teonimų, minimų *Sūduvių knygelėje*, etimologinė analizė – dievybių funkcijos, hierarchija: *Puschayts / Puschkayts*. *Res humanitariae* 3, 49–74.

Kregždys, Rolandas. 2008b. Teonimų, minimų *Sūduvių knygelėje*, etimologinė analizė – dievybių funkcijos, hierarchija: *Bardoayts / Gardoayts / Perdoytus*. *Res humanitariae* 4, 79–106.

Kregždys, Rolandas. 2009a. *Sūduvių knygelė* – vakarų baltų religijos ir kultūros šaltinis. I dalis: formalioji analizė. *Lituanistica* 55, 174–187

Kregždys, Rolandas. 2009b. Pruss. *Curche*: ėtimologija teonima, funkcii božestva; problematika ustanovlenija kuľtovyx sootvetstvij na počve obrjadovoj tradicii vostočno-baltijskix, slavjanskix i drugix indoevropejskix narodov. *Studia Mythologica Slavica* 12, 249–320.

Kregždys, Rolandas. 2009c. Baltų kalbų lingvistiniai ir mitologiniai duomenys lie. *kãktas/kaktà*, la. *kakts/kakta* rekonstrukcijai. *Vārds un tā pētīšanas aspekti* 13/1. Liepāja: Liepājas Universitāte, 256–269.

Kregždys, Rolandas. 2010. M. Stryikowskio veikalo *Kronika Polska, Litewska, Žmódzka i wszystkiej Rusi* teonimai: *Chaurirari*. *Acta Linguistica Lithuanica* 62–63, 50–81.

Kregždys, Rolandas. 2011a. Pr. *Romow*: tekstologinė, etimologinė, mitologinė analizė. *Baltų onomastikos tyrimai* 2. Red. L. Bilkis ir kt. Vilnius: Lietuvių kalbos institutas, 158–180

Kregždys, Rolandas. 2011b. Baltiškųjų teonimų perteikimo ir dievų funkcijų nustatymo problematika Jano Łasickio veikale „De diis Samagitarvm Cæterorvmque Sarmatarum, & falſorum Chriſtianorum. Item de religione Armeniorum": *Salaus, Klamals, Atlaibos, Tawals*. *Perspectives of Baltic Philology* 2. Poznań: Wydawnictwo „Rys" & Authors, 101–121.

Kregždys, Rolandas. 2012. *Baltų mitologemų etimologinis žodynas*, 1: *Kristburgo sutartis*. Vilnius: Lietuvos kultūros tyrimų institutas.

Kregždys, Rolandas. 2013. Ancient Baltic Religion: Evaluation of Archetypes Authenticity. In: *Oriental Studies. Between East and West. Scientific Papers. University of Latvia*, vol. 793. Rīga: Latvijas Universitāte, 91–98.

Kregždys, Rolandas. 2015. Baltų mitonimų kilmė: vak. bl. *Pargrubi(j)us* (*G[r]ubrium, Pergrubrius* ir kt.); lie. *maselis*. *Acta Linguistica Lithuanica* 73/1, 9–37.

Kregždys, Rolandas. 2016. *Sūduvių knygelės* etnomitologinė faktografija: mitonimų *Barstucke* 'die kleinen Mennichen, Erdleutlein, der Götter diener' ir *Marcopole* A 'die Edelleuthe' / C 'Erde leute resp. Subterranei dicti' etimologinė raida ir semantinė transformacija. *Baltu filoloģija* 25/1, 79–95.

Kregždys, Rolandas. 2018a. *Sūduvių knygelės* etnomitologinė faktografija: jtv. *Pockols* funkciniai alternantai (mitonimų v. dial. [RPr.] *Aitwars*, lie. *áitvaras* formalioji ir etimologinė analizė). *Prace Bałtystyczne* 7, 83–113.

Kregždys, Rolandas. 2018b. *Sūduvių knygelės* etnomitologinė faktografija: mitonimų *Swayxtix, Auschauts* etimologinė raida ir semantinė transformacija. *Baltu filoloģija* 27/1–2, 13–73.

Kregždys, Rolandas. 2019a. *Sūduvių knygelės* etnomitologinė faktografija: mitonimų *Potrimpus* (↔ *Autrimpus* [← *Natrimpus*]), *Pilnitis, Parkuns, Peckols, Pockols* etimologinė raida ir semantinė transformacija. *Baltu filoloģija* 28/2, 35–106.

Kregždys, Rolandas. 2019b. On the origin of the mythonyms OPruss. *Worskaito / Borsskayto* (S. Grunau) // Yatv. *Wourschkaite* (*Yatvigian Book*). In: *Komunikaty Mazursko-Warmińskie* 4(306). Olsztyn: Archiwum Państwowe w Olsztynie / Towarzystwo Naukowe i Instytut Północny im. Wojciecha Kętrzyńskiego, 780–807.

Kregždys, Rolandas. 2019c. Etymological Analysis and Transformation of the Semantic Value of the Mythonym Ockopirmus. *Annales Universitatis Mariae Curie-Skłodowska*, Sectio FF: *Philologiae* 37/1, 209–221.

Kregždys, Rolandas. 2020. *Baltų mitologemų etimologinis žodynas*, 1: *Sūduvių knygelė*. Vilnius: Lietuvos kultūros tyrimų institutas.

Kudirka, Juozas. 1993. *Lietuviškos Kūčios ir Kalėdos*. Vilnius: Vaga.

Kure, Henning. 2006. Drinking from Odin's Pledge: On an Encounter with the Fantastic in Völuspa 28–29'. In: *The Fantastic in Old Norse Icelandic Literature*. Preprint Papers Pt. 1, 533–540.

Kurschat, Friedrich. 1876. *Grammatik der littauischen Sprache*. Halle: Waisenhaus.

Kurschat, Friedrich. 1870–1883. *Wörterbuch der littauischen Sprache*, 1–2. Halle: Waisenhaus.

Kurschat, Alexander. 1968–1973. *Litauisch-deutsches Wörterbuch*, I–IV, hrgb. Wilhelm Wissmann & Erich Hofmann. Göttingen: Vandenhoeck & Ruprecht.

L = Pumpurs, Andrejs. 1975. *Lāčplēsis. Latyšskij epos, vossozdannyj po narodnym predanijam*. Iz latvijskogo perevodil Vladimir Deržavin. Moskva: Glavnaja redakcija vostočnoj literatury.

Larsson, Jenny Helena. 2002. Nominal compounds in the Baltic languages. *Transactions of the Philological Society* 100/2, 203–231.

Lasicius, Joannes (Łasicki, Jan) – viz Mannhardt 1868.

Latvija. Autoceļu karte. Rīga: Jāņa sēta 2008.

LD = Barons, Krišjānis. 1989–1994. *Latvju dainas* I, II, III (A, B, C), IV, V, VI.

First published in 1894–1915. Rīga: Zinātne. {The dainas are numbered; the figure accompanying the abbreviation LD indicates the number of the daina.}

Lehmann, Winfred P. 1986. *A Gothic Etymological Dictionary*. Leiden: Brill.

Lemeškin, Ilja. 2009. *Sovijaus sakmė ir 1262 metų chronografas (pagal Archyvinį Varšuvos, Vilniaus ir I.J. Zabelino nuorašus)*. Vilnius: Lietuvių literatūros ir tautosakos institutas.

Leskien, August. 1891. *Die Bildung der Nomina im Litauischen*. Leipzig: Hirzel.

Leskien, August. 1919. *Litauisches Lesebuch mit Grammatik und Wörterbuch*. Heidelberg: Winter.

Lexikon der indogermanischen Verben₂, eds. Rix, H. et al. Wiesbaden: Reichert 2001.

Lietuvių kalbos žodynas, I–XX. Vilnius: Minties / Lietuvių kalbos instituto leidykla 1968–2002.

Lietuvių mitologija, ed. Norbertas Vėlius. I–IV. Vilnius: Mintis 1995–2003.

LIV₂ = *Lexikon der indogermanischen Verben₂*, eds. Rix, H. et al. Wiesbaden: Reichert 2001.

LKŽ = *Lietuvių kalbos žodynas*, I–XX. Vilnius: Mintis/Lietuvių kalbos instituto leidykla 1968–2002.

LM = *Lietuvių mitologija* I.–IV. 1995–2003. Ed. Norbertas Vėlius. Vilnius: Mintis.

Lopez, Barry Holstun. 2004. *Of Wolves and Men*. New York: Scribner.

LPG = Mannhardt, Wilhelm. *Letto-Preussische Götterlehre (Latviešu-Prūšu mitoloģija)*. Written in 1880's, first published in Rīga: Latviešu literāriskā biedrība, 1936.

LPT = Šmits, Pēteris. 1925–1937. *Latviešu pasakas un teikas* I.–XV. Rīga: Latviešu folkloras krātuve.

LTD = *Latviešu tautas dziesmas* <https://latviandainas.lib.virginia.edu>

LTT = Šmits, Pēteris. 1940–1941. *Latviešu tautas ticējumi* I.–IV. Rīga: Latviešu folkloras krātuve. {The numbers following the abbreviation LTT indicate the concrete superstitions}.

Machek, Václav. 1971. *Etymologický slovník jazyka českého*. Praha: Academia.

Mannhardt, Wilhelm. 1868. Beiträge zur Mythologie der lettischen Völker. Johan Lasicii Poloni de Diis Samagitarum caeterorumque Sarmatorum et falsorum Christianorum. Mit Erläuterungen von W. Mannhardt und ‚Einige Bemerkungen' von A. Bielenstein. *Magazin der Lettisch-Literarischer Gesselschaft* XIV, St. 1. Mitau (Jelgava).

Mannhardt, Wilhelm. 1936. *Letto-Preussische Götterlehre*. Riga: Magazin der Lettisch-Literärischen Gesellschaft / Latviešu Literāriskā biedrība XXI (psáno v 80. letech 19. st.).

Martinaitis, Marcelijus. 2009. *Mes gyvenome: biografiniai užrašai*. Vilnius: Lietuvos rašytojų sąjungos leidykla.

Mayrhofer, Mannfred. 1976. *Kurzgefasstes etymologisches Wörterbuch des Altindischen*, Band III. Heidelberg: Winter.

Mayrhofer, Mannfred. 1986f. *Etymologisches Wörterbuch des Altindoarischen*, I–III. Heidelberg: Winter.

Mažiulis, Vytautas. 1981. *Prūsų kalbos paminklai* II. Vilnius: Mokslas.

Mažiulis, Vytautas. 1988, 1993, 1996, 1997. *Prūsų kalbos etimologijos žodynas*, I–IV. Vilnius: Mokslas.

Mažiulis, Vytautas. 2004. *Prūsų kalbos istorinė gramatika*. Vilnius: Vilniaus universiteto leidykla.

Mažiulis, Vytautas. 2013. *Prūsų kalbos etimologijos žodynas$_2$*. Vilnius: Mokslo ir enciklopedijų leidybos centras.

ME = Mühlenbach, Karl. 1923–1932. *Latviešu valodas vārdnīca. Lettisch-deutsches Wörterbuch*, I.–IV. Ed. Jānis Endzelīns. Rīga: Herausgegeben vom lettischen Kulturfond.

Meiser, Gerhard. 1986. *Lautgeschichte der umbrischen Sprache*. Innsbruck: IBS 51.

Melchert, H. Craig. 1993. *Cuneiform Luvian Lexicon*. Chapel Hill: Author.

MEnc = *Mitoloģijas enciklopēdija* I.–II. Rīga: Latvijas enciklopēdija, 1993–1994.

Mierzyński, Antonin. 1870. Jan Lasicki: źródło do Mytologii Litewskiej. *Rocznik Cesarsko-Królewskiego Towarzystwa Naukowego Krakowskiego* 18. Kraków.

Mierzyński, Antonin. 1878. Ian Lasickij i ego sočinenie: De Diis Samagitarum. In: *Trudy* III. *arxeologičeskogo s'ezda v Rossii*, T. II. Kyїv.

Mierzyński, Antonin. 1892–1896. *Mytologiae Lituanicae Monumenta. Źródła do mytologii Litewskiej*. 1. *Ot Tacyta do konca XIII wieku*. 2. *Wiek XIV i XV*. Warszawa: Kowalewski.

Mikkola, Josef Julius. 1896. Etymologische Beiträge. *Beiträge zur Kunde der indogermanischen Sprachen* 21, 218–225.

Miklosich, Franz. 1867. *Die Fremdwörter in den slavischen Sprachen*. Wien: K.K. Hof- und Staatsdruckerei.

Mitoloģijas enciklopēdija, I–II. Rīga: Latvijas enciklopēdija 1993–1994.

Mitologijos enciklopedija, I–II. From Latvian translated by I. T. Ermanytė, L. Kudirkienė, R. Kvašytė, Ž. O. Markevičienė, D. Murmulaitytė, I. N. Sisaitė, G. Šlapelytė, R. Zajančkauskaitė. Vilnius: Vaga, 1997, 1999.

MNM = *Mify narodov mira*, I–II, ed. S. A. Tokarev. Moskva: Sovetskaja enciklopedija 1988.

Mühlenbach, K. 1923–1932. *Lettisch-deutsches Wörterbuch*, I–IV, redigiert von J. Endzelin. Riga: Lettische Bildungsministerium.

MV = Mažiulis 2013.

Narbutt, Teodor. 1835. Mitologia Litewska. In: *Dzieje starożytne narodu litewskiego*. I. Vilnius: Marcinowski.

Nesselmann, Georg Heinrich Ferdinand. 1845. *Die Sprache der alten Preussen in ihren Überresten erläutert*. Berlin: Reimer.

Neuland, Lena. 1977. Jumis, die Fruchtbarkeitsgottheit der alten Letten. *Acta Universitatis Stockholmiensis. Stockholm Studies in comparative religion* 15, 1–186.

Niederle, Lubor. 1924. *Život starých Slovanů*, Díl II, svazek 1. Praha: Bursík & Kohout.

Novotná, Petra & Blažek, Václav. 2007. Glottochronology and its application to the Balto-Slavic languages. *Baltistica* 42/2, 185–210 & 42/3, 323–346.

Novotná, Petra & Blažek, Václav. 2009. Feno-sámské jazyky: test vzájemné příbuznosti. In: *Sámové – jazyk, literatura a společnost*, edd. Vendula Hingarová, Alexandra Hubáčková, Michal Kovář. Praha: Mervart, 81–114.

Orel, Vladimir E. 1997. Neslavjanskaja gidronimija bassejnov Visly i Odera. *BSI* [1988–1996/1997], 332–358.

Otrębski, Jan. 1965. *Gramatyka języka litewskiego*, Tom II. Warszawa: Państwowe wydawnictwo naukowe.

Ovid. 1931. *Fasti*. Translated by James George Frazer. Cambridge (MA): Harvard University Press – London: Heinemann (Loeb Classical Library Volume).

Parolek, Radegast. 1996. *Litevská literatura. Vývoj a tvůrčí osobnosti*. Praha: Bohemika.

Parolek, Radegast (ed.). 1998. *V kruhu krásy. Malá antologie z lotyšské a litevské lidové poezie*. Praha: Bohemika.

Pastoreau, Michel. 2011. *Medvěd. Dějiny padlého krále*. Praha: Argo.

Pike, Albert. 1992. *Indo-Aryan Deities and Worship as Contained in the Rigveda*. Whitefish (Montana, USA): Kessinger Publishing.

Pilāts, Valdis & Ozoliņš, Jānis. 2003. Status of Brown Bear in Latvia. *Acta Zoologica Lituanica* 13, No. 1. 65–71.

Piročkinas, Arnoldas. 2004. *Čekų-lietuvių / lietuvių-čekų kalbų žodynas*. Vilnius: Žodynas.

Pisani, Vittore. 1968. Rom und die Balten. *Baltistica* 4/1, 7–21.

PL = „Teksty, zapisannye u narodnych pevcov i skazitelej". „Paralleli k otdel'nym pesnjam eposa". In: Pumpurs, Andrejs. *Lāčplēsis. Latyšskij epos, vossozdannyj po narodnym predanijam*. Iz latvijskogo prerevodil Vladimir Děržavin. Moskva: Glavnaja redakcija vostočnoj literatury 1975.

Plāķis, Juris. 1926. *Leišu valodas rokas grāmata*. Rīga: Valters un Rapa.

Pokorny, Julius. 1959. *Indogermanisches etymologisches Wörterbuch*. Bern – München: Francke.

Polomé, Edgar C. 1995. Notes on the Baltic religious vocabulary. *Linguistica Baltica* 4, 35–40.

Popławski, P. A. 2001. Zachodni zasięg hydronimii typu bałtyckiego. *Onomastica* 46, 157–170.

Preussisches Urkundenbuch, ed. F. G. von Bunge. Königsberg: Hartung 1882.

Prosdocimi, Aldo L. 1969. Lituano *ēžeras*, latino *Egeria*. *Studi baltici* 10, 130–142.

PŠ = Šmits, Pēteris (Pēteris Šmitas). 2004. *Latvių mitologija*. From Latvian translated by Dainius Razauskas. Vilnius: Aidai.

Puhvel, Jaan. 1974. Indo-European Structure of the Baltic Pantheon. In: *Myth in Indo-European Antiquity*, ed. by G. J. Larson et al. Berkeley – Los Angeles: University of California Press, 75–85.

Pumpurs, Andrejs. 1975. *Lāčplēsis. Latyšskij epos, vossozdannyj po narodnym predanijam.* Iz latvijskogo perevodil Vladimir Deržavin. Moskva: Glavnaja redakcija vostočnoj literatury.

Pumpurs, Andrejs. 2008. *Lāčplēsis, latvju tautas varonis.* Rīga: Zvaigzne ABC.

Pūtelis, Aldis. 2019. *Domas par latviešu mitoloģiju. Kā tika meklēts latviešu panteons.* Rīga: Zinātne.

Radke, Gerhard. 1965. *Die Götter Altitaliens.* Münster: Aschendorf.

RB = Balsys, Rimantas. 2006. *Lietuvių ir prūsų dievai, deivės, dvasios: nuo apeigos iki prietaro.* Klaipėda: Klaipėdos universiteto leidykla.

Reichelt, Hans. 1911. *Avesta Reader. Texts, Notes, Glossary and Index.* Strassburg: Trübner.

Reichstäter, Jan. 2014. (Review of) Běťáková, M. E. & Blažek, V.: *Encyklopedie baltské mytologie* (Praha: Libri 2012). *Sacra* (Masarykova univerzita) 12/1–2, 67–70.

Reichstäter, Jan. 2015. Jak rozumět "pohanským reliktům": folklór baltských zemí jako zdroj pro studium předkřesťanských tradic starých Baltů. *Religio: revue pro religionistiku* 23/2, 161–185.

Reichstäter, Jan. 2019. *Předkřesťanská náboženství severních Indoevropanů. Tradice Keltů, Germánů a Baltů v kritické perspektivě humanitních věd.* Brno: Masarykova univerzita (Spisy Filozofické fakulty Masarykovy univerzity, č. 499).

RL = Rudzītis, Jānis. 1975. „*Lāčplēsis* i jego mesto v istorii latyšskoj kul'tury". In: PUMPURS, Andrejs. *Lāčplēsis. Latyšskij epos, vossozdannyj po narodnym predanijam.* Iz latvijskogo perevodil Vladimir Děržavin. Moskva: Glavnaja redakcija vostočnoj literatury.

Rudzītis, Jānis. 1975. Kommentarii. Iz latvijskogo prerevodil J. I. Abyzovy. In: Pumpurs, Andrejs. *Lāčplēsis. Latyšskij epos, vossozdannyj po narodnym predanijam.* Z lotyštiny přeložil Vladimir Děržavin. Moskva: Glavnaja redakcija vostočnoj literatury.

Rudzītis, Jānis. 1975. *Lāčplēsis* i jego mesto v istorii latyšskoj kul'tury". In: Pumpurs, Andrejs. *Lāčplēsis. Latyšskij epos, vossozdannyj po narodnym predanijam.* Iz latvijskogo perevodil Vladimir Deržavin. Moskva: Glavnaja redakcija vostočnoj literatury.

Ryžakova, Svetlana. 2009. Egle – koroleva užej: o sposobach interpretacii odnogo skazočnogo sjužeta v litovskoj kul'ture. In: *Mif v fol'klornych tradicijach i kul'ture novejšego vremeni.* Moskva: Rossijskij Gosudarstvennyj Gumanitarnyj Universitet, 49–70.

Schall, H. 1964. Berlin – ein slawobaltischer Flurname. *Zeitschrift für vergleichende Sprachforschung* 78, 126–146.

Schall, H. 1966. Baltische Gewässernamen in Flusssystem „Obere Havel" (Südost-Mecklenburg). *Baltistica* 2/1, 7–42.

Schall, H. 1970. Preussische Namen längs der Weichsel (nach Lucas David, ca. 1580). In: *Donum Balticum. to Prof. Ch.S. Stang on the occasion of his sev-*

entieth birthday, ed. Velta Rūķe Draviņa. Almqvist & Wiksell, Stockholm, 448–464.

Schleicher, August. 1856. *Litauische Grammatik.* Prag: Calve.

Schleicher, August. 1857. *Litauisches Lesebuch und Glossar.* Prag: Calve.

Schmid, Wolfgang P. 1979. Lett. *jumis*, eine sprachwissenschaftliche Nachprüfung. In: *Humanitas Religiosa.* Festschrift für Haralds Biezais zu seinem 70. Geburtstag dargebracht von Freunden und Kollegen. Uppsala: Almqvist & Wiksell international, 261–267.

Schrader, Otto & Nehring, Alfons. 1917–1929. *Reallexikon der indogermanischen Altertumskunde*, I–II. Berlin–Leipzig: Walter de Gruyter.

Shevelov, George Y. 1964. *A Prehistory of Slavic. The Historical Phonology of Common Slavic.* Heidelberg: Winter.

Simek, Rudolf. 2006. *Dictionary of Northern Mythology*, translated by Angela Hall. Cambridge: Brewer (first English edition 1993; first German edition 1984).

SKES = *Suomen kielen etymologinen sanakirja*, ed. Y. H. Toivonen et alii. Helsinki: Lexica Societatis Fenno-Ugricae XII (1955f).

SLDDG = Biezais, Haralds. 1998. *Seno latviešu debesu dievu ģimene.* Rīga: Minerva.

Smoczyński, Wojciech. 2000. *Untersuchungen zum deutschen Lehngut im Altpreussischen.* Kraków: Wydawnictwo Uniwersytetu Jagellońskiego.

Smoczyński, Wojciech. 2007. *Słownik etymologiczny języka litewskiego.* Wilno: Uniwersytet wileński.

Smoczyński, Wojciech. 2018. *Lithuanian Etymological Dictionary*, ed. by Axel Holvoet and Steven Young with the assistance of Wayles Browne. Berlin – Bern – Bruxelles – New York – Oxford – Warszawa – Wien: Peter Lang.

Stanevičius, S. 1967. {*Unfinished manuscript on history of Lithuania*}. In: *Raštai.* Vilnius: Vaga.

Stang, Christian S. 1966. *Vergleichende Grammatik der baltischen Sprachen.* Oslo – Bergen – Tromsø: Universitetsforlaget.

Stender, Gotthard Friedrich. 1783. *Lettische Grammatik*, including the chapter „Lettische Mythologie". Mitau (Jelgava): Steffenhagen.

Stender, Gotthard Friedrich. 1789. *Lettisches Lexikon.* Mitau (Jelgava): Steffenhagen.

Suomen kielen etymologinen sanakirja, ed. Y. H. Toivonen et alii. Helsinki: Lexica Societatis Fenno-Ugricae XII (1955n).

Szirwid, Konstantin (Szyrwid, Sirvydas, Širvydas, Konstantinas). 1629–1644. *Punktai sakimu* I–II. Vilnius.

Szirwid, Konstantin (Szyrwid, Sirvydas, Širvydas, Konstantinas). 1619/1713. *Dictionarium trium linguarum.* 1. vydání 1619; 5. rozšířené vydání 1713. Vilnius: Academicis Societatis Jesu.

Šmits, Pēteris. 1940–1941. *Latviešu tautas ticējumi.* Rīga: Latv. Kult. fonds.

Šmits, Pēteris (Pēteris Šmitas). 2004. *Latvių mitologija*. From Latvian translated by Dainius Razauskas. Vilnius: Aidai.

Švec, Luboš & Macura, Vladimír & Štol, Pavel. 1996. *Dějiny Pobaltských zemí*. Praha: Nakladatelství Lidové noviny.

Tacitus, Cornelius Publius. 1942. *Germany and its Tribes*. In: *Complete Works of Tacitus*, Translated and edited by Alfred John Church & William Jackson Brodribb. New York: Random House 1942.

Tacitus, Cornelius Publius. 1959. *Germania*, herausgegeben, übersetzt und mit Erläuterungen versehen von Eugen Fehrle. Heidelberg: Winter.

TDz = Šmits, Pēteris. 1936–1939. *Tautas dziesmas* I.–IV. Rīga: Latviešu folkloras krātuve.

Téra, Michal. 2009. *Perun – bůh hromovládce. Sonda do slovanského archaického náboženství*. Červený Kostelec: Mervart.

Thomsen, Vilhelm. 1890. *Beröringer mellem de finske og de baltiske (litauisk-lettiske) Sprog*. Kobenhavn: Dreyer.

Tischler, Johann. 1990. *Hethisches etymologisches Glossar*, Lieferungen 5–6 (L–M). Innsbruck: IBS 20.

Toporov, Vladimir N. 1966a. O baltijskix èlementax v gidronimii i toponimii k zapadu ot Visly. *Slavia Pragensis* 8, 255–263.

Toporov, Vladimir N. 1966b. K voprosu o toponimičeskix sootvetstvijax na baltijskix territorijax i k zapadu ot Visly. *Baltistica* 1/2, 103–111.

Toporov, Vladimir N. 1968. O baltijskom èlemente v gidronimii verxnego Nareva. In: *Studia Linguistica slavica baltica Canuto-Olavo Falk, sexagenario a collegis amicis discipulis oblata* (Lund 1966). Malmö: Slaviska och baltiska studier 8, 285–297.

Toporov, Vladimir N. 1970. K balto-slavjanskim mifologičeskim svjazjam. In: *Donum balticum. To Professor Christian S. Stang on the occasion of his seventieth birthday*, ed. by Velta Rūķe-Draviņa. Stockholm: Almqvist & Wiksell, 534–543.

Toporov, Vladimir N. 1972a. Zametki po baltskoj mifologii. In: *Balto-slavjanskij sbornik*, ed. V. N. Toporov. Moskva: Nauka, 289–314.

Toporov, Vladimir N. 1972b. „Baltica" Podmoskov'ja. In: *Balto-slavjanskij sbornik*, ed. V. N. Toporov. Moskva: Nauka 217–280.

Toporov, Vladimir N. 1974. Ob indoevropejskix sootvetstvijax odnomu baltijskomu mifologičeskomu imenu. Balt. *Puš(k)ait-* : dr.-ind. *Pūṣán*, dr.-greč. Πάν. In: *Balto-slavjanskie issledovanija*, ed. Tamara M. Sudnik. Moskva: Nauka, 3–36.

Toporov, Vladimir N. 1976. K frakijsko-baltijskim jazykovym paralleljam, II. In: *Balkanskij lingvističeskij sbornik*, ed. T. V. Civjan. Moskva: Nauka, 59–116.

Toporov, Vladimir N. 1980. Vilnius, Wilno, Vil'na: gorod i mif. *Balto-slavjanskie ètnojazykovye kontakty*, ed. Tamara M. Sudnik. Moskva: Nauka, 3–71.

Toporov, Vladimir N. 1982. Drevnjaja Moskva v baltijskoj perspektive. *BSI* 1981[1982], 3–61.

Toporov, Vladimir N. 1983. Galindy v zapadnoj Evrope. *BSI* 1982[1983], 129–140.

Toporov, Vladimir N. 1988. Baltijskij element v gidronimii Pooč'ja, I. *BSI* 1986[1988], 154–177.

Toporov, Vladimir N. 1989. Baltijski element v gidronimii Pooč'ja, II. *BSI* 1987[1989], 47–69.

Toporov, Vladimir N. 1993. Ešče raz o baltizmach v češskix zemljax. *Slavia* 62, 51–63.

Toporov, Vladimir N. 1997a. Baltijskij element v gidronimii Pooč'ja, III. *BSI* 1988–1996[1997a], 276–310.

Toporov, Vladimir N. 1997b. Baltijskie sledy po Verxnem Donu. *BSI* 1988–1996[1997b], 311–324.

Toporov, Vladimir N. 1997c. K voprosu o drevnejšix balto-finnougorskix kontaktax po materialam gidronimii. *BSI* 1988–1996 [1997c], 325.

Toporov, Vladimir N. 2000a. Iz indoevropejskoj etimologii, VI (1–2). Ètimologija 1997–1999, 172–185.

Toporov, Vladimir N. 2000b. K rekonstrukcii balto-slavjanskogo mifologičeskogo obraza zemli-materi *Zemia* & *Mātē (*Mati)*. *BSI* XIV, 1998–1999, 239–371.

Toporov, Vladimir N. 2002. K interpretacii nekotoryx motivov russkix detskix igr v svete osnovnogo mifa (prjatki, žmurki, gorelki, salki-pjatnaški). *Mythologica Slavica* 5, 71–112.

Toporov, Vladimir N. & Trubačev, Oleg N. 1962. *Lingvističeskij analiz gidronimov Podneprov'ja*. Moskva: Izdatel'stvo Akademii nauk.

Töppen, Max. 1846. Geschichte des Heidenthums in Preussen. *Neue preussische Provinzialblätter* 1, 297–316.

Töppen, Max. 1847. *Critica de historia Borussiae antiqua*. Königsberg: Regiomonti Dalkowski.

Töppen, Max. 1853. *Geschichte der preussischen Historiographie von P. von Dusburg bis auf K. Schütz*. Berlin: Hertz.

Töppen, Max. 1867. *Aberglauben aus Masuren*. Gdańsk: Bertling.

Trautmann, Reinhardt. 1910. *Die altpreussische Sprachdenkmäler*. Göttingen, Vandenhoeck & Ruprecht.

Trautmann, Reinhold. 1923. *Baltisch-Slavisches Wörterbuch*. Göttingen: Vandenhoeck & Ruprecht.

Trinkūnas, Jonas. 2009. *Lietuvių senosios religijos kelias*. Vilnius: Asveja.

Trubačev, Oleg N. 1967. Iz slavjano-iranskix leksičeskix otnošenij. Ètimologija 1965, 3–81.

Trubačev, Oleg N. 1968. *Nazvanija rek pravoberežnoj Ukrainy*. Moskva: Nauka.

Trubačev, Oleg N. et al. (ed.) 1974f. *Ètimologičeskij slovaŕ slavjanskix jazykov*. Moskva: Nauka.

Trubačev, Oleg N. 1981. Replika po balto-slavjanskomu voprosu. *BSI* 1980[1981], 3–6.

Tyszkiewicz (Tiškevičius), Eustachy. 1842. *Rzut oka na żródła archeologii krajowej*. Vilnius: Zawadzki.

Tyszkiewicz (Tiškevičius), Konstantin. 1868. *O kurhanach na Litwie i Rusi zachodniéj*. Berlin: Bock.

Untermann, Jürgen. 2000. *Wörterbuch des Oskisch-Umbrischen*. Heidelberg: Winter.

Usener, Hermann Karl & Solmsen, Felix. 1894. *Litauische und lettische Götternamen*. Bonn: Cohen.

Vaba, Lembit. 1983. Baltische Lehnwörter der Wolga-Sprachen im Lichte neuerer Forschungsergebnisse. *Sovetskoe finno-ugrovedenie* 19/2, 138–145.

Vaba, Lembit. 2011. Language contacts between Baltic and Finnic languages – an exhausted issue in linguistic research? In: *Congressus XI. Internationalis Fenno-Ugristarum* (Piliscsaba, 9–14. VIII. 2010), Pars VI: *Dissertationes symposiorum ad linguisticam*, ed. by Sándor Csúcs, Nóra Falk, Viktória Tóth & Gábor Zaicz. Piliscsaba: Reguly Társaság, 44–52.

Vaitkevičius, V. 2004. The main features of the state religion in thirteenth-century Lithuania. *BSI* XVI, 331–356.

Vanagas, A. 1980. Maksimaľnyj areal baltijskoj gidronimii i problema proisxoždenija baltov. In: *Ėtnografičeskie i lingvističeskie aspekty ėtničeskoj istorii baltijskix narodov*. Riga: Zinatne, 119–123.

Vanagas, A. 1981a. Litovskie gidronimy slavjanskogo proisxoždenija. *BSI* 1980[1981], 151–162.

Vanagas, A. 1981b. *Lietuvių hidronimių etimologinis žodynas*. Vilnius: Mokslas.

Váňa, Zdeněk. 1990. *Svět pohanských bohů a démonů*. Praha: Panoráma.

Vasmer, Max. 1986–1988. Ėtimologičeskij slovaŕ russkogo jazyka, I–IV. Moskva: Progress (translated from the German original *Russisches etymologisches Wörterbuch*, I–III, Heidelberg: Winter 1950–1958, by Oleg N. Trubačev).

Vėlius, Norbertas. 1977. *Mitinės lietuvių sakmių būtybės*. Vilnius: Vaga.

Vendryes, J. & Lambert, Pierre-Yves. 1996. *Lexique étymologique de l'irlandais ancien* (Lettre D). Dublin: Institute for Advanced Studies – Paris: CNRS.

Voigt, Johannes. 1827–1839. *Geschichte Preussens von den ältesten Zeiten bis zum Untergange der Herrschaft des deutschen Ordens*. Königsberg: Bornträger.

Vykypěl, Bohumil. 2011. *Studie k šlechtickým titulům v germánských, slovanských a baltských jazycích. Etymologie jako pomocná věda historická*, 2. vyd. Praha: Nakladatelství Lidové noviny.

Walde, Alois & Hofmann, Johann B. 1938–1954. *Lateinisches etymologisches Wörterbuch*. Heidelberg: Winter.

WLS = *Wörterbuch der litauischen Schriftsprache: Litauisch-Deutsch*, Bd. I, von Max Niedermann, Alfred Senn & Franz Brender. Heidelberg: Winter 1932.

West, Martin L. 2007. Indo-European Poetry and Myth. Oxford: University Press.

Wolff, Fritz. 1910. *Avesta. Die heilige Bücher der Parsen* (übersetzt von Fritz Wolff). Strassburg: Trübner.

Wölky, Carl Peter & Saage, Johann Martin. 1860. *Codex diplomaticus Warmiensis*, Bd. I. Mainz: Kirchheim.

Wolter, E. 1886a. Mythologische Skizzen. *Archiv für slavische Philologie* IX, 635–642.

Wolter, E. 1886b. Ein Westrussisches Zeugnis über litauische Götter. In: *Litovskij katichizis N. Daukši. Po izdaniju 1595 goda vnov' perepečatannyj i snabžennyj ob'jasnenijami E. Vol'terom. Priloženie k 52. tomu zapisok imp. Akademii Nauk*, Č. 3. Sankt-Petĕrburg.

ZBM = Toporov, V. N. 1972. Zametki po baltijskoj mifologii. In: *Balto-slavjanskij sbornik*. Moskva: Nauka, 289–314.

Zinkevičius, Z. 1984. Poľsko-jatvjažskij slovarik? *BSI* 1983, 3–29.

Alphabetical survey of abbreviated primary sources

1483: Anonymous from AD 1483. In: Voigt, Johannes. *Geschichte Preussens von den ältesten Zeiten bis zum Untergange der Herrschaft des deutschen Ordens.* Vol. I, *Die Zeit des Heidentums (mit Abbildungen altpreußischer Grabhügel).* Königsberg 1827.

Akel: Akeliewicz/Akielewicz/Akelaitis, Nikołaj/Mikalojus. *Uwag.* In: Lelewel, Joachim. *Pisma rozmaite.* Vol. III. Poznań 1863.

AnnLit1600: *Annuae Litterae Societatis Jesv ad Patres et Fratres ejusdem Societatis. Anni 1600. Anni 1605.* Antwerpen 1618. Some parts quoted in: Wolter, E. „Perkunastempel und litauische Opfer- oder Deivensteine". In: *Mitteilungen der litauisch-literärischen Gesellschaft*, IV. 1899, p. 393.

AnnLit1601: *Annuae Litterae Societatis Jesv ad Patres et Fratres ejusdem Societatis. Anni 1601.* Antwerpen 1618.

AnnLit1604: *Annuae Litterae Societatis Jesv ad Patres et Fratres ejusdem Societatis. Anni 1604.* Douai 1618.

AnnVen: *Annales Residentiae Vendensis soc.tis Jesu. 1618.* In: *Mitteilungen aus der Livländischen Geschichte.* Vol. IV. Rīga: Gesellschaft für Geschichte und Altertumskunde, 1849.

Artick: Brandenburg, Albrecht von (1490–1545) & Polenz, Georg von (1478–1550) & Speratus, Paul (1489–1551). *Artickeln der Ceremonien und anderer Kirchenordnung.* The edict from AD 1526. In: Jacobson, Heinrich Friedrich. *Geschichte der Quellen des katholischen Kirchenrechtes der Provinzen Preussen und Posen.* Königsberg 1837.

Baer: *Kirchenbuch zu Ronneburg* (today Rauna), dated to the Nov 3, 1717. In: *Protokoll der lettisch-literärischen Gesellschaft v. J. 1910 §4.*

Behm: Behm, Johannes († 1648). *Duae orationes historicae de duplici divinae gratiae fundamento.* Königsberg 1644.

Bend: Bender, Johannes. *De veterum Prutenorum diis. Dissertatio historico-critica.* Braunsberg 1868.

Ber: Beringer, Heinrich. *Die Predigt an den Hochmeister Paul von Russdorf.* Written AD 1428. In: *Scriptores Rerum Prussicarum.* Tom IV. Leipzig 1874.

Berkh: Berkholz, Christian August: „Etwas Kirchliches aus Riga, von 1604–1618." In: *Rigasches Kirchenblatt.* Vol. 6 (1869–1870), nr. 48.

Bert: Bertuleit, Hans. „Das Religionswesen der alten Preussen mit litauisch-lettischen Parallelen". In: *Sitzungsbericht Altertumsgesselschaft Prussia.* Heft 25. Konigsberg 1924.

Bezz: Bezzenberger, Adalbert. *Beiträge zur Geschichte der litauischen Sprache auf Grund litauischer Texte des XVI. und des XVII. Jahrhunderts.* Göttingen: R. Peppmüller, 1877.

BezzMythAltlit: Bezzenberger, Adalbert. „Mythologisches in altlitauischen Texten". In: *Beiträge zur Kunde der indogermanischen Sprachen,* I, 1877, 41–47.

BezzLitForsch: Bezzenberger, Adalbert. *Litauische Forschungen. Beiträge zur Kenntnis der Sprache und des Volkstums der Litauer.* Göttingen: R. Peppmüller, 1882.

BezzVeck: Bezzenberger, Adalbert, apud Veckenstedt, Edmund. *Die Mythen, Sagen und Legenden der Zamaiten (Litauer).* Heidelberg: E. Veckenstedt, 1883.

Biel: Bielenstein, August Johann Gottfried. *Lettische Grammatik.* Mitau (Jelgava) 1863.

BielGrenz: Bielenstein, August Johann Gottfried. *Die Grenzen des lettischen Volksstammes und der lettischen Sprache.* Sankt-Peterburg 1892.

BielMann: Bielenstein, August Johann Gottfried. „Einige Bemerkungen zu Dr. Mannhardts ‚Beiträge zur Mythologie der lettischen Völker'". In: *Magazin der Lettisch-Literarischen Gesselschaft,* XIV. Mitau (Jelgava) 1868.

Blum: Blumenau, Laurentius (c. 1415–1484). *Historia de ordine Theutonicorum cruciferorum.* Written AD 1457. In: *Scriptores Rerum Prussicarum.* Tom IV. Leipzig 1874.

Börg: Börger, Johann Ludwig from Ermes (today Ērģeme in North Latvia). *Versuch über die Altertümer Lieflands und seiner Völker, besonders der Letten.* Rīga 1774.

Brem: Bremen, Adam von. *Adami Bremensis Gesta Hammaburg. Ecclesiae pontificum* (AD 1075). In: *Scriptores Rerum Germanicarum in usum scholarum.* Hannover – Leipzig 1907. See also: Krantz.

Bretk: Bretkūnas, Jonas (Bretke, Bretkus, Johann) (1536–1602). *Historia Rerum Prussicarum.* Fragmentarily cited in: Praetorius, Matthaeus. *Deliciae Prussicae oder Preussische Schaubühne.* (Written AD 1684). Published as: *Matthäus Prätorius Deliciae Prussicae.* Berlin: W. Pierson, 1871.

BretkPos: Bretkūnas, Jonas (Bretke or Bretkus, Johann) (1536–1602). *Postilla, tatai esti trumpas ir prastas Ischguldimas euangeliu.* Königsberg 1591.

BretkRuk: Bretkūnas, Jonas (Bretke, Bretkus, Johann) (1536–1602). *Manuscript of sermons.* Preserved only one citation in: Praetorius, Matthaeus. *Deliciae Prussicae oder Preussische Schaubühne.* Written AD 1684. Published as: Matthäus Prätorius. *Deliciae Prussicae.* Berlin: W. Pierson, 1871.

Brod: Brodowski, Jakob (1692–1744). *Lexicon Germano-Lithvanicum et Lithvano-Germanum.* Vol. I–II. Ms. written in 1713–1744. The first volume was edited as: Brodovskis, Jokūbas. *Lexicon Germano-Lithuanicum et Lithuano-Germanum.* Sv. I, *Abtilgen die Gesetze – Futter unter Sattel.* Vilnius: Lietuvių kalbos institutas, 2009.

Brück: Brückner, Aleksander. „Osteuropäische Götternamen. Ein Beitrag zur vergleichenden Mythologie". In: *Zeitschrift für vergleichende Sprachforschung auf dem Gebiete der indogermanischen Sprachen,* 50, 1922, 161–197.

BrückBaltLas: Brückner, Aleksander. „Besprechung von Grienberger ‚Die Baltica des Libellus Lasicki'". In: *Kwartalnik historyczny* (Lvov), XI, 1897, p. 99.

BrückBei: Brückner, Aleksander. „Beiträge zur litauischen Mythologie". In: *Archiv für slavische Philologie,* IX, 1886, 1–35.

Bül: Bülow, Stephan. *Schreiben an Herzog Gotthard Kettler* (Written AD 1565). In: *Sitzungsberichte der Kurländischen Gesellschaft für Literatur und Kunst.* Mitau (Jelgava): Gustav Otto, 1905.

Cant: Cantimpre, Thomas von. *Thomae Cantipratani Bonum universale de apibus II.* (Written AD 1263). Douai: Colvenerius, 1597.

CDW: Wolky, Carl Peter & Saage, Johann Martin. *Codex diplomaticus Warmiensis I.* Mainz: Franz Kirchheim, 1860.

Cisz: Ciszewski, Stanisław. *Ognisko. Studium Etnologiczne.* Krakow 1903.

ConSyn: Brandenburg, Albrecht von (1490–1545), Polenz, Georg von (1478–1550) & Speratus, Paul (1489–1551). *Constitutiones synodales* (Edicts from AD

1530). In: Jacobson, Heinrich Friedrich. *Geschichte der Quellen des katholischen Kirchenrechtes der Provinzen Preussen und Posen.* Königsberg 1837.

Crit: Töppen, Max. *Critica de historia Borussiae antiqua.* Konigsberg 1847.

Dauk: Ledesma, Jakub. *Nauka Chrześciańska, abo Katechizmik dla Dźiatek etc.* Krakow 1572. Expanded and translated into Lithuanian by Daukša, Mikalojus (c. 1530–1613). *Katechismas arba Mokslas kiekwienam krikszczionii priwalvs.Paraszitas per D. Jakuba Ledesma theologa Societatis Jesu. Iszgulditas iż liecżuvio Laukiszko ing Lietuwiszka per Kuniga Mikałoju Daugsza kanonika Żemaicziu.* Vilnius 1595.

Dav: David, Lucas (1503–1583). *Preussische Chronik* (Written in 1573–1583). Königsberg 1812. Republished in: *Baltų religijos ir mitologijos šaltiniai*, Vol. II. Vilnius: Mokslo ir enciklopedijų leidykla, 2001.

Diar: *Rath und Abschiedbuch von 1531. Diarium curiae.* Foliant 284b of the archive of Königsberg B186.

Dl: Długosz, Jan (1415–1480). *Annales seu cronicae incliti Regni Poloniae.* Vol. 1–12 (Written in 1455–1480). In: *Joannis Długossii Opera Omnia.* Krakow: Alexander Przezdziecki, 1876–1877.

DomErm1325: Regulation of the Temple Chapter in Ermland, AD 1325. In: Wolky, Carl Peter & Saage, Johann Martin. *Codex diplomaticus Warmiensis.* I. Mainz: Franz Kirchheim, 1860. p. 375.

Dub: *Chronicon Dubnicense* (Till AD 1479). In: *Historiae Hungariae Fontes Domestici.* Vol. I, Script. III. Ed. M. Florianus. Budapest 1881, pp. 1–204.

Dusb: Dusburg, Peter von († 1326). *Cronica Terre Prussie* (Written AD 1326). Edited as: *Petri de Dusburg, Ordinis Teutonici Sacerdotis Chronicon Prussiae etc. auctore et collectore Christophoro Hartknoch, Jenae 1679* a *Chronicon Terrae Prussiae von Peter von Dusburg.* Ed. Max Töppen. In: *Scriptores Rerum Prussicarum.* Vol. I. Leipzig 1861, pp. 3–269.

Einh: Einhorn, Paul († 1655). *Historia Lettica (das ist Beschreibung der Lettischen Nation in welcher von der Letten als alten Einwohner und Besitzer des Lieflandes, Curlandes und Semgallen Namen, Uhrsprung oder Ankunfft ihrem Gottes-Dienst, ihrer Republica oder Regimente so sie in der Heydenschafft gehabt, auch ihren Sitten, Geberden, Gewonheiten, Natur und Eigenschaft en etc. gruendlich und uembstaendig Meldung geschickt). Der Teutschen Nation und allen der Historischen Warheit Liebhabern zu einem noethigen Unterricht zusammen getragen und in den Druck verfertiget durch Paulum Einhorn, Fuerstlichen Curlaendischen Superintendenten P.M.* Tartu: Johann Vogeln, der Koenigl. Acad. Buchdruker, 1649.

EinhAbg: Einhorn, Paul († 1655). *Wiederlegunge der Abgötterey.* Rīga 1627. Some passages appear in: *Scriptores Rerum Livonicarum.* Vol. II. Rīga – Leipzig 1853, pp. 639–652.

EinhAtax: Einhorn, Paul († 1655). *De ataxias incommodo et boni ordinis commodo et utilitate oratio, cum… M. Hermannus Toppius…ecclesiarum districtus Grobinensis Praepositus constitueretur.* Rīga 1648.

EinhRef: Einhorn, Alexander († 1575) & Paul († 1655). *Reformatio gentis Letticae in ducatu Curlandiae.* Message from Alexander Einhorn's visitation of parishes Selburg and Dunaburg (today Sēlpils and Daugavpils), AD 1570. Rīga 1636. In: *Scriptores Rerum Livonicarum.* Vol. II. Rīga – Leipzig 1853, pp. 605–637.

Engelb: *Executoriale Engelberts, Bischofs von Dorpat, als papstlichen Bevollmachtigten gegen den Deutschen Orden 1336 Nov 15.* In: *Livländisches, Esthnisches und Curländisches Urkundenbuch.* Vol. II. Ed. F. G. von Bunge. Königsberg 1853, p. 229.

Erl1693: Hastfer, Jacob Johann. Regulation dated Oct 4, 1693.

Fabr: Fabricius, Dionysius (1564–1617). *Livonicae historiae compendiosa Series.* Written AD 1611–1620. In: *Scriptores Rerum Livonicarum.* Vol. II. 1848. 2nd ed. Rīga – Leipzig 1853, pp. 427f.

Frey: Freyberg, Johannes. „Von dem Sudawen". In: *Preussische Chronik* (written AD 1548). Edited as: *Preussische Chronik des Johannes Freiberg.* Ed. F. A. Meckelburg. Königsberg 1848.

Fried1322: Wildenberg, Friedrich von. *Treaty with Bishop and Temple Chapter of the Sambian Diocese* dated to AD 1322. In: Voigt, Johannes. *Codex diplomaticus Prussicus.* Sv. II. Konigsberg 1836–1861.

Funcc: Funccius, Johannes (1518–1566). *Message about the year* 1217. In: *Commentariorum in praeced. chronologiam libri decem.* Written AD 1558. Wittenberg 1570.

Funck: Funcke, Johannes. *Protokoll der Kirchenvisitation, die… Johannes Funcke im… Gebiet Grobin… 1560, Juli 19–26 vorzog.* In: *Sitzungsberichte der Kurländischen Gesellschaft für Literatur und Kunst a. d. J. 1905.* Mitau (Jelgava): Oskar Stavenhagen, 1906.

Goe: Goebel, Severin (1530–1612). *Histori vnd Eigendlicher Bericht von Herkommen, vrsprung vnd vielfeltigem brauch des bornsteins.* Königsberg 1566.

GottCultPreuss: Anonymous author. *Gottesidee und Cultus bei den alten Preussen. Ein Beitrag zur vergleichenden Sprachvorschung.* Berlin 1870.

Grav1638: *Gravamina der H. Pastoren in Liefflandt, welche in dem Synodo zu Wenden gehalten Anno 1638 Dom. Esto mihi sindt afgenommen worden.* In: Lundström, E. H. J. *Bidrag till Livlands Kyrkohistoria under den svenska tidens första skede: från Rigas intagande 1621 till freden i Oliva 1660.* Supplement XXVI. Uppsala – Stockholm 1914.

Greg: *Bull of the Pope Gregorius IX.*, dated to the 23rd January 1232. In: Raynaldo, Odorico. *Annales ecclesiastici ad annum 1232*, nr. 6–7. Lucca: Leonardo Venturini, 1747–56. Reprinted in: *Preussisches Urkundenbuch.* Ed. F. G. von Bunge. Königsberg 1882.

Grenz1332: *Document determining the borders*, AD 1332. In: Voigt, Johannes. *Codex diplomaticus Prussicus.* Bd. II. Königsberg 1836–1861.

Grienb: Grienberger, Theodor. „Die Baltica des Libellus Lasicki. Untersuchungen zur litauischen Mythologie". In: *Archiv für slavische Philologie*, 18, 1896, 1–85.

Grimm: Grimm, Jacob Ludwig Karl. „Namen des Donners". In: *Grimm: Kleinere Schriften*, Bd. II, *Abhandlungen zur Mythologie und Sittenkunde.* Berlin: F. Dümmler, 1865, 402–438.

Grun: Grunau, Simon (1470–1530/1537). *Cronica und beschreibung allerlüstlichenn, nützlichsten und*

waren historien des namkundigenn landes zu Prewssen. Written in 1517–1529. Edited as: *Simon Grunau's preussische Chronik.* In: *Die preussischen Geschichtsschreiber des XVI. und XVII. Jahrhunderts.* Bd. IIII. Ed. M. Perlbach, R. Philippi & P. Wagner. Leipzig 1876–1896.

Hart: Hartknoch, Christoph (1644–1687). Transcript of *Constitutiones synodales* in: *Selectae dissertationes historicae de variis rebus Prussicis.* Frankfurt – Leipzig 1679.

HartDiss: Hartknoch, Christoph (1644–1687). *Selectae dissertationes historicae de variis rebus Prussicis.* Frankfurt – Leipzig 1679.

Heilw: *Message about the village called Heiligenwalde and circumstances called Silva sacra in Pomezania* (13th cent.). In: Voigt, Johannes. *Geschichte Preussens von den ältesten Zeiten bis zum Untergange der Herrschaft des deutschen Ordens.* Bd. I, *Die Zeit des Heidentums (mit Abbildungen altpreusischer Grabhügel).* Königsberg 1827.

Heilw1344: Kniprode, Winrich von. *Regulation about founding the village Heiligenwalde, entrusted to Volkwinu von Dobrin* (AD 1344). In: Voigt, Johannes. *Codex diplomaticus Prussicus.* Vol. III. Königsberg 1836–1861, p. 70.

Heilw1377: Kniprode, Winrich von. *Document dated to the* Nov 3, 1377. In: *Scriptores Rerum Prussicarum.* Vol. IV. Leipzig 1874.

Helm: Bosau, Helmold von (c. 1120 – c. 1177). *Cronica Slavorum.* Written c. 1167. First edited in print in Frankfurt: Siegmund Schorkel, 1556. Further e.g. Hannover: B. Schmeidler, 1909.

HennBes: Hennenberger, Caspar (1529–1600). *Kurtze und warhafftige Beschreibung zu Preussen.* Konigsberg 1584.

HennErc: Hennenberger, Caspar (1529–1600). *Erclerung der preussischen grössern Landtaffel oder Mappen.* Königsberg: Georg Osterbergern, 1595.

Herber: Herberstein, Siegmund von (1486–1566). *Commentarii Rerum Moscovitarum.* Wien 1549. Later editions were published in Basel: Johannes Oporinus, 1551; Basel: Johannes Oporinus, 1556. The German translation of the author: *Moscouia der Hauptstat in Reissen, durch Herrn Sigmunden Freyherrn zu Herberstain, Neyperg vnd Guetenhag Obristen Erbcamrer, und obristen Erbtruckhsessen in Kärntn, Römischer zu Hungern und Beheim Khü. May. etc. Rat, vnd Presidenten der Niderösterreichischen Camer zusamen getragen.* Wien: Michael Zimmermann, 1557.

Herv: Hervord, Heinrich von († 1370). *Liber de rebus memorabilioribus sive Chronicon Henrici de Hervordia.* Ed. August Potthast. Gottingen 1859.

Hon: *Bull of the Pope Honorius III,* dated to the 15th June 1218. In: Voigt, Johannes. *Codex diplomaticus Prussicus.* Vol. I, 12, nr. XII. Königsberg 1836.

Hup: Hupel, August Wilhelm (1737–1819). *Topographische Nachrichten von Liefund Ehstland.* Bd. I.–IV. Rīga: Johann Friedrich Hartknoch, 1774, 1777, 1782, 1789.

Idr: Idrisi. „Ein Abschnitt aus dem arabischen Geographen Idrisi", *Verhandlungen der Gelehrten Estnischen Gesselschaft .* Bd. VII, Heft 3/4, p. 1. Tartu 1873.

Inn: *Bull of the Pope Inocentius III,* dated to the 5th Oct 1199. *Innocentii III. PP. Epist. Prima Lib. II ep. 191.* In: *Scriptores Rerum Livonicarum.* Bd. I. Rīga – Leipzig 1848, p. 336.

InstKV: *Recessus Generalis der Kirchen-Visitation des Insterburgischen vnd anderen Littauschen Aembtern im Hertzogthumb Preuszen.* Record of visitation of the Prussian parishes. Königsberg: Lorentz Segebaden Erden, 1639. Some parts are cited in: Bezzenberger, Adalbert. „Zur litauischen Bibliographie". In: *Mitteilungen der litauisch-literärischen Gesellschaft,* I, 1883.

Instr1650: *Instructio ad Theodorum Praetorium.* Stockholm, Oct 29, 1650. In: Lundström, E.H.J. *Bidrag till Livlands Kyrkohistoria under den svenska tidens* *första skede: från Rigas intagande 1621 till freden i Oliva 1660.* Supplement XXXIX. Uppsala – Stockholm 1914.

InstrGen: Henning, Salomon (1528–1589) & Einhorn, Alexander († 1575). *Instructio generalis omnibus Pastoribus et Ecclesiae ministris praescripta etc.* (First edited AD 1570). In: Sehling, E. *Die evangelischen Kirchenordnungen des XVI. Jahrhunderts.* Bd. V. Leipzig 1913.

InstrPom: Instructions for Church visitations in the Prussian diocese Pomezania (14th cent.). In:. *Geschichte der Quellen des katholischen Kirchenrechtes der Provinzen Preussen und Posen.* Supplements LXXV & LXXVII, von Jacobson, Heinrich Friedrich. Königsberg 1837.

Jac: Jacobson, Heinrich Friedrich. *Geschichte der Quellen des katholischen Kirchenrechtes der Provinzen Preussen und Posen.* Königsberg 1837.

Jer: Jeroschin, Nikolaus von. *Kronike von Pruzinlant.* Extended translation of Dusburg's chronicle into German. Written AD 1340. In: *Scriptores Rerum Prussicarum,* Bd. I. Ed. Ernst Gottfried Wilhelm Strehlke. Leipzig 1861.

JL: Henricus de Lettis (c. 1187–1259). *Chronicon Livonicum vetus.* Written in 1225–1227. Edited e.g. as *Heinrici Chronicon Lyvoniae ex recensione Wilhelmi Arndt in usum scholarum ex Monumentis Germaniae historicis recudi fecit Georg. Heinr. Pertz.* Hannover 1874.

Jodoc: Willichius, Jodocus (1501–1552). *Commentaria in C. Taciti Germaniam.* 1560.

JohBrand: Brand, Johann Arnold von († 1691). *Johann-Arnolds von Brand Reisen durch die Mark Brandenburg, Preussen, Churland, Liefland, Pleskovien etc.* Ed. Heinrich-Christian von Hennin. Wesel: Heinrich-Christian von Hennin, 1702.

JohMal: Maletius, Johannes (Maeletius; Malecki, Jan) (1482–1567). *Epistola de sacrifi ciis et idolatria veterum Borussorum, Livonum, aliarumque uicinarum gentium, Ad Clarissimum Virum Doctorem Georgium Sabinum, Illustrissimi Principis Prussiae etc.* Ed. Georg Sabinus. Königsberg 1551. In: *Acta Borussica ecclesiastica, civilia, litararia.* Königsberg 1731. Other edition e.g. *Libellus. De sacrificiis et idolatria veterum Borussorum etc.* Ed. Hieronymus Maletius. Königsberg 1563.

Jung: Junge, Michael († 1443). *Articuli per Prutenos tenendi et erronei contra fidem abiciendi.* Command issued AD 1426. In: (Foliant of the archive in Königsberg) „Alte babstliche Privilegia", p. 215. Further Jacobson, Heinrich Friedrich. *Geschichte der Quellen des katholischen Kirchenrechtes der Provinzen Preussen und Posen.* Königsberg 1837.

Kadl: Kadłubek, Vincenc (1160–1223). *Chronica seu originale regum et principum Poloniae.* In: *Monumenta Poloniae Historica.* Bd. II. Ed. August Bielowski. Lvov 1872.

Kelch: Kelch, Christian (1657–1710). *Liefländische Historia oder kurze Beschreibung der denkwürdigsten Kriegs- und Friedensgeschichte Ehst- Lief- und Lettlandes etc.* Tallinn: Johannes Mehner, 1695.

KirchOr: Henning, Salomon (1528–1589) & Einhorn, Alexander († 1575). *De Doctrina et ceremoniis sinceri cultus diuini Ecclesiarum Ducatus Curlandiae, Semigalliaque etc. In Livonia – Kirchenordnung, wie es mit der LEHR/Göttliches worts, Ausstheilung der Sacrament, Christlichen Ceremonien, ordentlicher Ubung des waren Gottesdiensts, In den Kirchen des Herzogthumbs Churlandt und Semigallien in Lieflandt sol stets vermittelst Göttlicher hulff gehalten werden. Anno Salutis 1570.* In: Sehling, E. *Die evangelischen Kirchenordnungen des XVI. Jahrhunderts.* Bd. V. Leipzig 1913.

Klein: Klein, Daniel. *Grammatica Lituanica.* Königsberg 1653.

Kojal: Wijuk-Koialovicius, Albertus (Vijūkas-Kojalavičius, Albertas / Wijuk-Kojałowicz, Wojciech) (1609–1677). *Historiae Lituanae.* Selected Latin translation of Stryjkowski's *Kronika polska, litewska, żmudzka i wszystkiej Rusi.* Sv. I, *Historiae Lithuanae pars prior, de rebus Lithuanorum ante susceptam Christianam religionem conjunctionemque... cum regno Poloniae.* Gdańsk 1650. Vol. II, *Historiae Lithuanae pars altera a conjunctione cum Regno Poloniae ad unionem corum Dominiorum libri octo.* Antwerpen 1669.

Konr: Jungingen, Konrad von (1355–1407). *Law* dated to AD 1394. In: Voigt, Johannes. *Geschichte Preussens von den altesten Zeiten bis zum Untergange der Herrschaft des deutschen Ordens.* Bd. VI, *Die Zeit des Hochmeisters Konrad von Jungingen, von 1393 bis 1407. Verfassung des Ordens und des Landes.* Königsberg 1834, p. 17.

Konr1304: Sack, Konrad. *A document of Commander from* Guter, dated AD 1304. In: *Preussisches Urkundenbuch.* Bd. I. Ed. F. G. von Bunge. Königsberg 1882.

KozInv: Kozicki, Jozef (Joseph). „Inventarium". Edited on June 9, 1585. In: „Akta ziemskie Rosieńskie" in: Baliński, Michał a Lipiński, Tymoteusz. *Starożytna Polska pod vzgledem historycznym, jeografi cznym i statystycznym.* Sv. III. Warszawa: S. Orgelbrand Księgarz, 1846, p. 525.

Krantz: Krantz, Albert (c. 1450–1517). „Suetia liber I prologus" in: *Chronica regnorum aquilonarium Daniae, Sueciae, et Noruagiae.* Strassburg 1546–1548.

Kur1253: Lützelburg, Heinrich von. *Nach der Belehnung des Velthune, seines Bruders Reygyn, des Twertikine und des Saweyde mit der Burg Cretyn und der*

Hälfte der Burgsuchung überläßt Bf. Heinrich von Kurland dem Deutschen Orden das ihm verbliebene Drittel der anderen Hälfte, wofür der Orden ihm und der Stadt Memel ein Stück Weide- und Buschland zur Nutzung überläßt. Written in Memel (today Klaipėda), Apr 4, 1253. In: *Livländisches, Esthnisches und Curländisches Urkundenbuch.* Ed. F. G. von Bunge. Königsberg 1881.

Kursch: Kurschat, Friedrich. *Wörterbuch der littauischen Sprache.* Bd. 1, 2. Halle: Waisenhaus, 1870, 1883.

KurschGramm: Kurschat, Friedrich. *Grammatik der littauischen Sprache.* Halle: Waisenhaus, 1876.

Labiau: *The official letter of an administrative clerk to burggrave Christoph von Kreytzen,* dated to Nov 26, 1571. In: *Neue Preussische Provinzialblätter.* Serie I, Bd. II. Königsberg 1846, p. 227.

Land1422: Johannes VI. Ambundi & Spanheim, Siegfried Lander von. *Allgemeine Landesordnung.* Edited AD 1422. In: *Akten und Rezesse der livländischen Ständetage.* Bd. I, nr. 299. Rīga: Oskar Stavenhagen, 1907.

Land1434: Russdorf, Paul Belenzer von. *Neue Landesordnung.* Edited on the 24th January 1434. In: Töppen, Max. *Acten der Standetage Preussens unter der Herrschaft Deutschen Ordens.* Leipzig: Max Töppen, 1874.

Land1444: Erlichshausen, Konrad VI. von. *Landesordnung für das Niederland.* Edited on Oct 18, 1444. In: Töppen, Max. *Acten der Ständetage Preussens unter der Herrschaft Deutschen Ordens.* Leipzig: Max Töppen, 1874.

Land1503: Sachsen, Friedrich von. *Landesordnung.* Edited AD 1503. In: Jacobson, Heinrich Friedrich. *Geschichte der Quellen des katholischen Kirchenrechtes der Provinzen Preussen und Posen.* Königsberg 1837.

Landg1292: Brühaven, Berthold von. *Regulation about assigning a land to Konrad Koch,* AD 1292. In: *Preussisches Urkundenbuch.* Sv. I. Ed. F. G. von Bunge. Königsberg 1882.

Lang: Lange, Jakob (1711–1777). *Vollständiges deutsch-lettisches und lettisch-deutsches Lexikon.* Oberpahlen (today Poltsamaa, Estonia) – Mitau (Jelgava): Steffenhagen 1772–1777.

Las: Lasicius, Joannes (Łasicki, Jan) (1534 – c. 1600). *De Diis Samagitarum caeterorumque Sarmatorum et falsorum Christianorum.* In: *Michalonis Litvani de Moribus Tartarorum Litvanorum et Moschorum Fragmina X multiplici Historia referta Et Johan. Lasicii Poloni De Diis Samagitarum caeterorumque Sarmatorum et falsorum Christianorum, item de religione Armeniorum et de initio Regiminis Stephani Batorij nunc primum per J. Jas. Grasserum C. P. ex man-*

uscripto authentico edita. Basel: Conrad Waldkirch, 1615. Other edition: see LasMannBiel.

LasMannBiel: Lasicius, Joannes (Łasicki, Jan) (1534 – c. 1600). „De Diis Samagitarum caeterorumque Sarmatorum et falsorum Christianorum. Mit Erläuterungen von Wilhelm Mannhardt und ‚Einige Bemerkungen' von August Johann Gottfried Bielenstein". In: *Magazin der Lettisch-Literarischen Gesselschaft*, XIV. Mitau (Jelgava) 1868.

LD: Barons, Krišjānis (1835–1923). *Latvju dainas.* Bd. I, II, III (A, B, C), IV, V, VI. First edited in 1894–1915. Rīga 1922.

Les: Leskien, August. *Die Bildung der Nomina im Litauischen.* Leipzig: S. Hirzel, 1891.

LesLes: Leskien, August. *Litauisches Lesebuch mit Grammatik und Wörterbuch.* Heidelberg: Hirt und Streitberg, 1919.

LietDain: Juškevič (Juška, Juškevičius), Antanas. *Lietuviškos dainos.* Vol. I–III. Kazan 1880–1882.

LivOrd1677: Supreme Church Consistory for Livonia. *Verordnung* v. 1. Mai 1677.

Lub: Lubenau, Reinhold (1556–1631). „Beschreibung der Reisen des Reinhold Lubenau" (1585). In: *Mitteilungen aus der Stadtbibliothek zu Königsberg in Preussen.* Bd. IV. Königsberg: W. Sahm, 1912.

Lüb: Bardowik, Albrecht von. In: *Die Chroniken der niedersächsischen Städte Lübeck* (written 1298), Bd. II. Ed. K. Koppmann. Leipzig 1899.

Lyffl : Russow, Balthasar (c. 1536–1600). *Chronica der Prouintz Lyfflandt.* Rostock 1578.

Mal: Anonymous West Russian priest. Supplement to „*Xronografija"* of Ioannis Malalas (AD 563). Written AD 1261. *Xronika Ioanna Malaly v slavjanskom perevode.* Ed. V. M. Istrin. Odesa: Ėkonomičeskaja tipografija, 1905–1911. The part about Lithuanian mythology also appeared in: Mierzyński, Antoni. *Mytologiae Lituanicae Monumenta. Żrodła do Mytologii Litewskiej.* Vol. I, *Ot Tacyta do konca XIII wieku.* Warszawa 1892, pp. 127–129.

Mann: Mannhardt Wilhelm (1831–1880). *Letto-Preussische Götterlehre.* Published posthumously in Rīga 1936 (abbreviated as LPG). Till the present time it serves as the richest collection of the primary texts about Baltic mythology.

MannLettSonn: Mannhardt, Wilhelm. „Die lettischen Sonnenmythen". *Zeitschrift für Ethnologie* 7, 1875, 73–104, 209–244, 281–330.

Mart: Martini, Wilhelm. „A lituo nomen ducis gens Littawa agresti." In: Klein, Daniel. *Gesangbuch.* Königsberg 1666.

ME: Endzelīns, Jānis & Mīlenbachs, Kārlis (Mühlenbach, Karl). *Latviešu valodas vārdnīca. Lettisch-deutsches Wörterbuch.* Sv. 1–6. Rīga 1923–1932.

Med1326: *A document from Prussia dated to AD 1326* in: Töppen, Max. *Historisch-comparative Geographie von Preussen.* Gotha 1858.

Miech: Miechow, Mathias de (Maciej of Miechow, alias Maciej Karpiga) (1457–1523). *Chronica Polonorum.* Krakow 1521.

Mierz: Mierzyński, Antoni. *Mytologiae Lituanicae Monumenta. Źrodła do Mytologii Litewskiej.* 1. *Ot Tacyta do konca XIII wieku.* 2. *Wiek XIV i XV.* Warszawa 1892, 1896.

MierzLas: Mierzyński, Antoni. „Jan Lasicki źrodło do Mytologii Litewskiej". In: *Rocznik Cesarsko-Krolewskiego Towarzystwa Naukowego Krakowskiego.* Sv. 18. Krakow 1870.

MierzLasKiev: Mierzyński, Antoni. „Ian Lasickij i ego sočinenie: De Diis Samagitarum". In: *Trudy III. arxeologičeskogo sjezda v Rossii.* Tom II. Kyiv 1878.

Mikk: Mikkola, Josef Julius. „Etymologische Beiträge". In: *Beiträge zur Kunde der indogermanischen Sprachen,* 21/2, 1896, 218–225.

Mikl: Miklosich, Franz (Miklošič, Franc). *Die Fremdwörter in den slavischen Sprachen.* Wien: K. K. Hof- und Staatsdruckerei, 1867.

Mis: Mislenta, Coelestin (1588–1653). Transcript of *Constitutiones synodales* in: *Manuale Pruthenicum seu Repetitio corporis doctrinae ecclesiarum Pruthenicarum.* Königsberg 1626.

MLLGI: *Magazin der Lettisch-Literarischen Gesselschaft,* I. Mitau (Jelgava) 1828.

Mosv: Mosvidius, Martinus (Mažvydas, Martynas) (1510–1563). *Catechismvsa prasty szadei, makslas skaitima raschta yr giesmes.* Königsberg: H. Weinreich, 1547. Published as *Katechismus vom Jahre 1547* in: *Litauische und Lettische Drucke des 16. Jahrhunderts.* Bd. 1. Göttingen 1874.

Nar: Narbutt, Teodor. „Mitologia Litewska." In: *Dzieje starożytne narodu litewskiego,* I. Vilnius 1835.

NarkGail: *Das Verhör von Anna Narkuwen und Catharina Geilawen aus der Stadt Tilsit in Herzogtum Preussen, die der Hexerei beschuldigt werden den* 29. Dezember 1559 – 16. Januar 1560. Published in: Augstkalns, Alvils. „Tilžės lietuvių burtai XVI a. teismo aktuose". In: *Tautosakos darbai,* Vol. 3. Kaunas 1937. See also the Lithuanian translation included in: *Baltų religijos ir mitologi-*

jos šaltiniai, Vol. II. Edited by Vėlius. Vilnius: Mokslo ir enciklopedijų leidybos institutas, 2001.

Ness: Nesselmann, Georg Heinrich Ferdinand. *Die Sprache der alten Preussen in ihren Überresten erläutert.* Berlin: F. Dümmler, 1845.

NessLied: Nesselmann, Georg Heinrich Ferdinand. *Littauische Volkslieder, gesammelt, kritisch bearbeitet und metrisch übersetzt.* Berlin: F. Dummler, 1853.

Nies: Niesiecki, Kasper (1682–1744). *Korona Polska przy złotey wolności staro-żytnemi Rycerstwa Polskiego y Wielkiego Xięstwa Litewskiego kleynotami nay-wyższymi Honorami Heroicznym, Męstwem y odwagą, Wytworną Nauką a nay-pierwey Cnotą, nauką Pobożnością, y Swiątobliwością ozdobiona Potomnym zaś wiekom na zaszczyt y nieśmiertelną sławę Pamiętnych w tey Oyczyźnie Synow podana Przez X. Kaspra Niesieckego Societatis Jesu.* Vol. II + Vol. IV. Lwow: Drukarnia Collegium Lwowskiego Societatis Jesu, 1728–1743.

Nik: Jacobson, Heinrich Friedrich. *Geschichte der Quellen des katholischen Kirchenrechtes der Provinzen Preussen und Posen.* Königsberg 1837; and Schö-neck, Nikolaus von. *Mandate dated to the* 4th Oct 1442. In: Foliant of the archive of Königsberg „Alte babstliche Privilegia", p. 125.

Ol: Olearius, Adam (1603–1671). *Offt begehrte Beschreibung der Newen Ori-entalischen Reise, so durch Gelegenheit einer hollsteinischen Legation an den König in Persien geschehen.* Including his description of the journey for Livonia AD 1635. Schleswig 1647.

OlDal: Dalins, Olof von (1708–1763). *Geschichte des Reiches Schweden.* Ger-man translation by J. Benzelstierna & J. C. Dahnert. Greifswald: Anton Ferdinand Rose, 1756.

OlPad: Scholasticus, Oliverus. *Oliverii Scholasticii Historia regum Terre sancte.* Written AD 1220. In: *Die Schriften des Kölner Domscholasters Oliverus.* Tübin-gen: Bibliothek d. Litterar. Ver. in Stuttgart, 1894.

Osterm: Ostermeyer, Gottfried. *Kritischer Beytrag zur altpreussischen Reli-gionsgeschichte.* Marienwerder 1775.

Pax: *Peace agreement of the Order of the Teutonic Knights with the Prussians* dated to the 7th February 1249. In: Wolky, Carl Peter a Saage, Johann Martin. *Codex diplomaticus Warmiensis I,* nr. 19. Mainz: Franz Kirchheim, 1860.

Pax1398: *Peace agreement of Lithuanian Grand Duchy Vytautas (Witold) with the Order of the Teutonic Knights,* AD 1398. In: *Livländisches, Esthnisches und Curländisches Urkundenbuch.* Bd. IV. Königsberg: F. G. von Bunge.

Picc: Piccolomini, Enea Silvio (Aeneas Sylvius) (1405–1464; later the Pope Pius II., who mediated the reports of Hieronymus of Prague). *Europa.* Written in

1458–1464. In: Voigt, G. *Enea Silvio de Piccolomini als Papst Pius II. und sein Zeitalter.* Bd. 1–3. Berlin 1856–1863.

Plak: Plāķis, Juris. *Leišu valodas rokas grāmata.* Rīga 1926.

Plett: Plettenberg, Walter (Wolter) von (c. 1450–1535). *Draggun und allen sinen rechten eruen twe Hakenn landes im gebede vnd Kerspel to Goldingen in dusser naskreuen scheidung gelegen. Interste antogaende an enem hilligen busche, genomet Elkewalke etc. De dato am avende Thomae 1503.* In: *Livländisches, Esthnisches und Curländisches Urkundenbuch.* Bd. II, nr. 589. Ed. F. G. von Bunge. Königsberg 1853.

Pobeten: Hennenberger, Caspar (1529–1600). „Pobeten" (AD 1531), in: *Erclerung der preussischen grossern Landtaffel.* Königsberg 1595.

Pol: Dzierzwa (Dirswa, Traska). *Annales Polonorum.* Written in 1440's. In: Mierzyński, Antoni. *Mytologiae Lituanicae Monumenta. Źrodła do Mytologii Litewskiej.* Sv. I, *Ot Tacyta do konca XIII wieku.* Warszawa 1892.

Prae: Praetorius, Matthaeus (1635–1704/1707). *Deliciae Prussicae oder Preussische Schaubühne.* Written AD 1684. Edited e.g. as: *Matthäus Prätorius Deliciae Prussicae.* Berlin: W. Pierson, 1871.

PraeLitArt: Praetorius, Matthaeus (1635–1704/1707). *Nachricht von der Littauer Art, Natur und Leben.* In: *Erleutertes Preussen.* Sv. I. Königsberg 1723.

PreussUr: *Preussisches Urkundenbuch.* Ed. F. G. von Bunge. Königsberg 1882.

Priv1286: Thierberg, Konrad von. *Privilege for the city of Königsberg*, dated to the 28th February 1286. In: *Preussisches Urkundenbuch.* Bd. I. Ed. F. G. von Bunge. Königsberg 1882.

Proc: *Record of a judical process in Prussia*, AD 1415. In: *Scriptores Rerum Prussicarum.* Bd. II. Ed. Theodor Hirsch. Leipzig 1863, p. 540.

ProtRig1637: *Protocollum Inferioris Consistorialis Iudicii Districtus Rigensis A. 1637 mense Maio.* In: Die *Bibliothek der Gesellschaft für Geschichte und Altertumskunde zu Riga* (Rīgas Vēstures un senatnes pētītāju biedrības bibliotēka).

RagAbg: *And den Haubtmann zu Ragnit wegen der Abgötterey, so von einigen Littawen bei einer Eichen zwischen Bojargallen und Rudschen mitten im Walde getrieben wird. Den 31: Juli A. 1657.* In: *Neue Preussische Provinzialblatter.* Serie III (1858–1866), Bd. 10. Königsberg, p. 159.

RatBul: *Document about the villages of Ratytien and Bulichien* (14th cent.). In: Voigt, Johannes. *Geschichte Preußens von den ältesten Zeiten bis zum Untergange der Herrschaft des Deutschen Ordens.* Bd. III, *Die Zeit vom Frieden 1249 bis zur Unterwerfung der Preußen 1283.* Königsberg 1828.

Reim: Anonymous author. *Livländische Reimchronik* (till AD 1290). First edited: Rīga: L. Bergmann, 1817. Also in: *Scriptores Rerum Livonicarum.* Bd. I. Rīga – Leipzig 1848, pp. 493–829.

Rez: Rėza, Liudvikas Gediminas Martynas (1776–1840). *Dainos oder Litthauische Volkslieder, gesammelt, übersetzt und herausgegeben von L. J. Rhesa.* Königsberg 1825.

Rost: Rostowski, Stanislaus (Stanisław) (1711–1784). *Lituanicarum Societatis Jesu historiarum provincialium. Pars I.* Vilnius: S.R.M. et Reipublicae Academicis Societatis Jesu, 1768. Later edited as: *Lituanicarum Societatis Jesu historiarum libri decem.* Ed. Jean Martinov. Paris: V. Palme, 1877.

Ruh: Ruhig, Philipp (Ruigys, Pilypas) (1675–1749). *Littauisch-Deutsches und Deutsch-Littauisches Lexicon.* Bd. I–II. Königsberg 1747.

Sab: Sabinus, Georg (1508–1560). *The letter to cardinal Pietro Bemba*, dated to December 1545. In: *Erleutertes Preussen.* Königsberg 1742.

SalHenn: Henning, Salomon (1528–1589), *Warhafftiger und bestendiger Bericht, wie es bishero und zu heutiger Stunde in Religionssachen im Fürstenthume Churland und Semigalen in Lieffland ist gehalten worden.* Rostock 1589. In: *Scriptores Rerum Livonicarum.* Bd. II. Rīga – Leipzig 1853, pp. 293–330.

Sam1322: Johannes. *Complaint concerning the 'sacred field'*, AD 1322. In: Voigt, Johannes. *Codex diplomaticus Prussicus.* Bd. II. Königsberg 1836–1861.

Sam1325: *Contract about the renting one land in Sambia to the Prussian Stagote*, dated to AD 1325. In: Voigt, Johannes. *Codex diplomaticus Prussicus.* Bd. II. Königsberg 1836–1861.

Sam1327: Johannes. *Ruling about assignation of a land*, AD 1327. In: Voigt, Johannes. *Codex diplomaticus Prussicus.* Bd. III. Königsberg 1836–1861.

Sam1334: *Ruling of the Sambian Chapter*, AD 1334 *1334*. In: Voigt, Johannes. *Geschichte Preussens von den ältesten Zeiten bis zum Untergange der Herrschaft des deutschen Ordens.* Bd. III, *Die Zeit vom Frieden 1249 bis zur Unterwerfung der Preußen 1283.* Königsberg 1828.

Sam1357: Jakob. *Ruling about assignation of a meadow to Heinrich von Regenwalde*, AD 1357. In: Voigt, Johannes. *Geschichte Preussens von den ältesten Zeiten bis zum Untergange der Herrschaft des deutschen Ordens.* Bd. I, *Die Zeit des Heidentums (mit Abbildungen altpreußischer Grabhügel).* Königsberg 1827.

SamDarg1327: *Document determining the borders of lands in Sambia*, dated to AD 1327. In: Voigt, Johannes. *Geschichte Preussens von den ältesten Zeiten bis zum Untergange der Herrschaft des deutschen Ordens.* Bd. I, *Die Zeit des Heidentums (mit Abbildungen altpreußischer Grabhügel).* Königsberg 1827.

SamLand1309: *Ruling about assignation of a land to two Prussians, Hermann Maldite and his brother Strambote*, AD 1309. In: Voigt, Johannes. *Codex diplomaticus Prussicus.* Bd. II. Königsberg 1836–1861.

SamLand1322: *Contract about the renting the 'sacred field' to the Order Convention, to establish a pasture in Sambia*, AD 1322. In: Voigt, Johannes. *Codex diplomaticus Prussicus.* Bd. II. Königsberg 1836–1861.

Samp: *Sampetrinum Erfurtense (Chronicon Sancti Petri).* (till AD 1355). In: *Scriptores Rerum Germanicarum.* Bd. III. Ed. Iohann Burchard Mencken. Leipzig 1730.

Schleich: Schleicher, August. *Litauische Grammatik.* Prag: Calve 1856.

Schultz: Schultz, Theophil of Kattenau (Katniava, today Zavety). *Compendium Grammaticae Lituanicae.* Königsberg 1673.

Siles: *Breve Chronicon Silesiae (Annales Cisterciensium in Heinrichow 970–1410).* In: *Scriptores Rerum Silesiacarum.* Bd. V. Ed. Gustav Adolf Harald Stenzel. Wrocław: Josef Max & Komp., 1847. Dale Mierzyński, Antoni. *Mytologiae Lituanicae Monumenta. Źrodła do Mytologii Litewskiej.* Bd. II, Wiek XIV i XV. Warszawa 1896, p. 69.

Stell: Stella, Erasmus († 2. 4. 1521). *Erasmi Stellae, de Borussiae antiquitatibus, libri duo* (first published AD 1518). In: *Acta Borussica ecclesiastica, civilia, literaria I.* Königsberg 1739.

Stend: Stender, Gotthard Friedrich (alias Vecais Stenders, 'Elder Stender') (1714–1796). *Lettische Grammatik*, including the chapter „Lettische Mythologie". Mitau (Jelgava) 1783.

StendWB: Stender, Gotthard Friedrich (alias Vecais Stenders, 'Elder Stender') (1714–1796). *Lettisches Lexikon.* Mitau (Jelgava) 1789.

StRi: Scharpenberg, Henning. *Statuta provincialia concilii Rigensis.* (Written in January 1428). In: *Livländisches, Esthnisches und Curländisches Urkundenbuch.* Ed. F. G. von Bunge. Königsberg 1881.

StRiJac: Jacobson, Heinrich Friedrich. Excerpts from *Statuta provincialia concilii Rigensis*, written by Henning Scharpenberg in January 1428. In: *Geschichte der Quellen des katholischen Kirchenrechtes der Provinzen Preussen und Posen.* Supplement VIII. Königsberg 1837, pp. 59–72.

Strib / StribTolg / StribTolg1608: Stribingius, Joannis. *Report from missian journey for Livonia & Latgalia*, AD 1608, paraphrased by Ertmanus Tolgsdorff († 1620). In: *Annuae Litterae* of the Jesuit Collegium in Riga. Edited as: Kurtz, Eduard. *Die Jahresberichte der Gesellschaft Jesu über ihre Wirksamkeit in Riga und Dorpat 1583–1614. Lateinischer Text mit deutscher Übersetzung.* Rīga 1925.

Stryj: Stryjkowski, Maciej (c. 1547 – c. 1593). *Ktora przedtem nigdy światła nie widziała, Kronika polska, litewska, żmudzka i wszystkiej Rusi kijowskiej, moskowiewskiej, siewierskiej, wołyńskiej, podgorskiej etc.* Königsberg: Georg Osterberger, 1582. 3rd Edition: *Kronika polska, litewska, żmudzka i wszystkiej Rusi etc.* Warszawa: Malinowski, 1846. Partially translated into Latin by Albertus Wijuk-Koialovicius: *Historiae Lituanae*, Vol. 1. Gdańsk 1650, Vol. 2. Antwerpen 1669. See Kojal.

StryjSarm: Guagnini, Alessandro (1538–1614). *Sarmatiae Europeae descriptio, quae Regnum Poloniae, Lituaniam, Samogitiam, Russiam, Masoviam, Prussiam, Pomeraniam… complectitur.* Krakow 1578. The chronicle was based on the chronicle of Stryjkowski, Maciej (c. 1547 – c. 1593).

Sud: Anonymous author. *Das Sudauerbüchlein.* Written probably in 1520's. First edited as: *Wahrhafftige Beschreibung der Sudawen auff Samland, sambt jhren Bockheiligen und Ceremonien.* Ed. Hieronymus Maletius. Konigsberg 1561. Further printed e.g. in: *Erleutertes Preussen.* Bd. 5. Königsberg 1742. Reprinted in: *Baltų religijos ir mitologijos šaltiniai*, Bd. II. Vilnius: Mokslo ir enciklopedijų leidykla, 2001.

Szir: Szirwid, Konstantin (Szyrwid, Sirvydas, Širvydas, Konstantinas). *Dictionarium trium linguarum* (Written c. 1620, extended edition 1642). Vilnius 1713.

SzirPunkt: Szirwid, Konstantin (Szyrwid, Sirvydas, Širvydas, Konstantinas). *Punktai sakimu.* Collection of sermons in Lithuanian with Polish translations. Vol. I Vilnius 1629; Vol. II Vilnius 1644.

Tac: Tacitus, Publius Cornelius (AD 56–117). *Germania.* (Written AD 98). Leipzig: Alfons Hölder, 1878.

Töpp: Töppen, Max. *Geschichte der preussischen Historiographie von P. von Dusburg bis auf K. Schutz.* Berlin 1853.

Töpp1846: Töppen, Max. „Geschichte des Heidenthums in Preussen". In: *Neue preussische Provinzialblätter.* Serie I. Königsberg 1846.

TöppCrit: Töppen, Max. *Critica de historia Borussiae antiqua.* Königsberg 1847.

TöppMas: Töppen, Max. *Aberglauben aus Masuren.* Gdańsk 1867.

Tysz: Tyszkiewicz (Tiškevičius), Konstantin. *O kurhanach na Litwie i Rusi zachodniej.* Berlin 1868.

TyszRzut: Tyszkiewicz (Tiškevičius), Eustachy. *Rzut oka na żrodla archeologii krajowej.* Vilnius 1842.

Us-Solm: Usener, Hermann Karl, & Solmsen, Felix. *Litauische und lettische Götternamen.* Bonn 1894.

Viln: Anonymous author. Latin report about the conquest of Vilnius by Lithuanian Grand Duchy Kęstutis, AD 1345. In: Voigt, Johannes. *Codex diplomaticus Prussicus.* Bd. VI. Königsberg 1861.

Vis1633: *Consistorial vnd Visitation Ordnungh, wie es in Liefflandt hinfüro zue halten.* Command of the Swedish Queen Christina I. about visitations for the Lutheran priests in Livonia. Edited on the 18th February 1633. In: Lundström, E. H. J. *Bidrag till Livlands Kyrkohistoria under den svenska tidens första skede: från Rigas intagande 1621 till freden i Oliva 1660.* Supplement XVI. Uppsala – Stockholm 1914.

Vis1636: *Articuli Visitationis Publicati et a Supremo Consistorio Approbati.* Questionnaire for Lutheran priests and their parishioners. Tartu, June 1636. In: Lundström, E. H. J. *Bidrag till Livlands Kyrkohistoria under den svenska tidens första skede: från Rigas intagande 1621 till freden i Oliva 1660.* Supplement XX. Uppsala – Stockholm 1914.

Vis1638: *Articuli Visitationis.* Questionnaire for Lutheran priests and their parishioners. Tartu, June 1638. In: Lundstrom, E. H. J. *Bidrag till Livlands Kyrkohistoria under den svenska tidens första skede från Rigas intagande 1621 till freden i Oliva 1660.* Supplement XXIV. Uppsala – Stockholm 1914.

Vis1668, Vis1677 etc. till **Vis1767:** Reports from visitations of the Lutheran parishes in Livonia . In: Die *Bibliothek der Gesellschaft für Geschichte und Altertumskunde zu Riga (Rīgas Vēstures un senatnes pētītāju biedrības bibliotēka).* Collection of the primary sources from the 14th – 18th cent.

VisKok1638–1641: *Acta Visitationis Consistorialis ao. 1638. Protocollum Visitationis districtus Kokenhusensis habit. anno 1640. Protocollum Visitationis districtus Kokenhusensis anno 1641.* Reports from visitations of the Lutheran parishes in the district of Kokenhusen (today Koknese). In: Die *Bibliothek der Gesellschaft fur Geschichte und Altertumskunde zu* Riga (Rīgas Vēstures un senatnes pētītāju biedrības bibliotēka). Collection of the primary sources from the 14th – 18th cent.

VisLiv1613: Tecnon, Johannes, (Wenden, today Cēsis). *Visitatio Livonicarum ecclesiarum facta anno 1613 a die Transfi gurationis Domini usque ad 11am Octobris per R. D. Archidiaconum Vendensem et Romi Episcopi Livoniae Vicarium.* Report about visitations of the Livonian parishes Rositen (Rēzekne), Ludsen (Ludza) and Marienhausen (Viļaka). In: *Archiv für die Geschichte Liv- Esth- und Curlands.* Bd. I. Ed. F. G. von Bunge. Königsberg 1842.

VisRig1638, VisRig1671: *Protocollum Consist. Districtus Rigensis A. 1638 Mense Januar. Protocollum Consist. Districtus Rigensis A. 1671.* Reports from visitations of the Lutherans parishes in the district of Riga. In: *Die Bibliothek der Gesellschaft für Geschichte und Altertumskunde zu Riga (Rīgas Vēstures un senatnes pētītāju biedrības bibliotēka).* Collection of the primary sources from the 14th – 18th cent.

VoigtPreuss: Voigt, Johannes. *Geschichte Preussens von den ältesten Zeiten bis zum Untergange der Herrschaft des deutschen Ordens.* Königsberg 1827–1839.

Vojt: Canaparius & Bonifacius, Bruno. *Vita S. Adalberti episcopi. Vita secunda auctore Brunone archiepiscopo.* Written AD 999, 1000, 1004. In: *Scriptores Rerum Prussicarum.* Bd. I. Leipzig 1861.

Vol: *Galician-Volhynian Chronicle,* covering the years 1201–1292 (preserved in the *Hypatian Codex* from the 15th cent.*).* In: *Polnoe sobranie russkixъ Letopisej,* Tom II. Sankt-Peterburg: Archeografi češskaja komisija, 1843. The part connected with Lithuanian mythology was published in the German translation by Brückner, Aleksander. „Beiträge zur litauischen Mythologie". *Archiv für slavische Philologie* 9, 1886, pp. 1–12.

Wag: Wagner, Erhard of Insterburg. *Vita et mores Lithvanorum, in Borussia sub districtu Insterburgensi et Ragnitensi degentium, brevi delineatione adumbrata per Erhardum Wagner Insterburg. Borussum.* Königsberg: Georg Osterberger et Johannes Fabricius, 1621. Reprinted in: *Acta Borussica ecclesiastica, civilia, literaria.* Bd. I. Königsberg 1790, pp. 532–550.

Wais: Waissel, Matthäus (1543–1602). *Chronica Alter Preussscher, Eifflendischer und Curlendischer Historien etc.* Including fragments from *Sudauerbüchlein.* Königsberg: Georg Osterberger, 1599.

Warm: Ruperti, Andreas. *Collatio episcopi Warmiensis facta coram summo pontifi ce per dominum Andream plebanum in Danczk.* Written AD 1419. The part devoted to Prussian mythology was published in: Voigt, Johannes. *Geschichte Preussens von den ältesten Zeiten bis zum Untergange der Herrschaft des deutschen Ordens.* Bd. I, *Die Zeit des Heidentums (mit Abbildungen altpreußischer Grabhügel).* Königsberg 1827, p. 587.

Weg: Rabe, Engelhard & Tettingen, Werner von. *Wegeberichte.* Reports from spying expedition on the enemy Lithuanian territory. Written in AD 1384–1402. In: *Scriptores Rerum Prussicarum.* Bd. II. Ed. Theodor Hirsch. Leipzig 1863, pp. 662–708.

Wig: Marburg, Wigand von. *Gereimte Chronik des Deutschen Ordens in deutscher Sprache von 1294/95 an, verfasst 1393/94,* preserved in fragments. Written AD 1394. In: Schütz, Caspar. *Historia Rerum Prussicarum.* Gdańsk 1592. Further

„Die Chronik des Wigand von Marburg". In: *Scriptores Rerum Prussicarum*. Bd. II. Ed. *Theodor Hirsch*. Leipzig 1863.

Wolt: Wolter, E. „Mythologische Skizzen". In: *Archiv für slavische Philologie*, 9, 1886, 635–642. Further „Ein Westrussisches Zeugnis über litauische Götter". In: *Litovskij katixizis N. Daukši. Po izdaniju 1595–goda vnov' perepečatannyj i snabžennyj ob 'jasnenijami E. Vol'terom. Priloženie k 52. tomu zapisok imp. Akademii Nauk*. Č. 3. Sankt-Peterburg 1886.

Wulf: Wulfstan's Voyage (Written c. AD 890). In: *Scriptores Rerum Prussicarum*. Vol. I. Leipzig 1861, pp. 732–735.

Wund: Wunderer, Johann David (1570 – c. 1622). *Reise nach Dennemark* (1589); *Reise nach Moskau* (1590). In: *Frankfurtischen Archiv für ältere deutsche Literatur und Geschichte*, Bd. II. Frankfurt am Main: J. C. von Fichardt genannt Bauer von Eyseneck, 1812, pp. 163–255.

Zedel: Anonymous author. „Zedel zu einem verlorenen Briefe" (16th cent.). In: *Neue Preussische Provinzialblätter*. Serie I, Bd. II. Königsberg 1846, p. 224.

Abbreviations of languages:

Avest. Avestan, Balt. Baltic, Beloruss. Belorussian, Eng. English, Est. Estonian, Finn. Finnish, Germ. German, Gmc. Germanic, Goth. Gothic, Gr. Greek, Hitt. Hittite, Hom. Homeric, Ind. Indic, Ir. Irish, Karel. Karelian, Lat. Latin, Latv. Latvian, Lith. Lithuanian, Liv. Livonian, Mordv. Mordvinian, O Old, OCS Old Church Slavonic, OHG Old High German, ONor. Old Norse, Pers. Persian, Pol. Polish, Pruss. Prussian, RCS Church Slavonic of Russian redaction, Russ. Russian, Skt. Sanskrit, Sl. Slavic, Ved. Vedic.